Thinking About Research
Methods and Tactics
of the Behavioral Scientist

Thinking About Research
Methods and Tactics
of the Behavioral Scientist

Francis T. Durso
University of Oklahoma

Roger L. Mellgren
University of Texas-Arlington

WEST PUBLISHING COMPANY

St. Paul   •   New York   •   Los Angeles   •   San Francisco

COPYEDITING: *KATHLEEN PRUNO*
TEXT DESIGN: *ROSLYN M. STENDAHL, DAPPER DESIGN*
COMPOSITION: *G & S TYPESETTERS, INC.*
ART: *ROLIN GRAPHICS*

Library of Congress Cataloging-in-Publication Data

Durso, Francis Thomas.
    Thinking about research.

    Includes bibliographies and index.
    1. Psychology—Research—Methodology.   I. Mellgren,
Roger L., 1944–   II. Title.
BF76.5.D87   1989   150 .72   88–33798
ISBN 0–314–47598–2

To our children who continually remind us of the fun of discovery:
Andy, Sara, Scott, and Jill

Preface

The stumbling way in which even the ablest of the scientists in every generation have had to fight through thickets of erroneous observations, misleading generalizations, inadequate formulations, and unconscious prejudice is rarely appreciated by those who obtain their scientific knowledge from textbooks.

—*James Bryant Conant*
Science and Common Sense

Why would any author of a textbook begin with this quote by Conant? It is because we firmly believe that to become a good scientist you must do science, not merely read about it. In this text we begin each chapter with a problem. We then try to illustrate the thought processes a psychologist would go through to solve the problem. In the context of solving the problem, we introduce several general methodological tools. In fact, the text presents quite an array of valuable methodological principles, but it does so in the context of solving a specific, concrete problem. Thus, you, the student, should gain some insight into not only what the methods of scientific psychology are, but also when to employ them.

The skills and knowledge contained in this book are basic to an appreciation of the essence of psychology. Regardless of your career goals, what you learn in this course will be valuable to you. The knowledge gained will be valuable to those few of you who plan a research career in science. However, this knowledge is also essential to the practitioner—the clinician and the counselor; success in these vocations depends on the ability to evaluate the research findings of others. Even those of you who have no aspirations in psychology will benefit from these skills in your role as a consumer of scientific information. Those basic skills we promise are the ability to understand, design, analyze, communicate, criticize, and appreciate research. If you do your part by being an active participant in the course, the things you learn will be valuable to you for the rest of your life.

Each chapter (with the exception of chapter 1) of the book is designed to give you a research project or projects to do, totally planned and described. The plan and description are concerned not only with the implementation of the experiment, but also with the underlying thought processes involved before the experiment is conducted. We supply you a FRAME, which becomes increasingly complex, that should prove useful in reconstructing the thinking involved in experimentation. As each chapter introduces new concepts, the Frame will include additional items you should consider. Regardless of the format of your class, whether it is a lecture format, a laboratory format, or a discussion section, you should attempt to do at least some of the experiments. Your instructor may require that you conduct some or all of them. If you do conduct an experiment by yourself or with a friend, however, note that each experiment that is spelled out for you is very simple to do, requiring little or no equipment.

Progressing from one chapter to the next, the concepts introduced become increasingly complex. The methodological concepts, as well as the required statistical tests, increase in sophistication. We have also introduced "Writing Boxes" that should help you develop into a skillful writer of technical reports. These writing boxes also tend to increase in the level of detail. We have designed these writing boxes so they can be put together to form a reference for use with the course and in the future.

By the end of chapter 6, you will be able to conduct a simple experiment. By the end of chapter 11, you will be able to conduct more sophisticated experiments, including theory-driven experiments, experiments involving more than one factor, and more powerful experiments. Finally, the next four chapters deal with special situations, such as what to do when the subject tries to outguess the experimenter (chapter 12), what to do when you have only one subject (chapter 13), what to do when you must do an experiment but your subjects already belong to predefined groups (chapter 14), and what to do with quantitative independent variables (chapter 15). The final chapter (chapter 16) discusses the processes one set of researchers went through from the time they had the idea until the time the work appeared in print. Thus, these last five chapters can be read selectively. Although all chapters are required for a complete understanding of experimental methods, your instructor may choose to omit one or two of the final chapters without loss of continuity.

The book is designed to be "user friendly" and still maintain the quality of thinking typified by experimental psychologists. As one means toward that end, you will find very few citations in the text. We did not want citations to detract from the stream of consciousness we tried to maintain in our writing. The reader will, however, find recommended additional readings at the end of each chapter; these readings will be aimed at the particular content area used as a vehicle in the chapter. The few citations do not, of course, belie the contribution of methodologists and teachers of methodology. The several methodological articles, books, and textbooks used to construct the current text are referenced at the end of the book.

We are covering research in psychology rather than experimental psychology. Although this distinction may seem unclear to you at this point, you will probably gain a fuller understanding of the distinction by the end of the semester. The research techniques we will cover include those that are often thought of as being more appropriate to applied problems, as well as those designed to assess basic research questions. Our philosophy is that good research is good research. The question addressed may be of concern to society, or of concern only to the scientist. The criteria that determine the correctness of the research do not change as a result of the kind of question that is addressed. One of the things we have attempted to do in writing this book is to include problems of the real world in most chapters. We do this to show how it is possible to do research in this setting. There are difficulties of trying to go out in the world to do research. Ethics, lack of control of relevant variables, practical problems, and inconvenience are all problems we will have to overcome. Research in the lab is more straightforward than research done in a natural setting, but the lessons to be learned from the experimental design required by the natural setting and the inherent interest in questions that can be asked in this setting (often bordering on the gee-whiz sort), offset the disadvantages, in our opinion.

Several people have contributed to making this textbook possible. Charles Gettys and Terry Steele are two brave colleagues who were willing to try the book under an installment plan as we rewrote the manuscript. Kirby Gilliland helped us in our literature search of multiple personalities and Rich Reardon's ideas made Chapter 16 possible. Larry Toothaker lent us his statistical expertise and his experience with publishing a textbook. Joanna Harris sacrificed some of her own teaching and research time to supply several valuable suggestions throughout the manuscript, not to mention continual moral support.

We are grateful to the Literary Executor of the late Sir Ronald A. Fisher, F.R.S. to Dr. Frank Yates, F.R.S. and the Longman Group Ltd, London for permission to reprint Tables III and IV from their book *Statistical Tables for Biological, Agricultural and Medical Research* (6th Edition 1974).

This text would have remained only an idea if it were not for then chair, N. Jack Kanak, who let us team-teach the course so that we could write this text, and for the current chair, W. Alan Nicewander, who gave us the time and resources to finish the book. One of those resources was Susan Shull who has our special thanks for her extraordinary help in preparing the manuscript. Thanks also to Terri Snodgrass, Janie Mooney, and Kamran Sadeghi who would not let broken computers, slow mail, or red tape keep us from meeting deadlines, and to Paul Kleine, Steve Brown, Kathy Coggins, Barbara Krause, Karen Palmer, and Terri Thomas for their ideas and time.

We also received considerable support from our teaching assistants over the years who helped shape the ideas and structure of this textbook, and from the University of Oklahoma undergraduates in Psychology 3114 who suffered through bad photocopies, typos, and hand-drawn figures. They too offered valuable suggestions which have improved our original work. Our graduate students were helpful throughout this project even when they sometimes took backseats to deadlines and publishers timetables: Steve Brown, Kathy Coggins, Tom Dayton, Judi Jones, and Wendy Shore.

It was a pleasure to write this text for West Publishing Company. We were supported and encouraged every step of the project, from the advice and guidance of our editors, Tom LaMarre and Teresa O'Dell, to the expertise of our production staff headed by Jeff Carpenter, to the reviewers West located—Mary Ann Foley, Blaine Peden, Keith Rodewald, Robert Burke, Thomas W. Turnage, Mark Olson, and Charles Brewer who provided insightful, in-depth comments and suggestions on the text. The book is better for their efforts.

We hope that each of you finds the excitement in conducting research that we feel in our work. To us, there is nothing one can do with the lights on that gives the same feeling as does the process of discovery. Good luck and happy experimenting!

F. T. D.
R. L. M.

How to use this book

The Chapters

Each chapter describes an experiment in enough detail to allow you to conduct the experiment. None of the experiments require any sophisticated equipment. Several, or all, of the experiments can be viewed as "thought experiments," which the student and instructor can modify and improve without actually collecting data. If data collection is a part of the course, the chapters can be used to support other experiments of the instructor's or class's choosing; or the experiments detailed in the chapter or instructor's manual can be used. Data sheets are supplied in several chapters to acquaint the student with the details required in this often overlooked, but essential, organizational device and to provide an easy-to-use form should data for that chapter's study be collected.

Frame for Research

Each chapter contains a frame for research that requires the student to review the chapter and fill in sections of the frame. This device provides an *active* review of the chapter and allows the student to consider information assimilated from previous chapters. These frames provide a review of the methodological concepts *in the context* of a specific experiment. These pages can be removed and organized prior to an examination or in a notebook to provide a synopsis of the concepts necessary in psychological research.

TOGS, TOSS, and Writing Appendix

Each chapter has boxes giving Tips on General Style (TOGS) and Tips on Specific Style (TOSS). The TOGS boxes supply advice on technical writing style in general. The TOSS boxes supply information specific to the recommended format of the American Psychological Association (APA) for psychological manuscripts. These TOSS boxes can substitute quite nicely for the *Publication Manual* of the APA, especially in courses where students are first exposed to APA style. Both boxes appear on the same sheet in the chapter to allow them to be removed and organized in a way to match the needs of the student. The boxes are currently organized from the most basic elements of composition to the more advanced elements. However, a particular student having difficulty with one concept may wish to organize a notebook on writing in a way to fit his or her particular strengths and weaknesses.

In addition, two manuscripts are presented in the writing appendix. One manuscript contains errors typical of those found in initial attempts at technical writing. This error-filled manuscript also contains references back to the appropriate TOGS or TOSS boxes to provide the student with an easy index to the material supplied in those boxes. Students can determine the error in this manuscript, attempt to correct it, and then refer back to the referenced TOGS or TOSS box. The second manuscript is a corrected version of this manuscript, which the student can use to compare with his or her solution to the error. When students find themselves more comfortable with APA style, they can then use this correct, unannotated manuscript as a quick check on the format of their own manuscript. Both manuscripts can be removed and placed in the TOGS/TOSS notebook.

Statistics Review

Statistics are a valuable tool of the research scientist. Most students using this text will have had some experience with the basic statistical concepts. Some students may not have had any formal training in statistics. The reviews of statistics are not intended as a substitute for this formal training, but instead serve two purposes: (1) For the student with some statistical background, these reviews can serve as reminders of the computational steps required. They can be used in conjunction with the student's text, but they can stand alone for those students simply needing a device to refresh memory. (2) For the student with no statistical training, these reviews supply, in a step-by-step format, the procedures necessary to compute the statistic. These students will receive enough exposure to statistics to allow them to understand the methodology more fully and to prepare themselves for a more conceptual approach to this integral tool.

Additional Reading

The additional readings at the end of each chapter have been chosen to serve as a springboard into the literature. All of these articles are concerned with the topic of the experiment discussed in the chapter, rather than the methodology employed. (References for those students interested in exploring methodological issues can be found at the end of the text.) The articles referred to in the chapter can easily be used by the student who has mastered the techniques of searching the literature (chapter 2) to find additional references for his or her research report. Some of the readings are quite current, whereas others are from the beginning of the century. These two starting points provide experience with different methods of the literature search.

Contents

T Science & Psychology

Overview

Four different approaches to understanding our world are discussed, including the authority approach, analogy approach, rule approach, and scientific method approach. Scientists are viewed as a community: They share assumptions, goals, and rational rules to go from the assumption to the goal. Description, explanation, prediction, and control are increasingly sophisticated goals of science. The goals are achieved in science by creating a hypothesis and testing it by changing one variable (predictor) and measuring the effects on a second variable (dependent). The criteria that scientific data and scientific reasoning must meet are discussed: Data must be empirical, public (precise), and repeatable. Inductive and deductive methods of thinking are presented. Conventional rules are discussed including the idea of a science as a community, scientific revolutions, and the ethics of science.

There are no statistics mentioned in this chapter.

Tips on General Style discusses basic sentence structure. Throughout the text advice from these TOGS boxes provides general guides for effective technical writing.

Tips on Specific Style describes the basic formatting of a paper written according to the guidelines of the *Publication Manual* (3rd) of the American Psychological Association. Advanced psychology majors should have access to a personal copy of the *Manual*. Speak to your instructor or write to the Order Department, American Psychological Association, P.O. Box 2710, Hyattsville, MD 20784.

Throughout the text these TOSS boxes will supply advice specific to writing a manuscript in psychology.

The TOGS and TOSS boxes are ordered to provide manageable amounts of information with each chapter. They can be removed and placed together for easy reference. In addition, a completed manuscript is included in the appendix. This manuscript refers the reader to the appropriate TOGS and TOSS boxes.

How Scientists Know

"Rather than love, than money, than fame, give me truth."

—*Henry David Thoreau*

Recently, a colleague in our department found himself in the market for a new car. In the course of making a decision, he was faced with a small version of what faces each of us everyday: the task of obtaining more knowledge. "More knowledge" can take many forms. It can be additional facts about something, or it can be a new way to organize facts you already know. The desire to *know* motivates scientists and nonscientists alike to acquire new information with which to organize their world.

Approaches to Understanding

For our friend, more knowledge was needed about cars. In particular, he had narrowed his selection to either a large, American-made car (i.e., Chevy Impala) or a less expensive, smaller Japanese-made car (i.e., Toyota Tercel). At a basic level, the approaches taken by our colleague before buying a car are the same as the approaches that could be taken in any situation, including science. We will use the trials and tribulations of our car-buying friend to illustrate four approaches to understanding that are used by both scientists and nonscientists.

Authority Approach

The first approach our friend encountered was the reliance on an authority. His family, his friends, and the salesperson all told him which of the two cars was better. Accepting what we are told is an approach we use quite often to acquire and organize knowledge. If you come across an "Out of Order" sign on a vending machine, you are likely (and wise) not to deposit your money. In this case, you rely on authority, the sign, to supply you with knowledge concerning the vending machine's condition.

The authority approach is one of the oldest methods for gaining "truth" about the world. It is still present today in the form of newspapers, superstitions, expert opinions, and religious dogma to mention a few. As evident in buying a car, the authority approach has both strengths and weaknesses. Clearly the opinion of others might be biased or simply incorrect. On the other hand, accepting the opinion of *Motor Trend* magazine as fact makes the decision easy. Given the vast amount of information available on even the narrowest subject, we cannot possibly function without some reliance on authority. The authority approach allows us to assimilate knowledge and prevents us from reinventing the wheel. Scientists use authority, but they use it as a starting point, not an ending point. One use of the authority approach, the literature search, will be discussed in detail in chapter 2. There the scientist tries to determine what information is already available on a topic. Clearly he or she is forced to rely on the reports of others. Science would never progress if each scientist had to prove every "fact." Although it is very difficult to do, scientists try to keep in mind the underlying assumptions and question those assumptions. If they do not question that information, there is a very real danger that understanding will not be advanced.

Can you think of examples where your knowledge or understanding is based on authority? Can you think of logical arguments that you have heard or participated in that never questioned the underlying axioms? What were those unquestioned assumptions?

Analogy Approach

Another way of understanding and organizing the world is to note the similarities, to draw an **analogy,** between some new event and a more familiar, understandable event. Our car buyer was the owner of an older-model Chevy Impala and so had had much experience with a car presumably similar to the new Impala he was thinking of purchasing. A person may begin to understand something by saying that it is similar to something else. In our example, the new Impala is assumed to be similar to the old Impala. Unlike the authority approach, the analogy approach emphasizes observation of the world. However, unless we agree on the way we are going to observe our world, we will "see" different analogies; thus one problem with an analogy is that it is open to a number of interpretations. Our friend reasoned that his old Impala had many repair problems so therefore, by analogy, the new Impala should also. The old Impala had lots of room; therefore, so should the new Impala. Although some of his inferences would prove correct and some would not, the analogy between the old and the new, nevertheless, gave him more of an understanding of the purchase than he would have had without it.

Scientists also use the analogy approach, but they try not to rely totally on it. A complex problem may be made more comprehensible by pointing out an analogy to a simpler system. For example, "electricity is like water" may help understand aspects of the *flow* of electricity. However, taking water as the extreme example will lead to a number of misunderstandings about electricity: can it leak? does it go uphill? This example shows that an analogy may suggest interpretations, some of which may be incorrect. Further, an analogy can be stretched too far. In science, analogies are only helpful in understanding *part* of the more complex system.

What do you understand a little better because you realize that it is similar to something else? What aspects of the analogy are particularly good? Particularly bad or even nonsensical? Can you think of one analogy between some complex psychological process and some simpler physical system? For example, how is the eye similar to a camera? How is it different?

Rule Approach

The third approach to knowledge that we use in everyday life is the rule approach. The rule approach stresses the organization and order of the universe and tries to find laws or rules that cover a number of different specific observations. Dr. X gives easy tests. The restaurant is always crowded on Fridays. Toyotas are better than Chevrolets. Because "I know" Toyotas are better than Chevrolets, and the Tercel is a make of Toyota, then the Tercel is the better car. If we use these rules, without actually observing the situations, then we are trying to understand something by fitting it into an existing rule.

The advantages and disadvantages of the rule approach are clear from the above reasoning. The advantage of having a rule is that the rule may prove to be correct, and thus using the rule will save time and effort in making many decisions. However, because there are exceptions to rules, the particular make of car may not conform to the rule. If the rule is followed blindly, then the threat to the advancement of understanding is as great as in the authority approach, perhaps greater. Prejudice toward other races, other religions, or other ethnic groups makes the danger of the rule approach all too evident. If you feel that you are reasonably immune to such biases, try answering the following questions: (1) Which is further east, Los Angeles, California, or Reno, Nevada? (2) Which is further east, the Atlantic entrance to the Panama Canal or the Pacific entrance? For each of these questions, did you use the rule that California is west of Nevada? or that the Pacific Ocean is west of the Atlantic Ocean? If you did, you may want to check with an atlas to see if your rules led you to answer the questions incorrectly.

Scientists also use rules and laws in their pursuit of truth. Theories, hypotheses, models, and the goals of science themselves are intricately tied to the rule approach. However, as we will see, what is allowed as a rule in science and what is acceptable as evidence for that rule must meet several criteria. A scientist will see if the rule is correct by testing some of the implications of the rule. Thus, the scientist questions the rule and does not use the rule in place of observation; rather he or she continuously uses the rule and observation together as partners in the search for truth.

Can you think of other knowledge that you have that is based on the rule approach? Do you recognize situations in which you use the rule? Are any of these situations ones in which the rule does not apply?

Scientific Approach

The final approach we use in acquiring knowledge from day to day is the ultimate topic of this course. Although scientists use all four methods of acquiring truth, the scientific method is characterized by several principles, goals, methods, and assumptions, which we will consider more fully throughout the book. We can begin, however, by considering what most people associate with scientists: the experiment.

In our car-buying example, a simple experiment is the test drive. Before purchasing a car, most people will drive two or more cars around town and make mental notes or get a feel for how the car performed and make a judgment of how the car will perform when they get it home. During the drive, we would also probably make an effort to make the test drives as similar as possible. We would not drive one car down a dirt road and then compare it with the car we drove on an interstate. The test drive is a very crude experiment in that it begins with a research question about which car is the best; the scientist in us then manipulates or varies something of interest (the cars), without allowing other things to change (similar test drives), and then tries to assess changes in some variable (the evaluation of the drive) that are thought to depend on the variable we manipulated.

Our car buyer, being a scientist, used science to make his final decision. He conducted a more complicated experiment than the one represented by the test drive. The reason for each of our friend's actions may not be immediately apparent to you now (it certainly was not to the salespeople). However, by the end of the course each of the actions will make perfect sense. For now, you should understand that these efforts were to make certain that the difference in cars, and *only the difference in cars,* was responsible for the differences in the quality of the test drives. Let us consider his experiment.

Our friend began by inviting both of us to participate in his experiment. He told us that he was going to compare Chevy Impalas and Toyota Tercels to see how they differed on riding comfort, handling, and engine performance. We were to come with him and rank the cars on these three dimensions. One of us was to drive all of the cars while the other one recorded information about comfort, handling, and engine performance. Our friend just went along for the ride.

At the Toyota dealership, there were 8 Tercels on the lot. There were 10 Impalas at the Chevy dealership. Our friend numbered the Tercels 1 to 8 and the Impalas 1 to 10. He then put numbered slips of paper into a hat and drew four from the Tercel hat and four from the Impala hat. We then asked to test-drive these eight cars. We drove two Tercels, then went to the Chevy dealer and drove four Impalas, and finished at the Toyota dealership by driving the other two Tercels.

Each test drive involved the same course, and each time the driver tried to pass a tractor-trailer truck traveling at approximately 60 mph. We were told to measure the time from when the driver started to pass until he returned to the right lane. We also tried to parallel park with each vehicle, and we were to count and record the number of maneuvers required. Finally, for each vehicle we judged passenger comfort by giving each car a number from 1 to 7, where 1 meant very uncomfortable and 7 meant very comfortable.

Then, the time-to-pass, the number-of-maneuvers, and our comfort ratings were analyzed statistically to see if there was a real difference between Tercels and Impalas or whether our numbers were too similar to warrant claiming that one car was better than another.

Our friend's car-buying procedure has many characteristics of good science. He began with a research question that led him to compare Impalas and Tercels. He used several Impalas and several Tercels (rather than one of each), which he chose in an unbiased way from the ones available on the lot. He decided in precise ways how the Tercels and Impalas would be compared, and he tried to make everything the same on all the tests except for the difference between Impalas and Tercels. This last step was an attempt to ensure that any differences he found in the measures we recorded were due to differences between Tercels and Impalas, and not to some other factor. (Imagine if he had one person drive the Impalas and another person drive the Tercels.) Finally, he did not drive nor did he make judgments, but instead had two people who were unaware of his personal beliefs.

As with all science, our friend began with a question or **hypothesis.** He then varied the **predictor variable** (the makes of the cars) to see if it would cause a change on the **dependent variable** (e.g., riding comfort) for a **sample** of the cars on the lot. He tried to **control** everything else: If any differences were observed on the dependent variables, they could have been caused only by the predictor variable.

Can you think of experiments you have conducted informally to make a decision, find the cause of a problem, or understand something better?

The Rational Side of Science

Although science is only one of four methods of organizing and understanding the world we live in, it is quite different from any of the others. Scientists share assumptions about the world, goals they hope to reach or approach, as well as how to go from assumptions to goals. Their work is conducted according to a number of rules and a number of restrictions. They collect facts, but they do not settle for a collection of facts. Because they share a great deal, we can view scientists as a community.

A Rational Assumption

The scientist begins with one very simple assumption: There is order to the universe. Events in the universe do not occur randomly. This assumption suggests that one event leads to (or causes) some other event and that these chains of events can be observed (provided we eliminate other events that work in the opposing direction or that fog our view of the event.

Like the scientist, you probably share this assumption. For example, although you probably can accept that you do not know why you have a headache or where it came from, you probably cannot accept that there was no cause of the headache.

Goals

The goal of a scientist is to organize, simplify, understand, and improve our world. This understanding usually takes place in four steps, each of which is composed of hundreds of smaller steps. An individual scientist may make some of the smaller steps, but the larger steps often take the equivalent of several lifetimes.

The first step is **description,** where the scientist is able to characterize a situation. At this point the scientist might feel comfortable answering the question "What is it?" This may seem quite simple, though tedious—such as describing the weather. However, anxiety, emotion, or learning do not lend themselves easily to description. The second step is **explanation,** where the scientist attempts to answer "Why did it happen?" This step usually involves ideal situations in which the scientist does not have to be concerned with other factors that may complicate the basic explanation. For example, Boyle's law describes the relationship of pressure and volume of a gas in a vacuum. Here the vacuum is the ideal situation. In psychology, the scientific investigator uses the laboratory experiment to try to create such an ideal condition. The third step, **prediction** in the real world, follows closely after explanation. Here the scientist answers "What will happen?" Meteorology, for example, is somewhere within this stage; the weatherperson can often (sometimes?) predict the weather, but for the most part has no control over it. The final step is one in which no questions are left—**control.** At this step the scientist can make some event in the chain occur.

Many of the mature sciences, such as physics and chemistry, have achieved enough understanding to allow the scientist to control the events that occur in a less-than-ideal situation.

Psychology, unlike the more mature sciences, is relatively young. Scientific psychology is only a little over 100 years old, tracing its birth to the year 1879 in Leipzig, Germany. It is not surprising that many areas of psychology are at the descriptive step of research. In some areas, explanation may be possible in ideal situations such as in the laboratory. Prediction outside of the laboratory is only now being attempted in some areas, and even in these areas there has not been a great accumulation of information that can be used to argue for general psychological laws. We will consider one of psychology's few laws in chapter 15.

Science progresses through these steps by recording observations of particular situations and then making conclusions about classes of situations. Observations are made of events actually occurring, and our recordings of the observations are the data. However, not every observation is acceptable to the scientist or the scientific community, and not every conclusion or generalization from the observations is acceptable. Both the observations and the generalizations are guided by rules and criteria adopted by the scientific community.

Scientific Data

If an event actually occurs and is recorded, then these records may be **data.** However, not every recorded event qualifies as a datum. Scientists usually demand that data meet certain basic criteria before they are willing to accept them.

The first criterion is that the observations must be *real* or *objective* and not a figment of the observer's imagination. The observation must be based on the senses. The data that meet this criterion are called **empirical.** For example, thoughts and electrons do not meet the criterion. No one has ever *seen* a thought or, for that matter, an electron. Thus thoughts and electrons are not scientific data. However, the scientist will accept a *report* of a thought and will accept certain data that suggest the presence of electrons. Electrons and thoughts are **hypothetical constructs.** Many experiments indicate that matter behaves *as if* it is made up of electrons, and that people behave *as if* they have thoughts. The idea of hypothetical constructs is inextricably tied to data, but constructs are not data.

This difference between empirical data and hypothetical constructs is often ignored by the public. For example, "I saw an unidentified flying object" is a statement indicating that I saw something flying (presumably) that I could not identify. Such a statement can be a datum (but not an interesting one, because it only says that someone claimed to see something fly that they could not identify). However, people are often willing to treat a possible construct (e.g., extraterrestrial visitors) as if it were the datum rather than an interpretation of the datum.

A second criterion for events to be accepted as scientific data is the requirement of a high degree of agreement among different people on the description of the events. The data that meet this criterion are **public.** If you and I observe an event, we should be able to agree on the description of the event. Remember, it will be this description and not the event that will be entered as datum. Both you and I are able to observe the event, and it is not entirely personal to either you or me. This second criterion requires that I will agree with your description.

For example, both of us can, in principal, observe Halley's comet. In addition, I am likely to agree with your description. Now there will be parts of your description that I and others will be more likely to agree with than other parts. For example, you might simply say that Halley's comet had a tail. The description is public and empirical, but not very informative. In other words, the description is not very precise. The high degree of agreement required to be public means that the more **precise** the statement is the more agreement will result. The most accurately and specifically an event can be described along relevant dimensions, the more precise it will be and the more acceptable it will be to scientists. Nonscientists, on the other hand, often accept imprecise statements. The most obvious example is astrological predictions. These predictions are often so vague that they apply to everyone, even presidents. The more precise a statement, the easier it is to disconfirm. Astrological predictions, being imprecise, are difficult to disconfirm. To make certain that their data meet the criterion of precise public statements, scientists rely on operational definitions. We will cover operational definitions in more detail in chapter 3.

To illustrate the problem of making an observation public, consider the task faced by the Amazing Randi. The Amazing Randi has become famous for exposing persons who claim to have certain magical or mystical powers. In one case, a woman claimed to be able to see an aura around people that extended some 2 ft all around the person. This aura was not one that others could see (obviously), and thus the observation was not public. How could Randi decide if, in fact, she had some special visual ability?

Cleverly, Randi simply stepped behind a divider that was approximately 1 ft taller than he was. Thus, the 2 ft aura should have extended about 1 ft over the divider. He asked the woman to indicate where he was standing based on his aura; when she failed several attempts, he reached the conclusion that she was, in fact, a charlatan.

The final criterion for scientific data is that observations must be **repeatable.** *In principle*, it should be possible to make the same observation again. Everyone, scientists and nonscientists alike, find repeatable observations more compelling than unique events. However, nonscientists are often willing to accept unique events as fact. For example, a psychic received a great deal of notoriety after she successfully predicted the assassination of President Kennedy. If one makes enough predictions, some of them are bound to be confirmed. In fact, hundreds of other predictions by this psychic did not materialize. Scientists use **statistics** to determine if an event is one that could be expected based on **chance** or luck.

However, unique events have occurred in our history. Are once-in-a-lifetime events acceptable to the scientist? What about the destruction of Pompeii by the eruption of Mount Vesuvius? Do you believe it happened? What about the sinking of the city of Atlantis? Most scientists accept the former once-in-a-lifetime event, but not the latter.

Many pieces of data exist supporting the validity of the destruction of Pompeii, but no convincing evidence exists concerning the destruction of

Atlantis. Related events can supply **converging evidence** for the questioned observation. That is, related events come together to suggest the destruction of Pompeii. If an event is absolutely unique, open-minded scientists will not flatly reject it, but they will be skeptical.

In summary, scientific data must meet several criteria. Data are recorded statements of actually occurring singular events. The events must, in principle, be available for public scrutiny, and the description must be such that different individuals can know, as precisely as possible, what the event was that is being described. With these criteria met, scientists attempt to recreate the conditions that allow reobservation of the event.

Try to think of a number of reported events and decide why they would or would not be acceptable to a scientist. What about the reports of ghosts? The claim that "I flew to the moon in 1940, but I will never do that again!" ESP?

Scientific Conclusions

From individual events, scientists hope to make conclusions about classes of events. These conclusions about classes of events distinguish science from the humanities. In the humanities, events are considered unique and, as many would argue, attempts to classify these events would not do justice to them. For example, there was one *Hamlet* and one *Tom Sawyer*. These works can be studied, but not by grouping them together and not by speaking of causal chains of events. If someone did take this approach to the humanities (and some have), the endeavor would be more like a "literary science" than a liberal art.

In science, observations within a class may be tentative or they may be so well established that most or all scientists accept the conclusion. How do scientists go from observations of single events to conclusions about classes of events? In general, scientists might begin with a general hypothesis, theory, or gut feeling. From this, the scientist observes events (collects data) that are relevant to an aspect of the hypothesis. If the data do not support the hypothesis, then the hypothesis might be rejected or modified. If the data do support the hypothesis, then more data will be collected. Some of these additional experiments will be under conditions similar to the first observations, whereas others will be under what seem to be very different conditions.

Scientists go through the procedure using both *induction* and *deduction*. Scientists group observations of particular events into classes of events that share properties, and in the process they eliminate unimportant or irrelevant aspects. Here **induction** (reasoning from the specific to the general) yields a summary of the events observed thus far. An example of reasoning by induction would be:

> Roger likes Susan.
> Frank likes Susan.
> therefore All men like Susan.

After this process of induction, the scientist employs the process of **deduction** (reasoning from the general to the specific). He or she examines the summaries for gaps and generalizes from what is known to fill in the gaps. These lead to predictions the hypothesis makes that have not been observed. Additional data are then collected to test these predictions, and the hypothesis might be rejected, modified, or strengthened. An example of deduction would be:

> All men like Susan.
> Fred is a man.
> therefore Fred likes Susan.

If we discover that Fred does not, in fact, like Susan, then our hypothesis that "All men like Susan" should be changed. If Fred did like Susan, we would not say that we *proved* our hypothesis, because it is always possible that we could find some man who did not like her. This cycle is known as the **hypothetico-deductive** process. We will consider this process in more detail in chapter 7.

The Conventional Side of Science

Although scientists share rational assumptions, goals, and procedures, like any community of people, they also are held together by **conventional rules** that they agree on and beliefs that they share. Not subscribing to the conventional rules of science is just as likely to make you a social outcast in science as it is with your peer group or with society in general. Some violations of conventional rules of your peer group would indicate that you had bad taste, bad judgment, poor upbringing, or that you were just an oddball. While the "oddball" that marches to a different drummer has sometimes been proven to be ahead of his or her time, this does not negate how he or she is treated by contemporaries. Other violations of conventional rules, however, are more extreme and brand you as a criminal, rather than an oddball. In science, where open-mindedness is encouraged, very few violations are considered criminal, but those that are considered criminal carry the highest penalty; these are violations of ethics.

Ethics

Science has conventions that are so central to its moral fiber that violations of them would be comparable to theft or murder in general society. In psychology, these ethical guidelines are published by the American Psychological Association. Here we discuss some of the capital crimes.

Plagiarism.   Plagiarism is stealing someone else's thoughts or words without acknowledging the contribution. This crime can be as blatant as lifting pieces of text word for word from someone else's article, book, or lab report. Paraphrasing someone else's *idea* without acknowledging that person is also unethical. A more subtle example of this crime is reading about a study in a textbook and then citing that study in your paper as if you had read the original article.

Misreporting.   When you conduct your study, you must report all relevant details of that study. A blatant offense of this law is "dry-labbing" where the scientist makes up the data. This offense may hurt science for a time; however, in most cases it is so obvious that the offense is discovered immediately. In fact, modern statistical techniques can be used to prove that a person made up the data rather than collecting it. This crime also occurs when a scientist omits a part of the data or the procedure that goes against the theory or that makes the scientist appear, in hindsight, foolish. This does not mean that you should necessarily report all of the experiments you conducted on a particular question. Perhaps your first experiments were flawed. You should not burden the reader by tracing through all of the false starts and mistakes that you made.

Human Subjects.   The people who agree to be in your experiment have inalienable rights that the psychologist cannot violate. The risk of participation may include not only physical harm and discomfort, but also social and mental harm. These are considerations uppermost in the scientist's mind. The subject has a right to know all the risks, if any, and to give **informed consent.** The subject also has the right to refuse to continue at any time. A good rule of thumb is to ask yourself if the risks associated with your experiment are greater than what would be experienced by the person in ordinary life. Certain subjects may be especially vulnerable. For example, special care should be taken when working with children. The privacy of the subject must also be protected. Finally, you should **debrief** the participants in your study. They should be told at the end of the study (1) what the experiment was about, (2) what value it may have to psychology, and (3) what value it may have to them. You should also be prepared to answer any questions your subjects might have. Remember, they are doing you a favor. Finally, the data you collected should be available only to authorized personnel and should be destroyed after it is no longer needed. (Some journals require that the data be retained for a few years after the work has been published.) Universities have an **Institutional Review Board (IRB)** established for the protection of human subjects. The University of Oklahoma form appears at the end of this chapter.

Animal Subjects.   Just as there are guidelines for treating human subjects, so are there guidelines for the ethical treatment of animals. Although most states have legal guidelines for the care and treatment of animal subjects, most ethical researchers go beyond these legal requirements in the care and treatment of their animals. The American Psychological Association publishes guidelines for the humane care of laboratory animals. Care should be taken that cruelty is absent not only from the experiment but also from the living conditions of the animals. Clean cages, no overcrowding, and a general understanding of the habits of the species are imperative. The University of Oklahoma form for permission to use infrahuman subjects appears at the end of this chapter.

Peer Pressure

Whereas ethics and rational rules can be viewed as guidelines telling the scientist how to do research, other conventional rules can be viewed as guidelines telling the scientist what to research. For example, psychologists within a particular area will tend to agree on what the important research questions are, on what things they are willing to take for granted, on what questions are uninteresting, and on what are good analogies and what are not good. These guidelines are not written anywhere, but rather exist in the minds (and hearts) of the scientists. In fact, the scientist is responsible for these rules. Just as your peer group adopts some of your views and you adopt some of its, so a scientist has an influence on the community of scientists and is influenced by it.

What happens if someone in your peer group does not conform? If it is only one person, then the peer group will remain intact and that person will cease to be a functioning part of it. However, what happens if a large number of people cease to accept a belief or behavior as acceptable? Then the peer group changes. What if a large number of people question a large number of beliefs? Then the peer group changes so dramatically that it no longer resembles the original group: a revolution has occurred. Science progresses in the same way. The image of science accumulating knowledge in a continuous, steadfast way is in large part misleading. Science undergoes revolutions.

Some of you reading this text will become part of the next revolution in psychology. You will bring to your science predispositions, personal history, and gut feelings and beliefs that will become part of the conventional rules of the new generation of psychology. With the rapid advances in psychological science, your community will be as much like ours as ours is to the philosophers who asked how many angels can sit on the head of a pin.

Key Words

analogy	hypothetical constructs
chance	hypothetico-deductive
control	induction
conventional rules	informed consent
converging evidence	Institutional Review Board (IRB)
data (singular: datum)	precise
debrief	prediction
deduction	predictor variable
dependent variable	public
description	repeatable
empirical	sample
explanation	statistics
hypothesis	

Additional Reading

Kuhn, T. S. (1970). *The structure of scientific revolutions* (2nd ed.). Chicago: University of Chicago Press.

McCain, G., & Segal, E. M. (1977). *The game of science* (3rd ed.). Monterey: Brooks/Cole Publishing Company.

Stevens, A., & Coupe, P. (1978). Distortions in judged spatial relations. *Cognitive Psychology, 10*, 422–437.

The Basic Sentence

The sentence is the basic unit of the composition. All parts of a sentence contribute to the development of a single idea or impression.

A *simple* sentence contains one independent clause and thus by its nature contains a single idea. The student wanted to pass the course.

The other basic sentences do, however, present situations where the sentence could lose unity.

A *compound* sentence contains two or more independent clauses. The data were tabulated, and a mean was computed.

A *complex* sentence contains one independent clause and one or more dependent clauses. The apparatus that was used in Experiment 1 was replaced in Experiment 2.

Use independent clauses of equal importance. Subjects in the experimental condition studied pictures, whereas subjects in the control condition studied words.

Use dependent clauses for ideas of secondary importance. Subjects responded by pressing a button, while the computer recorded the response time.

Develop unrelated ideas in separate sentences or show the relationship.

Inexact: The subjects were over 60 years old, and the reaction time to the tone was long.

Better: Because the subjects were over 60 years old, the reaction time to the tone was long.

Avoid superfluous details.

Weak: The subjects, who volunteered to participate, were recruited from an introductory psychology class that was taught in the morning and had approximately 500 students.

Better: The subjects were volunteers from a large introductory psychology class.

Basic Formatting

All manuscripts must, of course, be TYPED.

Spacing: DOUBLE SPACED (everything).

Margins: 1.5 inches all the way around.

Pagination: Number ALL pages (except figures) consecutively.

Page numbers: Place in the upper right-hand corner using arabic numbers (e.g., 1, 2, 3) just below the short title.

Short Title: One or a few key words of the title. Place in upper right-hand corner above the page number. (Used to identify manuscript pages.)

Hyphenation: Do NOT hyphenate a word at the end of a line.

University of Oklahoma
Summary of Research Involving Human Subjects

Title _____

_____

Principal Investigator(s) and Department(s) _____

_____

Faculty Advisor (if student) _____

Proposed Starting Date _____ Project Duration _____

Potential Sponsor(s) _____

To provide adequate review information for the Institutional Review Board, thus avoiding unnecessary delays, please complete the following, attach 11 copies of any available project proposal, and send to the Office of Research Administration, Buchanan Hall, Room 314, *not later than the 5th day of the month in which you wish the proposed project reviewed.* If you have any questions, please call 325-████.

1. Briefly describe the project's overall purpose and primary objectives:

2. Briefly describe the subject population to be used (specifically noting if any will be from "vulnerable" categories; e.g., minors, prisoners, mentally or physically infirm). Also, describe the procedures for identifying/obtaining the subjects, subject compensation (if any), and the research procedures to be used in treating or obtaining information from the subjects: (Attach continuation sheets if necessary.)

3. Briefly describe the procedures to be used to assure the confidentiality of subject data, specifically addressing whether subjects will be identifiable from raw and/or re-fined data, how such data will be protected from non-project personnel (e.g., stored in locked cabinets), whether the identifiable data will be destroyed when no longer needed, and whether project publications (theses, papers, videotapes, etc.) will allow identification of individual subjects:

4. Describe the potential risks to subjects that may result from the project:

5. Describe the potential benefits to subjects or society that may result from the project:

6. Attach 11 copies of the planned "Informed Consent" (see Appendix A) or "Agreement to Participate" (see Appendix B) form that you plan to use for the project.

7. Attach 11 copies of any available questionnaires, other instruments/materials, and/or comments that would be of value to the Board in its review.

Appendix A

This is an approved Informed Consent format. Use only as a guide to prepare your own.

University of Oklahoma
Informed Consent Form

Title of Project:

Investigator(s): (Give name(s), title(s), department(s), and telephone number(s).)

This is to certify that I, __(print full name)__ , hereby (give permission to have my child or legal ward) agree to participate as a volunteer in a scientific investigation (experiment, project, study) as part of an authorized research program of the University of Oklahoma under the supervision of __(principal investigator)__ .

The purpose of this research is to: . . . The procedures to be followed are: . . . (This section must include a fair and understandable explanation of the nature of the activity, its purpose, the duration of the subject's participation, and the procedures to be followed, including identification of any procedures which are experimental.)

I understand that I may expect the following (physical and/or mental) discomforts during the course of this research: . . . I understand that, by participating in this research, I may be subjected to the following (physical, mental, and/or social) risks:

I understand that this research may result in the following benefits to me: . . .

The following are alternative investigative procedures which might be more advantageous to you: . . .

I understand that the information obtained from or about me will be kept confidential to the following extent: . . . (if subject information is not to be kept fully confidential, indicate the extent to which it will be protected).

I understand that I am free to refuse to participate in any procedure or to refuse to answer any question at any time without prejudice to me. I understand that I am free to withdraw my consent and to withdraw from the research at any time without prejudice to me.

I understand that by agreeing to participate in this research and signing this form I do not waive any of my legal rights.

I understand that the research investigator(s) named above will answer any of my questions about the research procedures, my rights as a subject, and research-related injuries at any time.

(For projects containing physical risks to subjects only.) I understand that, for any physical injury I may suffer as a result of and during the course of this research investigation, the University (will, will not) provide compensation (in the following types and amounts) and (will, will not) provide medical treatment (in the following types and amounts). (If either compensation or medical treatment is provided, also provide a source where additional information on the limits and restrictions can be obtained by the subject.)

_____   _____
Date   Subject or Parent/Guardian Signature

Appendix B

This is an approved Agreement to Participate format. Use only as a guide to prepare your own.

University of Oklahoma
Agreement to Participate

Title of Project:

Investigator(s): (Give name(s), title(s), department(s), and telephone number(s).)

I, __print full name__ , hereby agree to participate (give permission for my child or legal ward to participate) as a volunteer in the above named research project, which has been fully explained to me.

I understand that I (my child or legal ward) is free to refuse to participate in any procedure or to refuse to answer any question at any time without prejudice to me (him/her). I further understand that I am free to withdraw my consent and to withdraw (my child, legal ward) from the research project at any time without prejudice to me.

I understand that by agreeing (for my child, legal ward) to participate in this research and signing this form I do not waive any of my legal rights.

_____   _____
Date   Subject or Parent/Guardian Signature

NOTE: This form may be used *only* when the Institutional Review Board has determined that the research contains no risk to subjects beyond those of normal, everyday life and when the Board specifically approves its use.

Laboratory Animal Use Statement
University of Oklahoma, Norman Campus

Principal Investigator   Date

_____

Department   Telephone

_____

Title of Project

_____

Sponsoring Agency   / / New   / / Continuing

_____

Effective Period

_____ to _____
Investigator's Signature   Account # (when assigned)

_____

Action Taken   ACUC Reviewer   Date
/ / Approved   / / Disapproved

_____

Please check one of the following categories that best describes this study:
/ /   Study involves no pain or distress to animals
/ /   Study involves the use of appropriate anesthesia, analgesic, or tranquilizer to
      avoid pain or distress
/ /   Study involves pain or distress without administration of appropriate anesthetic,
      analgesic, or tranquilizer

_____

A. Justification for Use of Proposed Animal Model:
   1. List the species and the approximate number of each to be used.

Species and/or strain	No.	Source
_____	____	_____
_____	____	_____
_____	____	_____
_____	____	_____

   2. Briefly describe your rationale for the use of animals in this study and for the ap-
      propriateness of the species and the numbers to be used:

   3. Give a complete description of the proposed use of the animals, include daily
      care, caging systems (size), etc.:

4. Are anesthetic, analgesic, or tranquilizing drugs used on animals during actual studies to relieve pain and distress? / / Yes / / No
If yes, list drugs and dosages:
If no, give justification:

5. Describe method of euthanasia to be employed at conclusion of study.

6. Present evidence of experience and/or training of personnel conducting the procedures on the proposed animal model. (This includes investigators and/or technicians.)

7. Surgical Procedures:
a. Will this proposed study involve surgical procedures?
/ / Yes / / No
b. If yes, complete the following:
Will surgery be performed under aseptic conditions?
/ / Yes / / No If no, please explain:

c. Will the animals be allowed to recover from anesthesia?
/ / Yes / / No
If yes, will appropriate measures be taken to alleviate post-operative pain and distress? / / Yes / / No
Please describe the post-operative therapy for pain.

Housing Requirements:
/ / Individually Housed / / Group Housed / / Other facility, list:

Special Requirements, include special diets, handling procedures required above routine care:

ACUC-NC 1: Revised 1-87

2 Literature & Ideas

Overview

In this chapter, the literature search is discussed in depth. An example of how to find references is developed through the formulation of an idea about multiple personality. There are many different sources in which to get ideas to do research: colleagues and professors, books, journal articles, and conventions and talks. Journal articles are a primary source of information and supply clues to previous work (treeing backward). *Psychological Abstracts* (*PA*) is a useful way to search for relevant journal articles. Finding articles that cite a critical article (treeing forward) can be done by using the *Social Science Citation Index* (*SSCI*). Electronic searches of the *PA* and the *SSCI* can also be done, although electronic searches are sometimes expensive and are not foolproof.

There are no statistics required in this chapter. Tips on General Style addresses common sentence construction problems. Tips on Specific Style gives advice about the four major sections of the psychology paper.

Learning About the Community of Psychologists

"Even speculation requires some data, Captain."

—Mr. Spock

"I'm not a psychologist!", you say? "How can I possibly know about the conventional rules of psychology?" "How will I ever know on *what* to do a study?"

Before any experiment can be conducted, the experimenters must have a reason for conducting it, a question they wish to answer, or a problem they would like to solve. Getting an idea for an experiment is like playing poker: You can begin with very little training, but it is something you can spend a lifetime mastering. Of course, there are those scientists, as there are those poker players, who believe that success will come without thought and without practice. Some believe that quantity can substitute for quality; they are likely to suffer rejection several times or have their experiments published in places where they have little impact on the field. Only a few scientists produce a great number of high-quality publications. These leaders of the field devote considerable thought to their ideas.

Pursuing the Idea

Most researchers do, in fact, continuously attempt to polish their ideas and improve on the quality of the ideas they entertain. Initial ideas can come from several places. You may casually observe something on the street and wonder *Why?* or *What if?* Ideas can also come from readings in psychology or other classes. Any experience, whether direct or indirect, that deals with thinking or behaving organisms may produce the *seed of an idea.*

For example, the other day a person who suffered from multiple-personality disorder was being interviewed on a radio talk show. During one part of the interview, the interviewer asked about the guest's early childhood. She conveyed much information, but one thing that was particularly interesting was that she had been abused as a child. Had there been any research done on the incidence of child abuse in people diagnosed as having multiple personalities? Could this actually be what caused the development of these other personalities?

This is clearly the seed of an idea. To stop here and design a study prematurely would be like the poker player with a low pair who decides not to draw any more cards. It will make a good bluff, but the probability of raking in the pot is very low. The first thing needed is to determine how good the idea is. That is, has it already been done, does it fit with the literature and the other studies that have been done, where does it fit, and will anyone care? Several sources can help to answer these questions. The first four sources listed below may also be especially good at helping you come up with the initial idea as well as helping you develop the idea. Each of the suggestions in this chapter are an appeal to authority as we discussed in chapter 1. However, here authority is the beginning of the process, not an end.

In reading the following, do not assume that the steps to an idea always follow this order. For example, your idea may begin after hearing a talk at a convention; from there you could speak with the researcher of the talk or with one of your professors.

Colleagues and Professors

One of the easiest ways to begin to answer questions about your idea is to talk it over with someone who might know more than you. This is always true, but it is especially helpful at the earlier stages of your career. Often you may find it difficult even to determine in which large subarea of psychology your ideas belong. Talking to a graduate student or professor, for example, may help you take this initial step.

When you speak with this person, you should go with a concrete idea, even if the concreteness is somewhat artificial. Then be prepared to listen and modify your idea. We took our interest in multiple personality to Dr. Kirby Gilliland, a member of our faculty who specializes in experimental personality research. Although multiple personality is not his specialty, we thought he might provide us with a good starting point for our idea.

Dr. Gilliland told us a great deal about multiple personality, but he did not have much detailed information about the incidence of child abuse in that population. However, several things suggested to him that such an idea was worth pursuing, such as the fact that there are more women than men suffering from multiple personalities and that they develop during adolescence. He also warned us that the incidence of this diagnosis is very rare. He gave us a textbook, *Abnormal Psychology* by Goldstein, Baker, and Jamison, as well as the *Diagnostic and Statistical Manual of Mental Disorders* (3rd ed.; DSM-III), to begin our search of the literature.

Books

Textbooks, review books, and introductory books are all good sources for the initial idea and the development of the idea. A good textbook will have the advantage of including the most important work in an area, although this research will have been done some time ago (often 10 years or more for textbooks). When you locate a book or two by talking to someone or using the card catalog, you should use the index and table of contents to isolate parts of the book that are particularly relevant (if you already have an idea) or particularly interesting (if you do not). Read those sections or chapters very carefully. Do you really understand what was said? Can you answer Why?, What?, How?, and So? If you have mastered this introductory material, you can now use the bibliography at the end of the book to help you start investigating primary sources, such as journal articles. You may find that your good idea has been heavily researched. Do not despair; if your idea has already been researched, it just means you are on the right track.

The DSM-III book borrowed from Dr. Gilliland stated under "predisposing factors" that "Child abuse and other forms of severe emotional trauma in childhood may be predisposing factors" for multiple personality. We took this as evidence that our idea had some merit. Further, in the *Abnormal Psychology* text we found citation of two articles: Wilbur, 1984, and Bliss, 1984. From the narrative, both seemed to deal with child abuse. We looked up the complete references in the reference section of the book; unfortunately, the Wilbur reference had been omitted, but the Bliss reference led us to the library.

Articles

At some point in your idea development, you will come across the **journal article** (sometimes the articles will appear in edited books). You will eventually rely on the journal article as your primary source for information. In addition to containing information in the body of the article, the journal article gives you an important section that can make your search of the literature easy: the **reference section.**

By using the list of references cited by the author, you will be able to **tree backward** through the literature. The reference section tells you at least three things that will assist you in your task: (1) The particular articles of relevance to the problem will be listed here. If a certain reference is cited by a number of articles, it is probably a classic and should definitely be included in your reading. (2) Names of other authors doing work in the area can be found in the references. You can now locate other works by the author or actually write to the author using a **reprint request card** to ask for a

Figure 2–1   Reprint Request Card

Department of Psychology
University of Oklahoma
455 West Lindsey, DAHT 740
Norman, OK 73019

Dear

      I would appreciate receiving _____ reprint(s) of

your article _____

_____

and any other related materials. Thank you.

                     Sincerely,

copy of the article (i.e., a **reprint**) or to find out if anything new is in the works. The reprint request card is simply a postcard with some standard information on it. A copy of one used at the University of Oklahoma is pictured in Figure 2-1. (3) Journals that tend to publish work in the area will be listed several times in the references. You can go to recent issues and past issues of this journal to see what other studies have been published that did not happen to be cited in the article(s) you already have. In our search, we decided to look up several articles cited by Bliss in his article. In one of those we also found some articles that were cited that did not appear in the original work. In this way we were able to tree backward through the literature and collect several articles relevant to multiple personality. We also sent a reprint request card to one of the authors asking for a copy of the article and any recent work. By this point, we were beginning to modify our original idea. We began to focus on Bliss's idea that along with abusive life situations the person must have a capacity for self-hypnosis. In other words, it seemed that abuse alone would not invariably lead to multiple personalities. The victim must also be able to "escape" through an ability akin to self-hypnosis.

Conventions and Talks

Another easy way to get ideas and develop the ideas is to attend presentations given by psychologists. Sometimes these talks are given within your department by your faculty, by job candidates, or by visiting scholars. They are almost always open to the public. Other times, usually annually, groups of psychologists get together and spend 2 to 7 days reporting their research and listening to others (or at least that is what they are supposed to do).

Such a **convention** might be statewide, regional (several adjacent states), or national. For the University of Oklahoma, the state meeting is the Spring Conference to Encourage and Develop Psychological Research. As the somewhat convoluted name implies, it is strongly focused at novice researchers. Perhaps your state has a similar meeting for undergraduates. The regional meeting is organized by the Southwestern Psychological Association (SWPA). State and regional meetings are usually cost effective for students on a budget, as registration costs ($5 to $10) and travel costs are minimal. In fact, SWPA allows students to register free. The national organizations include the American Psychological Association (APA), which holds a huge 7-day affair taking place in several hotels in a large city. If feasible, a student would find such a trip very informative. (Students can join any of these organizations for a nominal fee. APA is especially good if you want to subscribe to journals at student membership rates.) Attending a convention allows you to hear about research that has just been completed or that is in the process of being completed. You can also talk to the participants after their talk or, in the case of poster sessions, while they stand next to a display of their study.

In our search for more information about multiple personalities, we went to a poster session at the Southwestern Psychological Association meeting that was held in Tulsa. There we attended a poster session where a talk by Betty Everett and Vicki Green on "Physical abuse and interpersonal problem-solving skills in preschoolers" gave us some insight into abuse and coping.

Psychological Abstracts

By now we felt comfortable with the question and issues that were implicated by that radio talk show. We knew what multiple personality was, how it was diagnosed, something about its incidence, and most important something about its predisposing factors. The Bliss article had led us to modify our idea about childhood abuse. Bliss's idea that abuse and an ability to escape mentally from the abuse led us to start thinking about the interrelationship of abuse and hypnotism and how these factors might work in multiple personality. It was time to do a serious review of the literature in preparation for our final steps in formulating a good, well-thought-out study.

We turn now to *Psychological Abstracts,* a publication of the American Psychological Association that is maintained in the reference section of college and university libraries. It is issued monthly in journal form and will thus appear in your library as either softbound issues (for the recent editions) or large hardbound collections (for the past years).

The key to using the abstracts is its index. It has both a subject index and an author index. In addition, there are indexes for each issue as well as indexes for an entire year (or several years) of work. These indexes, which cover several issues of *Psychological Abstracts,* are particularly useful and are called *Cumulative Indexes.* Figure 2-2 is a sample from the subject index, volume 66. We see that some work has been published on multiple personality. Further, the work has been broken down by subtopics. We decided to ex-

Figure 2–2   A page from the subject index of *Psychological Abstracts*.   Four abstracts fall under the topic of multiple personality (i.e., numbers 10893, 5944, 3772, and 1671). This material is reprinted with permission (fee paid) of the American Psychological Association, publisher of *Psychological Abstracts* and the PsycINFO Database (Copyright © 1967–1987 by the American Psychological Association), and may not be reproduced without its prior permission.

gies & informa-
gies & informa-
·rred & nonpre-
; 4th vs 6th grad-
  preacademic &
8
performance on
ican 5–8 yr olds,
idition, learning
nale college stu-
ucationally sub-
7 yr olds, 10075
·ncidence antici-'

choice tests, college students, 6695
preference for assigned notetaking vs full vs partial distributed notes,
    multiple-choice vs essay test scores, college students, 13555
short-answer vs multiple choice format, retention of research concepts & procedures, college students, 6759
technically worded options, multiple choice test performance, college
    students, implications for testwiseness, 4459
Multiple Personality
behavior therapy, transient dual personality, female 33 yr old, 10893
diagnosis & characteristics, multiple personality syndrome, 5944
history of multiple personality & early examples from B. Rush, 3772
hypnosis & psychotherapy, multiple personalities resulting from
    childhood & adolescent trauma, 29 yr old female, 1671
Multiple Sclerosis
click stimuli repetition rate, auditory brainstem responses, normal
    hearing 14–26 yr olds vs 19–47 yr olds with multiple sclerosis vs
    70–91 yr olds, 13151
critical flicker fusion thresholds, 22–56 yr old females mildly impaired by multiple sclerosis, implications for diagnostic use
    10692
hyperbaric oxygen therapy, multiple sclerosis, 10782

plore further the work done relating "hypnosis and psychotherapy, multiple personalities resulting from childhood and adolescent trauma": abstract number 1671 from volume 66 (the same volume as the index, of course).

We now turn to the abstracts and look for the appropriate number. Because the abstracts are organized based on the abstract number, it is easy to find the one abstract of interest. Figure 2-3 shows the abstract number 1671 found in volume 66 of the *Psychological Abstracts*.

We can tell a great deal about the article before we even decide whether to go to the library, retrieve the journal, and read the article. Following the abstract number we are given information about the author or authors, their affiliation (particularly valuable if we want to write to them or send a reprint request card), and the title of the article. Following the title we find information about where the article was published; we will use this information to find the article if the description of the article, the **abstract,** indicates it would be relevant. From the abstract, we can see that it was a report of a case study. We also can expect to see in the article some information or argumentation for our original thesis that abuse in childhood is a predisposing factor in the development of multiple personalities. Further, we note that there are 14 other references cited in the article that may be of further use in our quest. Thus, this one seems as if it would be worth exploring further.

We also want to see if Salama, the author of this paper, has done anything else that might be useful. We can find out easily by consulting the

Figure 2–3   Abstract 1671 taken from Volume 66 of *Psychological Abstracts*.   Following the abstract number, and preceding the description of the work, information is provided about **Author(s)**, (Affiliation) **Title**, *Journal*, Year, Volume, pages. Following the description of the work is the number of references cited by the author (e.g., 14 ref). This material is reprinted with permission (fee paid) of the American Psychological Association, publisher of *Psychological Abstracts* and the PsycINFO Database (Copyright © 1967–1987 by the American Psychological Association), and may not be reproduced without its prior permission.

licted amputation.
/ol 25(2), 143–150.
f-inflicted amputa-
eplanted. Three of
iloyed and pleased
nitted suicide. The
ion surgery is re-
ole of the psychia-
(French summary)

ıh, Salt Lake City)
nsulting & Clinical
—112 chronic pain
the MMPI upon
chiatric treatment
e was found to be
average of 20 mo
g Attitude), Hypo-
Femininity scales
e strength of this
ure of the outcome
MMPI differences
their body in pain
pain complaints.
nd in comparisons
back), and type of
atric vs anesthesio-

by BDI. The HRSD on a subsample did not result in between-groups differences at posttreatment. The addition of medication to individual therapy did not reduce end-of-treatment symptom levels. The symptom response pattern during active treatment suggests that group therapy initially produced as rapid symptom reduction as other treatments, but a less complete response was obtained by end of treatment. (23 ref) —*S. Dargahi Hampion.*

1671. **Salama, Abd El Aziz A.** (Southern Illinois U School of Medicine, Springfield) **Multiple personality: A case study.** *Canadian Journal of Psychiatry,* 1980(Nov), Vol 25(7), 569–572. —Presents a case study of a 29-yr-old woman with multiple personalities that developed from traumatic childhood and adolescent experiences and discusses how the therapist's attention can reinforce the development of new personalities. Hypnosis, psychotherapy, and advancing age are viewed as affecting resolution. In this case, there was only partial success in resolving all the personalities because of earlier reinforcement. (French abstract) (14 ref)

1672. **Schneider, P.-B. & Wulliemier, F.** (U. Lausanne, Psychiatric Policlinic, Switzerland) **The psychotherapy of the psychosomatic patient.** *Psychotherapy & Psychosomatics,* 1979, Vol 32(1–4), 112–117.—Describes some of the reasons why psychotherapy is seldom used for psychosomatic patients, either on an individual or group basis. Two treatments that contain some elements of psychotherapy and that have been developed as a consequence of the analysis of the early

ada) **Replantation**
Canadian Journal (
—Describes 4 case
tion of the upper li
the 4 patients are
with the surgical re
literature on self-i
viewed, and psych
trist in replantatio
(18 ref)

1677. **Strassberg**
he MMPI and chi
Psychology, 1981(⁄
patients (mean aç
entering either an
program. Pretreatr
successful in predi
following treatmen
chondriasis, Hyste
accounting for m
relationship varied
and type of treatm
were found when :
were compared w
Significant MMPI
based on Ss' sex, t
treatment for whicl

author index. Figure 2-4 shows a page from one such index. During this year Salama did not publish anything else; however, if we had come upon the name in some other way, we would discover in a different way that Salama had published a paper on multiple personality: abstract number 66:1671.

Social Science Citation Index

Whereas *Psychological Abstracts* is ideal for treeing backward through the literature, it is not very useful if you want to go forward in time. For example, it would be useful to know if anyone has included the Salama article in his or her reference section (sort of like treeing forward). Because the article was published in 1980, we may find related work done from 1981 to the present. We could look up each abstract in the *Psychological Abstracts* and then read each article to see if it included Salama in its references. However, there is an easier way: ***Social Science Citation Index***. This index will allow us to see if anyone has cited an article of interest to us. For example, if

Figure 2–4   A page from the author index of *Psychological Abstracts*.   Only the abstract reproduced in Figure 2.3 was found when looking for contributions by author's name. This material is reprinted with permission (fee paid) of the American Psychological Association, publisher of *Psychological Abstracts* and the PsycINFO Database (Copyright © 1967–1987 by the American Psychological Association), and may not be reproduced without its prior permission.

Safran, Joan, 11338
Sagar, H. Andrew, 5578
Sagberg, Fridulv, 4736
Sager, Clifford J. et al. 7975, 13256
Sages, Roger 5166
Sagi, Abraham, 2795
Sagvolden, Terje, 531
Sahakian, B. J., 7689
Sahay, M., 7067
Saheb, S. Jaleel, 6810
Sahib, S. Jaleel, 8849
Sahlin, Nils-Eric, 2421
Sahu, S., 5525
Saigh, Philip A., 7092, 11391
Sailinger-Holle, R., 12234
Saint-Germain, Gisèle, 3686
Saint-Jean, Heliette, 13109
Saisa, Jouko, 2624
Saisangjan, Upatham, 7119
Saito, A., 12036
Saito, I. et al, 6798
Saito, M., 4534
Saito, Masahiko, 390

Sakinofsky, Isaac, 2040
Sakitt, Barbara, 365, 2700, 11603
Saklad, Stephen R., 13341
Saklofske, D. H., 2523, 9121, 13046
Sakowski, Cyril J., 4821
Sakurai, Melvin M., 9458
Sala, Linda S., 7257
Salafia, W. Ronald, 827, 3092
Salafia, W. Ronald et al. 605
Salajpal, Tereza, 6165, 6274
Salama, Abd El Aziz A., 1671
Salamero, Manuel, 2468
Salamy, A., 8367, 9799
Salamy, Alan, 12225
Salapatek, Philip, 12504
Sale, Ian, 10518, 10519
Saleh, Joseph, 4737, 12417
Saleh, S. D., 6748
Sales, Bruce D., 8789
Salibi, N. A., 9795
Saligaut, C., 3143

Sanberg, Paul R., 3208, 5398
Sanchez, Victor C., 4749, 9371
Sanchez-Sosa, Juan J., 6672
Sanchez Turet, M., 3454, 5354
Sandall, Susan R., 8984
Sandell, Rolf G., 12422
Sander, Louis, 6275
Sanders, A. F., 3052
Sanders, C., 11554
Sanders, C. J., 9698
Sanders, Catherine M., 5887, 10190
Sanders, Connie H., 9400
Sanders, D. C., 5095
Sanders, Glenn S., 1242, 5718, 10360, 12703
Sanders, Jeffrey L., 7093, 8368
Sanders, Jill D., 6304
Sanders, Joseph R., 11121
Sanders, Judith A., 10183
Sanders, Mark S., 2278, 13782
Sanders, Matthew R., 4324

an article published in 1980 were cited by someone in 1985, we would want to investigate the contents of the 1985 article and add it to our list of articles.

Figure 2-5 is the page that contains information about all the articles published by Salama that were cited by someone in the year 1985 and part of 1986. Salama had one of his articles cited this year. It happens to be the one that we found using *Psychological Abstracts*. We see that one person has since listed that paper in his or her reference section. We can now go to that journal (i.e., *Psychopathology*, 1985, volume 18, page 237) and determine the exact relevance of this more recent study by Alzenber to our work.

The *SSCI* is perhaps the most important index to consult right before you invest a great deal of effort in a study. If you read an article written in 1978 and get a great idea about an experiment or study, it is quite possible that someone else may have already had the same idea. If that is true, then they probably would have cited that 1978 article. You can determine this very easily using the *SSCI*.

Electronic Searches

Our initial searches through *Psychological Abstracts* and the *Social Science Citation Index* were conducted by hand. We believe this manual approach has much to recommend it. We obtain a good feel for the area for a relatively low cost. However, an extensive consideration of the literature would be greatly aided by using some computer assistance. Today most research databases have been computerized, allowing a search of massive amounts of literature in a short period of time. These searches are sometimes expensive. In addition, the researcher must plan quite extensively *before* he or she sits down at the computer terminal: The selection of **key words** will be critical to the success of the search. The computer will search the comput-

Figure 2–5   A page from the *Social Sciences Citation Index.*   In the effort to find other researchers who had cited the work of A.E.A. Salama (the author of the abstract in Figure 2.3), one additional article was uncovered. Following information about the cited article (e.g., Salama's) is information about the Author, Journal, Vol, page, and year of the citing article. Reprinted with permission from the *Social Sciences Citation Index* ® GSL1986 annual. Copyright 1987 by the Institute for Scientific Information, Philadelphia, PA, U.S.A.

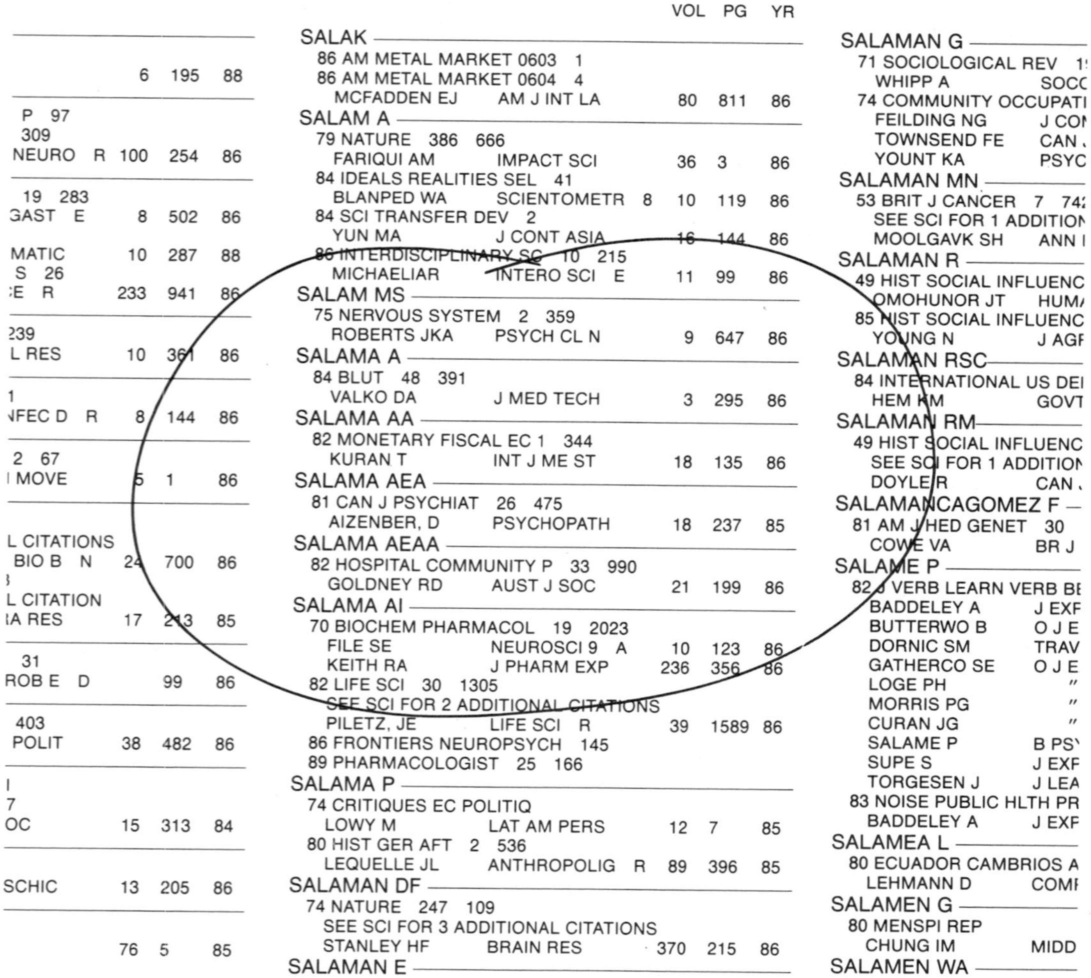

A page from the Social Sciences Citation Index showing the following entries:

	VOL	PG	YR
SALAK			
86 AM METAL MARKET 0603 1			
86 AM METAL MARKET 0604 4			
MCFADDEN EJ AM J INT LA	80	811	86
SALAM A			
79 NATURE 386 666			
FARIQUI AM IMPACT SCI	36	3	86
84 IDEALS REALITIES SEL 41			
BLANPED WA SCIENTOMETR 8	10	119	86
84 SCI TRANSFER DEV 2			
YUN MA J CONT ASIA	16	144	86
86 INTERDISCIPLINARY SC 10 215			
MICHAELIAR INTERO SCI E	11	99	86
SALAM MS			
75 NERVOUS SYSTEM 2 359			
ROBERTS JKA PSYCH CL N	9	647	86
SALAMA A			
84 BLUT 48 391			
VALKO DA J MED TECH	3	295	86
SALAMA AA			
82 MONETARY FISCAL EC 1 344			
KURAN T INT J ME ST	18	135	86
SALAMA AEA			
81 CAN J PSYCHIAT 26 475			
AIZENBER, D PSYCHOPATH	18	237	85
SALAMA AEAA			
82 HOSPITAL COMMUNITY P 33 990			
GOLDNEY RD AUST J SOC	21	199	86
SALAMA AI			
70 BIOCHEM PHARMACOL 19 2023			
FILE SE NEUROSCI 9 A	10	123	86
KEITH RA J PHARM EXP	236	356	86
82 LIFE SCI 30 1305			
SEE SCI FOR 2 ADDITIONAL CITATIONS			
PILETZ, JE LIFE SCI R	39	1589	86
86 FRONTIERS NEUROPSYCH 145			
89 PHARMACOLOGIST 25 166			
SALAMA P			
74 CRITIQUES EC POLITIQ			
LOWY M LAT AM PERS	12	7	85
80 HIST GER AFT 2 536			
LEQUELLE JL ANTHROPOLIG R	89	396	85
SALAMAN DF			
74 NATURE 247 109			
SEE SCI FOR 3 ADDITIONAL CITATIONS			
STANLEY HF BRAIN RES	370	215	86
SALAMAN E			

Left column entries:

	VOL	PG	YR
	6	195	88
P 97			
309			
NEURO R 100		254	86
19 283			
GAST E 8		502	86
MATIC 10		287	88
S 26			
E R 233		941	86
239			
L RES 10		361	86
1			
NFEC D R 8		144	86
2 67			
MOVE 5		1	86
L CITATIONS			
BIO B N 24		700	86
L CITATION			
IA RES 17		213	85
31			
ROB E D		99	86
403			
POLIT 38		482	86
I			
7			
OC 15		313	84
SCHIC 13		205	86
	76	5	85

Right column entries:

SALAMAN G	
71 SOCIOLOGICAL REV 1	
WHIPP A SOCC	
74 COMMUNITY OCCUPATI	
FEILDING NG J CO	
TOWNSEND FE CAN	
YOUNT KA PSYC	
SALAMAN MN	
53 BRIT J CANCER 7 74	
SEE SCI FOR 1 ADDITION	
MOOLGAVK SH ANN	
SALAMAN R	
49 HIST SOCIAL INFLUENC	
OMOHUNOR JT HUM	
85 HIST SOCIAL INFLUENC	
YOUNG N J AG	
SALAMAN RSC	
84 INTERNATIONAL US DE	
HEM KM GOVT	
SALAMAN RM	
49 HIST SOCIAL INFLUENC	
SEE SCI FOR 1 ADDITION	
DOYLER CAN	
SALAMANCAGOMEZ F	
81 AM J HED GENET 30	
COWE VA BR J	
SALAME P	
82 J VERB LEARN VERB B	
BADDELEY A J EXF	
BUTTERWO B O J E	
DORNIC SM TRAV	
GATHERCO SE O J E	
LOGE PH "	
MORRIS PG "	
CURAN JG "	
SALAME P B PS	
SUPE S J EXF	
TORGESEN J J LEA	
83 NOISE PUBLIC HLTH PR	
BADDELEY A J EXF	
SALAMEA L	
80 ECUADOR CAMBRIOS A	
LEHMANN D COM	
SALAMEN G	
80 MENSPI REP	
CHUNG IM MIDD	
SALAMEN WA	

erized database for the occurrence of your key words. The **Thesaurus of Psychological Index Terms** is a document containing key words useful for a computer search. Even with this resource, however, some relevant articles will be missed and a number of irrelevant articles will be included. By relying on all of the methods discussed in this chapter, you will be better able to determine if your electronic search has been successful and complete. Despite these limitations, the computerized literature search is a valuable tool that will allow you to obtain references, and even the abstracts, for a number of articles.

In the rest of the text, we supply a number of additional readings at the end of each chapter. These readings should be used, along with the techniques described in this chapter, to search the literature for those topics that you plan to research further.

Key Words

abstract	reprint
convention	reprint request card
journal article	*Social Science Citation Index (SSCI)*
key words	*Thesaurus of Psychological Index Terms*
Psychological Abstracts (PA)	tree backward
reference section	

Additional Reading

American Psychiatric Association. (1980). *Diagnostic and statistical manual of mental disorders* (3rd ed.). Washington, DC: APA.

Bliss, E. (1984). Spontaneous self-hypnosis in multiple-personality disorder. *Psychiatric clinics of North America, 7,* 135–138.

Everett, B., & Green, V. (1988, April). *Physical abuse and interpersonal problem-solving skills in preschoolers.* Paper presented at the Annual Meetings of the Southwestern Psychological Association, Tulsa, OK.

Goldstein, M. J., Baker, B. L., & Jamison, K. R. (1986). *Abnormal Psychology: Experiences, origins, and interventions* (2nd ed.). Boston: Little, Brown.

Salama, A. A. (1980). Multiple personality: A case study. *Canadian Journal of Psychiatry, 25,* 569–572.

Common Mistakes in Sentence Construction

Does every string of words form a sentence?
A common mistake is

> *Subjects.* Fifteen undergraduate psychology majors.

Have you used primarily active voice?

"Smith (1900) investigated differences between . . ." NOT "Differences between . . . were investigated by Smith (1900)."

Have you used past tense everywhere in the methods and most of the rest of the paper?

Do the verbs and subjects of your sentences agree in number?

> "The **responses** of the subject **were** . . ."
> "The **set** of responses **was** . . ."

Does each pronoun have a clear referent and do they agree?

> "The **group** improved **its** score."
> "The children **who** . . ."
> "The rats **that** . . ."
> "The children were separated from the parents. **They** fussed and cried." (WHO fussed and cried?)
> "Although it was an interesting finding, I did not use the same apparatus in Experiment 2 because it was broken." (It is used to refer to two different entities in the same sentence.)

Can the noun of your sentence perform the action specified by your verb?

> "The experiment predicted . . ." Can an experiment predict? "The stimuli suggested a possible problem." Can stimuli suggest? "Experiment 1 disagreed . . ." Can experiments disagree?

The Four Basic Sections

All empirical reports have four basic sections: the introduction, methods, results, and discussion. These four sections form a sort of hourglass, beginning with broad issues and concerns, funneling into the specifics of the study, and ending with the results in their broader context.

The introduction begins very broadly, then funnels into a consideration of studies specific to your research problem, and finally presents a preview of your experiment. The writer's concern in the introduction is to make certain that the reader has been told what the problem is and why it is important (see TOSS 7).

The methods section follows the introduction and is like a narrow tube where the reader learns exactly what you did in your experiment. The writer's concern here is with making certain that a reader who wished to do exactly what was done, could. To facilitate this, there are often several subsections explicitly presented in the methods section (see TOSS 4, 5).

The results section is the second half of this narrow tube. It tells the reader what you discovered during the experiment. The writer must be careful in this section not to speculate or go beyond the actual data (see TOSS 6).

With the beginning of the discussion section, the tube begins to funnel out again. This section starts with conclusions tied very closely to the results and then widens to consider implications of the research. The writer must be especially alert to connecting the discussion back to the introduction, so that the reader has a sense of closure (see TOSS 9).

How should you go about writing these sections? We have found that a good strategy followed successfully by experienced and novice scientists is to write the sections in the following order: method, results, introduction, discussion, abstract (discussed in TOSS 10). The methods section should be written soon after you begin running the study. This ensures that your memory will be precise and that you will not forget any details. This advice does not mean that the introduction is not planned until after the methods. It simply means that the researcher usually writes a better introduction after he or she has considered the methods and results in concrete terms. Also, because the discussion and introduction are written close together in time, it is easier to tie the two together.

Scavenger Hunts

As a vehicle for learning about the literature databases available to psychologists, we have prepared the following scavenger hunt sheets. If your instructor chooses to use this option, he or she will assign you a list. Your instructor may give some reward to the first student(s) who answers all of the questions correctly. Good luck!

DATA SHEET

Library Scavenger Hunt

1. Write the author and title of the article that appears first under the topic heading Memory Disorders in the index volume 54, 1975, in *Psychological Abstracts.*
   ANS. Author _____
   Title _____
   _____

2. Write the name of the journal that MacDonall, James S. published in, which is referenced in the index volume 62, 1979, of *Psychological Abstracts.*
   ANS. Journal Name _____

3. How many subjects are used in the experimental report?
   Harrison, R., & Dorcus, R. M. (1938). Is rate of voluntary bodily movement unitary. *Journal of General Psychology, 18,* 31–39.
   (First experiment only, if there is more than one.)
   ANS. Number of Subjects _____

4. In the article in question 3, find the first reference in the list of references at the end of the article. Find this reference and copy the first five words of the introduction of the article.
   ANS. First five words of the introduction
   _____

5. Who is the current editor of the following journal:
   American Psychologist
   ANS. Name of Editor _____

6. How many times was the article by Weber, S. J., published in the *Psychological Bulletin* (1972), cited in the year 1983?
   ANS. Number of Citations _____

7. What is the call number for the book *Handbook of Psychological Terms* by Phillip Lawrence Harriman?
   ANS. Call Number _____

Library Scavenger Hunt

1. Write the author and title of the article that appears first under the topic heading Anger in the index volume 65, 1981, in *Psychological Abstracts.*

    ANS. Author _____

    Title _____

2. Write the name of the journal that Eagley published in, which is referenced in the index volume 71, 1984, of *Psychological Abstracts.*

    ANS. Journal Name _____

3. How many subjects are used in the experimental report?
    Shea, J., Crossman, S., & Adams, G. (1978). Physical attractiveness and personality development. *The Journal of Psychology, 99,* 59–62.
    (First experiment only, if there is more than one.)

    ANS. Number of Subjects _____

4. In the article in question 3, find the first reference in the list of references at the end of the article. Find this reference and copy the first five words of the introduction of the article.

    ANS. First five words of the introduction

    _____

5. Who is the current editor of the following journal:
    The Journal of General Psychology

    ANS. Name of Editor _____

6. How many times was the article by Tesser, A., published in the *Journal of Personality & Social Psychology* (1976), cited in the year 1984?

    ANS. Number of Citations _____

7. What is the call number for the book *The Conference on Psychological Stress,* by Appley and Trumbell.

    ANS. Call Number _____

Library Scavenger Hunt

1. Write the author and title of the article that appears first under the topic heading Employee Turnover in the index volume 63, 1980, in *Psychological Abstracts*.

   ANS. Author _____

   Title _____

   _____

2. Write the name of the journal that A. Thompson published in, which is referenced in the index volume 61, 1979, of *Psychological Abstracts*.

   ANS. Journal Name _____

3. How many subjects are used in the experimental report?
   Park, D., & Mason, D. (1982). Is there evidence for automatic processing of spatial and color attributes present in pictures and words? *Memory and Cognition, 10,* 76–81.
   (First experiment only if there is more than one.)

   ANS. Number of Subjects _____

4. In the article in question 3, find the first reference in the list of references at the end of the article. Find this reference and copy the first five words of the introduction of the article.

   ANS. First five words of the introduction

   _____

5. Who is the current editor of the following journal:
   Journal of Experimental Child Psychology

   ANS. Name of Editor _____

6. How many times was the article by Weber, S. J., published in the *Psychological Bulletin* (1972), cited in the year 1982?

   ANS. Number of Citations _____

7. What is the call number for the book *Casebook on Ethical Standards of Psychologists* published by the American Psychological Association?

   ANS. Call Number _____

Library Scavenger Hunt

1. Write the author and title of the article that appears first under the topic heading Pain in the index volume 67, 1982, in *Psychological Abstracts*.

    ANS. Author _____

    Title _____

    _____

2. Write the name of the journal that Obrist, Paul A., published in, which is referenced in the index volume 66, 1981, of *Psychological Abstracts*.

    ANS. Journal Name _____

3. How many subjects are used in the experimental report?
    Heineman, E. G., Avin, E., Sullivan, M. A., and Chase, S. (1969). Analysis of stimulus generalization with a psychophysical method. *Journal of Experimental Psychology, 80*, 215–224.
    (First experiment only if there is more than one.)

    ANS. Number of Subjects _____

4. In the article in question 3, find the first reference in the list of references at the end of the article. Find this reference and copy the first five words of the introduction of this article.

    ANS. First five words of the introduction

    _____

5. Who is the current editor of the following journal?
    Developmental Psychology

    ANS. Name of Editor _____

6. How many times was the article by Weber, S. J., published in the *Psychological Bulletin* (1972), cited in the year 1975?

    ANS. Number of Citations _____

7. What is the call number for the book *Science and Human Behavior* by B. F. Skinner?

    ANS. Call Number _____

3
Observing
&
Defining

Overview

In this chapter, the requirements of what qualifies as a scientific observation are elaborated. Focus is placed on the operational definition. The problem of unobtrusive observation in the context of the natural observation is discussed. Natural observation is a method of research where the observations (data collection) are done in the real world without intrusion by the scientist. This chapter presents the thinking required to develop a study to observe "door-holding behavior."

A feature of experimental psychology is the translation of general ideas into specific, workable hypotheses. Most hypotheses stem from one or more of three sources: (a) personal experience and observation of the world, (b) theories, and (c) previous research results. Several practical concerns relevant to the issues of control and operationism are introduced in this context. Several command decisions must be made by the experimenter to implement an experiment. Among them, clear operational definitions specifying measurable characteristics of an event are important.

Statistics required are simple frequencies and relative frequencies. Tips on General Style points out common sentence faults. Tips on Specific Style gives advice about sections of the psychology paper and section headings.

Naturalistic Observation and Experimentation

"Perhaps I have trained myself to see what others overlook."

—*Sherlock Holmes*

- Who says chivalry is dead?
- Men unconsciously treat women as if they were the weaker sex.
- We are living in an era of equality between the sexes.
- In most ways behavior toward the opposite sex is the same as behavior toward the same sex.

All of the above statements are general hypotheses or statements about the relationship between males and females; contradictory statements at that! What we will do in this, and all the subsequent chapters of this book, is to translate a general hypothesis into an empirical study. In the process of designing an empirical study, the principles and concepts of experimental psychology will be defined and illustrated. At the end of the chapter, the hypothesis and experimental situation will be reviewed in a systematic Frame for Research.

Hypothesis

You may feel that males and females treat each other as equals. You may feel that a big difference still exists in the way males and females treat each other, reflecting the stereotypes and biases of our culture. Regardless of how you feel, these feelings are too general to be used as a research hypothesis. To do research to help decide the issue, these general statements must be made concrete. The translation of general ideas into specific, workable hypotheses is the distinguishing feature of experimental psychology.

A **research hypothesis** is a tentative statement about the way things are under certain specified conditions. It is *tentative* because we are not totally sure it is correct. If we were sure our statement was correct, it would be called a law, not a hypothesis.

We are concerned with the behavior of individuals under well-specified conditions. The behavior in which we are interested is objective, measurable, or empirical. For example, we might form the research hypothesis that women drive cars at a faster speed than men. The behavior of interest is the speed of a car being driven by a woman or a man. We could rent a radar gun and test the hypothesis by recording the speed of cars driven by a woman or a man on a particular street. The behavior is made objective, measurable, and empirical by the use of the radar gun, and the conditions are clearly specified by using a particular street.

Most of the hypotheses in which experimental psychologists are interested come from one of three sources. The example given above concerning differences in the speed of driving cars between men and women came from *personal experience and observation of the world*. Another source of research hypotheses is from formal *theories of behavior*. A third source is to base the hypothesis on *previous research results*. In this chapter we will develop our hypothesis based on personal experience and observation. In other chapters, theories (e.g., chapter 7) or past research (e.g., chapter 13) will serve as the basis for the hypotheses.

Our example of the speed of driving cars is designed to test a difference between males and females, but does not directly address our concern with the relationship between the sexes. To generate a hypothesis concerning the way men and women treat each other, we must think of a social and an observable behavior(s) for study. A traditional situation that meets these needs is the opening of a door and passage through it by males and females. According to the traditional manners of our culture, males should open a door and allow a female companion to enter first. Thus our hypothesis is that there will be a greater degree of door-holding behavior by males for females (male-female) than by females for males (female-male) or than by same sex pairs (male-male or female-female).

The hypothesis is more restricted than the idea that generated it. We began by considering how males and females treat each other in general, but the hypothesis we have arrived at is much more specific, dealing only with door holding. This is almost always the case in research. Rarely can the researcher test a **general idea.** Usually several tests must be done to evaluate the general idea. Science almost always moves in small steps. Even when a crucial bit of research provides the answer to a very general question, that bit is usually the culmination of a whole series of previous increments of knowledge. Thus our hypothesis that men will hold doors more often for women than for men, or that women will hold doors for men or other women, is a simplification of the more general notion that men treat women according to traditional cultural values. If we confirm our hypothesis by the research we are about to describe, then we have one piece of evidence in support of our general idea, but clearly we have not *proved* it.

Science is customarily thought of as a *conservative* process. General ideas are rarely proven by a single fact, for example. Once in a great while, the cumulative knowledge in an area of science allows a single experiment or fact to confirm or disprove a general hypothesis (or theory, see chapter 7). This rare occurrence usually involves a **critical experiment,** one that every scientist hopes to do, but one that is rarely achieved. The scientist is always careful to realize that his or her research is subject to error and must be confirmed by **replication**—doing the research over and getting the same result. Even if the research is replicated, it is usually only one piece of a larger puzzle. With these cautions in mind, we now develop the actual procedure for evaluating our hypothesis.

Natural Observation

Our research hypothesis helps us determine what procedure we should use to evaluate the hypothesis. In our case, we want simply to determine if there is a difference in a certain behavior (i.e., door holding) as a function of some **predictor variable** (i.e., gender) as it occurs in the natural environment. Thus, to investigate our research hypothesis, we simply need to observe people in appropriate situations. This method of investigation is the **naturalistic observation** or natural observation for short.

Translating our hypothesis into an actual research project might seem to be a simple matter. All we need to do is pick a suitable place, such as the entrance to a building, and observe people as they use the entrance. However, two important questions must be answered before the experimenter leaves the planning stage. One question is *how* you will observe and the other is *what* you will observe. We consider each in turn.

Unobtrusive Observation

In a natural observation study, the hope is to obtain an uncontaminated record of the behaviors of a subject in a natural environment. This means that we should observe people in the real world and not in some psychology laboratory. The problem is, however, that as soon as the observer enters the situation, it is no longer the natural environment. Take for example the situation of a psychologist interested in the play behavior of kindergarten children. In order to observe their behavior she comes to the class and watches the children play. What will she find? If you have ever been to a kindergarten, you know that she will discover that the children decide to play with the new "toy" (i.e., her) rather than with each other. By entering the situation as an observer, she has changed the situation.

In general, there are two solutions to this problem. Her best solution would be to observe the children without herself being observed. A one-way mirror would accomplish this. If this is not available, she may try to install a hidden videotape camera and observe the tape at a later date. If none of these **unobtrusive observation** techniques are feasible, she can try to minimize her impact in the classroom. She can, for example, attend class for 2 weeks prior to the start of her data collection. Although this is not an ideal solution, it is probably true that the children will adapt to her presence (particularly if she does not interact with the children), and thus she will no longer be the novelty that she once was. In our door-holding example, you should be aware of the effect that a person with a clipboard has on the public.

A team of students from an experimental psychology course wanted to see what effect obtrusive versus unobtrusive observation had on people. The entrance to the parking lots at this university are monitored by gates that require a magnetic card for entrance. The students put up signs on the gates that read "New gate system: Beep horn before inserting card." The gate would have opened with the magnetic card whether or not the driver beeped the horn. The interesting manipulation was whether the student stood by the gate with a clipboard or whether he or she stood behind some bushes nearby. Significantly more people beeped their horn in the obtrusive observation condition than in the unobtrusive one.

Operational Definition

Once the details are worked out to ensure that the observation will be unobtrusive, a decision must still be made about *what* to observe. We can count the number of times a male holds the door for a female and the number of times he does not and compare these frequencies with female-male, male-male, and female-female pairs. However, imagine yourself observing under these conditions. You see a male step forward, open the door and hold it while a female passes through. Count "one" for chivalry! As this male goes through the door a female is leaving the building so the male steps halfway through the door to allow her to pass. Is this a second instance of door holding? Now a second male shows up and our polite male who is halfway into the building continues in, but extends his arm backward to hold the door until the second male touches the door. Is this an instance of a male holding the door for another male? The problem is that door holding may occur in more than one way. What we need is a clear definition of door holding.

An **operational definition** specifies the observable and measurable characteristics of a term or concept. An operational definition of door holding requires that we can immediately decide on what counts as a "door hold" and what does not. Operational definitions are definitions in terms of conditions and the procedures used within those conditions to measure the variable. An operational definition of a cake would be the recipe for baking the cake. A good instructive exercise is to try to create operational definitions of old adages. For example, how would you operationally define Benjamin Franklin's adage: "Early to bed, early to rise, makes a man healthy, wealthy, and wise"?

Recall from chapter 1 that several characteristics were important for an observation to be scientific. The typical observation is empirical, public, and repeatable. We also discussed that the more precise a description, the more people will agree on the description, and thus the more scientific will be the observation. Operational definitions help us accomplish this. Operational definitions make abstract terms objective and specify measurement operations, but they are not always perfect. For example, in our experiment we could operationally define *male* as anyone over 5'10" tall. Clearly, this definition allows for easy classification of the individuals. However, most people would not accept this as a good definition of what is meant by the construct male. In other words, the definition lacks **construct validity,** because some individuals that should be classified as female will be classified as male because they are over 5'10". An operational definition gives a construct, or a concept, the property called *validity* when it gives a way of measuring and classifying events that prove to be useful. The operational definition limits the commonsense meaning of a concept, but it must also capture the essence of the concept. One of the best tricks of successful scientists is their ability to develop and use operational definitions that both capture the essence of an abstract concept and make the concept easily measurable. In the Franklin adage, do you think that "a score above 140 on a standard IQ test" captures the essence of "wise"?

For door holding, our operational definition is that door holding occurs when an individual opens the door, allows the other person who is going in the same direction as the holder to pass through first, and the person for whom the door is held never touches the door. This is a restrictive definition in that it eliminates some instances of door holding, such as the reaching back after you have already gone through the door. It also eliminates cases where a person is entering the building, opens the door, and allows another person to leave before he or she enters. An operational definition does restrict the range or richness of the defined term.

The operational definition we have made of door holding restricts it to the classical form of "I'll open and hold, and you go first." Using this as our operational definition is an arbitrary decision, but one based on our initial statements about the way the sexes treat each other. The classical form of door holding leaves little doubt as to the intent of the holder. There are no casual, halfhearted door holds as there might have been with a more liberal operational definition of door holding. Thus we justify our particular operational definition of door holding. As the experimenter, you are continually called on to make **command decisions.** There are no universal rules for how to make these decisions. The best scientists are the ones who make the best command decisions. Their common sense is often a background of experience and knowledge, but in the end there is still room for argument about the exact nature of command decisions.

Dependent Variables and Data Collection

We have an operational definition of what constitutes door holding. This is the behavior we will measure, and we call the behavior we measure the **dependent variable** (DV). In this situation the dependent variable is a **binary variable;** it takes on *one of two values.* Either the door is held or it is not. In other situations the dependent variable will have more than two **discrete** values. For example, we could have recorded partial door holds—such as those we described previously. Then the dependent variable would have three discrete values: no hold, partial hold, total hold. Even more common is for the dependent variable to have a **continuous** value. In our previous example of measuring the speed of driving by males and females, speed was the dependent variable; and because it can be anywhere within a range, it is a continuous dependent variable. Determining if the best measure should be a discrete dependent variable or a continuous one is important, because the statistical analysis of the results changes as a function of the type of dependent variable.

Because we are interested in how the gender of the subjects (predictor variable) affects door holding (dependent variable), we will record instances of the operationally defined behavior, or its failure, for same-sex and mixed-sex pairs of subjects. Once again some command decisions are necessary. What happens if three persons show up at the same time, say two males and one female. One of the males holds the door in the manner described by our operational definition of door holding. Do we score this as an instance of door holding for both a same-sex male pair and a mixed-sex pair? Do we score it as a door hold only for the first person through the door and the holder (e.g., male holds and other male goes first followed by the female would count as a "male-male hold")? All this may seem like nit-picking, but without careful consideration of all possibilities the validity of the research will be in doubt. Research done in the real world is particularly open to unanticipated problems.

How should we decide who are subjects for our research? We will count, as subjects, only those persons who arrive in pairs. Three or more persons arriving at the same time will simply not be counted as subjects; they will be ignored. This may seem wasteful, but it is a simplifying procedure that is particularly important when the number of experimenters is large and they are relatively inexperienced. Thus the experimenters are not required to make judgments about group size, how to classify a door hold involving multiple subjects, and so forth. Yet, we still have a problem. How do we define a *pair* of subjects? What if they are a foot or two apart as they arrive at the door? Are they a pair or two individuals? Once again we need to define what we mean by a pair so that all the experimenters will be in agreement about what they record as the data.

The most straightforward approach to defining a pair of subjects is to require that they be within some well-defined distance of each other as they arrive at the door. One way to do this is to draw two lines on the sidewalk a fixed distance from the door and from each other. We suggest that two chalk lines, one 5 ft from the door and the other 7 ft from the door, be drawn on the sidewalk. To be considered a pair the subjects must both have one foot between or touching these lines at the same time. If they fail to meet this requirement, they are ignored and not counted as subjects.

Chalk lines on a sidewalk are not very noticeable on many college campus sidewalks. In doing the research described in this chapter, the fact that research is being conducted should not intrude or affect the behavior of the subjects. The experimenter should be as unobtrusive as possible, and any manipulation of the environment (such as chalk lines) should also be as unobtrusive as possible. If the experimenter is positioned next to the door with clipboard in hand and pen poised, the subject's behavior might be influenced in one way or another. Therefore, the experimenter should be able to see the subjects, but not be obvious—unobtrusive is the watchword. Depending on the particular door location chosen, the experimenter must use his or her best judgment to determine where to make the observations. Each situation will be different and will require one of those command decisions we have previously discussed, but this one will have to be made on the spot.

The final decision we must make is one that allows for the distinction between male-female and female-male pairs. Given our discussion above, we could make this discrimination by observing which person crosses our chalk line first. If a male crosses the line followed by a female, we could count this as a male-female opportunity. Similarly, if the female precedes the male, then it would be a female-male opportunity. Consider, however, the following scenario. A male crosses the line first, followed closely by a female. Thus far it would be a male-female opportunity. However, the female reaches the door first and holds the door for the male. Given our initial decision, we would have to count this as a male-female opportunity in which there was *not* a door hold. Clearly we would be missing some interesting data. Instead of distinguishing between the mixed-sex conditions by crossing the chalk line, we can distinguish them simply by who touches the door first. Now the scenario would place the observation in the female-male condition, and we would score it as a door hold. A data sheet is included at the end of this chapter for use in the actual data collection for the study.

Data Analysis

We presumably have figured out what we are observing and when we have observed it. Now the question becomes how do we make sense of our observations? A frequency count of the occurrence of door holds will not do, because there may have been more different-sex pairs than same-sex pairs. Therefore, just knowing the frequency of door holds would be biased in favor of the type of pair showing up most frequently as subjects. This is a relatively easy problem to solve, and perhaps you already know how it is done. We need to calculate the **relative frequency** of door holds among the different possible pairs of subjects. The relative frequency is *the number of occurrences of the event divided by the number of possible occurrences of the event.* This can be expressed as a proportion or a percentage, the difference being that a percentage = 100 × proportion.

Suppose that we see the following number of pairs of subjects and door holds.

| | Sex of Pairs | | | |
	Male-Male	Female-Female	Male-Female	Female-Male
Number of pairs appearing	24	18	28	5
Number of door holds	12	12	21	1
Proportion	12/24 .50	12/18 .67		
Percentage	.50 × 100 = 50%	.67 × 100 = 67%		

The last two columns in the table have been left for you to calculate, and you should do so now to ensure that you understand these methods of data handling. The proportion or percentage is a way of describing what happened in the research, and they are called **descriptive statistics.** If you have not bothered to fill in the missing parts of the table, do so now! You

---

Figure 3–1   Percentage of door holding for different pairs of subjects.

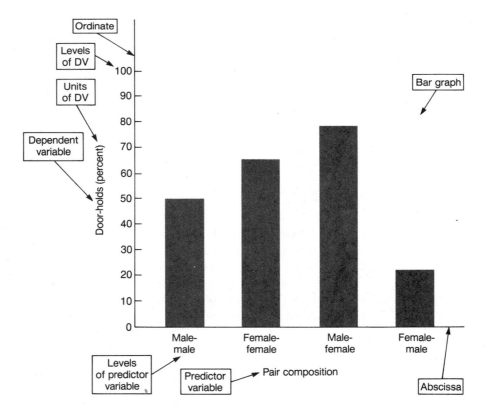

should come up with the proportion being .75 and the percentage 75% in the third column. The last column should be .20 and 20%.

The hypothetical data from this example could be presented as a bar graph. Virtually all bar graphs show the dependent variable—the measure of behavior—on the vertical axis of the graph. In that way, the height of each bar on the graph represents the results and makes for an easy comparison. Figure 3–1 shows how these results should be displayed in a bar graph.

Key Words

binary variable	general idea
command decision	naturalistic observation
construct validity	operational definition
continuous	predictor variable
critical experiment	relative frequency
dependent variable	replication
descriptive statistics	research hypothesis
discrete	unobtrusive observation

Additional Reading

Ashmore, R. D., Del Boca, F. K., & Wohlers, A. J. (1986). Gender stereotypes. In R. D. Ashmore & F. K. Del Boca (Eds.), *The social psychology of female-male relations* (pp. 69–119). New York: Academic Press.

Skrypnek, B. J., & Snyder, M. (1982). On the self-perpetuating nature of stereotypes about women and men. *Journal of Experimental Social Psychology, 18,* 227–291.

Yamada, E. M., Tjosvold, D., & Draguns, J. G. (1983). Effects of sex-linked situations and sex composition on cooperation and style of interaction. *Sex Roles, 9,* 541–553.

Door Holding

TYPE OF PAIR	PAIRS APPEARING	POSITIVE DOOR HOLDS	RELATIVE FREQUENCY
MALE-FEMALE			
FEMALE-MALE			
FEMALE-FEMALE			
MALE-MALE			

NOTES: Location of observations: _____

_____

    Special problems or comments: _____

_____

_____

_____

    Experimenter's/observer's name(s) _____

_____

    Time observation started: _____

    Time observation finished: _____

This worksheet and future worksheets provide you with a frame that reviews the study described in the chapter. The larger headings form the basic outline. In all the remaining chapters, the Frame for Research section will be featured. Later frames build on earlier ones. Thus, the frame of this chapter can be found as a part of all subsequent frames. New additions to a frame will be indicated by arrows. In some cases, we have asked specific questions within this outline that you should attempt to answer. In other cases, especially when the concept is new to the frame, we sketched an answer from something explicitly stated in the chapter's narrative or implied by the chapter and previous principles. As you become more familiar with a concept, we supply less guidance in completing that aspect of the frame. Finally, chapter 16 will include the complete frame for research that you can use in your own research endeavors.

General Idea (Previous Research, Curiosity)

The idea derived from *curiosity* and informal observations. In general, the population seems to hold the belief that men should be chivalrous toward women. On the other hand, the times are reportedly "a changing." How pervasive are the stereotyped sex roles of males and females?

Research Hypothesis

Males will hold the door for females more (greater relative frequency) than will other gender combinations.

Methods (Natural Observation)

Natural Observation

Dependent Variable

Door hold; it either does or does not occur, a binary event

Operational Definition

A door hold occurs when an individual opens the door and allows the second individual to go through the door in the same direction without the second individual touching the door.

Predictor Variable

The predictor variable is the gender constitution of pairs of subjects: male-male, female-female, male-female, female-male.

Operational Definition

Defining gender is trivial for these purposes. A pair can be defined by two people occupying a space (defined by chalk lines) at the same time. How was the distinction between male-female and female-male pairs made?

Continued

Continued
Subjects

Subjects for our experiment will simply be those who appear at the location chosen to do the observations.

Ethical Considerations

Natural observation raises the problem of obtaining informed consent without violating the integrity of the study. In the current study, the behavior measure does not seem to be a violation of privacy, especially given that only group data will be considered.

Procedural Command Decisions

Where will the observations take place?

How long will you observe?

List one other procedural command decision.

Data Analysis

Descriptive.   The statistic discussed was the use of relative frequencies for each of the four levels of the predictor variable. These could be displayed in a table or in a bar graph. Draw a bar graph of the hypothetical results *you* expect.

More Common Sentence Faults

Avoid splitting infinitives (e.g., to be, to see).

Incorrect: Subjects were told to rapidly respond . . .
Correct:　Subjects were told to respond rapidly . . .

Avoid misplaced and dangling modifiers.

Incorrect: *Being an often-used laboratory animal,* I decided to use the white rat. (The italic phrase modifies "I.")

Avoid faulty comparisons.

Incorrect: The theory leads to the prediction that subjects given caffeine will respond more quickly. (Than whom?)
Correct:　Subject 12 finished sooner than any *other* subject in the experiment.

Express parallel ideas in parallel structure.

Incorrect: Subjects were asked to read stories, listen to speeches, or wrote sentences.
Correct:　Subjects were asked to read stories, listen to speeches, or write sentences.

Avoid redundancy in the sentence.
In the examples below the italic words should be eliminated.

Subjects were 48 undergraduate volunteers *who were students attending college.*

a total of 68 subjects
absolutely essential
summarize *briefly*
very close

Avoid the and/or construction.

Incorrect: Subjects participated for course credit and/or $3.00.
Correct:　Subjects participated for course credit, $3.00, or both.

Section Headings

The sections of the manuscript (with one exception) are designated by headings. The headings help in the organization of the manuscript and serve the same function that an outline serves. Thus the headings simultaneously divide the paper into coherent units and place the sections in their relative positions of importance in the hierarchy. Consider the following outline:

I.   Introduction
II. Methods
     A. Subjects
     B. Materials (or in some cases Apparatus)
        1. Intelligence tests
        2. Performance tests
     C. Procedure
        1. Pretest
        2. Training procedure
        3. Posttest
III. Results
IV. Discussion

Where there is an A, there is a B; where there is a 1, there is a 2. Like any good outline, the headings of your paper should conform to these principles. Instead of arabic numerals, the most specific level is represented by PARAGRAPH HEADINGS; the next level is represented by SIDE HEADINGS; and the next level, the most general one in our example, is represented by CENTERED HEADINGS. (Exception: The introduction never has a head.) If you require more levels than this, see the APA Publication Manual. Below are examples of these headings for a piece of the above outline. The paragraph headings are specific to our example, whereas the side and centered headings will appear in all empirical papers.

Methods

A CENTERED HEADING is typed in upper and lower case.

<u>Subjects</u>

A SIDE HEADING is flush with the left margin and is underlined. It, like the other headings, is in upper and lower case. Important words should be capitalized.

<u>Materials</u>

   <u>Intelligence tests.</u> A PARAGRAPH HEADING is indented, underlined, and followed by a period. It forms the beginning of the actual paragraph.

   <u>Performance tests.</u> Only the first word of a PARAGRAPH HEADING is capitalized, unless there is a proper noun after the first word.

4 Sampling & Surveys

Overview

Research can be either basic or applied. Applied research is conducted to solve a problem of concern to a segment of society. Basic research is conducted to find answers to questions of any sort. Applied issues can use a survey to measure some characteristics of a group of individuals. Structuring a survey requires attention to the level of the questions (global or specific), the ordering of the questions, the responses required of the subjects, and the subjects' perception of the demands of the situation (e.g., social desirability). An opinion survey is developed to determine the opinions of "Greeks" and "Independents" about the academic and social well-being of members of each group.

A sample is usually drawn from a population of individuals to induce the nature of that population. Samples range from the ideal, but impractical, random sample, through stratified samples and cluster samples, to convenience samples. The validity of a convenience sample depends on the shared assumptions of the scientific community.

The level of measurement in a survey is discussed, and Steven's scales are presented: nominal, ordinal, interval, and ratio. Descriptive statistics for each scale are the mode, median, and mean. Each statistic is a type of average.

A scatterplot is illustrated to graph the relationship between social and academic opinion for each group (i.e., Greek or Independent).

Tips on General Style discusses proper punctuation. Tips on Specific Style focuses on the Methods section of the psychological research paper.

Inducing the Opinion of Many from Those of a Few

American televisions are on 7 hours and 8 minutes a day.
—Results of Nielsen 1982–83 Survey

When college students first arrive on campus, they are faced with a number of important decisions. Not the least important of these decisions is the social network they choose. On several campuses the decision is between joining a social fraternity or sorority and remaining an "independent." These first-year students might want to obtain some information about the pros and cons of joining and not joining the Greek system.

One of the attractive aspects of psychological research is that many practical or applied issues can be addressed, such as the advantages and disadvantages of joining social organizations. Traditionally, a distinction is

55

made between applied and basic research. **Applied research** is done to solve a problem or answer a question that is of concern to society, business, or some special group (like the first-year students above). **Basic research** is done to solve a problem or answer a question that may or may not have any immediate relevance to the concerns of society. Basic research ultimately has a considerable influence on society and our lives. Usually the results of basic research are not applied immediately, nor are the scientists necessarily concerned about the application of their work. Simply to understand the structure of matter, the organization of the DNA molecule, the processes of the mind, or the conditions influencing behavior are important contributions to science, even if we never invented the atomic bomb, oil-consuming bacteria, intelligent robots, or behavior modification. If it were not for advances in basic research on molecular biology, there would not be an applied area of genetic engineering, for example. Once established, an applied area can function to a large extent independently of the basic area until further advances are made.

Regardless of the purpose of research, the principles that allow us to decide when an answer has been reached, and the correctness of the answer, are the same. Good research and bad research can be done on applied problems or basic problems. In this chapter, we will be concerned with applied problems. In particular, we will discuss surveys and how to measure the attitudes, knowledge, feelings, and behavioral tendencies of people. The economic importance of being able to make such measurements should be obvious. Any company producing a product for commercial gain would give large amounts of money to be able to know the mind of the consumer. In fact, survey research has become so popular that it can be difficult to get a person to allow the interviewer to ask him or her questions.

Survey Research

In this chapter we will develop a survey appropriate for measuring the beliefs of college students concerning academic and social life. We will use a survey questionnaire to measure these beliefs, and in the process we will compare the responses of students affiliated with a fraternity or sorority (Greeks) and those living in a dormitory or off campus (Independents).

Samples and Populations

The purpose of doing a survey is usually to measure some characteristics of a group of individuals. The group might be as large as all adult citizens of the United States. This group would be of interest to many businesses. A car manufacturer might be interested in a somewhat smaller group of persons, such as those who plan on buying a new car within the next year. The entire group of individuals with a set of characteristics defines a **population.** The characteristics may be general, such as all persons who own a television set for the television networks concerned with the popularity of their programs, or they may be specific, such as all persons whose height is 7 ft or more. Most of the time including the entire population in the survey would be impractical, because there would simply be too many people. A **sample** is a subset of a population and is used to estimate the nature of the population.

There are several ways of obtaining a sample from the population. The particular method of creating a sample depends on such things as the nature of the information to be derived from the sample, the convenience and feasibility of different types of samples, and the nature of the population. In the perfect situation the researcher would have a complete list of the population. With the whole population on a list, a **random sample** of the population may be chosen. In a random sample each person in the population has an equal probability of being included in the sample, and the selection of one person does not affect the other selections. When a truly random sample can be obtained, the accuracy of the survey is excellent at a relatively low cost. The 200 million plus persons living in the United States can have their opinions accurately measured by a random sample of only a few thousand persons. The problem is that obtaining the *truly* random sample is not easy. Subtle and not-so-subtle biases can creep into the sampling procedure, creating distortions in the results.

A famous example occurred during the 1948 presidential race. Harry Truman and Thomas Dewey were the candidates. Public opinion surveys were just becoming popular, and the most influential pollsters of the time showed Truman, the Democrat, trailing Dewey, the Republican. Of course, Truman won the election to the complete surprise of the pollsters. What had happened was that the polls were conducted by making phone calls. In 1948, telephones were not nearly as common as they are today, so the persons interviewed by the pollsters tended to be the more affluent members of society. Voters had been operationally defined by the fact that they owned a phone. Traditionally, the poorer persons in our country have voted Democratic. In the opinion survey they were never asked who they would vote for because they had no phones. When they went to polls, their votes were counted, which resulted in a major "upset."

Figure 4–1 illustrates how faulty induction from the sample to the population can occur. Because phone-owners were overrepresented in the sample, the correct induction was to the population of phone-owners, not to the desired population of all American voters. If we wanted to generalize to the population of college students at a particular college or university, our sample could lead to similarly faulty induction if members of the Greek system were disproportionately represented.

If our sample was large enough, and truly random, then we could be fairly confident that the characteristics of the population appeared in our sample in roughly the same proportions. However, there are methods of obtaining samples of subjects that would *guarantee* that our sample, even if it were small, had Greeks and Independents proportionately represented. A **stratified random sample** involves choosing people according to some characteristic(s) they represent. For example, the Nielsen ratings concerning the television viewing habits of Americans uses a representative sample of households based on various economic and social characteristics. These characteristics are known and the proportion of households with the particular combination of characteristics is chosen to be representative of the entire country.

Figure 4–1.   The relationship between sampling and induction.

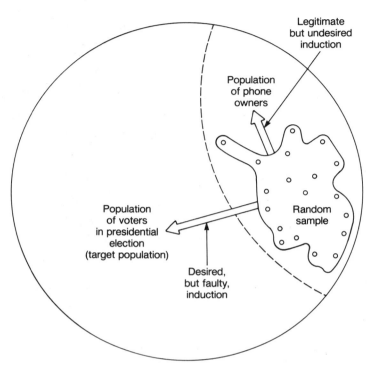

We refer to the known characteristics of the individuals we include in our sample as **demographic variables.** Things such as age, annual income, size of family, and type of residence are some examples of demographic variables. To create a stratified random sample, we would define the set of demographic characteristics making up each class we wanted represented in the sample and then randomly sample from individuals in each class.

For the survey comparing Greeks and Independents, a stratified random sample might be accomplished by first determining the proportion of Greeks and Independents in the population. If, for example, 75% of the population belonged to a sorority or fraternity, then we would make sure that our sample also contained 75% Greek and 25% Independent.

Both random sampling and stratified random sampling are often difficult to implement. Because of these difficulties, scientists often compromise by using techniques that approximate the truly random situation, but that are more practical. These methods, the convenience sample and the cluster sample, offer trade-offs between good sampling and practicality.

The rubric **convenience sample** covers a wide range of particular sampling procedures, most of which do not meet the spirit of good sampling practices. At its broadest level, a convenience sample is just what the name implies: you use whatever subjects are handy. For example, if you were interested in the opinions of people toward the military and chose students and colleagues at the university as the sample because they were convenient people to ask, the survey would clearly be biased. Why? Because there is good reason to believe that people in academia have different opinions than other people about a number of things, possibly including the military.

What if, instead, you were interested in how quickly a person could press a button when he or she heard a tone played over headphones? Again, a decision to use the convenience sample of university students is needed. Would you be more likely to accept these findings as being generally true? Probably. Most people, psychologists included, accept results such as these from a convenience sample because they assume that the auditory system of university students is really not different from the population as a whole. Thus, whether the use of a convenience sample is justified or not depends on whether the community of psychologists is willing to share your assumption that the sample is representative of your population. This discussion can also be related to Figure 4–1, showing the relationship among samples, populations, and induction.

One final sampling technique is the **cluster sample.** In this technique a compromise is reached between the theoretical advantages of random sampling and its practical disadvantages. Assume, for example, that we want a sample of all the people in the United States. In cluster sampling we may begin by randomly selecting 10 states. From each of these 10 states, we may randomly sample 5 counties. From each of these 5 counties, we randomly sample a 100 people. Figure 4–2 illustrates this cluster sample.

The requirements of a truly random sample are not met in this cluster sample. That is, once Wyoming is excluded from the sample, no person in Wyoming has any chance to be in our study. However, because the clusters are sampled randomly, there is some effort to reduce the introduction of bias. If we wanted to get an idea of the frequency of drug use among high school students in Denver, we could pick one inner-city high school and one suburban high school. We could then go to these schools, randomly pick a senior, junior, and sophomore class, and ask all the students in each class about their use of drugs. Obviously, the cluster sampling technique may allow bias to occur in the characteristics of the subjects sampled.

We now turn to the specific research question to be developed in this chapter to illustrate how these ideas can be put to use.

Measuring Opinions

We have stressed the importance of the way a sample of the population is made for determining the results of a survey. We will not develop a procedure for evaluating this idea. Pretend, for the moment, that you are a reporter for the student newspaper and your assignment is to find out if students feel that living in a Greek house—a fraternity or sorority—results in a more satisfying social life and higher perceived academic achievement than living as an Independent—in the dormitory or off campus. You are being asked to determine if students *feel* that the Greek versus Independent classification makes a difference, not if there is an *actual* difference. We might measure an actual difference in academic achievement by comparing the grade point averages (GPA) for the two groups. It is hard to know how we would interpret any difference we might find. For example, if Greeks had a higher GPA than Independents, is it because of the housing

Figure 4–2.   An illustration of cluster sampling.

100 people from
Cleveland county,
Oklahoma

CLEVELAND
● Norman

difference or is it because the fraternities and sororities recruited students
with higher academic achievement orientation? Or because they enrolled in
easier courses or with less strict instructors? Answers to questions such as
these require a controlled experiment described first in chapter 6.

We want to measure how students feel the Greek versus Independent
affiliation affects social and academic life. How will we obtain a sample of
students for our survey? We could go to the registrar of the university and
obtain a list of all currently enrolled students. Using an appropriate procedure (e.g., assign students numbers and then use a table of random numbers to select them, or a computer-generated random selection), we could

produce a sublist of randomly selected students. Each student selected would then be approached (by phone or mail) and asked to answer a questionnaire designed to measure their feelings about academic and social life for Greeks and Independents. As a practical matter this would be a tough assignment for you as a student of experimental psychology (or as a reporter for the student newspaper) to accomplish. The list of students would be large and potentially not that easy to obtain. It might contain names of students who do not appropriately fit our population. For example, many graduate students come from different universities or colleges, and if they are included in the sample, they may distort the results because the Greek system is exclusively for undergraduates and the graduate students' experiences reflect a different situation.

Another problem with obtaining a truly random sample of all students is that some of the sampled subjects are going to reject our request to give an interview and others will be unreachable because they have moved or changed phone numbers. What kinds of biases might occur given these problems? A fraternity or sorority may keep close track of its members, making it easier to obtain interviews from Greeks because they are more easily located. Independents, who may live in apartments or rooming houses, may not be reachable if they move. Even if we choose a random sample of students to interview, we will be hard-pressed to actually obtain the sample. The same problems would apply to any attempt at obtaining a stratified random sample with the additional problem of determining who was and who was not a member of a fraternity or sorority.

Given the constraints of time and money that might be needed to overcome the problems of obtaining a truly random sample of students, what should we do? We can obtain a sample of Greeks and Independents in a fairly easy manner by asking students as they are encountered, at "random," to fill out our survey and have them classify their affiliation (Independent or Greek). The "randomness" of our sample will not be the truly random one we discussed before. Rather, we will ask persons entering the library, the student union, or a classroom building to fill out our survey. Because traffic into these buildings is liable to be high, every other person, every third person, or every tenth person might be chosen as a subject. Such a sample will not be random, but will be satisfactory for comparing the responses of Greeks and Independents because each type of person will be included as a subject. Clearly this is a sample of convenience. By having a reasonably large sample of Greeks and Independents, we can compare their responses to our survey and evaluate our research hypothesis that "members of a group (Greek or Independent) will rate the academic and social lives of persons who are part of that group more positively than they rate the lives of comparable persons who are not."

We could do our survey by asking one question of the subject: "Do you agree or disagree with the statement that members of fraternities and sororities do better academically and have better social lives than Independents?" However, we won't use this single question, because it does not provide a sensitive answer to our research hypothesis. In other words, the answer we receive will be at such a general level that we will not obtain enough information about people's opinions. Sensitivity of measuring attitudes can be increased in two ways. First, we can measure the separate components of the attitude (i.e., social life and academic life). Second, we can get finer levels of measurement of the attitude (i.e., how much better).

Our question tries to address two separate issues in one question: academic life and social life. The Greek system may work to enhance the social life of its members, but not the academic (or vice versa), relative to being an Independent. If we ask the question posed above, no distinction is made between social and academic characteristics. Such a question is referred to as a **double-barreled question** and should be avoided in surveys. We clearly need at least two questions in our survey. Will two questions suffice to measure what we want to measure?

Consider the social issue first. What do we mean if we state, "Members of sororities and fraternities have better social lives than Independents"? Do we mean they have more parties? They have more friends? They have more fun? They are more likely to marry someone they met in college? The question is what constitutes a "better social life"? We can distinguish two levels of information: *global* and *specific*. A global question is broadly phrased and is presumably based on a number of specifics. Thus if we were interested in people's attitudes toward the president of the United States, we might ask specific questions about the person's attitudes about tax cuts, military spending, and other specifics and compare the responses with the president's position on each. We might also ask a global question, such as do you agree with the following statement: "Overall I agree with and support the president and his policies."

For our case we can ask a global question about social and academic attitudes and specific questions about each. This will increase the sensitivity of our survey. Sensitivity can also be increased by measuring the subjects' responses in finer detail. Rather than asking the subjects if they agree or disagree with a statement, we can ask the extent to which they agree or disagree. A discrete 5-point scale is often used (called a **Likert scale**) for this purpose. Thus the response alternatives for the global statement, "Members of sororities and fraternities have better social lives than Independents" are:

strongly agree	moderately agree	there is no difference	moderately disagree	strongly disagree

By using this scale we can convert each response to a number and then apply the principles of measurement to summarize and compare results. We can also create more specific questions to be answered on a Likert scale for the academic side of the coin.

Influences on Survey Responses

One final problem must be considered before we complete our discussion on the construction of the survey. Whenever we ask people for their opinion, the way we ask the question and the context in which we ask it can influence the answer we receive. The respondent may see the situation as one that demands a response other than he or she would normally give. The **demand characteristics** of a study can influence responses to the survey.

One possible influence on answers comes from **social desirability.** A person may respond to a question with the answer he or she feels is the expected or desirable response to make him or her appear in the best light. For example, a student in a philosophy class might answer the question "Do you believe in God?" by saying "I don't know" or "I'm not sure," but if asked the same question by his or her minister might answer "of course."

Another influence on responses to a survey can be produced by a **response set** creating a halo effect. When a series of questions are asked, they may have a cumulative effect; therefore, the person's earlier responses may affect the latter responses. For example, suppose we ask a person the following questions: "Do you favor a system of communism or capitalism?", "Do you feel that the Soviet government is a threat to the American way of life?", and "Do you feel that no price is too high to pay to protect our freedom and way of life?" Now we ask the person, "Do you favor a strong military and increased defense spending?" The questions coming prior to the last one may create a response set for the individual to answer more positively to the last question than would have been the case had it been asked without the preceding questions.

Because the way a question is asked and the context in which it is asked can affect the response an individual has to it, we have prepared separate forms of the survey to be used in our research on academic and social attitudes. You should read over the different forms of the survey found at the end of this chapter.

Demographic Questions

In addition to these opinion questions, we should obtain demographic information from our respondents. Because these are personal questions, they should be placed at the end of the survey to insure the greatest number of respondents.

In particular, it might be valuable to know (1) their social affiliation (i.e., Greek or Independent), (2) their class (i.e., Freshman, Sophomore, Junior, Senior), (3) their financial budget, and (4) their age. Consider the following questions and answers:

1. I (am) (~~am not~~) a member or pledge of a social fraternity or sorority. (Cross out the one that does not apply.)

2. I am a: _____ Freshman
    __X__ Sophomore
    _____ Junior
    _____ Senior
    _____ Other

3. At the end of each month, how much money are you able to save (positive number) or must you borrow (negative number)?
    −$150.00

4. How old are you?   20

After the respondents answer each question, we will record some number for each answer and then summarize their answers. We could, as we did in chapter 3, tally the frequency of responses in each category. For example, we might tally 35 Greek respondents and 60 Independents. In other cases, however, a simple frequency tally would not supply us with much information. Instead we want to use other measures to characterize our groups of subjects. When we summarize the responses of an entire group with a single number, we are using simple descriptive statistics to describe our sample. In particular, we want to compute an **average** response for each group. However, there are different types of averages, and which average we use will depend on how the responses were measured in our survey.

Measurement and Scales

Whenever we assign a number to something according to a rule we are using **measurement.** However, not all measurement rules are equally useful. According to S. S. Stevens, all measurements fall into one of four classes: nominal scales, ordinal scales, interval scales, and ratio scales. The scale underlying the dependent variable makes some conclusions possible and other conclusions not possible.

The **nominal scale,** as the name implies, refers to the use of numbers to name or classify responses, people, and so forth. For example, the numbers on the uniforms of baseball players constitute a nominal scale. What can we say about the person wearing number 4 compared with the person wearing number 2? Nothing, except that they are not the same person. In our study, we have the nominal variable of academic affiliation: Greek or Independent. We can assign all the Greeks number 1 and all the Independents number 2 or vice versa. The only thing that we cannot do is to assign some of each to the number 1.

The appropriate average for a nominal scale is the **mode.** The mode is simply the category with the greatest frequency. With 35 Greeks and 60 Independents, the mode would be Independent.

The **ordinal scale** tells us something about the order of the measured entities. For example, the finishers of a race can be given the numbers 1, 2, 3, and so forth. From this, we can tell not only that 1 is different from 2, as with the nominal scale, but also that 1 finished before 2. However, we cannot tell how much before. That is, we have no information about the distance between 1 and 2 other than the order. We can change the numbers in any way that we want as long as the order of the numbers is the same. In our study, academic class is on an ordinal scale. We can assign Freshmen a 1, Sophomores a 2, Juniors a 3, and Seniors a 4.

The appropriate average for an ordinal scale is the **median,** although the mode can also be used. The median is the number below which 50% of the respondents fall. In the data below, the median class for the Greeks was Sophomore and for the Independents was Junior.

	Freshman	Sophomore	Junior	Senior
Greek	12	9	10	4
Independent	15	12	23	10

The **interval scale** tells us something about the distance between our measurements, and it also contains all the information of the nominal and ordinal scale. For example, if it were 10°F outside on Monday, 20°F on Tuesday, and 30°F on Wednesday, we can say that the temperature difference between Monday and Tuesday was the same difference as that between Tuesday and Wednesday. Because we can now make statements such as this, the interval scale allows us access to a powerful system: mathematics. We can now add numbers together, multiply them, and so forth to form means and other statistics. We can change the numbers only linearly: $Y = mX + b$. In other words, we must preserve the distance information if we want to transform the data. In our study, demographic question 3 is an interval variable (the respondent's budget). We can use the actual numbers given by the respondents in the calculation of the average. Positive numbers and negative numbers can both be entered into the calculations.

The appropriate average for the interval scale is the **arithmetic mean,** although the median and mode are also permitted by this type of scale. The mean is the average with which you are probably most familiar and simply involves summing all of the scores and dividing by the number of respondents. We might discover in our survey that the mean budget for Greeks is −$100 and for Independents is +$50, suggesting that Greeks have a tighter budget than do Independents.

The **ratio scale** tells us all the information of the previous scales. As the name implies, it is a scale where we can make statements about the ratio of two numbers. This may not seem much better than the interval scale until you realize that only with a ratio scale can you claim that some quantity is twice as large as another. The ratio scale has this added property because there is an absolute zero point. In other words, there can be no negative numbers. You can see why our budget scale is not a ratio scale by trying to answer the question "How much more did the Independents have at the end of the month than did the Greeks?" Clearly the answer of "Negative two times as much" does not make much sense. For a ratio scale the only way we are allowed to change the number is by multiplying by a constant (e.g., changing inches to feet, months to years). In our survey, the person's age can be considered to be on a ratio scale.

The average usually used for a ratio scale is the same mean as used for interval-scaled data. Although other, more-restrictive means can be used with a ratio scale, the mean will almost always serve your purposes. In chapter 15, we will introduce you to the geometric mean that takes advantage of the characteristics of ratio-scaled data.

Psychological Scales versus Physical Scales

Before we leave the topic of measurement, consider the old puzzle: Which is heavier a pound of feathers or a pound of lead? The correct answer is a pound of lead, because heaviness is a psychological property not a physical one. Of course a pound of lead and a pound of feathers *weigh* the same, but they are not equally heavy. This illustrates the point that, as psychologists, we are interested in the psychological scale, not the physical one. If, for example, we wanted to measure people's intelligence, we could give them a test where the scores range from 0 to 200. What can we say about those who receive a 150 compared with those who receive a 75? Clearly we could say that their score was twice as large because the scores are on a ratio scale. But could we say that they were twice as intelligent? or 75 units smarter? At best we could say that those with an IQ of 150 were smarter: an ordinal conclusion.

Data Analysis

After we collect the data from our respondents, we want to summarize the data by finding averages for each question. The averages for the demographic questions will vary depending on the type of scale, but all of the opinion questions will be on an ordinal scale, so the median response of each group, Greek and Independent, should be calculated for these questions. We may also want to know the percentage of Greeks versus the percentage of Independents for a number of the questions on our survey. We should also remember to group the specific questions around the appropriate general question.

This survey also asks a question about the relationship of academic and social satisfaction. We can answer this by trying to determine if the answers to the general social question tend to be answered in the same way as the answers to the general academic question. There are three possibilities: (1) People may believe that a better social life and a better academic life *go together;* that is, they show a **positive correlation** or positive relationship. (2) People may believe that a better social life *goes against* a better academic life; that is, they show a **negative correlation** or negative relationship. (3) People may believe that a better social life is not related, in one way or the other, with a better academic life; that is, there is **zero correlation** or no relationship.

The correlation can be quantified by computing a **correlation coefficient,** which gives you an index of the strength and direction of the relationship. In lieu of calculating this statistic, the general direction of the correlation can be determined by constructing a **scatterplot.** A scatterplot is a graph with one variable (e.g., social opinion) on the ordinate (i.e., y-axis) and the other variable (e.g., academic opinion) on the abscissa (i.e., x-axis). Each subject contributes a point to the graph. If more than one subject falls on the same point of the graph, the point is represented by the number of subjects located at that point. Figure 4–3 shows the hypothetical relationship between general social opinion and general academic opinion for the Greeks and the Independents.

Greeks tended to show a positive relationship between social and academic life, whereas the Independents tended to show a negative correlation. These relationships are indicated by the dashed lines drawn through each scatterplot. For the Greeks, there was one person (represented by the "*") who responded with a 5 for social life and a 1 for academic life. On the other hand, there were 8 Greeks who responded with a 5 for social life and a 4 for academic life.

Figure 4–3. Scatterplots of the relationship between general social and academic opinions for members and nonmembers of social organizations.

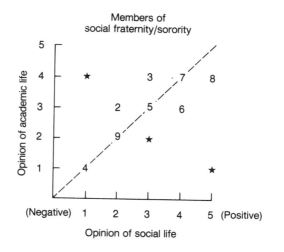

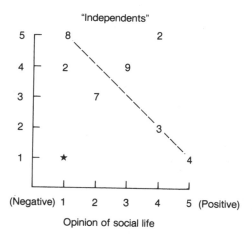

Key Words

applied research
average
basic research
cluster sample
convenience sample
correlation coefficient
demand characteristics
demographic variables
double-barreled question
interval scale
Likert scale
mean
measurement
median

mode
negative correlation
nominal scale
ordinal scale
population
positive correlation
random sample
ratio scale
response set
sample
scatterplot
social desirability
stratified random sample
zero correlation

Additional Reading

Byrne, D. (1971). *The attraction paradigm.* New York: Academic Press.

Festinger, L., Schachter, S., & Back, K. (1950). *Social pressures in informal groups: A study of human factors in housing.* Stanford University Press.

Jones, W. H. (1982). Loneliness and social behavior. In L. A. Peplau & D. Perlman (Eds.), *Loneliness: A sourcebook of current theory, research and therapy* (pp. 238–254). New York: Wiley-Interscience.

Sarason, I. G., Sarason, B. R., & Shearin, E. N. (1986). Social support as an individual difference variable: Its stability, origins, and relational aspects. *Journal of Personality and Social Psychology, 50,* 845–855.

The Surveys

Some questions about the survey forms follow. Look over the forms and then answer the following questions.

1. Which are the global and which are the specific questions?

Global (Form A1) ——————

Specific (Form A1) ——————

2. What changes are made between forms A1 and A2 and between forms B1 and B2?

———————————————————————————

3. What changes are made between the A and B forms of the survey?

———————————————————————————

4. Given the differences between the A and B forms of the survey, how would you scale the responses to make them comparable? That is, A and B should measure the same thing. How would you assign numbers to the scales for A versus B to make them comparable?

———————————————————————————

———————————————————————————

5. What, if anything, should you say or ask your subjects before giving them the survey?

Survey: Social and Academic Attitudes (Form A1)

Please answer the following questions by putting the number that most closely summarizes your feelings in the appropriate space next to each statement. "Greeks" refers to students who are members of a fraternity or a sorority. "Independents" are not members of a fraternity or sorority. The scale and numbers are:

1	2	3	4	5
strongly agree	moderately agree	there is no difference	moderately disagree	strongly disagree

———— 1. Greeks have more parties and attend more social functions than Independents.

———— 2. Greeks are more likely to have a regular boyfriend or girlfriend than are Independents.

———— 3. In general, Greeks have a better social life than Indepedents.

———— 4. Greeks attend classes more regularly than Independents.

———— 5. Greeks have higher grade point averages than Independents.

———— 6. In general, Greeks do better academically than Independents.

7. I (am) (am not) a member or pledge of a sorority or fraternity. (Cross out the one that does not apply.)

8. I am a: Freshman, Sophomore, Junior, Senior, Other

9. At the end of each month, how much money are you able to save (positive number) or must you borrow (negative number)?

10. How old are you?

Survey: Social and Academic Attitudes (Form A2)

Please answer the following questions by putting the number that most closely summarizes your feelings in the appropriate space next to each statement. "Greeks" refers to students who are members of a fraternity or a sorority. "Independents" are not members of a fraternity or sorority. The scale and numbers are:

1	2	3	4	5
strongly agree	moderately agree	there is no difference	moderately disagree	strongly disagree

_____ 1. Greeks attend classes more regularly than Independents.

_____ 2. Greeks have higher grade point averages than Independents.

_____ 3. In general, Greeks do better academically than Independents.

_____ 4. Greeks have more parties and attend more social functions than Indepedents.

_____ 5. Greeks are more likely to have a regular boyfriend or girlfriend than Independents.

_____ 6. In general, Greeks have a better social life than Independents.

7. I (am) (am not) a member or pledge of a sorority or fraternity. (Cross out the one that does not apply.)

8. I am a: Freshman, Sophomore, Junior, Senior, Other

9. At the end of each month, how much money are you able to save (positive number) or must you borrow (negative number)?

10. How old are you?

Survey: Social and Academic Attitudes (Form B1)

Please answer the following questions by putting the number that most closely summarizes your feelings in the appropriate space next to each statement. "Greeks" refers to students who are members of a fraternity or a sorority. "Independents" are not members of a fraternity or sorority. The scale and numbers are:

1	2	3	4	5
strongly agree	moderately agree	there is no difference	moderately disagree	strongly disagree

———— 1. Independents have more parties and attend more social functions than Greeks.

———— 2. Independents are more likely to have a regular boyfriend or girlfriend than are Greeks.

———— 3. In general, Independents have a better social life than Greeks.

———— 4. Independents attend classes more regularly than Greeks.

———— 5. Independents have higher grade point averages than Greeks.

———— 6. In general, Independents do better academically than Greeks.

7. I (am) (am not) a member or pledge of a sorority or fraternity. (Cross out the one that does not apply.)

8. I am a: Freshman, Sophomore, Junior, Senior, Other

9. At the end of each month, how much money are you able to save (positive number) or must you borrow (negative number)?

10. How old are you?

Survey: Social and Academic Attitudes (Form B2)

Please answer the following questions by putting the number that most closely summarizes your feelings in the appropriate space next to each statement. "Greeks" refers to students who are members of a fraternity or a sorority. "Independents" are not members of a fraternity or sorority. The scale and numbers are:

1	2	3	4	5
strongly agree	moderately agree	there is no difference	moderately disagree	strongly disagree

_____ 1. Independents attend classes more regularly than Greeks.

_____ 2. Independents have higher grade point averages than Greeks.

_____ 3. In general, Independents do better academically than Greeks.

_____ 4. Independents have more parties and attend more social functions than Greeks.

_____ 5. Independents are more likely to have a regular boyfriend or girlfriend than Greeks.

_____ 6. In general, Independents have a better social life than Greeks.

7. I (am) (am not) a member or pledge of a sorority or fraternity. (Cross out the one that does not apply.)

8. I am a: Freshman, Sophomore, Junior, Senior, Other

9. At the end of each month, how much money are you able to save (positive number) or must you borrow (negative number)?

10. How old are you?

Summary Data Sheet: Survey

Sub	Form	Social	Parties	Friends	Acad	Classes	GPA	Frat?	Class?	Money?	Age?

Note: Questions 1 to 6 should be rescaled so that responses are consistent across the four different surveys. That is all low numbers could be changed to reflect, for example, a positive feeling toward fraternities.

Experimenter _____ Date _____

Comments:

General Idea (Previous Research, Curiosity)

The general idea came from *curiosity*. We would like to measure how being Greek versus being Independent affects someone's opinion of his or her social and academic life.

Research Hypothesis

One possible hypothesis you may hold is: Members of the Greek system will perceive their social and academic life as superior to Independents. Further, those who rate the Greek social life as superior will also tend to rate the Greek academic life as superior.

What is another research hypothesis you may hold prior to conducting the survey?

Methods (Natural Observation, ➤ Survey)

Survey

Dependent Variable

The dependent variable will be the responses to the questions on the survey.

Operational Definition.   Pro or con feelings about social and academic achievement are measured by both global and specific questions on the survey to which subjects will respond on a Likert scale.

Predictor Variable

Affiliation or lack of affiliation with a social fraternity or sorority.

Operational Definition.   An undergraduate who is a pledge or a member of a fraternity or sorority will be considered a Greek. An undergraduate not affiliated with any such organization will be considered an Independent. Subjects will self-report their affiliation with the Greek or Independent life-style.

Subjects

Ethical Considerations.   The subject must agree to answer the questions. He or she could refuse to continue at any time. The subject should be informed that no individual answers would be released; only group averages.

Continued

Continued

► ***Characteristics and Availability.*** Any student enrolled as an undergraduate in the school can be considered. Demographic variables will be obtained to help assess the characteristics of the sample.

► ***Sampling Procedure and Number of Subjects.*** Students will be randomly sampled by order of appearance at various locations. The number of Greeks and Independents is a command decision that will depend on the size of the school, the amount of time available to the researchers, and the cooperativeness of the population. The sample should be large enough to obtain a good representation of both Greeks and Indepedents.

Procedural Command Decisions

What size sample would be minimally acceptable?

Where will you survey students and how will the locations be chosen?

Data Analysis

Description. Appropriate averages are computed for the opinion questions and the demographic questions. Percentage of each affiliation holding certain opinions can be computed. The relationship between global opinions about social life and academic life will be investigated by constructing a scatterplot of the data for each group.

Punctuation

Your ability to write effectively can be vastly improved by studying a few simple rules of punctuation. The comma, especially, seems to present problems to neophyte and expert alike. Below are some guidelines.

Exclamation point: Never use it!

Comma:

Separates independent clauses. The study of imagery has a long history, but only recently have psychologists considered it an important area.

The study of imagery has a long history but a short future. (The word *but* in this sentence does not separate independent clauses.)

Separates adjectives that could have been presented in either order. The *unusual, unexpected* pictures were responded to more slowly than were the *loud pure* tones.

Separates nonrestrictive clauses. The finding of Experiment 1, which supported our hypothesis, was not replicated in Experiment 2.

Separates a parenthetical comment that is closely related to the sentence. It was, however, interesting data.

Sets off sharp contrasts. The control group, not the experimental group, performed better.

Prevents misreading. After tabulating the data, analyses were conducted. (When in doubt put a comma between two nouns that occur together but not simply for "a place to breathe.")

Semicolon:

The semicolon is a compromise between the period and the comma; it separates two **sentences** that are relatively highly related.

The semicolon can also substitute for the comma between independent clauses when one of the clauses has several commas. The data from Experiments 1, 3, and 4 were combined, summarized, and transformed; but the data from Experiment 2 was omitted.

Colon:

Introduces a sequence or a clarifying phrase or sentence. Three responses were permitted: yes, no, and maybe. The prediction was straightforward: Control subjects should fail.

Methods Section

The methods section of an article is the operational definition of an experiment. Thus, it is specific and precise throughout. The methods section should reflect the tight logic of the experiment. Here the experimenter tells the reader exactly what was done. If this section is not clear, the remainder of the paper—the results and discussion—will be difficult to interpret, and the reader will not have much confidence in your conclusions. The methods section should be regarded as the *recipe* for the experiment. It contains both the necessary ingredients and the steps used to combine those ingredients. The appropriate test for evaluating any methods section is: *Could someone else repeat the experiment on the basis of this description?*

The methods section usually contains subsections (as implied in TOSS 3). In particular the subjects, materials or apparatus, and procedure are described separately. Other subsections may also be used depending on the experiment. Here the ingredients (subjects and materials) are discussed. The steps of the recipe (i.e., procedure) are discussed in TOSS 5 of the next chapter.

Subjects

The number of subjects in your sample should be stated. The procedure used to sample the subjects (e.g., volunteers, random) should be reported. This sampling procedure should indicate what caused volunteers to agree to participate (e.g., payment, did they know what the experiment was about?). The relevant characteristics of the population from which they were drawn should also be defined. For example, gender affects the results of many studies, and thus the reader should know the male-female composition of your experiment. Political affiliation affects the results of only certain studies and thus is usually not an important characteristic of the sample or population. In short, the reader must be able to determine the characteristics of the subjects that may be relevant to the outcome of the research.

Materials or Apparatus

This section should allow the reader to reproduce or to obtain equivalent materials as were used in the experiment. The detail necessary to do this may be supplied in prose, in a figure, or in a reference to standard materials (e.g., WAIS) with an appropriate citation. Characteristics of the materials should be highlighted, and any steps taken to construct materials should be detailed. If words, sentences, or other materials are used, a complete list can often be presented in an appendix.

In some cases, an apparatus subsection is used in place of, or in addition to, the materials subsection. Sufficient details of the physical environment of the research situation should be described so that they could be replicated, or at least known by others trying to do future work. Reliance on brand names of products, manufacturer names, or other commercial descriptions are usually inappropriate because the product may become unavailable or the company may go out of business, thereby preventing a future researcher from being able to replicate the experiment.

5 Causes & Validity

Overview

Chapter 5 discussses several concepts at the center of experimentation including internal and external validities, causality, and confounding variables.

The reader is taken through the development of a field experiment designed after Ellen Langer's work on "mindless" behavior. A natural observation study (no independent variable) is contrasted with the field experiment (independent variable), and the former is shown to be high in external validity but low in internal validity.

Being able to generalize findings to other settings gives a study high external validity. Doing an experiment that allows statements about causality gives a study high internal validity. The three types of causation discussed are a necessary cause, a sufficient cause, or a contributory cause.

Besides the independent variable, confounding variables can also be the cause for a change in the dependent variable. Those confounds could be selection, mortality, history, maturation, instrumentation, or reactivity. These causes can be eliminated in well-designed experiments.

The first inferential statistic is required in this chapter: the chi-square. A brief discussion of the null hypothesis and Type I errors in conjunction with this statistical procedure is also included.

Tips on General Style focuses on the structure of the basic paragraph. Tips on Specific Style focuses on the procedure subsection of the methods section.

Causality, Confounds, and Validity

"Something cannot emerge from nothing. This is profound thinking if you understand how unstable 'the truth' can be."

—*Paul Muad'Dib*

If science could advance only by asking people for their feelings or opinions (as in chapter 4) many questions could not be answered. If science always had to wait for a predictor variable to be manipulated by nature (as in chapter 3), it would progress very slowly indeed. Although several interesting variables cannot be manipulated by the scientist, fortunately many can. Our ability to control the variation of a predictor variable makes that variable an **independent variable (IV)** and brings us a step closer to achieving our goal of determining which variables (under which circumstances) **cause** changes in behavior.

79

Consider the following story a friend told us. While I was at the super-market the other day I noticed a woman trying to get in line at the checkout stand. The lines were quite long that day, and the woman was obviously in a hurry to get out. She headed for my aisle, and with a brusk "I'm in a hurry!" she shoved her overloaded cart in front of me. I stood there with my mouth open while she loaded her myriad products in front of my box of cereal, liter bottle of soda, and loaf of bread. By the time she left, I was just beginning to recover. I reached into my wallet to pay for my groceries when the girl at the checkout stand looked at me and said, "Keep your money. I charged these to her."

From this event, one could think of a thousand possible research questions. An intriguing one was how could the woman have gotten in front without rudely shoving her way in line? If she had asked and had a good reason, would she have been allowed in line without anyone feeling emotional distress?

As a simple hypothesis, let us begin by making the unoperationalized statement that "People will do what you want if you give them a reason for doing it." According to this hypothesis, the woman could have cut in line by asking and stating that she was late for an appointment. In fact, according to our hypothesis, the reason would not even have to be a good one in order for compliance to ensue. Let us now operationalize our hypothesis: A person will allow someone to cut in front of him or her in line if asked "May I cut in front of you?" and given some reason for the request.

How could we test this hypothesis using naturalistic observation as in chapter 3? What would such observation tell us? As with door holding, we would have to wait until someone requested to cut in line, record whether that person gave a reason and then observe whether he or she were allowed to cut in. Assume you and a lab partner decide to do just that. You and your partner note at the end of the study that of the 500 cases (remember, this is only a hypothetical outcome) where a reason was involved, the person was allowed to cut in line 400 times; of the 50 cases that did not involve a reason, only 10 received the favor of cutting in line. Thus, 80% of the people in the Reason condition complied and a mere 20% of the people in the No-Reason condition complied.

Correlation and Causation

Types of Relationships

A relationship clearly exists between reason-giving and compliance with the request. As we discussed in chapter 4, there is a correlation between the two variables, and by using the correct statistics we could obtain a measure of the strength of the relationship. However, did the line-jumper's reason cause people already in line to comply? Before we can even think of talking about causation, we must have a **correlation.** If half the people in each group complied, there would have been no correlation, and we would have no suggestion that our hypothesis was true. However, as Campbell (1974) details, a correlation does not mean that we have definitely identified a cause.

Figure 5—1.   Types of relations that could be responsible for a correlation in a particular set of observations of *X* and *Y*.

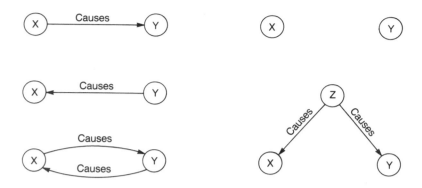

In general, two variables, *X* and *Y*, can vary together for any one of five reasons (see Figure 5–1):

1. *X* is a cause of *Y;* smoking is a cause of cancer.

2. *Y* is a cause of *X;* a rooster crows (*X*) before sunrise (*Y*) and yet the causal connection is clearly from *Y* to *X*.

3. *X* causes *Y*, which in turn causes *X;* advertising a product leads to increased sales, which leads the company to purchase more advertising.

4. *X* and *Y* are related by chance; in some cases, for example, with only a few observations, *X* and *Y* just happen to be related; washing your car causes it to rain.

5. *Z* causes both *X* and *Y;* for example, when more ice cream is consumed, more drownings occur. This correlation is true, not because ice cream consumption causes drowning (or that drowning causes ice cream consumption), but because people swim more and eat more ice cream during the summer (*Z*).

A correlation must be present to imply causality, but because a correlation alone might or might not be due to a causal relation, scientists say that correlation is necessary, but not sufficient, for causation. Can you think of other examples of each of the five relationships?

Types of Causation

If it did turn out that reason-giving *caused* compliance, what would this mean? The answer will depend on what type of cause is identified. One possibility is that the reason was a **necessary cause.** A necessary cause means that *X* (the reason) *must be present* for *Y* (compliance) to occur. Other conditions might also be needed, such as the person must ask politely, but without a reason there would be no compliance. In our data, because some people (although only a few) complied without receiving a reason, the reason was not necessary.

Another possibility is that the reason was a **sufficient cause.** A sufficient cause means that X (the reason) is all that is needed to ensure that Y compliance) will occur. There may be other ways to gain compliance, such as with a gun, but giving a reason will always result in compliance. In our data, because some people did not comply, even when given a reason, the reason was not sufficient, because something else was needed.

A final possibility is that reason-giving contributes to gaining compliance. A **contributory cause** is one where X (the reason) makes it more likely that Y (compliance) will occur. In our data, because there is a correlation between reason-giving and compliance, it is possible that reason-giving is a contributory cause of compliance. In fact, almost all causes in psychology are contributory causes. Figure 5–2 illustrates different relations between independent and dependent variables.

Before completing this discussion, let us consider more familiar examples. Suppose I am interested in what causes rain. Clouds must be present for rain to fall. Clouds are a necessary cause of rain, but they are not sufficient. We must have clouds (necessary condition or cause) for rain, but the presence of clouds does not guarantee it will rain (that is, it is not a sufficient condition or cause). A T-bone steak is sufficient to satisfy our hunger, but it is not a necessary condition. A lobster, a bowl of cereal, and many other foods are sufficient to cause a reduction in hunger, but they are not necessary. Finally, consider the relationship between smoking and lung cancer. Some people who smoke will not get cancer, and thus smoking is not a sufficient cause. Some people who do not smoke will get cancer, and thus smoking is not a necessary cause. However, smoking does increase the likelihood of having lung cancer, making smoking a contributory cause of lung cancer.

Internal Validity

Unfortunately, we cannot even say that reason-giving is a contributory cause of gaining compliance. As in the relationship between ice cream and drowning, another factor could have caused the results. For example, perhaps people who are self-confident are more verbal (and therefore are more likely to give a reason as part of casual conversation) than people who are not. Or maybe good-looking people are more likely to give a reason than ugly people. Or perhaps the person making the request assessed whether the person he or she asked was friendly. If that person looked friendly, the requester would give a reason; if he or she did not look friendly, the line-jumper simply pushed in first. In other words, it was actually the demeanor of the requestee that caused the requester to give a reason or not. These are alternative explanations for the results of our study and are called **rival hypotheses.** Any of these rival hypotheses could be the true underlying cause.

To the extent that a scientific study can identify the cause of a change, it is said to have **internal validity.** Because of the existence of these rival hypotheses, our study would have very low internal validity; naturalistic observation does not allow us to conclude that the changes in the dependent variable (allowing the person to cut in front of the line) were caused by changes in the predictor variable (reason or no reason for wanting to cut in).

Figure 5-2.   Possible patterns that implicate different types of causes. If the pattern were observed in a controlled experiment, casual claims could be made rather than merely being implicated.

No relationship

	DV Present	DV Absent
IV Present	50	50
IV Absent	50	50

	DV P	DV A
IV Present	100	0
IV Absent	100	0

IV is Both **NECESSARY AND SUFFICIENT**
for observation of DV

	DV P	DV A
IV P	100	0
IV A	0	100

IV is **NECESSARY** for observation of DV

	DV P	DV A
IV P	50	50
IV A	0	100

IV is **SUFFICIENT** for observation of DV

	DV P	DV A
IV P	100	0
IV A	50	50

IV **CONTRIBUTES** to observation of DV

	DV P	DV A
IV P	80	20
IV A	20	80

Confounding Variables

Other factors also varied (or could have varied) when the predictor variable changed. These other factors are called **confounding variables.** Scientists use the slang **confound** to refer to these variables. The change in the dependent variable could be due to the predictor variable or to the confound. The problem is that we cannot tell which caused the change.

To illustrate confounding variables and their effect in the study, imagine that women were always the ones who gave a reason and men never gave a reason.

	Gave a reason (Women)	Did not give a reason (Men)
Person complies	400	10
Person denies	100	40

From the data above, what caused compliance? Was it the reason or the gender of the person making the request? Clearly there is no way to tell. Gender is a confounding variable that, in this case, is perfectly correlated with the give-a-reason and give-no-reason variable.

There are many possible confounds in the world, but they tend to fit into one of a few categories. They occur in natural observation studies and in inadequately controlled experiments. Below we consider some of these categories. Others are discussed and given special consideration in later chapters. In particular, statistical regression, testing, and sequencing are problems in special cases and are discussed in detail in subsequent chapters.

Selection. **Selection** refers to differences due to biases in the assignment of subjects to conditions. Most (or all) of the people in the No-Reason condition were deaf, men, brunettes, unemployed, or dressed badly. All of these characteristics of the subjects are confounding variables that could lead to the creation of rival hypotheses.

Consider the following study. A scientist is interested in whether a Drug A or Drug B results in the greater improvement in the spatial ability of rats. He goes to the city dump and catches 10 rats, which he injects with Drug A. He then goes to the same dump and catches 10 more rats, which he injects with Drug B. He then places all the rats in a maze and observes that the B rats learn the maze faster than the A rats.

What is a rival hypothesis for this study? The B rats were harder to catch (that is why they were not caught first) and so probably had better spatial ability initially.

Mortality. **Mortality** is the differential loss of subjects from the conditions. People who had to listen to a long reason may have decided to continue shopping rather than stay in line, thus removing themselves from the experiment. Even if we assume that the groups started out equal, if more people leave the experiment in one condition compared with another, there is a chance that the groups will be different in the end.

Consider the following study. A scientist wants to compare a Gradual Diet Plan with an Intensive Diet and Exercise Program. He starts with 50 people on each plan who were similar at the beginning. At the end, the 10 people left in the Exercise Program had lost an average of 75 pounds, whereas the 50 people left in the Gradual Plan had lost only 15 pounds.

What is a rival hypothesis for this study? Everyone who was not losing weight in the Exercise Program decided to quit the plan. Perhaps they found it too rigorous for too little payoff. Only those losing great amounts of weigh continued on the Exercise Program. Thus, as with the selection confound, the final comparison is biased by the characteristics of the subjects.

History.   **History** refers to specific events external to the subject that distinguish one condition from another condition besides the independent variable. Most (or all) of the people in the No-Reason condition may have been late for an appointment, been paying by check, had a child with them.

Consider the following study. An experimenter is interested in the effects of hunger on aggression. She removes 10 cats from a group kennel and places them in individual cages so that she can monitor their food intake. She leaves 10 cats in the group cages and allows them to eat freely. She then pairs the cats and observes that the hungry cat was more aggressive.

What is a rival hypothesis for this study? The hungry cats also were socially isolated for a period of time, while the other cats remained in a social situation, the kennel. The animals differed in their history as well as in their hunger, so the experimenter could not conclude which caused the aggression.

Maturation.   **Maturation** involves processes internal to the subject that are due to the passage of time (e.g., growing older, getting tired). Most (or all) of the people in the No-Reason condition may have just gotten off of work.

Consider the following study. A researcher believes that exercise will give people increased lung capacity. She has one group of people skip rope for 10 minutes and another group of subjects watch a 10-minute videotape on exercise. Following the 10 minutes, she asks each person to hold their breath while she records the length of time. To her surprise, she finds that the members of the group watching the videotape held their breath longer.

What is a possible rival hypothesis? Clearly, because there was no rest period for the members of the exercise group, they may have been winded or otherwise tired; therefore, changes internal to the subject had occurred.

Instrumentation.   **Instrumentation** refers to changes in the instrument used to measure the dependent variable. The instrument may be a paper-and-pencil test, a human observer, or a machine. Your lab partner may have observed most (or all) of the No-Reason instances and may have a stricter criterion for what he or she counted as being allowed to cut in front of the line or what he or she counted as a reason.

Consider the following study. A researcher is interested in whether a lecture-style class or a discussion-style class leads to better understanding of course material. He compares Professor A, the lecturer, with Professor B, the discussion leader. He asks both professors to give the same essay test, grade their tests, and then return the tests to him. He discovers that the grades in the lecture class were higher.

What is a possible rival hypothesis? Because each instructor graded his or her own tests, it is possible that Professor A is simply an easier grader. Because the instruments used to measure the dependent variable were different professors, a confounding variable is present.

Reactivity. **Reactivity** occurs when subjects react differently in different conditions because of biases or expectancies of the subject or of the experiment. A person giving a reason for his or her request may also have an expectation that the person will comply. This may be manifested in other behavior besides the actual statement of the reason (e.g., nonverbal cues). It may be these nonverbal cues that produced the effect. We encountered a specific example of this class of confounds in chapter 4 when we discussed demand characteristics and social desirability.

Consider the following study. A doctor wants to determine if a new drug will increase the activity level of geriatric patients. She gives one group of elderly patients an injection of the drug and compares their activity level with the activity level of other patients of the same age. She finds increased conversation and social interactions among the patients receiving the drug.

What is a possible rival hypothesis? Those receiving the drug had a topic of conversation that the other patients did not have, namely the drug injection. They may have discussed what it felt like or speculated on the purpose of the drug. The patients may have even guessed the purpose of the drug and behaved accordingly. Reactivity confounds often require special procedures to eliminate them; chapter 12 is dedicated to those procedures.

For all of the above confounding variables, we may experience them as a **local** or as a **global** effect. A local confound, sometimes referred to with the adjective **differential,** means that the confound is having a disproportionate effect on some, but not all, of the conditions. For example, a local history effect, or differential history, in our study might be due to one group hearing a joke and the other group not hearing one. Local effects will threaten the internal validity of the study. Global effects, on the other hand, are more likely to affect the population to which you can generalize. This will be discussed in more detail when we consider external validity.

Finally, these confounding variables can combine in complex ways to produce a rival hypothesis. For example, if ROTC students were compared with other college students (a selection confound) about their opinion of war, they may suspect that they should respond in a socially acceptable way (a reactivity confound) or they may refuse to answer the questions (a mortality confound).

Many of the above scenarios for our reason study seem unlikely. However, only one of these needs to be present to prevent us from making conclusions about causality. Further, less bizarre scenarios could be constructed that have a high probability of occurring that would also make causal conclusions impossible.

So why would someone do a study if causality could not be determined? Often, researchers are interested in the presence of a relationship and do not care about the causal implications. Our survey from chapter 4 was such a study. In other cases, such as in the health services, the clinical psychologist is interested in getting an idea about the possible cause without necessarily being concerned with being able to prove scientifically what the cause was. The **case study,** where a practitioner studies a long history of the patient to get an idea of the *cause* of the problem, is sometimes useful for the patient even though speculations about cause are never proven. In some cases, as in chapter 3, some causal relationships would be contaminated if we manipulated the variables. In other cases, we would not want to manipulate the variables (e.g., suicide) for ethical reasons.

External Validity

Our reason study has none of these rationales, however; we wanted to see if reason-giving was a causal agent. Does our study have any advantages at all? Yes, it does. It has an important characteristic that we will weaken as we gain more internal validity. We can be reasonably certain that the pattern of results we found would apply to other settings and other subjects; our study has a lot of **external validity;** our findings are generalizable.

The more an experimenter interferes with a situation, the less external validity there will be. The more restrictions an experimenter places on his or her subjects, the less external validity there will be. Recall from chapter 4 our discussion concerning induction and sampling. When we restricted our sample (e.g., to phone owners), we also restricted the population to which we could generalize (e.g., all phone owners). External validity is the same concept in a different guise. If we test reading comprehension of adults using a short children's story, our findings may only apply to short children's stories, not to all stories. However, external validity is not restricted by every decision we make. For example, if we tested memory in a blue room, our findings would probably generalize to other colored rooms. This should remind you of our discussion of convenience sampling in chapter 4. Sometimes a convenience sample was acceptable because scientists would agree that your sample was representative of the population. Similarly, for some factors in your study, scientists would agree that they would not restrict your ability to generalize to other situations (such as red rooms). It may turn out that room color does have an effect on memory, but this will be discovered when other people try to see if your data are repeatable (see chapter 1) and just happen to use a red room.

External validity is greatest with the least amount of interference. However, as we discussed, internal validity is lowest with the least amount of interference. Almost always, internal validity and external validity must be balanced against each other in a study. A natural observation (chapter 3) has high external validity but low internal validity. A laboratory experiment has high internal validity, but often has low external validity. The case study mentioned above lacks both external and internal validity.

In our reason study, if the same person allowed one identical twin (who gave a reason) to cut in and the other identical twin (who did not give a reason) not to cut in, and the person had the same time pressures, amount of groceries, and so forth, we would be less doubtful about whether reason-giving was the cause, but the cause we discover would be so limited in scope that it would be of no real use. To what other situations would you generalize?

In some cases, external validity is not a concern at all. For example, if one theory predicts one effect and a second theory predicts the opposite effect, external validity may not concern us. In other situations, the researcher wants to demonstrate the existence or possibility of an effect (such as teaching chimps to use sign language). Mook (1983) discusses situations where external validity is not an important issue.

A Field Experiment

To investigate the role of reason-giving in gaining compliance, we are going to do a **field experiment.** In a field experiment, the experimenter manipulates an independent variable and attempts to eliminate as many confounding variables as possible. This is usually done by trying to treat subjects in each condition in as similar a manner as possible, except for the independent variable. However, because the experiment is conducted in the real world rather than a laboratory, there is the possibility of rival hypotheses. The manipulation of an independent variable reduces the external validity of the study compared with a natural observation, but because the study is in the real world, the field experiment will usually have more external validity than a laboratory experiment.

Let us begin with our general idea:

People will do what you want if you give them a reason for doing it.

We can then convert it into a specific research hypothesis:

A person will allow someone to cut in front in a line at a photocopier if he or she is asked "May I cut in front of you?" and given some reason (e.g., "I have to make copies") for the request.

Independent Variable

When we manipulate the independent variable (as opposed to letting it happen), we have several options that we did not have before. One thing that we must do is introduce variability into the independent variable. But how should we introduce the variability and how much variability should we introduce? For our study, we need only two conditions to test our research hypothesis: one where the line-jumper gives a reason and one where no reason is given. The Reason condition would require the requester not only to state a reason, but also make eye contact, speak politely, and follow the conventions of conversation.

If those are the characteristics of the Reason condition, what should the No-Reason condition be like? One approach is to make the No-Reason condition have a **qualitative** difference from the Reason condition. In this case, the No-Reason condition would consist of a different type of reason or perhaps something totally different, such as a verbal insult. For example, we could compare a simple reason with a complex reason or a personal reason with a nonpersonal one. We could also compare a reason with a comment about the person's choice of clothing. A second way to make the No-Reason condition is to make it have a **quantitative** difference from the Reason condition. In this case, the No-Reason condition would offer fewer reasons than the Reason condition. Both conditions involve reasons, but the number or quantity of the reasons vary. A final approach is to make the No-Reason condition, as the name implies, the *absence* of any reason. In this case, the No-Reason condition would not include a follow-up statement after we said "May I cut in front of you?" This presence/absence manipulation is both qualitative and quantitative in a sense.

Which Reason and No-Reason conditions should we adopt? The quantitative technique for introducing variability in the independent variable is often useful when some initial information is already known about the variable and finer-grained information is desired (see chapter 15). It is also useful when the independent variable is on an interval or ratio scale of measurement, such as drug dosage. Because this is our first study involving reason-giving, we want to begin more simply by seeing if a reason has any effect at all. Thus, we should probably not use a quantitative manipulation (such as 1 versus 2 reasons).

The command decision between the presence/absence approach and the qualitative approach is more difficult. On the one hand, if we choose the qualitative approach (e.g., reason versus verbal abuse) and find that reasons are better than verbal abuse, we would not know if the reason led to more compliance or if the verbal abuse led to less compliance. Even if we compared two types of polite reasons, we still could not be sure if one type helped or if the other type hurt. If, on the other hand, we chose the presence/absence approach, we would know that any differences were due to the reason, but the effect we observe is likely to be smaller than it would be in the verbal abuse situation.

Which comparison should we make? The presence/absence comparison is a good first start when you are just beginning to explore a question and have no previous information. It is not a sophisticated comparison because it does not tell you specific information about how, for example, one reason differs from another or how two reasons differ from one. As we will see in chapter 6, the conclusions you can make from a study depend on both the experimental condition and the control condition. Nevertheless, because we are just starting in this area, we will compare a Reason with No-Reason.

Some of you may object to the definition of a reason as "I need to make copies." Clearly, this is not a good reason, because why else would you need to use a photocopier? However, a social psychologist named Ellen Langer has argued that people do not evaluate a reason when deciding whether to comply with a request. In other words, as long as some reason is provided, it does not make any difference what that reason is. If Langer's thesis is correct, then we should find that more people will comply in our reason condition, even though the reason is quite uninformative.

Dependent Variable

For our dependent variable, we need some measure of compliance, or more specifically, "cutting in line." A simple, and acceptable, variable would be the presence or absence of compliance. If a person allows the experimenter in line, it is scored as a "hit"; if he or she does not, it is scored as a "miss." This has the advantage of simplicity (which should never be overlooked). However, what do we do with the person who wants to help but also has a deadline? or only a few sheets left? Should this be considered compliance?

One solution to this is to collect the additional information during the experiment. In other words, if a person rushes through his or her remaining copies, you could record that fact. If the additional data are uninteresting, you can always use the original, simple "hit" and "miss" data. On the other hand, you may find that the reason leads people to try to comply (i.e., rushing behavior) even though he or she does not actually let you cut in.

In general, then, using a more sensitive dependent measure compared with a less sensitive one is usually better. The time it takes people to do something may reveal more than whether they complete the task; a 7-point scale for coffee preference may tell you more than simply asking people whether they like the brand. The 5-point Likert scale used in chapter 4 is another example of a dependent variable that is more detailed than simply having the subject agree or disagree with a statement.

Subject Variables

Of the techniques discussed in chapter 4, we clearly will use a convenience sample of some kind, perhaps with some modification. We should systematically skip over all potential subjects who could have seen us cut in earlier. We will try to keep as much of a random element in our sampling procedure as possible, but as is usually the case in psychological research, the theoretical random sample will be pragmatically prohibitive.

In addition, for our particular concerns, we should probably restrict our population in a couple of ways. First, we probably do not want to generalize to people photocopying in groups, because these people may be more or less likely to comply than an individual (more complex designs to be studied in chapter 11 allow us to do both). More generally, we need to make a decision about whether to cut in when there is a line or only when one person is using the machine. If possible, the one-person restriction would prevent any peer pressure from the other people in line. We should also skip over any people whom we know, which restricts our population further to that of strangers. Finally, our subjects must be sensitive to the manipulation; that is, they must be able to tell the difference between a reason and the lack of a reason. Except for these restrictions, however, we should do our best to select our subjects randomly. To do this effectively we must overcome any experimenter biases (reactivity); we cannot pick friendly looking people to be in our Reason condition. The only way to accomplish this is to decide beforehand who will be the subject.

One approach is to come prepared with some random numbers. Pick a random number, wait until that many *eligible* subjects have used the copier, and then ask the next stranger using the machine if you could cut in. After this subject, wait until people near by who heard or saw you have left and then repeat the procedure.

Our final consideration for our subjects is how many should we ask. If we expect a big difference (between Reason and No-Reason), we can ask fewer subjects than if we expect a small difference (between one type of reason and another). Because the total number of subjects asked will depend on the size of your class, you or your instructor will make a command decision.

Procedural Details

Finally, you will need to work out the details of your experiment. All of these details should be exactly the same for the Reason condition and the No-Reason condition. Some things to think about are when will you conduct the experiment? What will you wear? Will you be carrying anything to photocopy? Will you actually do the photocopying? What will you do if asked "How many copies?" How will such a response be scored?

In our study, students at the University of Oklahoma who were using a photocopier were approached while trying to make copies. All subjects were approached between 9:30 in the morning and 9:30 at night on a weekday. The confederates wore standard student attire and asked a subject "May I cut in front of you"? Control subjects were told nothing else, and experimental subjects were also told that "I have to make copies." If a person asked "How many copies do you have to make?" or any other vocalization, the confederate simply repeated the request (and reason if appropriate) until the subject either complied or denied.

The Data

Subjects were classified as either having complied or not. These frequency data can be summarized in a 2-by-2 table where the entries indicate the number of people falling into each of the categories. The data may be analyzed using the chi-square statistic.

	Outcomes		
	Compliance	No Compliance	Total
Reason	10	8	18
No-Reason	2	16	18
Total	12	24	36

The chi-square is an **inferential statistic.** That is, it allows you to determine how likely it is that the pattern you observed was due to chance. How likely would such a pattern be if there was no difference between Reason and No-Reason conditions? That is, how likely would such a pattern be if compliance was independent of reason-giving?

The no-effect assumption of the independent variable is called the **null hypothesis** and is made as a part of the statistical procedures. It should not be confused with your research hypothesis. In fact, it is usually the statement that goes against your research hypothesis. The chi-square statistic gives us a value for our data that we will compare with a table that indicates the probability of observing that value if the null hypothesis is true. There is always some chance that any value (even a very large one) will occur even when the null hypothesis is true. However, scientists have adopted the convention that if the value would have occurred by chance 1 time in 20 or less (alpha = .05), then the null hypothesis assumption is not valid. In such a case, the scientist rejects the no-difference assumption and would claim that there was a difference between the Reason and No-Reason conditions even though this claim will be wrong 1 in 20 times, or .05. The scientist is willing to accept this type of error at this frequency of occurrence. Such an error is called **Type I error** or an **alpha error.**

If you have not had a course in statistics, the steps to compute the chi-square are presented below to provide you with a cookbook method for calculation. If you have had statistics, these steps can be used as a reminder, but you should refer to a statistics book for detailed information about the uses and abuses of this statistic. The table of chi-square values appears in the statistical appendix.

Key Words

alpha error	internal validity
case study	local
cause	maturation
confounding variable (slang: confound)	mortality
contributory cause	necessary cause
correlation	null hypothesis
differential	qualitative
external validity	quantitative
field experiment	reactivity
global	rival hypothesis
history	selection
independent variable	sufficient cause
inferential statistic	Type I error
instrumentation	

Additional Reading

Cialdini, R. (1985). *Influence: Science and practice.* Glenview, IL: Scott, Foresman.

Freedman, J. L., & Fraser, S. C. (1966). Compliance without pressure: The foot-in-the-door technique. *Journal of Personality and Social Psychology, 4,* 195–202.

Langer, E. J., Blank, A., & Chanowitz, B. (1978). The mindlessness of ostensibly thoughtful action. *Journal of Personality and Social Psychology, 36,* 635–642.

The chi-square statistic (χ^2) is used to determine if the observed frequencies (O) are different from expected frequencies (E). The formula for chi-square is:

$$\chi^2 = \frac{\Sigma (O - E)^2}{E}$$

STEP 1. Make a table of the observed data.

	Outcomes		
	Compliance	No Compliance	Total
Reason	10	8	18
No-Reason	2	16	18
Total	12	24	36

STEP 2. Compute the expected frequencies.

What is expected depends on what assumption you want to make (and test) about the data. Sometimes the researcher has specific theoretical predictions (e.g., chapter 7). Other times, as in the experiment in chapter 5, the researcher wants to see if a relationship exists between the predictor variable and the dependent variable. In other words, we want to assume that the two variables are independent and then determine if we can reject that assumption.

Consider the following table:

	Outcomes		
	Compliance	No Compliance	Total
Reason	?	?	18
No-Reason	?	?	18
Total	12	24	36

If the Reason variable is independent of the Outcome variable, what would we expect in each of the four cells? We can calculate these expected scores using the following formula:

$$\frac{\text{row total} \times \text{column total}}{\text{grand total}}$$

Thus, the expected score of the Reason-Compliance cell is found by multiplying the frequency of people giving a reason (18) by the frequency of compliance (12) and dividing by the total number of observations (36). If reason-giving was independent of compliance, we would expect the following table:

	Outcomes		
	Compliance	No Compliance	Total
Reason	(18 × 12)/36 = 6	(18 × 24)/36 = 12	18
No-Reason	(18 × 12)/36 = 6	(18 × 24)/36 = 12	18
Total	12	24	36

STEP 3. Compute chi-square.

Subtract the expected scores from the observed scores, square each difference, divide by the expected scores, and add them together.

$$\frac{(10-6)^2}{6} + \frac{(8-12)^2}{12} + \frac{(2-6)^2}{6} + \frac{(16-12)^2}{12} = 8.00$$

STEP 4. Compare the observed chi-square (8.00) with the critical chi-square.

There are many distributions of critical values of chi-square. The one you use depends on the number of rows and number of columns you have. More specifically, you must compute the degrees of freedom of the statistic using the following formula:

$$(\text{number of rows} - 1) \times (\text{number of columns} - 1) = 1$$

Table A in the Appendix shows that the critical value of χ^2 (1) is 3.841 if we are willing to accept a Type I error only 5% of the time. Our observed χ^2 was 8.00. Thus, because we observed a value greater than the critical value, we would reject the hypothesis that reason-giving and compliance are independent.

STEP 5. Compute the size of the relationship.

If there is a relationship between the two variables, we would like to know how large it is. The magnitude of the relationship can be computed by calculating the contingency coefficient (C):

$$C = \sqrt{\frac{\chi^2}{\chi^2 + \text{grand total}}} = .4264$$

We already know from the χ^2 test that the coefficient, .4264, is significantly larger than 0.0.

Compliance

Subject Number	Request Maker*	Dependent variable Comply/Failed	Other variables of interest		
			Gender	Copy amount	Time

NOTES:

Location: _____

_____

*Characteristics of request maker(s). Indicate code if more than one: _____

_____

Special problems or comments: _____

_____

_____

Experimenter's/Observer's Name(s): _____

_____

Time(s) of experiment: _____

_____

SUMMARY DATA SHEET

Compliance
Summary of observed data:

	Complied?		
	Yes	No	Total
Reason			
No-Reason			
Total			

Computed expected frequencies:

	Complied?		
	Yes	No	Total
Reason			
No-Reason			
Total			

Chi-square observed: _____ Chi-square critical: _____

Comments:

General idea (Previous Research, Curiosity)

The general idea in this chapter came from both previous research and curiosity. State the general idea and specify how the two sources gave rise to the idea.

Research hypothesis

How was the research hypothesis stated in the chapter?

Methods (Natural Observation, Survey, ► Field Experiment)

Field experiment. Why is the method *not* a natural observation? or a survey?

Dependent variable

The dependent variable is whether or not the subject complies.

Operational Definition.   Operationally define: Compliance

Continued

Continued
Predictor or ► Independent Variable

Whether or not the experimenter accompanies the request with a reason.

Operational Definition. What was the operational definition of Reason given in the chapter? No-Reason?

Create another operational definition of Reason and No-Reason.

Evaluate the two sets of operational definitions using the criteria discussed in the chapter. Does the definition of Reason depend on the definition of No-Reason?

Subjects

Ethical Considerations. You will be unable to obtain informed consent from your subjects without contaminating the study. Yet, most psychologists would accept this as an ethical study because it does not put subjects in a situation unlikely to be encountered in everyday experience.

Characteristics and Availability. Anyone who appears at the copy machine could be considered a subject in this experiment. We might eliminate those people who are familiar to the experimenter or who might have overheard an earlier request.

Continued

Continued

Sampling Procedure and Number of Subjects.   A convenience sample of those people appearing at the copy machine can be used. Would you argue for a large sample or a small one? Defend your answer.

Procedural Command Decisions

Some command decisions about what time of day to conduct the experiment, the exact question to ask the subject, and what reason to give the subject should be considered.

Data Analysis

Descriptive.   Frequency of compliance

Inferential.   The chi-square statistic is done on the frequency data of subject compliance in the two conditions.

The Basic Paragraph

We have spent much time discussing techniques for improving the quality of the sentences you write. This box focuses on how to combine those sentences into a coherent, interesting paragraph. We assume that you know that a paragraph is a series of related sentences organized around a single topic. Knowing this alone eliminates problems such as single-sentence paragraphs and loosely organized paragraphs. Below we give some additional specifics about the paragraph.

Each of your paragraphs must have a central thought and a topic sentence. If your paragraph has two thoughts, make two paragraphs. If neighboring paragraphs have the same thought, combine them.

Each sentence should relate to and develop the central thought. A paragraph can be developed in many ways. You could:

1. Supply scientific examples or pieces of literature to support the topic sentence.

2. Make specific comparisons.

3. Define, describe, or explain a concept, procedure, or result.

4. Argue from examples to the general case (topic sentence at end).

5. Argue from general case to specific instance.

Vary the sentences in their structure and length. By using all the different structures we have discussed, you can supply interest and dramatic effect.

Use transition paragraphs when one central thought does not follow from the previous one.

Procedure Subsection

Procedure

This subsection is the crucial part of the recipe. It describes the step-by-step processes involved in conducting the experiment. From the time the subject begins the experiment until the subject finishes, all *important* aspects should be described. No detail is too small in the procedure. However, you must distinguish between small and irrelevant. A good strategy is to pretend that you are describing, blow by blow, the adventures of your subject. Does the reader know exactly what it was like to be a subject in your experiment? The procedure should include the experiences of the subject from the subject's point of view.

Even earnest attempts to present the information step by step can fail. Failures take three forms. One is the attempt to include too much irrelevant information. For example, the room in which the experiment takes place is rarely described. This reflects the author's belief (as well as his or her belief that no one else would believe differently) that the room will not affect the results. A second failure occurs because the author does not "step back" from the actual procedure. For example, you may note that the instructions were read to the subject, but fail to supply a paraphrase of those instructions. Or you may note each step of the experiment, but fail to supply any indication of the timing of the steps. In some cases (e.g., memory experiments), timing information is critical. A third failure occurs because, even though all the information is there, the author has not highlighted the differences between the experimental and the control group. Remember, just because the information is "in there somewhere" does not mean the reader will easily grasp the difference.

6 Control & Conclusions

Overview

This chapter discusses the role of control in eliminating rival hypotheses of the type encountered in chapter 5. If a factor cannot be regarded as irrelevant, then it must be controlled through experimental control, random assignment, or statistical control. In addition to general procedures for control, the chapter focuses in detail on the relationship between the experimental and control conditions of an experiment. Both the experimental condition *and* the control condition dictate the conclusions that can be reached. The laboratory experiment is the methodological vehicle of the chapter. The student is led through the development of an experiment designed to investigate a mnemonic strategy used by ancient Greek orators: the method of loci. Concepts of placebo, ceiling and floor effects, and demand characteristics are discussed in the implementation of the experiment.

The independent groups *t*-test is introduced in this chapter.

Tips on General Style focuses on a number of troublesome words often misused in technical writing.

Tips on Specific Style addresses the structure and substance of the results section of a manuscript.

Control

Children who brushed with Crest had 26% fewer cavities.

—*Television commercial*

All of us are constantly bombarded by claims from people who want to convince us of something. Commercials want us to be convinced to buy one product over another; politicians want us to support one view over another; proponents of self-help programs want us to buy their records to improve our vocabulary, their books to improve our memory, and their videotapes to improve our shape. A good scientist is able to evaluate these claims, because these claims are no different from the conclusions that they must come to when doing their research.

As an example, consider the claims made by some authors of books designed to give people super memories. Call this memory improvement program BUYME. As we consider the possible claims, decide for yourself whether you would purchase the BUYME program over other programs of similar price. If you decide not to purchase the BUYME program, try to specify your reasons.

103

Claim 1. In a clinical study at a major university, 900 people who studied the BUYME program of memory improvement were able to remember perfectly a list of 25 names.

Obviously, this claim is uninformative because we have no idea how many people studied the BUYME program and were unable to remember the 25 names. So let us try another claim.

Claim 2. In a clinical study . . . 900 people who studied the BUYME program were able to remember the 25 names and only 100 people using BUYME failed to remember the names.

This claim is a little more informative. We now know, for example, that 90% of the BUYME people were able to remember the names. But, is 90% good? Good compared with what? The problem with this claim is that we have no idea how people using some other program, call it BRAND-X, would have done. Is this a strange example just for the purpose of this course? How about the advertising claim that "4 out of 5 dentists recommend Trident for their patients who chew gum"? How many dentists? Did they also recommend BRAND-X or perhaps all sugarless gums? In fact, the claim quoted at the beginning of this chapter was an experiment comparing Crest with fluoride against Crest without fluoride. Thus, the fewer cavities was due to fluoride, not to Crest.

Claim 3. . . . 900 BUYME people passed the test, but only 90 BRAND-X people passed the test.

Now we know something about the other group. The proponents of the BUYME program want you to jump to the conclusion that their program is better. In fact, most people would give them the benefit of the doubt and assume that the two groups had an equal number of subjects. However, what if there were 1,000 BUYME people and only 100 BRAND-X people? Then for both groups, 90% would have passed the test. Again, such situations occur in advertising in which the consumer is invited to make the comparison and jump to the wrong conclusion: "No toothpaste fights cavities better than Crest" (but most do just as well). "More people buy GM auto parts than any other auto part" (More people own GM cars than any other kind, and thus you could actually interpret this negatively—more GM cars break down; but even with equal breakdowns you would still expect more GM parts to be sold.).

Claim 4. Ninety percent of the people who passed the test were in the BUYME program and 90% of the people in the BUYME program passed the test.

This claim is perhaps the trickiest one of all. It supplies no more information than does claim 3, but it sounds good. Consider the following tables of frequencies (not percentages):

	BUYME	BRAND-X	BUYME	BRAND-X
PASSED	90	10	81	9
FAILED	10	90	9	1

The advertisers want people to infer that the table on the left characterizes reality as given in claim 4. However, the table on the right also agrees with claim 4. Here again both programs yield a 90% success rate.

Although commercials try to hide their failure rate, several do imply that they are better than some other product.

Claim 5. In a clinical study of 1,000 college students conducted at a major university, 450 of the 500 people in the BUYME program passed the memory test, while only 50 of the 500 people in the BRAND-X program passed the test.

Now we have a claim that supplies us with a great deal of information. Which is the better program? Under the conditions of the clinical study (about which we know very little), BUYME was the better program. So we would start thinking about the possibility that the BUYME program actually caused an improvement in memory. We cannot say for certain that BUYME was the cause until we know more about the clinical study.

The Concept of Control

As we learned in the last chapter, to be able to claim that our independent variable *caused* a change in our dependent variable (i.e., that our experiment has internal validity), we must show that the independent variable *and only the independent variable* produced the change. To do this, we must control all other possible changes.

The best way to accomplish this amount of control is to perform your research in the laboratory. When you do this, you often lose a lot of external validity; but scientists are often willing first to determine the cause under the ideal situation created in the laboratory and then to see how this cause works in the real world. For example, Boyle's law tells us about how gases behave in a vacuum—a very unrealistic world; but physicists are then able to apply this in more complex situations.

In this chapter an experiment is designed to determine if we can give people advice that will improve their memories. Consider first whether a field experiment (chapter 5) would be appropriate. We could give advice to half of our subjects and no advice to the other half. We could then let these subjects go about their business. But how could we measure their memories? We could do something right then and there: We could give them a list of words to remember. But notice how unrealistic our "realistic" field experiment has become. Alternatively, we could invite people to a free workshop where they could improve their memories. We could then compare them with another group of people randomly sampled from the community. However, the people who signed up for our workshop are going to be different from our random sample of other people. For one thing, they may have poorer memories to begin with, or at least they are more concerned about their memories than are the people whom we randomly picked for our control group.

Achieving Control

We want a study with a good amount of internal validity. Because we want to be able to conclude that the difference in the independent variable produced our results, we must attempt to make certain that the *only* difference between the Advice and No-Advice conditions is the advice they receive.

The attempt to do this is called **control**. Much of the mastery of experimental methodology involves the mastery of the techniques that control for the possibility of confounds.

Some differences may occur between the Advice condition and the No-Advice condition that are so unlikely to have an effect on the dependent variable that you can *assume the factor is unimportant*. For example, it may be discovered that, despite your best efforts, there are more red-headed people in the Advice condition than in the No-Advice condition. It is *so* unlikely that this could be a causal agent that most people would ignore it. Whether something can be assumed to be irrelevant is not entirely up to you. If the scientific community thinks it is important, then your assumption will not be shared. Assuming a factor is not important does not require any active involvement by the experimenter and is therefore not a control technique. We now consider the things an experimenter can do to counteract potential confounds in an experiment.

What do you do if the confound is important? The remaining methods deal with these more common situations. The first method of control, **experimental control**, is when the experimenter makes certain that the confound is equally represented in both conditions. For example, the gender of the subject could possibly affect the amount remembered. The experimenter would make certain that any effects of gender that occurred in the Advice condition would also be present in the No-Advice condition.

One approach is to use only males or only females in the study. In this way, gender of the subjects could not possibly have different effects on the Advice condition than on the No-Advice condition. However, external validity will be decreased because the findings are generalizable to only one gender. A second approach is to make certain that the proportion of males is the same in both conditions: If there are 75% males in the Advice condition, there should be 75% males in the No-Advice condition. This should be reminiscent of stratified random sampling discussed in chapter 4. There are other options here, but we will wait until a later chapter to discuss and until a later experiment to employ them.

The second method of control is a most important one in scientific methodology: **random assignment** or **randomization.** (This should not be confused with random sampling.) In this technique subjects are randomly assigned to be in either the Advice or the No-Advice condition. As with random sampling, this decision is made before the subect arrives. Assuming that you have a reasonable number of subjects scheduled for the experiment, random assignment is all that is needed to ensure that the experiment is internally valid. It is also *the only technique that can control for confounds you have failed to consider.* Random assignment must be done in all experiments that attempt to determine the cause of an effect. It is sometimes called controlling by chance, because it ensures that *in the long run* all confounds will be equally represented in both, or all, conditions. *In the long run* is important because it highlights that random assignment depends on a number of subjects to guarantee internal validity.

Random assignment is the prerequisite for a **true experiment.** Other experiments (called quasi-experiments) are conducted without random assignment. For example, subjects may naturally belong to, or choose, one condition over the other. If we wanted to compare ROTC students with other students, we could not randomly assign, and thus the conclusions from the experiment would be restricted to statements about correlation rather than causation. (Quasi-experiments are discussed in chapter 14.)

Randomization will be the method of control in our experiment. *Before* each subject arrives for the experiment, flip a coin and decide whether he or she will be in the Advice condition or the No-Advice condition. Do this for each subject until the quota of one of the conditions is filled; the remaining subjects may then be assigned to the other condition.

The skeptical experimenter may be interested in seeing if, in fact, random assignment controlled for variables that were not explicitly considered. If you simply record the gender of the subjects without using that information in any way, you should find that randomization placed roughly equal numbers of males in the Advice condition and the No-Advice condition. Figure 6.1 shows how the confound "evenness" is controlled with random assignment.

Figure 6–1   Illustration of how random assignment distributes an unknown confound (i.e., evenness) following a random sample and a biased sample.

1	2	3	4	5	6	7	8	9	10	11	12	13	14	15	16	17	18	19	20	21	22	23	24	25
26	27	28	29	30	31	32	33	34	35	36	37	38	39	40	41	42	43	44	45	46	47	48	49	50
51	52	53	54	55	56	57	58	59	60	61	62	63	64	65	66	67	68	69	70	71	72	73	74	75
76	77	78	79	80	81	82	83	84	85	86	87	88	89	90	91	92	93	94	95	96	97	98	99	100

RANDOM SAMPLE OF SIZE 40
(without replacement):

10	09	73	25	33	76	52	01	35	86	34	67
48	80	95	17	39	29	27	49	45	37	54	20
36	05	64	61	18	71	24	71	24	72	100	15
93											

BIASED SAMPLE OF SIZE 40
(without replacement):
(15 odd digits from sample on left were replaced with 15 even digits)

10	8	12	68	44	76	52	98	84	86	34	66
48	80	16	90	62	40	32	50	38	92	60	37
54	20	36	05	64	61	26	51	65	18	71	24
72	100	15	93								

RANDOM ASSIGNMENT TO EXPERIMENTAL AND CONTROL CONDITIONS:

	EXP	CONT			EXP	CONT	
	73	10			12	10	
	33	09			68	8	
	52	25			44	76	
	01	76			52	84	
	86	35			98	34	
	34	67			86	66	
	48	80			48	90	
	95	90			80	50	
13 Odd	17	91	10 Odd	16 Even	16	92	16 Even
7 Even	39	45	10 Even	4 Odd	62	60	4 Odd
	29	54			40	54	
	27	36			32	20	
	49	05			38	64	
	37	64			37	61	
	20	26			36	51	
	61	51			5	24	
	65	71			26	72	
	18	24			65	100	
	72	15			18	15	
	93	100			71	93	

What if, after completing the experiment, random assignment had given you a bad shuffle and by chance there were many more females in the Advice condition than in the No-Advice condition? Although this is unlikely and becomes increasingly unlikely with increasing numbers of subjects, it may happen. Must we throw up our hands and throw out our data and hours of work? Not necessarily. There is a third control technique that can actually be used after the data have been collected: **statistical control.** Discussion of statistical control is beyond the scope of this book. Should this situation arise, you should be aware of its existence so that you can learn more about the techniques (e.g., analysis of covariance) or consult with a statistician.

Creating the Experimental Condition: Half of the Independent Variable

In an experiment, we must have a plan for applying the independent variable to the subjects to determine the effect on some dependent variable. This plan requires consideration of (1) the independent variable and the number of levels for the variable and (2) how the levels of the independent variable will be distributed to the subjects. Such a plan is called the **design** of the experiment. Here we will discuss a design with one independent variable having two levels, and the subjects will participate in only one level of the independent variable. This design is referred to as a **completely randomized design** or **between-subjects design,** because subjects are randomly assigned to only one level of a factor.

In any experiment, there must be at least two conditions. In our case, the Advice condition is called the experimental condition or the treatment condition. The No-Advice condition should be exactly the same as the Advice condition except for the advice. The No-Advice condition is called the control condition, because it controls for all other possible explanations for any effects that we may find. We know already that subjects must be randomly assigned to the experimental condition and the control condition (a between-subjects design).

We now turn to the nature of the memory advice we will give the subjects. A technique for improving memory called the method of loci was used by the great orators of ancient Greece. If you were using this technique to remember a list of things to buy at the grocery store, you would first think of an area that was familiar to you and that had a number of landmarks, such as your campus. You would start at one building and associate the first object on your shopping list with that building. You would do this by trying to make a bizarre image, or mental picture, of the object interacting in some way with the building. If, for example, you started at the student union and the first object on your list was a pepperoni pizza, you might image a pizza hovering over the building with little "pepperoni Martians" climbing down to the roof. Or you might imagine a giant pizza buzz-saw cutting the building in half. From the student union you would "walk" to the next building in your map and place the second object there. When you got to the grocery store, all you would have to do is "walk around campus" in your mind, picking up the correct objects.

When the orators used this technique, they would associate parts of their speech with different locations. A famous memory expert (called a mnemonist) was able to listen to a list of 200 objects and to later remember 198 of them—in order. What is even more amazing is that he recalled them 10 years after he first heard the list! So from this evidence we might expect that subjects given this advice would remember very well.

Creating the Control Condition:
The Other Half of the Independent Variable

You will recall from our criticisms of the BUYME program that we will need a comparison condition to evaluate the effectiveness of the Advice condition. The first thought might be to tell the people in the control condition absolutely nothing about the experiment (as we did in chapter 5). Thus, the experimental group gets instructions about the method of loci and the control group gets no instructions. We then read our shopping list and ask both groups to remember as many of the words as they can. Assuming that the experimental group remembers more than the control group, what can be concluded? We would like to conclude that the method of loci improved people's memory. However, how else are the two conditions different?

The experimenter spent more time with the experimental group than with the control group. Maybe this leads people in the experimental condition to take the experiment more seriously than the people in the control group. In other words, the demand characteristics (chapter 4) of the experiment differ for the two groups (a differential reactivity confound). If we literally tell the control subjects nothing, then they may not even expect a memory test at the end. The difference could be due merely to intention to remember and not to the method of loci.

Clearly both groups should be told that there will be a memory test, and the experimenter should spend about the same amount of time with each group. What do we tell the control group? One possibility is to give the control subjects **placebo** instructions. They can be told to pay close attention to the words, to think about the words, and to try their best to remember the words. We are telling the subjects little more than to try to remember the words. The instructions accomplish what we want in that they take time to administer, but they are a placebo—not a real technique or manipulation.

The best way to think of placebo conditions is to think about the typical drug study. In a drug study, we want to give our experimental group an injection of a drug, and we want to give the control group no drug. However, the administration of the drug (e.g., visit to a nurse, puncture in the arm, trauma of injection) can have effects independent of the actual drug. A good solution is to inject the control subjects with an inert substance such as saline (salt) solution that is similar to the drug in all respects except its active ingredients. Such an inert substance is called a placebo. Our instructions to "pay attention" are analogous to the placebo saline solution used in drug experiments.

What if the control subjects use the method of loci without being told to do so? Obviously, to the extent that this happens, we will be less likely to find a difference between our two groups. We *assume* that in our experiment it is unlikely that people will spontaneously adopt the experimental strategy, but it may be more likely to occur in other experiments. For example, in an experiment where the subjects were asked to remember a phone number by repeating it over and over to themselves, probably no effect of this advice would be found because the control subjects would repeat the number to themselves without being told to do so. In such cases, it may be advisable to force control subjects to do something else or to prevent them from repeating the phone number to themselves. In the current experiment, if you do not share our assumption about the spontaneous use of the method of loci, you may want to be more directive with your control subjects. For example, the subjects may be required to repeat each word to themselves as many times as possible in the control condition.

Before leaving the construction of the control condition, consider what can be concluded from the experiment. A conclusion depends on both the experimental condition and the control condition. The control condition will allow us to conclude that the method of loci is better than just trying to remember, but it will not tell us what it is about the method of loci that makes it work. Is is the bizarre imagery? Is it that the items are integrated with familiar locations? To answer these questions, we would need additional and different control conditions. What can be concluded from an experiment depends not only on the experimental condition but also on the control condition(s).

Thus far it has been suggested that experimental subjects be given method-of-loci instructions and the control subjects be given pay-attention placebo instructions. Subjects are to be randomly assigned to either the Method-of-Loci condition or the Pay-Attention condition. Subjects will be treated similarly except for the difference in instructions.

More Confounds

The experimenter must make certain that all of his or her effort to equate the groups is not destroyed by events that happen after the experiment begins. We encountered these potential confounds in the previous chapter.

The selection confound is one that was controlled by randomly assigning subjects to conditions. This confound would have been a serious one if we tried to compare volunteers who signed up for a workshop on memory with randomly selected subjects. However, a selection confound can appear under the guise of a different confound: mortality or differential attrition. Recall that mortality refers to the fact that subjects will sometimes drop out of experiments and that this dropout may be different for different conditions. In our experiment, we may find that some of the method-of-loci people cannot make images and therefore choose not to participate after they hear the instructions. The pay-attention instructions do not mention imagery so those people unable to make images would remain in that condition. Notice what happens to the random assignment if more people drop out of the experimental condition than the control condition. The ones who drop out are likely to have poorer memories, leaving a disproportionate number of people with good memories in the experimental group.

Thus, by the end of the experiment the control group and the experimental group may be different even though random assignment equated them at the beginning of the experiment.

If the number of dropouts is very different for the two conditions, changes in our experiment are needed and it should be run again with the necessary changes. If the number of dropouts is about the same and only a few, and if we can assume the subjects dropped out for reasons unrelated to the experiment, we can equate the conditions by randomly dropping out a subject or two from the condition with the large number of subjects. However, even if the number is the same in both conditions, but several people have dropped out, there should be concern about the external validity of our study even though the internal validity is not threatened. Unequal numbers of subjects is also a problem for a number of statistical tests, and for this reason also psychologists try to have "equal Ns."

Another possible confound that we should watch for is the history confound. Recall that a history confound is any change that occurs external to the experiment. Imagine that we are collecting data from a group of method-of-loci subjects and we happen (very innocently) to tell a joke that day. This may relax those subjects and make it easier for them to concentrate on the word list. We might assume, perhaps, that the effect is irrelevant and proceed. As another example, you might supply one group of subjects with an extra example in answer to a question. What if one of your subjects talks out loud while trying to recall words? Simply assuming irrelevance will not suffice. However, most of these problems can be avoided by the alert experimenter. One procedure that greatly reduces the chances of history effects producing important differences is to test the subjects one at a time or in small groups. This way a history effect would not affect a large number of subjects.

Try to think of other confounds that could be unintentionally introduced after assignment of subjects to conditions. Remember, if the effect is local, that is, if it affects only one condition, then it certainly will threaten internal validity. If the effect is global, that is, if it affects all the conditions, then it certainly will affect external validity.

The Experiment

Let us turn now to other details necessary to conduct the experiment. We will begin with the choice of dependent variable.

Dependent Variable

The choice of dependent variable is relatively simple for this experiment. We want some measure of people's memory. A good choice is to have the subjects remember as many items as they can. The subject may recall the words in the order presented or in any order they can. Because there are many things that must be remembered in order (e.g., speeches, logical arguments, telephone numbers), we will make the command decision to ask our subjects to recall in order, but we will be prepared to score our data in two ways. One scoring method we will call *strict:* Subjects will only get credit if they recall the item in the correct position on the list. The other scoring method we will call *liberal:* Subjects will get credit for any word on the list that they remember regardless of the order in which is recalled. Thus, while collecting only one set of data, there are *two dependent variables* to analyze.

Subject Variable

Sampling will be strictly a matter of convenience. We will use any people we can, including other people in the class, freshmen from the subject pool, and so forth. Your instructor can give you information about the procedure for your college.

All Else Being Equal

Although we have already spent a good deal of thought on the control condition, a few more issues must be noted on the procedure for the experiment. Remember, everything discussed now should be implemented for both the experimental group and the control group in exactly the same fashion.

The first command decision is to pick the words that we want the subjects to remember. First, how many words should the subjects be given to remember? If we pick too small a number (say 5), the task may be so easy that everyone will be able to remember all five. If the control group remembers all five, then how could the method of loci help memory when memory needs no help? This problem is referred to as a **ceiling effect.** There is no room for the independent variable to have an effect, even if it really could help memory. Similarly, if the subject is given 2,000 words to remember, performance may be so poor that everyone will do badly. As you may have guessed, this is referred to as a **floor effect.** Both problems should be avoided.

If this were the first study ever done on memory, then it would be a wise idea to do a **pilot study.** A pilot study is a small version of the experiment that researchers conduct to give them the necessary information before they throw a lot of time and effort into a full-blown version of the experiment. Alternatively, as is the case for the current study, a lot of research may have already been done. The literature, rather than a pilot study, can help make the command decision about the number of words. A good number of words for our purposes is 20. This turns out to be a good number to remember and yet is not so many that subjects will perform poorly. Also, method-of-loci people should not have much trouble thinking of some area with 20 buildings, landmarks, or locations.

What type of words should be used? To be fair to the method-of-loci group, we may want to make certain that people can make a mental image of the word's referent. For example, it is more difficult to make an image of the word *honesty* than the word *bookshelf.* Again the literature helps us out by supplying lists of *concrete* and *abstract* words. If we use only concrete words, it may be interesting in a later experiment to see if our conclusions also hold for the harder-to-image, abstract words.

We also want to minimize any natural associations or relationships among the words in the list. For example, if the words *bacon, lettuce,* and *tomato* are on the list, these words would tend to go together, and thus using a technique such as the method of loci to help the words "go together" may be redundant. Again, such a manipulation would be an interesting one in a subsequent experiment; but for now, the command decision is to make a list of unrelated words. A list that meets these criteria appears at the end of the chapter.

Finally, a number of smaller command decisions will need to be made. Before the words are presented to the subject, tell the subject:

> You are about to participate in an experiment designed to test people's memory. I will read a list of words to you, and I want you to try to remember them. After I read the list, I will say "remember," which will be your cue to write down as many of the words as possible that you can remember. We would like you to try to remember the words in order. However, if you remember a word but don't remember where in the list it occurred, take a guess but be sure to write the word down somewhere.
>
> Okay, please take out a sheet of paper and number it from 1 to 20. Then put down your pencil.

At this point you would read the instructions that were relevant to the particular condition, making certain that the group hears only its instructions:

Loci Instructions

While I read the list of words to you, I would like you to try to remember them by following a special procedure. First, I want you to think of a place, area, or building that is familiar to you and has many separate locations. For example, the area around your home or neighborhood or the campus. Each time I read a word I want you to make a picture in your head of the object and to place it at one of the locations in your map. When I read the next word, I want you to mentally walk to the next location and do the same thing. These pictures you make should be vivid, bizarre, and show the object interacting in some way with the location. For example, if you started at the student union and the first object I said was pizza, you might image a pizza hovering over the building with little "pepperoni Martians" climbing down to the roof. Or you might imagine a giant pizza buzzsaw cutting the building in half. From the student union you would walk to the next building in your map and place the second object there.

Pay-Attention Instructions

While I read the list of words to you, I would like you to try to remember them by following this procedure. I want you to concentrate on the word and try to remember it. You should try your best to remember them because it is important to the success of the experiment. Listen carefully to the word, think about the word, and repeat the word over to yourself several times. When I read the next word, I want you to do the same thing.

For the final command decisions, say the words out loud at a rate of one every 8 seconds. At the end of the list, wait 8 seconds and then say "remember." This will be a cue for the subjects to "write down in order as many of the words as you can remember." Give them 5 minutes to recall the list.

Data Analysis

For each subject, score the number of words recalled under the strict criterion (order counts) and under the liberal criterion (any order). Then calculate the mean number of words recalled for the subjects in the Method-of-Loci condition and compare it with the Pay-Attention condition. The appropriate statistical test for this comparison is the independent *t*-test. The independent *t*-test is used when comparing exactly two conditions and when the subjects in one condition cannot be paired with subjects in the other condition. One *t*-test should be conducted on each dependent variable.

An outline of the independent *t*-test procedure follows for those interested in calculating the statistic and for those needing a reminder of the test. The table of *t*-values can be found in the statistical appendix.

Key Words

between-subjects design	floor effect
ceiling effect	pilot study
completely randomized design	placebo
control	random assignment (randomization)
design	statistical control
experimental control	true experiment

Additional Reading

Atkinson, R. C. (1975) Mnemotechnics in second language learning. *American Psychologist, 30,* 821–888.

Bower, G. H. (1970). Analysis of a mnemonic device. *American Scientist, 58,* 496–510.

Groninger, L. D. (1971). Mnemonic imagery and forgetting. *Psychonomic Science, 23,* 161–163.

Luria, A. R. (1968). *The mind of a mnemonist.* New York: Avon.

Paivio, A. (1979). *Imagery and verbal processes.* New Jersey: Lawrence Erlbaum Associates.

Pavio, A., J. C. Yuille, and S. A. Madigan (1968). Concreteness, imagery, and meaningfulness values for 925 nouns. *Journal of Experimental Psychology Monograph Supplement, 76,* 1–25.

Independent t-test

Students t-test for independent groups is useful in determining if the independent variable produced a difference between your two groups of subjects greater than would be expected simply because there are different subjects in the two groups or because of chance. The formula for the independent groups t-test is:

$$t = \frac{\bar{X}_1 - \bar{X}_2}{\sqrt{\frac{SS_1 + SS_2}{(n_1 - 1) + (n_2 - 1)}\left(\frac{1}{n_1} + \frac{1}{n_2}\right)}}$$

where SS stands for the sum-of-squared-deviations or sum-of-squares:

$$SS_1 = \Sigma X^2 - \frac{(\Sigma X)^2}{n_1}$$

n_1 = number of subjects in condition 1
$\bar{X}_1$ = arithmetic mean of condition 1

STEP 0.   Decide on the null hypothesis.

In most cases using the t-statistic, the null hypothesis will be that the means of the two conditions are equal. This is a nondirectional hypothesis, meaning that if condition 1 is significantly larger than condition 2, or if condition 2 is significantly larger than condition 1, you would reject the null hypothesis. Directional hypotheses (e.g., condition 1 is equal to or greater than condition 2) are also possible, but these are rare in psychology.

STEP 1.   Table the Data.

Condition 1		Condition 2	
s1	5	s6	10
s2	1	s7	3
s3	6	s8	9
s4	10	s9	11
s5	3	s4	5

STEP 2.   Square each value of X. *Then compute the sums of the* Xs *for each condition and the sums of the squared* Xs *for each condition.*

X	X^2	X	X^2
5	25	10	100
1	1	3	9
6	36	9	81
10	100	11	121
3	9	5	25
25	171	38	336

STEP 3.   Compute the SS *for each condition.*

$$SS_1 = 171 - (25)^2/5 = 46$$
$$SS_2 = 336 - (38)^2/5 = 47.2$$

STEP 4.   Compute the means for each condition.

$$X_1 = 25/5 = 5.0$$
$$X_2 = 38/5 = 7.6$$

STEP 5.   Compute t.

$$\frac{5 - 7.6}{\sqrt{\frac{46 + 47.2}{(5 - 1) + (5 - 1)}\left(\frac{1}{5} + \frac{1}{5}\right)}} = 1.20$$

STEP 6.   Compare the observed t *with the critical* t.

There are many distributions of critical values of t. The one you use depends on the number of subjects in each group. The degrees of freedom for an independent t in our example is:

$$(n_1 - 1) + (n_2 - 1) = 8$$

Using Table B in the Appendix shows that the critical value of $t(8)$ is 2.306 if we are willing to accept a Type I error at alpha .05 for a nondirectional (i.e., two-tailed test). Because our observed t of 1.20 is smaller than 2.306, we would conclude that there is not a real difference between our two conditions. Therefore, we would not reject the null hypothesis.

Method of Loci

Instructions: Method of Loci

Exp. Initials	Subject #	Strict	Liberal	Comments

$\bar{X}_{strict} =$

$SS_{strict} =$

$n_{MOL} =$

$\text{Variance}_{strict} = SS/(n-1) =$

$\bar{X}_{liberal} =$

$SS_{liberal} =$

$\text{Variance}_{liberal} = SS/(n-1) =$

Method of Loci

Instructions: Placebo

Exp. Initials	Subject #	Strict	Liberal	Comments

$\bar{X}_{strict} =$

$SS_{strict} =$

$n_{Placebo}$ instructions $=$

Variance $= SS/(n - 1) =$

INDEPENDENT t OBSERVED: _____

$\bar{X}_{liberal} =$

$SS_{liberal} =$

Variance $= SS/(n - 1) =$

t CRITICAL _____

General Idea (Previous Research, Curiosity)

State the general idea and how it arose.

Research Hypothesis

State the research hypothesis from the text as specifically as possible.

Methods (Natural Observation, Survey, Field Experiment,
► Lab Experiment)

Lab experiment: How does this differ from the field experiment of chapter 5, besides the lab/field differences? Why is this a true experiment?

Dependent Variable(s)

The number of words recalled will be operationalized in two different ways.

Operational Definition Operationally define:
Strict:

Liberal:

Continued

Continued
Predictor or Independent Variable

The independent variable was memory instructions.

Operational Definition Operationally define the experimental condition given in the chapter:

The control:

Give a different operational definition of the placebo condition. Then discuss how this change in the control condition changes how the operational definition of the experimental condition and the conclusions that can be reached have changed.

► Design (Between)

This is a between-subjects design because a subject will be in the Advice condition or the No-Advice condition, but not both.

Continued

Subjects

Ethical Considerations   Is there any reason *not* to follow procedures of informed consent and debriefing? How much will subjects be told before the experiment? After?

Characteristics and Availability   If someone forced you to collect data tomorrow, what subjects would you use? What subjects would you use in an ideal situation?

Sampling Procedure and Number of Subjects   Following the assumptions above, what sampling procedure is involved in each assumption? What about external validity?

► Control

► *Subject Assignment (Randomization)*   Random assignment: Before each subject arrives, he or she will randomly be assigned to the experimental or control condition by a coin toss.

► *Environment (Insured Equivalence)*   The placebo instructions were included to equate the Advice and No-Advice groups in a number of ways. List those considerations.

Continued

Continued
Procedural Command Decisions ► (Floor Effect, Ceiling Effect)

For the procedural command decisions below, state the decision from the chapter. Then indicate if increases would lead to a ceiling or a floor effect.
Number of words in the list:

Presentation rate:

Time allowed to recall:

One other command decision:

► Retrospective Confound Check (Assumed, Statistical, Rethink)

(Selection, Mortality, History, Maturation, Reactivity, Instrumentation)
Even in the most carefully planned experiment, there is a utility in reviewing the entire design and procedure before collecting data. This review is often beneficial if done by considering the confounding variables or rival hypotheses that might be circumvented with a little thought. Do you agree with the following logic?

Selection: Okay. Random assignment.
Mortality: Short experiment for both conditions. Should be okay.
History: Might be a problem if we run all method-of-loci people in one big group and all placebos in another. Might use smaller groups if time permits. If this is not practical, we will have to be certain that the experimenter interacts minimally with the groups. *Rethink* the experiment with this in mind.
Maturation: Short experiment. Should be okay.
Reactivity: Not much to react to? Should be okay, provided experimenter is well-rehearsed and automated? *Rethink* about minimizing reactivity, perhaps by tape recording instructions and word lists.
Instrumentation: Scoring should be relatively simple. Probably okay.

Data Analysis

Descriptive   What data points should be recorded for each subject?

Inferential   The independent *t*-test.

Troublesome Words

Below are a list of words that students (and others) often use incorrectly.

Irregardless vs. Regardless: "Irregardless" is not an English word.

Data vs. Datum: The word *data* is the plural form of *datum*. ("The data *are* relevant to the theory" is correct usage.)

Phenomena vs. Phenomenon: *Phenomena* is the plural of *phenomenon*.

Criteria vs. Criterion: *Criteria* is the plural of *criterion*.

Since vs. Because: *Since* implies that time has passed. It should not be used as a substitute for *because*, which implies that a reason will follow.

While vs. Whereas: *While* implies that two events are occurring simultaneously. Do not use as a substitute for *whereas, although,* or *but*.

Which vs. That: A clause beginning with *that* is essential to the meaning of the sentence (e.g., The state that was chosen for the first survey provided financial support to the research.) The *that* clause in the above example restricts the class of states to the one chosen for the first survey. A clause beginning with *which* adds additional information, but the sentence could stand even if the clause was removed (e.g., Oklahoma, which was chosen for the first survey, provided financial support to the research). The *which* clause in the above example assumes there is only one state about which the reader is aware, and thus is merely supplying additional information about that state. **As a general rule, if you could use either word in the sentence choose *that*.** So, except in cases such as ". . . of which," use *that*. You will be right 99.44% of the time.

Compared to vs. Compared with: Use *compared with*.

Effect vs. Affect: As a general rule, *effect* is used as a noun and *affect* as a verb. *Affect* is a noun when it refers to emotion, and *effect* is a verb when it means "causing something to come into being" as in "she effected a change."

Results Section

The results section is the second part of the narrowing of the research report. At the end of this section, the reader should have learned about the facts of the experiment. In this section, the outcome of the study is simply presented. The presentation here will form the foundation of the conclusions that will be presented in the discussion section. This presentation, at a minimum, involves the following.

The Dependent Variable

Begin by telling the reader what data were actually analyzed. Do not make the mistake of diving right into the statistical analyses or a figure of the results. Are the data means? Percentages? Any data not analyzed? Why?

Inferential Statistics

The reader must be convinced as well as informed. Thus, statistical tests and significance levels must be reported. The specific analysis should be described as well as the input data. Typically, reporting of the statistical test takes the form, $t(\mathrm{df}) = t$-observed, $p <$ smallest alpha (e.g., .05), or as it might actually appear $t(15) = 4.19$, $p < .01$.

Figures or Tables

The actual data must appear in some summarized form. With only a small number of means to report, this information is often included in the prose: Men (8.5) scored higher than women (3.2) on the test. With more data, a table or figure is appropriate to use. The tables and figures go at the end of the report, each on a separate page (see TOSS 8 for further discussion of figures and tables). The reader should be told when to refer to a particular figure, and the printer should be told where to place the figure by:

Insert Figure 1 about here

Describing Patterns

The author's job in the results section is to describe to the reader what has happened. The author should not make conclusions at this point or try to interpret the data. Simply state the results. With a large data set, the reader must be directed to the part of this complex that the author wishes understood. The test of a good results statement is: MUST everyone agree with the statement? If yes, then it is a description and appropriate for the results. These simple statements need not be dull repetitions of the figures. For example, "As expected, subjects trained with the method of loci remembered more words than those left to their own devices, and this was especially true when words were recalled in order."

Items selected from Paivio, Yuille, and Madigan, 1968 norms.

	Word	Concreteness Rating
1.	accordian	7.00
2.	beast	6.51
3.	wheat	7.00
4.	priest	6.59
5.	corpse	6.89
6.	cranium	6.45
7.	edifice	6.56
8.	engine	6.76
9.	flag	6.94
10.	foam	6.73
11.	glacier	6.93
12.	frog	6.96
13.	toy	6.63
14.	infant	6.76
15.	macaroni	7.00
16.	lawn	6.96
17.	journal	6.69
18.	iron	6.87
19.	lice	6.36
20.	machine	6.75

7 Theory & Data

Overview

This chapter introduces the concepts of explanation and theory. Comparisons of descriptive and explanatory statements are followed by the development of a theory created to explain the method-of-loci findings of chapter 6. The characteristics of good theories are that they are parsimonious and sufficient; they explain existing data and predict new results. Theories are not proven by experiments; they are either supported because they correctly predict the results or falsified because they are inconsistent with the results. A theory may be modified or discarded when results fail to confirm it, or the results may be disregarded. An experiment designed to test one aspect of the theory of memory developed in the chapter is discussed.

The one-way ANOVA with post-hoc tests is introduced.

Tips on General Style provides suggestions on how to avoid sexist language in technical writing. Tips on Specific Style specifies guidelines for using numerals or words to represent quantity.

From Theory to Data and Back Again

"There is nothing so practical as a good theory."

—Kurt Lewin

The ideas for our experiments in previous chapters have come from our personal observations of the world or, in the case of the last chapter, from having read about a procedure used by Greek orators. Although these approaches to science are useful, science often progresses most rapidly by doing experiments to test a **theory.** In this chapter, we are going to develop and test a theory that could explain why the method of loci from the last chapter helps people's memories.

The term *theory* as used and discussed by a scientist has little to do with the term as the general or lay public uses it. When most people think of theories, they think of ideas that have not been put into practice (e.g., "It looks good in theory") or ideas that are not associated with reality (e.g., "It's just a theory"). The better term for these uses is *hypothesis*. A scientist, on the other hand, would be unlikely to bestow the term *theory* on something until it has received a good amount of support from experimentation. Theories *are* based on facts and they *are* important.

Explanatory Statements: A Step Toward Theories

Before designing the experiment for this chapter, we will consider theories in some depth. First, we will discuss explanation as the starting point of theory construction. We will then expand the discussion into a rough sketch of a theory.

Let us begin with a descriptive statement, call it D1, of the results of the last experiment:

> Subjects who were instructed to use the method of loci (experimental group) re-   [D1]
> called a list of words better than those not so instructed (control group).

As a starting point, we want to explain this result; that is, we want to create an **explanatory statement.** There are two general ways to proceed. One way is to generalize the independent and dependent variables to other instances of the same general category (category technique). Another way is to propose a mechanism that operates between the independent and the dependent variable (underlying mechanism; intermediate mechanism).

Using the category technique, we could explain the results by generalizing method of loci to a broader category. Method of loci is a special case of telling people to "integrate two ideas," and "recall a list of words" is a special case of "remembering" in general. Thus, by substituting these concepts into the descriptive statement, D1, we could now generate the following explanatory statement, E1:

> Instructing people to integrate two ideas leads to superior memory.   [E1]

If this is a good explanatory statement, it should predict. To predict means we should be able to generate another descriptive statement. In this case another example of "instructing people to integrate two ideas" is to tell people to "associate each word with a person you know." Another example of remembering is to ask subjects to recognize (rather than recall) the stimuli. Now we have a testable research hypothesis, or another descriptive statement, D2:

> People told to associate words with a person they know will recognize the words   [D2]
> better than the appropriate control.

The intermediate mechanism differs from the category technique in that it tries to explain by adding a construct that mediates the action of the independent variable on the dependent variable. Starting with the same descriptive statement D1, we can propose that a construct called an "image" is involved. This leads immediately to the explanatory statement:

> People instructed to use the method of loci form images that in turn improve recall   [E2]
> of a list of words.

In E2 we did not generalize the independent or dependent variables. Instead we inserted the construct of an image as an explantory device. To generate predictions, we must now think of independent variables that would affect images and then see if recall of a list of words is in turn affected.

If images do exist, then one way to affect them should be to show people pictures of objects and compare their performance with a group

Figure 7–1   Two explanatory statements for the casual statement: "Eating potato chips makes me drink lots of Coke." The dotted figures are hypotheses or predicted descriptive statements.

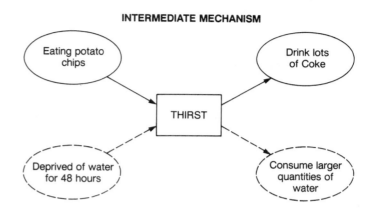

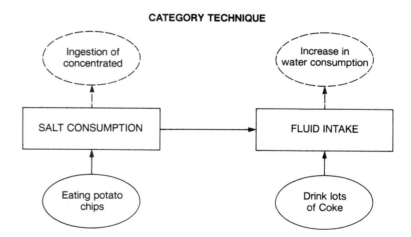

that sees only the words for those objects. Images should be more likely to be formed when we see a picture than when we see the word. We can then test recall by having subjects write down all the labels or words that they remember. Thus, a prediction might be:

People who view pictures of objects will be better able to recall them than subjects   [D3] who read the word representing the object.

Explanatory statements are, at best, simple theories. Most theories are considerably more intricate than simple explanatory statements. However, explanatory statements will be especially useful in conducting experiments, in constructing your own theories, and in testing theories of other scientists. Although serious theory construction is beyond the scope of this book, we sketch out a simple theory drawing on the explanatory construct of images.

Theories: An Explanation of the Method of Loci

As we create a theory to explain the results of the last experiment, consider what we need to create a theory, what a theory can do for us, and what makes a good theory. To create any theory, we must first make some statements about the basic terms that we will use. Second, we must interrelate these statements. Third, we must relate at least some of the terms to the world (possible observations). At the beginning of your research career, most of your work will be experiments that test other people's theories. Later as you gain more experience and collect your own data, you may choose to develop your own theory for other people to test. With this last disclaimer in mind, let us begin to sketch out a theory of memory.

First, begin by defining the basic theoretical terms of the theory. *Memory* is an internal storehouse of information. A *trace* is the internal representation in memory of some experience. An *image* is a trace that has many characteristics in common with actual perception. A *nonimage* is a trace that has many characteristics in common with language. *Distinctiveness* is a characteristic of a trace that makes it different from other traces. *Integratedness* is a characteristic of two traces such that the two traces behave functionally as one trace. *Retrieval* is the process of outputting a particular trace from memory. Retrieval consists of two phases: *find*—the process of locating a memory trace, and *decide*—the process of deciding whether that memory trace is the correct one to output.

Next, we can interrelate the statements. (Much interrelationship already exists in the definitions.) An image, because it closely reflects perception, and because perceptions are very different, tends to be distinctive compared with a nonimage. During retrieval, a distinctive trace is not any easier to find than is a nondistinctive trace; however, it is easy to decide if the distinctive trace is one to be outputted. For integrated traces, once you have found one of the constituent traces it would be easy to find the second. However, integration would be of little benefit to the decide process.

If the above rather abstract theory is difficult to digest, try rereading it after we relate the terms to the real world: In the method of loci, memory is improved because subjects are instructed to integrate an image of the to-be-remembered word with some familiar location. Some locations are easy to find because they are so familiar. This makes the to-be-remembered word easy to find because it is integrated with the familiar location. In addition, subjects are told to make a bizarre (distinctive) image of the two. This should aid the decide stage of the search process. Thus, according to our theory, the method of loci is effective because it improves the find stage of retrieval (through the use of integration with a familiar location) *and* because it improves the decide stage of retrieval (through the use of distinctiveness).

Evaluating and Testing a Theory

How good is this theory? Scientists evaluate theories on the basis of how useful the theory is to the field. To reach a judgment on the usefulness of a theory, the scientist will employ a number of criteria. Employing these criteria without some other theory to compare is often difficult. However, you can decide for yourself how the theory fares against the following criteria.

Is the theory **parsimonious?** It should make only the minimal number of assumptions and no more to be parsimonious.

Is the theory **sufficient?** It should not leave any important terms undefined or vaguely defined. A sufficient theory would not be open to alternative interpretations because of vagueness of the meanings of terms.

Does the theory correctly summarize or *explain* existing knowledge? It should provide a summary of existing knowledge by being consistent with facts.

Does the theory predict new facts? It must be **testable,** meaning that it must predict the outcome of experiments. By making predictions the theory can be tested and falsified—shown to be wrong.

What have we gained by formulating this theory? First, it gives us an organized view of the world. We can probably find other data already in the literature that can be explained, **post hoc** (after the fact), by the theory. Second, we can now make predictions about what should happen in other situations; that is, we can test the theory.

When we collect data to compare a theory's predictions with the actual behavior of subjects, many things can happen. First, consider the case where the data are consistent with predictions. Should we be happy with this supporting evidence? Well, yes and no. We personally may have a little more faith in the theory, but have we proved that the theory is correct? Or even that it is more likely to be true than before? No!

Confirming a theory is like trying to find the murderer from a number of suspects. Let us assume that Colonel Mustard was murdered in the ballroom with a lead pipe. The following people are suspects: Miss Scarlet, Mr. Green, Professor Plum, and the butler. What is the probability, currently, that the butler did it? One chance in four or .25. Now you discover during your investigation that the butler was seen arguing with Colonel Mustard. What is the probability now? Well, it is still .25. Why? Others could have argued with the Colonel as well; just like other theories could explain the results of your study. What if you discover that Miss Scarlet was in her experimental psychology class at the time of the murder? What is the probability that the butler did it? Now it is one out of three or .33 because Miss Scarlet has been eliminated as a suspect. We can now state an important principle: We can never prove a theory; but by eliminating alternatives, we gain support for a theory. Thus, in an ideal situation, we try to do an experiment that disproves a theory or that pits one theory against another. To design such a critical experiment requires considerable thought and is a major goal of the scientist.

Despite this warning about the importance of eliminating alternative theories, you must fight the tendency for humans to fall back on trying to prove a theory correct rather than eliminating incorrect theories. Try the following exercise to see how susceptible you are to this human bias.

Below are four cards. Each card has a letter on one side and a number on the other. Your task is to turn over as few cards as possible that will determine whether the following rule is correct: If there is a vowel on one side, there is an even number on the other. Which card or cards will you turn over?

Cards: E   7   K   4

The answer appears at the end of the chapter.

So theory and data can agree or disagree. If they agree, you have some support (circumstantial evidence?) for the theory. If they disagree, should you throw out the theory? Not necessarily. This theory has already explained a number of facts, and we may be reluctant to throw out the baby with the bathwater. One possible decision would be to *modify the theory*. Perhaps the experiment reveals some evidence that you could account for with a simple change in the theory. Another possible decision is to *ignore the data*. Perhaps the experiment is flawed; you believe it is a statistical anomaly; or it represents data that do not really bear in an important way on the theory. In astronomy, Copernican theory was adopted even though it was known at the time that it did not explain the motion of the planets. Finally, it is possible that the data (along with other data) are so damaging to the theory that the *theory must be abandoned.*

One quality of a theory that may save it from the scrap pile even when data from experiments fail to support it is the beauty or aesthetic value of the theory. You may think, along with much of the general public, that science is always a cut-and-dried matter, that things are either right or wrong. All along in this book we have tried to stress the importance of the decisions a researcher must make to do research. We call these decisions *command decisions* and acknowledge that there is no single command decision that is correct while all others are incorrect. Some are better than others, and the best scientist makes the best command decisions. Similarly, theories do not represent absolute truth (at least not at the beginning), but may be an approximation to truth. Theories contain many assumptions, definitions, and concepts, and interrelations among these elements. A failure to support the theory in a particular experiment does not mean that the whole theory is inadequate. But, you might ask, how many failures will cause the scientist to abandon the theory, and how many successes of the theory are needed to counteract the failure? These kinds of questions have no universally agreed upon answers. What we can say is that the more elegant, the more pleasing a theory, the greater is the tendency to hold on to it in the face of adversity.

What constitutes an elegant theory? There are several characteristics that make a theory influential or popular and make scientists unwilling to abandon the theory. Elegant theories: (1) make a small number of plausible assumptions and a larger number of surprising predictions, (2) cover a broad range of interesting situations, (3) are precise, often mathematical, in their structure, and (4) have implications for the real world as well as the controlled experiment. When a theory has the above qualities, scientists are less willing to abandon the theory than when these qualities are absent.

A Theory-Driven Experiment

As with explanatory statements, a theory should lead to some predictions. In fact, there are a number of possible predictions that we could test. Some of these predictions deal with imagery, some with integration, some with distinctiveness, some with retrieval, and so on. We are going to test a prediction of our theory that has nothing to do with imagery. We do this partly to show that a good theory should be able to cover a number of different situations that go beyond the original study that generated it. In the following experiment we are going to test the part of the theory that claims that attaching new information to something familiar makes it more memorable than attaching it to something in memory that is not as familiar or that is completely unfamiliar. When the subject attempts to find new information that is attached to something familiar, the new information will be found; if it is attached to something less familiar, the new information will be harder to find.

In general then, we would like people to study some list of to-be-remembered information. Sometimes this information will be associated with a very familiar concept, sometimes with a less familiar concept, and sometimes with an unknown concept. After the subjects have studied these concepts—information pairs—they will then be asked to remember all that they can.

As a first step we must determine the to-be-remembered information and the concepts to which this information is attached. Most learning requires that we associate a new piece of information with some already existing concept. For example, when we learn a new fact about experimental methodology, we usually try to associate it with something we previously learned. More simply, when we learn a friend's phone number, we are associating a string of digits with the concept of the person. But how can we manipulate the familiarity of the concepts we carry around inside our heads?

One possibility is to have subjects learn some information about very famous people, not so famous people, and completely unknown people. The concept is now the person, and we will add new information for the subject to remember. The very famous people will be most familiar and the unknown people will be least familiar. This sounds like a good idea, but first we have to define operationally what is meant by familiarity. One operational definition immediately springs to mind. Have judges view the names of people and decide "How familiar is the person?" or "How many people in the world know this person?" or "How many facts can you list about the person?" These methods have the advantage of being relatively straightforward but may create reactivity problems. Subjects want to present their most positive side and may thus feel that they should know these people but in fact do not. The subject does not want to appear stupid, so he or she claims to know who the people are. The subject has reacted to the instructions of the experiment. A simple way around this problem is to have people actually give a fact or facts about each person they claim to know. For example, if a person claims that Barry Goldwater is familiar, he or she should be able to list some facts about him. Perhaps the best operationalization of familiarity would be to give the judges 30 seconds to write down as many facts as they can about a person. We can then average the number of facts for each stimulus person and classify the people as well-known, little-known, and unknown individuals.

Operationalizing familiarity in the above way involves what psychologists refer to as a **norming study.** In such a study, the experimenter collects some information about the materials to be used before actually trying to conduct the primary experiment. The information then becomes the norms that define the relative familiarities of the individuals in question.

In presenting the names of different people to the subjects, what information do we want them to associate with the individuals? In other words, what should the to-be-learned material be? One possibility is to have them learn the phone number of each person. Although this is a perfectly reasonable task, we could run into a problem or two. First, phone numbers are all very much alike, and according to the theory this would not make the information very distinctive. We may find that all of the subjects perform poorly. Second, we may run into a problem when we try to score the data: If Barry Goldwater's phone number is 555-1236 and a subject remembers it as 555-6321 or 555-1234, is the answer wrong or do we give them partial credit? Your class may wish to try to resolve these problems and actually use phone numbers for the to-be-learned material. However, we will use another type of information in this chapter: true but unknown facts about the person (alias trivia).

By having people learn trivia about a person, we minimize both the problems we encountered with phone numbers. The trivia facts need not be similar to each other, and scoring the fact will be simply right or wrong. A list of people appear at the end of the chapter as well as trivia facts about each person. The norming study was conducted in 1980, so you may wish to renorm them for your population and year. The trivia facts are all true about the person and were normed to ensure that they were unknown facts about the individual.

Thus far we plan to present subjects with a list of person-fact pairs in the form of simple sentences, such as: Adolph Hitler was a vegetarian. Some of the people will be well known, some little known, and some unknown. We then want to see if the subjects' memory of the trivia facts is better for the well-known people. According to the theory, memory should be best for the facts associated with the well-known people, next best for the little-known people, and poorest for the unknown people.

According to the theory, people should more easily recall the information about the well-known people, because the familiar items in memory are easier to *find*. Once the information is found, however, the theory predicts that only distinctiveness would have an effect on the *decide* stage. For example, if a person studied "Adolph Hitler was a vegetarian" and "James Logan was the son of a Frenchman" and was later asked to "recall everything you remember," the Adolph Hitler fact should be remembered better than the James Logan fact because it was easier to *find* Hitler than Logan.

On the other hand, if the experimenter gave the subject the names Adolph Hitler and James Logan as cues (e.g., "remember all the facts you can about Adolph Hitler" or ". . . about James Logan"), the theory predicts that the subject would *not* be more likely to remember the fact about Hitler than about Logan because the *find* stage, which is affected by familiarity, has been bypassed by the cue. In other words, the cue has "found" the name for the subject. From this point on, the theory predicts that only the distinctiveness of the facts should be important.

How should we test the theory? One way is to ask subjects to remember as much as possible with no cues given; the theory predicts that we should observe differences in the number of facts remembered. A second way is to supply the subjects with cues; the theory predicts that we should not observe differences in the number of facts recalled under these conditions. Assume that we take the second approach. When we are finished, we find that, as predicted, there were no differences among the conditions. This supports the theory, but can we be sure?

There are many ways to do an experiment and obtain **null results** (no difference among the conditions of the experiment). First, and most important, is that there are probably many other theories that would also predict no difference in the particular experimental situation. Thus, obtaining null results would not eliminate the other theories and therefore not add any support to your theory. If you can identify another theory that *does* predict a difference when yours does not, then you can learn something from a null finding.

Second, statistical considerations make null findings difficult to interpret. Consider the extreme case where only one subject is tested in the well-known condition, one in the little-known, and one in the unknown. Would you still be willing to say that the lack of an effect was support for the theory? No, you would not, because you did not have enough subjects to let the statistics show an effect even if one were present. Statistically, the experiment would have low **power.** Power is the probability that a difference between conditions will be detected if one really exists. Would a failure to find a difference be because there really is no difference (supporting our theory) or because there is not enough power? With low power we are likely to say that our conditions are the same when they are really different. In statistics, such a mistake is called a **Type II error.** There are advanced statistical techniques that allow you to calculate the power of your experiment and the probability of making a Type II error. Table 7–1 presents a summary of the relationship between the real world and the results of the experiment and what the experimenter concludes about this relationship, as discussed here and in previous chapters.

Finally, there is the possibility that your null effect is due to ceiling effects or floor effects. What if we discovered that the result of no difference between conditions was because nobody remembered anything (a

Table 7–1 Statistical decision making and the state of the world.

	State of the World	
	No effect of IV (null hypothesis)	Effect of IV
Researcher's Decision: Not significant	Correct [1 − p(Type I)]	Type II Error (beta level can be determined with advanced statistics)
Significant	Type I Error (alpha level conventionally set at .05)	Power [1 − p(Type II)]

floor effect) or alternatively that everybody remembered all the facts (a ceiling effect). Again, this would not be strong support for the theory because the experiment was too hard (or too easy) to permit any change in the dependent variable. In general, the psychological community prefers experiments that predict and find a difference rather than reporting null results.

On the other hand, if we do find a significant difference among the conditions, what can we say? We clearly have found a problem in the theory because the theory predicted that there should have been no difference. In this case, *our* theory could be rejected, supplying support for other theories.

The other way to do the experiment is to ask the subject to recall everything without any cue. In this case, if we do not find a difference, it is a problem for the theory. If we do find a significant difference, it supplies some confirmatory evidence for the correctness of the theory.

At this point the scientist would make a command decision. Some scientists, especially when first working with a theory, will choose to conduct an experiment in which a significant finding will support their theory (but remember that support for a theory can only occur by eliminating other theories). Other scientists will choose to conduct an experiment in which a significant finding will eliminate their theory; being only human, however, they are hoping that their theory is supported and thus they are hoping for null results—a catch-22 situation. This discussion of theories, predictions, and outcomes is captured in Figure 7–2.

Although either of the above approaches are acceptable and either may be done in your class, we will choose the memory test without cues. Remember that in this case a null result will go against the theory and a significant result (if it is the right one) will support the theory.

After the subjects hear a list of facts about people, they will be asked to recall as many of the facts as possible. A subject will hear only one type of list: a list consisting of well-known people, a list consisting of little-known people, or a list consisting of unknown people. The list of facts will be read aloud at a rate of one fact every 10 seconds. After the last fact, the subjects will be told to recall. They will be told that they should try to recall both the name and the facts associated with the name. Subjects will be allowed 10 minutes to recall as many facts as possible.

Data Analysis

Data analysis will begin by tallying the number of correct responses. A correct response will be the recall of the person's name together with the appropriate fact (an "appropriate" fact being one that was in the list). Other ways of summarizing the data are also possible and should be contemplated. For example, it may be of interest to ignore the number of facts recalled and tally only the number of names recalled. We assumed that more familiar individuals will be better recalled than less familiar ones. Clearly this result is fundamental to the prediction that more facts will be recalled about famous persons than less well-known ones. The analysis of the number of names recalled is therefore of interest to analyze separate from the number of facts recalled.

The analysis requires that we compare three different conditions. Up to this point, we have used only the *t*-test. With three conditions, we could

Figure 7–2   Illustration of how testing the predictions of one theory depends not only on the outcome of the experiment but also on the nature of the alternative theories, if any, considered. Theory I is a theory developed by the experimenter. Theories II and III already exist.

Theory I predicts: A ≠ B and C = D

Outcome
of experiment

	A ≠ B	A = B	C = D	C ≠ D
No alternative in mind	Because no alternatives are considered, this finding would be "circumstantial" evidence for Theory I. However, it would presumably eliminate several "unstated" theories that would not have made this prediction. If the result is viewed as surprising to someone it, at least, eliminates that person's intuitive view of the process which might have existed before Theory I.	Because Theory I predicted a difference, but none was found, this may either be a problem for Theory I or an indication of lack of power. Because Theory I was the product of the experimenter, it will probably undergo more such tests before it is abandoned. Like all parents, the theorist wants to give his or her "baby" every fair chance to succeed. Without an alternative theory, however, it is always possible that only the author of the theory will be surprised by the finding.	Because Theory I predicts no difference and no alternative is in mind, this is unlikely to be viewed as any support for the theory because there are likely to be many "unstated" theories which would make the same prediction. In addition, a null finding may always be due to a lack of power in the experiment.	This would be a definite problem for the experimenter's Theory I. However, whether or not the finding is of value depends on whether the finding is surprising to people other than the author of Theory I.
Theory II A = B C ≠ D	This outcome now becomes strong support for Theory I because it is inconsistent with Theory II. Assuming Theory II has supporters in the literature, they should be surprised by the finding, and thus must consider the finding in one of the ways discussed in the text.	This result is support for Theory II because it creates problem for the experimenter's theory. The experimenter is likely to make certain the null finding does not have problems of power before trying to publish the experiment. In motivating this study in the introduction, the experimenter can use the thinking behind Theory I to introduce the experiment as an interesting test of Theory II.	This result is support for Theory I because it is inconsistent with the established theory from the literature, Theory II. However, the null finding allows the possibility of not enough power in the experiment to give Theory II a "fair chance." If additional experiments show a null effect when Theory II expects one, the proponents of Theory II may be surprised. This type of finding is often thought of as a boundary or limitation of the theory.	This would be a problem for Theory I, especially now that it is consistent with Theory II from the literature. However, because Theory I may have only one supporter (the experimenter) it is possible that only he or she would be surprised by the finding. Nevertheless, the thinking behind Theory I may be used to motivate a test of Theory II by asking if Theory II applies in a new situation. The results would suggest that it does.
Theory III A ≠ B C = D		Notice that because Theory III makes predictions identical to Theory I, none of the outcomes will distinguish between the two theories. If there are many theories like Theory I and Theory III, consistent results will be viewed as trivial, or already known—even if the particular experiment was never conducted. For example, no one has probably compared the ability of goldfish to learn math with the ability of humans to learn math because so many alternative theories exist which could explain the advantage of humans that no information would be supplied. The results would surprise no one. However, the impact of inconsistent results (i.e., A = B, C ≠ D) could imply either serious problems with basic assumptions of the field, or serious flaws in the experiment. For example, finding that goldfish learned math faster than humans would require considerable rethinking on the part of us all, including the experimenter and the goldfish.		

use the t-test and make three comparisons. However, if each test was made with a .05 probability of a Type I error, the probability of a Type I error by the end of the experiment would be .15 (.05 + .05 + .05), not the conventional .05. Instead, we rely on the analysis of variance (ANOVA). The ANOVA and how to interpret its results are discussed at the end of the chapter. If the ANOVA reveals a significant effect, we can then perform **pairwise comparisons** using various derivatives of the t-test to determine which particular condition is different from which. These post-hoc comparisons, which are conducted after finding a significant effect in the ANOVA, are also discussed at the end of the chapter.

Finally, there may be a number of other procedural details that you would like to work out in class or on your own. For example, should the list of facts always be presented in the same order? What should we do about the fact that the last fact that is read will always be remembered no matter what condition it is from? Are there any confounds that we can take care of before it is too late?

When this experiment was conducted in our laboratory using 60 students in an experimental methodology class, we found that recall was different for the different materials; that is, we obtained a significant F statistic. Further, post-hoc comparisons revealed that, although recall of the statements about well-known persons was greater than recall about the little-known persons, these two groups were not statistically different. However, both of these groups showed better recall than the subjects in the Unknown condition.

This pattern of results suggested that the theory may be in large part correct. However, because the Little-Known and Well-Known conditions did not differ, the theory should be modified to account for this lack of difference.

Answer: E and 7. The most common errors are E alone or E and 4. If there is an odd number behind the E, then the rule has been disconfirmed. If there is a vowel on the other side of the 7, then, again, the rule has been disconfirmed. Consider the common mistake of turning over the 4. If there is a consonant on the other side, it tells us nothing about the theory because the theory does not say that consonants must have odd numbers on the reverse. This example illustrates that people have a difficult time designing experiments that will disconfirm a theory.

Key Words

explanatory statement	post hoc comparisons
norming study	power
null results	sufficient
pairwise comparisons	testable
parsimonious	theory
post hoc	Type II error

Additional Reading

Klatzky, R. L. (1975). *Human memory: Structures and processes.* San Francisco: Freeman.

Paivio, A. (1979). *Imagery and verbal process.* New Jersey: Lawrence Erlbaum Associates.

Shepard, R. N. (1967). Recognition memory for words, sentences, and pictures. *Journal of Verbal Learning and Verbal Behavior, 6,* 156–163.

Wollen, K. A., Weber, A., & Lowry, D. H. (1972). Bizarreness versus interaction of mental images as determinants of learning. *Cognitive Psychology, 2,* 518–523.

One-Way, Between-Subjects ANOVA

The analysis of variance (ANOVA) allows the researcher to make comparisons among more than two conditions. Here we discuss the one-way, between-subjects ANOVA, which is used when there is one independent variable and subjects have been randomly assigned to one of three or more conditions. The ANOVA involves a series of steps that yield an F statistic.

Although only the F is typically reported in the research report, the ANOVA is summarized as follows:

Source of Variance	Degrees of Freedom	SS	Mean Square	F
Knowledge	$k - 1$	$\dfrac{\overset{k}{\sum}(\overset{s}{\sum}X)^2}{s} - \dfrac{(\overset{k}{\sum}\overset{s}{\sum}X)^2}{ks}$	SS/df_K	MS_K/MS_e
Error	$k(s - 1)$	$\overset{k}{\sum}\overset{s}{\sum}X^2 - \dfrac{\overset{k}{\sum}(\overset{s}{\sum}X)^2}{ks}$	SS/df_e	

where k = the number of levels of the independent variable
s = the number of subjects in each condition

STEP 0. State the null and alternative.

Extending the t-test, we have a null hypothesis stating that all of the conditions are drawn from the same population; that is, there are no differences. The alternative hypothesis is that there is a difference, but the alternative does not specify where the difference lies.

STEP 1. Table the data.

Well-known	Little-known	Unknown
7	5	1
6	4	0
5	6	2
4	5	3

STEP 2. Sum each column; square each sum; divide each squared sum by the number of subjects in that condition; total these values.

	$\overset{s}{\sum}X$	$(\overset{s}{\sum}X)^2$	$\dfrac{(\overset{s}{\sum}X)^2}{s}$
Well	22	484	121
Little	20	400	100
Unknown	6	36	9
			230 $= \dfrac{\overset{k}{\sum}(\overset{s}{\sum}X)^2}{s}$

STEP 3.   Sum all data in table; square that sum; divide it by total number of data points.

$$\frac{(\Sigma \overset{k}{\Sigma} \overset{s}{X})^2}{k \times s} = \frac{(48)^2}{3 \times 4} = \frac{2304}{12} = 192$$

STEP 4.   Square each data point in the table; sum these squared values.

$$\overset{k}{\Sigma}\overset{s}{\Sigma} X^2 = 7^2 + 6^2 + 5^2 + \ldots + 0^2 + 2^2 + 3^2 = 242$$

STEP 5.   Calculate the SSs.

$$SS_K = [\text{Step 2}] - [\text{Step 3}] = 230 - 192 = 38$$

$$SS_e = [\text{Step 4}] - [\text{Step 2}] = 242 - 230 = 12$$

STEP 6.   Calculate DFs.

$$df_K = k - 1 = 3 - 1 = 2$$

$$df_e = k(s - 1) = 3(4 - 1) = 9$$

STEP 7.   Compute mean squares.

$$MS_K = 38/2 = 19$$

$$MS_e = 12/9 = 1.33$$

STEP 8.   Compute F.

$$F = 19/1.33 = 14.28$$

Source	DF	SS	MS	F	Sig Level
K	2	38.3	19.15	14.28	.01
ERROR	9	12.0	1.33		

STEP 9.   Compare the observed F with the critical F.

The observed $F(2, 9) = 14.40$. This should be compared with the critical F in Table C with 2 degrees of freedom in the numerator and 9 in the denominator. The observed F could have occurred if the three conditions were equal less than 1 chance in 100. Clearly, we would reject the null hypothesis and conclude that the conditions are not equal.

Memory

Experimenter _____ Date: _____

Condition (circle one):   Unknown   Little-Known   Well-Known

Presentation rate: 10 sec   Recall time: 10 min

Order of presentation: _____

List length (number of possible correct): _____

Subject #	Number Correct	Comments or Other Information

$\bar{X} =$ _____   Variance $SS/(N\text{-}1) =$ _____

Comments:

Memory

Experimenter _____ Date: _____

Condition (circle one):   Unknown   Little-Known   Well-Known

Presentation rate: 10 sec   Recall time: 10 min

Order of presentation: _____

List length (number of possible correct): _____

Subject #	Number Correct	Comments or Other Information

$\bar{X}$ = _____   Variance $SS/(N-1)$ = _____

Comments:

Memory

Experimenter: _____ Date: _____

Condition (circle one): Unknown Little-Known Well-Known

Presentation rate: 10 sec   Recall time: 10 min

Order of presentation: _____

List length (number of possible correct): _____

Subject #	Number Correct	Comments or Other Information

$\bar{X}$ = _____   Variance $SS/(N-1)$ = _____

OBSERVED $F(2,$ _____$)$ =

CRITICAL $F(2,$ _____$)$ =

TUKEY'S *HSD* STATISTIC: _____

Comments:

General Idea (Previous Research, Curiosity, ► Theory)

The idea came from a theory induced from the method-of-loci findings of a previous study. The general idea is that the method-of-loci mnemonic works because it involves connecting distinctive images to familiar locations.

► Explanatory Statement

Recall of recently studied information depends on the number of facts already known about the target stimulus.

Research Hypothesis/► Descriptive Statement

Recall of statements studied about well-known persons will be better than recall of information about little-known persons, which will be better than recall of information about unknown persons.

State one more descriptive statement that follows from the explanatory statement.

Methods (Natural Observation, Survey, Field Experiment, Lab Experiment)

Lab experiment: Lab experiments often concede some external validity. Should this concern us in this particular study?

Dependent Variable(s)

State the dependent variable:

Continued

148

Continued

Operational Definition Define the DV in a way that will allow responses to be classified easily as right or wrong. If you wanted a more sensitive dependent variable, how would you define the DV to give partial credit?

Predictor or Independent Variable

The independent variable went from familiarity to amount of prior knowledge associated with the stimulus person. Why?

Operational Definition How was amount of knowledge defined? What was required to be well-known? Little-known? Unknown?

Continued

Design (Between)

Between: Subjects were randomly assigned to one of three levels of amount of prior knowledge.

Subjects

Ethical Considerations   Usual procedures about securing the subjects' consent, informing them of the procedures, and so on should be followed. What ethical advantage is achieved by using only true facts?

Characteristics and Availability   The characteristics of subjects are constrained by the norming study. How so? Why?

Sampling Procedure and Number of Subjects   If you used a large convenience sample, how far would you be willing to generalize? If generalization was limited, would the purpose of your study be compromised? Why or why not?

Control

Subject Assignment (Randomization)   Random assignment: Before arriving at the experiment, a random number table would be consulted or a chit drawn to determine the materials the subject would receive.

Continued

Continued

Environment (Insured Equivalence) Presentation rate of the materials and instructions given to the subjects are two aspects of the environment controlled by ensuring that all subjects are treated equivalently. List one other factor that should be controlled.

What insured equivalence is lost by using true facts?

Procedural Command Decisions (Ceiling Effect, Floor Effect)

The number of facts to be recalled is an important procedural command decision to ensure that the task is not too easy (potential ceiling effect). It is unlikely that the task will be too hard, so a floor effect (recalling nothing) is unlikely. List one other procedural command decision.

Retrospective Confound Check (Assumed, Statistical, Rethink)

(Selection, Mortality, History, Maturation, Reactivity, Instrumentation) Assuming good research practices after the subjects are assigned to groups, most of the confounds are unlikely to lead to rival hypotheses after the random assignment. However, instrumentation is a possible confound that could threaten the internal validity of the study. Specifically, paraphrases of the facts and misspellings of names could affect the conditions differently. *Rethink:* Formal rules for scoring the facts should be established prior to the beginning of the study.

Continued

Data Analysis

Descriptive Total number of facts recalled will be computed for each subject. Means should be computed for each condition.

Inferential A one-way, between-subjects ANOVA with three levels should be conducted to determine if there are any significant differences among the means. Post-hoc comparisons should follow a significant F to determine more specifically which conditions differ.

► Hypothetical Outcome Analysis

What results do you expect? If you get unexpected results, what might they look like and what would they mean?

Expected Well-known > little > un	Unexpected well-known = little > un
The pattern above would support the original hypothesis and thus be confirming evidence for our explanatory statement.	The pattern above would supply some support for the explanatory statement but would be inconsistent with the specific descriptive statement. This might suggest that recall depends on having a previous memory of a person, regardless of how many facts you know about the person. Any familiarity compared with completely new material aids memory.

Sexist Language

Scientists "are committed both to science and to the fair treatment of individuals and groups" (from *Guidelines for Nonsexist Language in APA Journals*). To this end, authors avoid common usages that reflect even subtle biases and prejudices. In the following, an example of sexist language is followed by revisions that eliminate the sexism.

Sexist: The *subject* was asked to complete *his* questionnaire.
Revised: The subject was asked to complete the questionnaire.
          The subjects were asked to complete their questionnaires.
          The subject was asked to complete his or her questionnaire.

Sexist: Politicians reported being less responsive to their *wives.*
Revised: Politicians reported being less responsive to their *spouses.*

Sexist: Freshmen
Revised: No alternative if academic standing is meant, but *first-year student* will often be an acceptable alternative.

Sexist: Coed
Revised: Female student

Sexist: Mothering
Revised: Parenting; Nurturing

Sexist: The men chose male occupations.
Revised: The men chose _____ (specify the occupations).

Sexist: History of mankind, history of man
Revised: History of humankind, . . . of humans

Introduction Section

The introduction begins with a statement of the general problem as discussed in the literature. You can show the importance of your problem by (1) tracing the history of the problem, (2) illustrating a real-life example, (3) tying into theory, or (4) tying into previous empirical findings. From here the introduction rapidly proceeds to a review of the literature on a specific aspect of the general problem. After the first paragraph or so, it is important to consider the recent literature on *your* problem. By eliminating some articles and highlighting others, you can lead into the problem section of the introduction.

In the problem section, your particular issue is placed in context. You should show how your question or hypothesis has evolved from previous work. A common misconception held by new authors is that they must convince the reader that this is the first study (or at least first good study) in an area. This is not necessary, and in fact often indicates a lack of sophistication. *Build* on the old! Don't tear it down. You must convince the reader at this point that your work is a valid next step in the progress of science. Make a general statement, then follow it with a supporting statement from the literature. Continue to focus in until you come to the purpose of your study. Fit the purpose into the context of the prose as well as the context of the literature. Your purpose may be simply to answer the question, "I wonder what will happen if . . ." or it may be to test a theory, extend previous research, solve a practical problem, and so on.

After the statement of the purpose, the introduction will become increasingly specific—focusing the reader on your particular experiment. At the very end of this section, the reader should be given an overview of what is going to happen in the experiment. This overview should be good enough that the reader can tell (1) what the variables involved will be, (2) what the subject will do or experience, and (3) what hypotheses will be evaluated. In other words, a person should be able to read *only* the introduction and the discussion of your paper and still have an understanding of what you have done. The methods and results will supply the scientific details, but the introduction and discussion should be capable of supplying the general ideas.

The following materials are the result of a norming study designed to assess how much information people knew about different celebrities. The number in parentheses next to the name indicates the mean number of facts listed in 1 minute by 28 undergraduates attending the State University of New York at Stony Brook in 1980. The two sentences following the name are true statements about the celebrity that were least likely to be recognized by a group of 28 subjects from the same population. Subjects were presented with a variety of sentences, including false statements, and were asked to indicate whether the fact was "definitely known," "vaguely familiar," or "unknown." Because these norms were collected some years ago, you may wish to gather your own normative information. To do this, first collect a pool of names that you feel will span the range from unknown to well known. Then give people 1 minute for each name to write down as many facts as they can about the person. It is probably less critical that you renorm the actual sentences; simply find facts that you feel intuitively none of your subjects will know.

Unknown Personalities

Donald MacMillan (0): was a polar explorer; was awarded a medal of honor.
Henry Maine (0): wrote books on society; worked in India.
James Logan (0): was a friend of the British; was a Cayuga Indian.
Mary Ann Johnson (0): has red hair; has appeared on Broadway.
Paul Graggs (0): acts on soap operas; worked on a mink ranch.
Arthur Burghardt (0): supports Black rights; has a moustache.
Jack Brymer (0): enjoys photography; is a clarinetist.
Henry Barnes (0): taught at universities; enjoys hunting.

Little-Known Personalities

Neil Armstrong (2.16): was a pilot at sixteen; joined the Navy.
Johann Sebastian Bach (1.70): was imprisoned for a month; married a soprano.
Julius Caesar (2.54): entered the priesthood; was married three times.
Christopher Columbus (3.25): worked as a weaver; was appointed governor.
Barbara Walters (2.93): likes flower arrangements; has an award named for her.
Alexander Graham Bell (1.54): was the son of a scientist; had almost black eyes.
Sigmund Freud (2.86): had six children; was the son of a merchant.
Walter Cronkite (2.25): enjoys mysteries; is the son of a doctor.

Well-Known Personalities

Farrah Fawcett (5.21): usually is asleep by ten; was born on Ground Hog Day.
Jane Fonda (3.71): studied painting in Paris; dropped out of Vassar.
Clark Gable (3.89): was an only child; wanted to be a doctor.

Adolph Hitler (3.50): suffered from lung disease; begged in the streets.
John F. Kennedy (4.29): worked as a secretary; quit business school.
Zsa Zsa Gabor (3.96): had a Swiss education; wrote three books.
Dean Martin (4.46): worked as a gas attendant; was once a mill hand.
Muhammad Ali (3.86): was a marble champ; is a son of a sign painter.

8 Matching & Yoking

Overview

The idea of more precision in experimentation is discussed in terms of matching and yoking procedures. The precision or power of the experiment is increased when a preexisting characteristic that is correlated with the dependent variable is used to match the subjects in different experimental conditions. Subjects may be matched on an individual-to-individual basis, or a group of subjects may be matched to another group so that each group has equal representation of some important characteristic. Yoking equates two or more conditions on important characteristics that occur as part of the experiment (not a preexisting characteristic, as in matching). A field experiment concerned with spatial memory with controls for gender and the use of yoking is developed. Primacy and recency effects on memory are mentioned.

The correlated *t*-test is introduced.

Tips on General Style enumerates five general principles useful in writing any technical manuscript. Tips on Specific Style focuses on the figures and tables necessary in the report of any empirical results in psychology.

Equating People and Experiences

"Thou hast the same hair, the same eyes, the same voice and manner, the same form and stature, the same face and countenance, that I bear. Fared we forth naked, there is none could say which was you, and which the Prince of Wales."

—The Prince to the Pauper

Where did I put my sunglasses? Have you ever asked yourself this question? Have you found yourself driving to a house you visited once before, but you are not quite sure where it is? Both of these problems are common in our everyday experience and have been of interest to psychologists. We call the ability to remember where things are *spatial memory,* and this will be the topic for the experiment developed in this chapter.

I may want to know why it is that I never remember where I put my sunglasses. Or why it is that when I ask my wife she always knows where *I* left them. Perhaps people's spatial memory is not very good. Obviously mine is bad, so I prefer a hypothesis that includes all people. However, if spatial memory is poor in humans, why can my wife remember? Maybe it has something to do with the fact that I'm male and my wife is female. Maybe it is because I was the person who left the sunglasses and my wife

157

was the passive observer of where I put them. In this chapter we are going to investigate people's spatial memory and how this memory is affected by whether a subject was actively involved in the placement of an object or whether he or she merely observed it being placed.

One ability we have is the ability to use, organize, and represent space by forming *cognitive maps,* accounting for our ability to navigate from one point in space to another. Another spatial ability is an ability of subjects to remember where in space some event took place or where some object was left. This latter ability, to remember the location of objects, reaches a new level of importance when we consider its use to many nonhuman species. We are all familiar with squirrels that hide nuts in the fall for recovery during the winter when they are required to maintain life. Bird species also do similar things. One, the Clark's nutcracker, is particularly impressive in its behavior. This species lives in the higher altitudes of Arizona, and during the late summer and fall it collects and stores seeds in literally thousands of locations. It then flies to Mexico for the winter, returning to the stored seeds in the spring. It then recovers the seeds, often when there is still snow on the ground. A failure of spatial memory for this species would result in almost certain death.

We distinguish two types of spatial processes: those called "cognitive maps" which tell us in large scale where we are in the world (e.g., my house is three blocks in that direction, the grocery store is a mile away) and those called "spatial memory" which identify the location of specific objects in a place (e.g., I left my sunglasses in the desk drawer, my car is the third row of the parking lot). In the experiment developed in this chapter the focus is on spatial memory: the location of specific objects within a larger space.

Do we human beings have an accurate spatial memory? What might be important in determining the accuracy of such memories? At the time of this writing, the answers to these questions are not well known. First, we must develop a procedure for testing spatial memory and then a manipulation to begin to determine those factors that might affect the accuracy of spatial memory.

We begin with the assumption that to test spatial memory we will need a substantial chunk of space in which to work, and the space should not be uniform in appearance (holding constant the cognitive map aspects). A college campus meets the requirement of a large and varied chunk of space. Therefore, the location for the study is easy to choose. The campus also is familiar to the subjects (you), and therefore we eliminate the potential problem of an inaccurate memory caused by the subject getting lost or confused as to where he or she is. The formation of the map of the campus is a topic of study in its own right (i.e., how is the map learned?), and this will be considered in chapter 9. For now, we want to study the ability of subjects to remember specific locations in a familiar space.

Given that the space is the campus, what is it that is to be remembered in different locations, and how should we determine the actual locations? We will use a stick-on colored dot that can be purchased at any variety store as the hidden, to-be-remembered object. These colored dots come on sheets and are analogous to the seeds that a Clark's nutcracker would store. Each dot should be numbered and initialed in case other members of the class place dots in similar areas of the campus. Also, the order in which the dots are hidden and recovered is of importance. We will collect data on the order by numbering the dots from 1 to 50 and hiding them in order and recording the order in which they are found.

The general plan is to have a number of objects, stick-on dots, hidden in space, to remember where they are, and to find them. The hypothesis is that the way in which the dots are hidden will affect the subjects' ability to remember where they were hidden. In particular, one of our conditions will require subjects to hide dots and later to attempt to find them. We will call this condition the Hiders. The other condition will require subjects to attempt to find dots that they watched someone else place. We will call this condition the Observers.

Experimental Control

How do we decide who will be a hider and who will be an observer? By randomly assigning subjects to conditions in an experiment, it is assumed that the difference between subjects that might affect the outcome of the experiment will be even, or averaged out, by the randomization procedure. Random assignment is particularly useful when we do not know what subject characteristics might affect the outcome of the experiment. In our ignorance of what might be important, randomization is the best way to proceed. When we do have an idea about what might affect behavior in the experiment, a technique called **matching** could be *added to* (*not* substituted for) randomization. If some subject characteristic is known to be important for the experiment, then it makes sense to match the subjects in the conditions of the experiment on that characteristic. By matching, we mean that each condition of the experiment will be equated by the experimenter on some relevant subject characteristic.

A quick look through the literature will make it evident that a number of studies have found differences between males and females on spatial ability. Thus, we would like to deal with this potential confound explicitly in our experiment and not rely on randomization.

Matching + Randomization Compared with Randomization

Recall from chapter 5 that randomization and experimental control were both ways to control for confounds. We argued then, and wish to reinforce now, that randomization is sufficient to insure the internal validity of a study. So why should we add an experimental control method (i.e., matching)? The answer requires an understanding of the difference beween systematic error and random error.

Systematic error is a bias in an experiment that systematically favors one condition over the other. For example, in our experiment if we had all the females as observers and all the males as hiders, we would have introduced a systematic error. Systematic error threatens the internal validity of a study, preventing us from making any conclusions about the cause of an event (in other words, it is the type of error produced by a confound.) In the table below, we assume that there is a true effect of hiders versus observers that gives an advantage to the hiders. In addition, we assume that being male allows you to find an extra two dots (+2), whereas being female means that you will find two dots fewer regardless of the condition you are in (−2). If we put all the females in the Hider condition, we clearly have a confound. The numbers in parentheses represent this systematic bias, which in our example gives a benefit to the observers. Finally, the sums of the numbers are the data that the experimenter actually observes.

S#	True	Hiders Confound (female subjects)		Data	S#	True	Observers Confound (male subjects)		Data
#1	10	+	(−2)	=	8	#3	8	+	(2)	=	10
#2	10	+	(−2)	=	8	#4	8	+	(2)	=	10

The experimenter will reach the wrong conclusion that observers are better than hiders. The data have been distorted by the systematic error of having all male hiders and all female observers.

Random error differs from systematic error in that random error will average out to zero in the long run. If we randomly assigned our subjects to the two conditions, we would in the long run have an equal number of each gender in each condition. Thus, random error does not distort the results (as far as the mean score for each condition) as indicated in the following table.

True		Random		Data	True		Random		Data
10	+	(−2)	=	8	8	+	(+2)	=	10
10	+	(+2)	=	12	8	+	(−2)	=	6
10	+	(−2)	=	8	8	+	(−2)	=	6
10	+	(+2)	=	12	8	+	(+2)	=	10
		Mean	=	10			Mean	=	8

The experimenter will conclude that the hiders are 2 units better than the observers; the same conclusion that would have been reached had the experimenter the godlike ability to look directly at the true scores. However, without access to the true scores, the experimenter can be adversely affected by the random error. Although the same conclusion is reached, determining if the two conditions are really different is more difficult because the random error introduces a lot of variability into the scores. Some observers did do better than some hiders. Thus, random error does cloud the true score, but it does not systematically distort it when a large sample of subjects is used. What this all means is that the statistics will be less likely to find a difference when one is really present because of random error. In the statistical terms we discussed in chapter 7, an experiment with a large amount of random error lacks power. Recall that with low power we are likely to say that the two conditions are the same when they are really different (i.e., a Type II error).

Matching on an A Priori Basis

With a strong reason to suspect gender as a contributor to spatial ability, we can do one of two things to evaluate the possibilities. We can do a factorial experiment that involves manipulating both factors in the same experiment (to be discussed in chapter 11) or we can match subjects on one factor (e.g., gender) to evaluate the contribution of the other (e.g., hider vs. observer) in the experiment. If we match subjects, we can eliminate much of this random error. That in turn makes it easier for our statistics to find a difference if one is truly there.

Matching should be used when there is a subject characteristic that is *highly correlated with the dependent variable.* So, in our experiment, we would not want to waste our time matching people on their shoe size or hair color because neither of these is correlated with spatial ability. If you want to match on more than one variable, say, gender and familiarity with the campus, you can do so but it becomes increasingly difficult to match as the number of matching variables increase. In addition, when matching on more than one variable, both should be correlated with the dependent variable, but *not* correlated with each other. For example, if we matched on gender and whether or not the subject wore pantyhose, we would have wasted our time. Whereas it is probably true that wearing pantyhose is correlated with spatial ability, this correlation is only because of the correlation between gender and spatial ability. Thus we have actually matched on the same variable twice.

Consider one additional example. Suppose we were interested in a special math training program and how it could help students do math more effectively. Our dependent variable will be how well the subjects perform on a standardized test of math ability. We might use a class of fourth-grade students, half of them in the math program and half in a control group. We could randomly assign subjects to the two conditions, but we might get all the best math students in one of the two groups, thus introducing a source of systematic error in the experiment. Because we are using an intact group of students as the subjects, we should capitalize on the fact that there are known characteristics of these students that will ensure an equivalence between the two groups of subjects. The teacher has math achievement scores compiled from tests similar to the one we will give at the end of the experiment. We could match the subjects on this basis, thereby insuring an equivalent level of math achievement at the start of the experiment. We have matched on the basis of the dependent variable—math ability. When the matching occurs on a measure of the dependent vriable obtained before treatment is administered, we would be matching on a **pretest.** We focus on an experimental design that uses a pretest, the pretest-posttest design, in the next chapter.

Individual-Individual Matching

There are some variations on the exact way we can go about matching subjects. We can try to match one individual to another, thereby creating a kind of pairing of subjects. The quintessential individual-individual matching would be identical twins. We could randomly assign one twin to the Observer condition and one to the Hider condition. In this way we would be matching on a number of variables, including some we did not realize. Although matching twins is easy (once the twins agree to be in your experiment), trying to match individual for individual is usually more cumbersome, especially when there are more than two conditions in an experiment. It can also become cumbersome when the matching variable can take on a range of values. For example, in a five-condition experiment where we wanted to match on IQ, it would be difficult to find five people with an IQ of exactly 111. If we also wanted to match on another variable, the problem would become more difficult.

Group Matching

An alternative to matching individual to individual is to match the averages of the subjects in the experimental conditions to each other. Matching the group averages is less desirable than matching individuals, because group averages can hide some important differences between the makeup of the groups. For example, four scores of 10 and one of 60 make an average score of 20. This group of subjects would be different from a group of subjects who all had scores between 18 and 22, even though the average score would be the same, 20. In practice, it is a good idea to match both the means of the groups and the standard deviations of the two groups. Actually doing an experiment where matching is used is much simplified if the population of subjects and the measure on which they are to be matched is known before the start of the experiment.

Thus, matching subjects on some a priori basis can increase the precision of an experiment by ensuring that the conditions of the experiment have equal representation of the matched characteristic. When subjects are matched, we do not have to rely on randomization to control the characteristic; therefore we do not have to worry that by chance there are differences between groups by the (bad) luck of the randomization process. Remember that matching *does not* do away with randomization. Once a pair of matched subjects has been obtained, one member is randomly placed in the control group and one in the experimental group.

Standardized tests of spatial ability indicate that there are some differences linked to gender. To control for possible differences in spatial memory, we will use a matching procedure to control for gender effects. We will make pairs of same-gender subjects and then randomly assign one to the Hider condition and one to the Observer condition.

Yoked Control: "Matching" Experiences

Now returning to our two conditions: Hiders and Observers. A simple way to implement these two conditions is to have subjects in one condition hide some dots and later try to find them. The subjects in the Observers condition could watch the *experimenter* hide some dots and then try to find them. However, are there problems with this procedure? For one thing, the experimenters may hide the dots in places that are harder to remember than the places used by the hiders, thus making the observers' task more difficult than the hiders'. The experimenter could also hide the dots according to a different time pattern; that is, the experimenter may tend to hide a cluster of dots, wait a while and then hide another cluster; the hiders may, as a group, tend to space their hidings more evenly. How can we equate the two groups on these types of variables?

Essentially we want to equate, or match, for the experience the subjects have in the experiment. The normal procedures of the experimental design usually provide such an arrangement, because the experimenter usually has an experimental protocol already arranged for the subject. The only thing that varies between one condition and another is the prearranged experimental conditions of the experimenter. Sometimes, however, the subject determines aspects of the experimental situation (as in our study where the subjects actually choose the location where the dot will be hidden).

One way to control for subject-controlled effects is to use a **yoked-control** procedure. This procedure involves matching subjects on some important aspects of the experience they have in the experiment. Thus, just as two oxen yoked together to pull a cart experience the same events, so do two yoked subjects. Usually, the experimental subject dictates the yoking. For example, if the experimental subject takes 50 minutes to do a task, then the yoked-control subject is allowed only 50 minutes to do a task. In our case, if the hider must find a dot hidden under the water fountain in the psychology building, then the yoked observer subject must find a dot hidden under the same water fountain. We will yoke an observer to a hider in the current experiment to control for the experiences during the placement of the dots. A pair of subjects, one hider and one observer, will be asked to go around campus with the hider placing the dots in different places and the observer watching.

With these procedures we can be certain that any event that happened to the hider also happened to the observer. Every time the experimental subject hid a dot, the yoked subject would watch the dot being hid. Thus, the yoked subject receives the identical pattern and amount of experience as the experimental subject. The difference between the two would be only that one person actively hid the dot while the other simply watched.

Some have argued that the yoked-control procedure has some flaws, mainly revolving around the idea that the experimental subject has the advantage of something happening at just the right moment, but the yoked subject does not have such an advantage. Although this may be true, the yoked-control procedure is the most effective method we have of controlling response-dependent events in an experiment. For our particular experiment, the fact that the hiders can take advantage of the right moment can be considered an integral part of the effect we are trying to investigate.

Matching and yoking are procedures that allow greater precision in the control of extraneous variables than randomization allows. By matching (either for preexisting characteristics or experimental experience as in yoking), we ensure an equivalence between conditions of the experiment. Matching and yoking also allow us to analyze the data in somewhat different ways than the more common randomization techniques allow. When we have subjects matched either for some preexisting characteristic or for experimental conditions, the differences between subjects can be analyzed by direct comparison of the pairs. In statistical terms, there is a dependence between subjects in the experimental and control groups that allows us to use powerful statistical tests (e.g., dependent t-tests).

Thus far, pairs of subjects will go out to hide dots. One member of the pair will determine where a dot is to be placed. The other subject will observe but not determine where the first subject places the dot. Thus the experimental subject will place the dot, and the other subject will receive the same information but not decide where the dot is placed. This is the independent variable: whether the person generated the hiding place or simply perceived the hiding place.

The Experiment

The requirements for hiding the dots are (a) that they be out of sight from normal viewing perspectives, (b) that they be placed where they will do no harm to the object on which they are stuck (e.g., not stuck to a page of a book where its removal might damage the book), (c) that they will not cause any problem if left attached indefinitely (we may not find all of them), (d) that one dot not be hidden within 20 feet of another (obviously the purpose of the experiment would be undermined if all the dots were hidden in close proximity to each other), and finally (e) that they *not* be hidden in the hider's home building or place of work. This last restriction is to help ensure that the area of placement is about equally familiar to the hider and observer.

To have a reasonable analog to the seed storage problem faced by Clark's nutcracker, the dots will be hidden on one week and recovered next week. When recovering the dots, the same pair of subjects cannot be used, because they are both trying to find dots in the same place and the success of one person would be dependent on the other. To make the data collection appropriate for each subject, the pairs will be reassigned at the time of data collection. When one subject is relocating the dots, he or she (or the original partner) hid, the new member will record data. They will then reverse roles, and the first data recorder will now be the searcher and the original searcher will record data. This procedure means that the data collector is "blind" with respect to the actual location of the dots the subject is trying to find. Thus, the data recorder could not provide intentional or unintentional cues to the subject because they were not together at the time the dots were hidden.

Because each dot will be searched for twice (experimental and yoked subjects), the first searcher should not remove the dot, but the second should. Who will search first from each pair of subjects will be decided at random. Every attempt should be made to locate lost dots, because we do not want to clutter the campus with hidden colored dots. In recording data, the searcher gets only one try for each dot. The searcher should declare when he or she is making a search (e.g., "I'm looking at the middle of this shelf," or "I'm looking on the top of this door sill"). If the search is incorrect, the data recorder should record it as an error. If the searcher can, he or she should locate the dot that was not in the expected place, but does not receive credit for a correct response. In other words, the searcher gets one crack at each dot but should try to find the lost dots anyway.

Other procedural details such as the number of dots, when subjects will place them, and other concerns will be left to the reader. Below is a summary of the experiment with some suggestions for the final procedure.

1. Match subjects for gender, forming pairs of males and pairs of females.
2. Randomly assign a member of the pair to hider and the other to observer.
3. Obtain 50 colored dots, number them from 1 to 50, and put the initial of the experimental subject on each one.
4. The hider hides the dots, beginning with number 1 and continuing, in order, to the end. The hider will follow the rules for hiding dots as outlined in the chapter. The observer watches where the hider hides the dots.
5. The following week, subjects are matched as before but with a different partner. Each subject tries to find the dots. For the original pair of hider-observer (who are now in different pairs), randomly determine who will search first. The second searcher removes the dots.
6. Subject and data recorder change roles and repeat the procedure. Use the provided data sheet to record the data.
7. Try to find all lost dots to keep the campus "dot-less."

Data Analysis

Because we have *pairs* of subjects, the appropriate statistical analysis is the dependent *t*-test for the total number of dots correctly found. This statistical procedure is slightly different from the independent *t*-test procedure used in previous chapters, although the meaning of a significant dependent *t* is exactly the same as for the independent *t*. The difference lies in the calculations. Information to remind you of the necessary computation in a dependent *t* appears at the end of the chapter.

In addition to the total number of dots recovered, we also have data on the order of hiding-recovery. When things are experienced serially, there are often "primacy" and "recency" effects noticeable. These effects refer to the finding that the first (primacy) and last (recency) items of a serially presented set of items are more often remembered than those in the middle of the set. Primacy effects are particularly well known in various areas of psychology. For example, a job applicant is often told to dress appropriately because one of the first pieces of information the employer receives from the applicant is his or her appearance, and the primacy effect means that the first item (the applicant's appearance) of information is better remembered than the later items.

Are there primacy and recency effects in spatial memory? To evaluate the existence of these effects, we need to consider the probability of correct recall as a function of the order in which the dot was hidden. We can look at the recall of the first dot, the second, third, and so on. One problem we may have with this arrangement is that there will be variability from one to the next dot. There are techniques for dealing with variability of this sort. The one we consider here is called **classification.** Consider the following example.

					When the dot was hidden:					
	1	2	3	4	5 . . .	46	47	48	49	50
Subject 1	1	1	0	1	0	0	0	0	0	1
Subject 2	1	0	1	0	1	0	0	0	1	0

In our experiment we will have a total of 50 positions for each subject. We could begin our summary of the data by averaging over subjects to produce 50 means, one for each condition. This is more data than we can digest (it is also difficult to analyze statistically). A way of simplifying and summarizing is to classify the data within an interval. This means we could consider the first five positions hidden as one data point and take an average of these. The process is classifying data into intervals of size five:

	When the dot was hidden:	
	1–5 . . .	46–50
Subject 1	3	1
Subject 2	3	1

The size of the interval is a command decision, as is the decision whether to reduce your data in this fashion. In this example we have used an interval of size five. The goal is to simplify the data without hiding or obscuring effects that might be important. (There is also an advantage in analysis because we will not have to analyze data that can only take on the values of 0 or 1.)

Key Words

classification   pretest
matching   yoked control (yoking)
preexisting characteristics

Additional Reading

Kamil, A. C., & Balda, R. P. (1985). Cache recovery and spatial memory in Clark's nutcrackers (Nucifraga columbiana). *Journal of Experimental Psychology: Animal Behavior Processes, 11,* 95–111.

Neisser, U. (1982). *Memory observed.* San Francisco: W. H. Freeman.

Shettleworth, S. J., & Krebs, J. R. (1982). How marsh tits find their hoards: The roles of site preference and spatial memory. *Journal of Experimental Psychology: Animal Behavior Processes, 8,* 354–375.

Correlated t-test

The Student's t for correlated samples, called the correlated groups t-test or simply the dependent t-test, is useful when comparing two distributions that have been matched in some way. Like the independent groups test, the correlated t-test will indicate if the means of two conditions are significantly different. Generally, this test is more powerful than the independent groups test, provided the matching has been effective in removing some of the random error. To illustrate this power, we will use the same hypothetical data as that used in the independent t-test where we failed to reject the null hypothesis.

The formula for the dependent t-test is:

$$t = \frac{\bar{D}}{\sqrt{\frac{SS_D}{(n-1)}\left(\frac{1}{n}\right)}}$$

STEP 0.   Decide on the null hypothesis.

We will use a two-tailed test and assume that there is no difference between the two conditions. We will test at the .05 alpha level.

STEP 1.   Table the data, pairing subjects according to the results of matching.

	Condition 1	Condition 2
Pair 1	5	10
Pair 2	1	3
Pair 3	6	9
Pair 4	10	11
Pair 5	3	5

STEP 2.   Compute a difference score for each subject, square each difference score, and compute the sum of Ds and sum of D^2s.

X_1	X_2	D	D^2
5	10	5	25
1	3	2	4
6	9	3	9
10	11	1	1
3	5	2	4
		13	43

STEP 3.   Compute the SS_D. (See review for independent t for the formula for SS.)

$$SS_D = 43 - (13)^2/5 = 9.2$$

STEP 4.   Compute the mean D.

$$\bar{D} = 13/5 = 2.6$$

STEP 5.   Compute t.

$$t = \frac{2.6}{\sqrt{\frac{9.2}{(5-1)}\left(\frac{1}{5}\right)}} = 3.833$$

STEP 6. Compare the observed t *with the critical* t.

In this test we have 4 degrees of freedom (# of pairs − 1). Assuming a nondirectional (two-tailed) test at the .05 level, we find in Table B of the Appendix a value of 2.776. Our observed value is larger than the critical value, indicating that there is a difference between the two conditions.

Comparison of independent and dependent ts.

The alert reader may have noticed several interesting differences between this test and the independent *t*-test, even though we used the same data in both exercises. First, the two *t*-tests had the same numerator (i.e., 2.6). Second, the dependent *t*-test had a much smaller denominator, suggesting that we removed a large amount of random error from the test, thus producing a much larger $t_{observed}$. Third, the critical value for the dependent *t*-test was larger than for the independent *t*-test, indicating that the dependent *t*-test had fewer degrees of freedom. Nevertheless, with the dependent *t*-test we concluded that there was a significant difference, whereas with the independent *t*-test we failed to reject the null hypothesis.

Spatial Memory Experiment

Subject name: _____

Recorder name: _____

Subject is EXPERIMENTAL or YOKED (circle one)

The subject gets 50 searches, each is either an error (no dot found) or the number of the dot is recorded. Therefore, next to each number on this data sheet there should be either an E for error or a number representing the number on the dot that was found.

1.	2.	3.	4.	5.	6.	7.	8.	9.	10.
11.	12.	13.	14.	15.	16.	17.	18.	19.	20.
21.	22.	23.	24.	25.	26.	27.	28.	29.	30.
31.	32.	33.	34.	35.	36.	37.	38.	39.	40.
41.	42.	43.	44.	45.	46.	47.	48.	49.	50.

Buildings or general location where dots were hidden:

_____

_____

_____

_____

_____

Spatial Memory

Hiders Subject #	Dots Recalled	Yoked Observers Subject #	Dots Recalled	D

$\bar{X}_{Hiders} =$　　　　　　$\bar{X}_{Observers} =$　　　　　　$\bar{D} =$

$SS =$　　　　　　　　　　　　$SS =$

. Variance $=$　　　　　　　　Variance $=$

OBSERVED $t\,(\underline{\hspace{1cm}}) =$　　　　CRITICAL $t\,(\underline{\hspace{1cm}}) =$

Comments:

Spatial Memory

Each pair will hide 50 dots. Below is a way of tallying the number of people who recalled the first dot, second, and so forth. After the frequency data have been tabulated, a graph plotting frequency as a function of serial position will reveal if the two groups happen to differ on their recall of the first dots, middle dots, or final dots hidden. If there appears to be a difference on some of the dots but not others, recompute the dependent *t*-test from the previous page using only the dots of interest. Was there really a significant difference between the groups? If so, why?

Dot #	# of Hiders Recalling	# of Observers Recalling	Dot #	# of Hiders Recalling	# of Observers Recalling
1			26		
2			27		
3			28		
4			29		
5			30		
6			31		
7			32		
8			33		
9			34		
10			35		
11			36		
12			37		
13			38		
14			39		
15			40		
16			41		
17			42		
18			43		
19			44		
20			45		
21			46		
22			47		
23			48		
24			49		
25			50		

Comments:

General Idea (Previous Research, Curiosity, Theory)

Certain species of birds are phenomenally able to recall where they have stored food. Humans also have spatial memory that is often quite good. It is unclear, in humans, the factors that influence memory for spatial location. If birds are born with this ability, perhaps it is "hardwired" and innate in humans as well.

Explanatory Statement

Notice how the following two explanatory statements lead to different predictions. By eliminating one of the statements, we can gain support for the other.

Explanatory statement 1 (active involvement explanation): Storing an object in a spatial location requires active interaction with the environment, which in turn should lead to better memory of the spatial location.

Explanatory statement 2 ("hardwired" explanation): Storing an object in a spatial location automatically (without effort or without intention to remember) registers information about the spatial position in memory.

Research Hypothesis/Descriptive Statement

Hypothesis 1: Subjects who actively place an object will be more likely to recall the location of that object than subjects who merely observe the placement.

Hypothesis 2 (generate a descriptive statement predicted by the "hardwired" explanatory statement):

Methods (Natural Observation, Survey, Field Experiment, Lab Experiment)

Most field experiments give up some internal validity for external validity. Discuss this trade-off for the current experiment.

Dependent Variable(s)

The chapter discusses a primary dependent variable and a secondary one. What were they?

Operational Definition   Operationally define the main dependent variable:

Continued

Continued

Predictor or Independent Variable

Involvement: Hider vs. Observer

Operational Definition   Operationally define *involvement:*

Design (Between)

Between: Why is this a between-subjects design if the subjects are yoked?

Subjects

Ethical Considerations

Characteristics and Availability

Sampling Procedure and Number of Subjects
Stratified random sample. What is the strata?

Continued

Control

Subject Assignment (Randomization, ► Matching)
Matching: Each pair will comprise same-gender subjects.

Randomization: Members of a pair will be randomly assigned to the Hider or Observer condition.

Environment (Insured Equivalence, ► Yoking)
Insured equivalence: (List the potential rival hypotheses controlled in this way.)

Yoking: The observer member of each pair will be yoked to the hider in that the former will observe each placement by the latter in the same order and same timing intervals.

Procedural Command Decisions (Ceiling Effect, Floor Effect)

Some command decisions that need to be made would be where to hide the dots, how far apart the dots must be from one another, how many dots can be in one general area, and how long the hiders/observers have to retrieve the dots. Should subjects be restricted in the locations they are allowed to choose, or could the hider "drag" the yoked-observer anywhere?

Retrospective Confound Check (Assumed, Statistical, Rethink)

(Selection, Mortality, History, Maturation, Reactivity, Instrumentation)   Review the experiment as discussed in the chapter. By considering the following confounds, make suggestions, where necessary, about what might require rethinking.

Selection:

Mortality:

History:

Maturation:

Reactivity:

Data Analysis

Descriptive   Mean number of dots recalled is one descriptive statistic computed. What descriptive statistic might be computed to analyze serial position effects?

Continued

176

Continued

Inferential   Correlated (dependent) *t*-test comparing members within a pair.

Hypothetical Outcome Analysis

Discuss what each pattern below would mean for the two hypotheses.

Active Involvement Hypothesis	Hardwired Hypothesis
Hider > Observer	Hider = Observer

Principles of Technical Writing

Technical writing must be precise yet easy to comprehend. Page limitations of journals are severe, making it imperative that you say what you need to say and say it clearly. This does not mean that technical writing is cryptic or convoluted; nor does it imply that the prose must be boring. Rather, technical writing requires intense efforts at organization, rewriting, and good grammar. Do not worry about your personal style: That will develop as you go. And above all, do *not* try to write "scientifically." This will lead to convoluted, overly complicated, jargon-filled papers.

Below are five basic principles of good technical writing.

1. Did you have in mind a specific reader who is intelligent but uninformed? (This rules out your instructor.)

2. Did you "tell the readers what you are going to tell them, then tell them, then tell them what you told them"?

3. What is the purpose of the report? Does every paragraph, sentence, and word contribute to that purpose?

4. Did you use language that is simple and familiar to the psychologist?

5. Is your report attractive?

Citing the Literature

Every journal article includes citations or references to existing literature. The APA has a standard style for both the citation of literature in the text and the listing of references in the reference section.

One important point to keep in mind is that the citations in the text and the articles listed in the references are completely overlapping: All cited works, and *only* cited works, should appear in the reference section. If you are relying on a secondary source to cite primary material, you must give credit to the secondary source (see plagiarism discussion in chapter 1).

There are basically two forms of citation: in-text and parenthetical. They differ slightly in their format:

Heckle and Jeckle (1986) agreed with several other researchers (Abbot & Costello, 1949; Burns & Allen, 1948; Lewis, 1980; Lewis & Martin, 1955, 1956) when they . . .

There are several things to note about the above. First, if the citation is a part of the prose (not parenthetical) the word *and* is written out, whereas the *&* sign is used for parenthetical citations. With more than one citation, the citations are ordered alphabetically according to name of first author. If there is a tie, then order based on the second author, keeping in mind that sole authors precede double authorships, and so forth. If there is still a tie, then place the earlier publication first. In this latter case you need not re-peat the authors name (see Lewis & Martin example above).

The nice thing about all of this is that these are exactly the same rules used when you are ordering your reference list. In the reference section, an entry would look as follows:

Abbott, B., & Costello, L. (1949). Who really is on first? Journal of Comedy and Freudian Theory, 55, 217–235.

for a journal article published in 1949, volume 55, pages 217–235, or:

Lewis, J., & Martin, D. (1955). Slapstick: The early years. In M. Berle (Ed.), Comedy doesn't have to be funny (pp. 111–112). Las Vegas: Full Court Press.

for an article in a book edited by Berle and published by Full Court Press located in Las Vegas.

9 Pretests & Gain Scores

Overview

The pretest-posttest design is introduced as an alternative to designs that measure the dependent variable only after the treatment has been given. This design results in a gain score or difference score based on the pre-post differences. The use of the pretest-posttest design in preference to the after-only (no pretest) design is useful in determining the direction of the effect of the independent variable and the size of the effect; it also increases the sensitivity of the experiment. This design may also provide insurance against problems of mortality effects, faulty random assignment, ceiling and floor effects, and generalization of the results to inappropriate populations. The problem of a testing confound is discussed and the Solomon's four-groups design is briefly mentioned as is the idea of alternate forms. The experiment compares training techniques using a finger maze apparatus.

The concept of a planned comparison is discussed and compared with post-hoc comparisons.

Tips on General Style focuses on the use of transition devices to assist in keeping the discourse cohesive. Tips on Specific Style focuses on the final part of the narrative in a psychology paper: the discussion section.

Pretest-Posttest

"Young men's minds are always changeable, but when an old man is concerned in a matter, he looks both before and after."

—*Homer*

During the experiment discussed in chapter 8, you may have noticed that some people knew the campus better than others. Speaking with our subjects in that experiment revealed that some had been on campus longer, and thus had more practice finding their way around. Others seemed to differ in how they learned about the campus. Some had classes they attended from all around campus, whereas others seemed to have most classes in one part of campus or another. Still others claimed to have no spatial ability and were never able to learn their way around the campus.

Learning a route from one location in your town (e.g., home) to another (e.g., psychology classroom) is the sort of task, like so many other tasks, that should result in improvement with the right kind of practice. It should be possible to design a training program to facilitate learning how to get around in a new town or new campus and to then test whether the training program was effective.

Figure 9–1 Patterns that could lead to the same conclusion if the dependent variable were measured only after the independent variable. Even though the trained group supposes the control group during the test, the training could help (a), hurt less (b), or have no real effect (c).

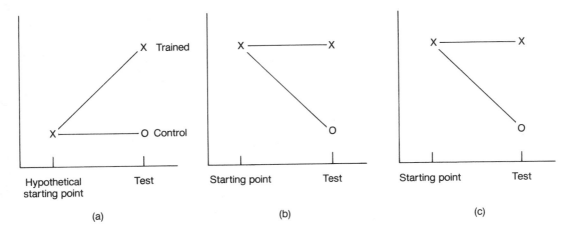

With the methodologies discussed thus far, we could proceed with a between-subjects design by forming two groups of subjects: a training group and a control group that receives no training. We could match on some variable of importance. Half of the subjects could then be randomly assigned to one group and half to the other. We could then measure performance on some task and compare the resulting scores. If the score for the training group was superior to that of the control group, we would conclude that the training program was effective.

Did the training program actually improve performance? The training group might outperform the control group on the final test in more than one way. Consider the graphs in Figure 9–1. In each case, the training group was better than the control group on the final test. The graphs also include hypothetical starting points for the groups. In each graph, we can assume the training group and the control group would start out at approximately the same level, because random assignment should equate the groups. In Graph A, the group receiving training improved, while the control group did not. This is the finding we would like to infer from our study. However, other patterns are possible. Both groups could get worse (Graph B), suggesting that our training program does not actually help but rather "hurts less" than no training. The training group might not change at all, while the control group gets worse (Graph C), again suggesting that the training is not really effective. To assess whether the training program improves performance, we must obtain a measure of performance before and after the training. The **pretest-posttest design** accomplishes this.

Pretest-Posttest Design

In this method we administer a test or measure some behavior. Following the first test some treatment is given, and following the treatment a posttest that is the same as, or highly correlated with (e.g., a different version of), the pretest is given. Thus the attempt is to measure a particular aspect of behavior prior to the treatment and following it to see how the treatment affected performance.

One common situation where pretests are used is in school systems. Achievement tests given at the start of the school year and readministered at the end are used to evaluate the effectiveness of the year of schooling the student has experienced. Because a specific test usually is the dependent variable, such as in this example, the method has been labeled a pretest-posttest design. A **difference score** or **gain score** can be calculated by subtracting the pretest score from the posttest score. If the student improves as a result of the year of study, then the difference score should be positive (the student should score higher on the posttest than the pretest). No improvement would be reflected by a difference score equal to zero.

If we are interested in evaluating how a special course affects the students' achievement, we would compare difference scores of students randomly assigned to the special course with those assigned to a standard course. We need two conditions (special course and standard course) and two measurements (pretest and posttest) to do the complete experiment. Further, students must be randomly assigned to one of the two classes, as has been the case in the previous experiments we have conducted. If there were only one group, the one receiving the special course of instruction, differences between the pretest and posttest may arise simply because the students have matured or numerous other possible reasons. Thus a simple pretest-posttest difference does not mean that the special course caused the difference. To show it was the special course that caused the difference, a control group is needed. So the pretest-posttest methodology does not substitute for those principles of experimentation we have already developed, but it adds a new dimension to them.

Comparing Designs

We might well ask why use the pretest-posttest methodology. In chapter 6 we developed the methods to do a two-group, between-subjects experiment. If we simply gave the students the achievement test at the end of their school year, we could compare the performance of those in the special course with those in the standard course. Comparing the performance of two distinct groups of subjects, measured once, is sometimes called an **after-only design.** The pretest-posttest design requires the collection of data at both time 1 (pretest) and time 2 (posttest) from the same subject. When subjects provide data for more than one condition, the design involves a **within-subjects manipulation.** In the pretest-posttest design, the variable of time (pre vs. post) is a within-subjects variable, whereas the independent variable (e.g., training vs. control) is a between-subjects variable. In other designs (see chapter 10), the independent variable can also be a within-subjects variable.

Reasons to Pretest

How can we choose between the pretest and the after-only designs? The pretest requires more effort on the part of the experimenter, but there are many reasons why the pretest-posttest procedure may be preferred to the between-group method for a particular study.

1. *Direction of the effect.* The special training we have been considering is assumed to improve the students' performance. By comparing pretest and posttest scores, we can confirm the direction of change. In many experiments, the direction of change may not be assumed. For example, if we were interested in how much attraction two persons have for each other, we might have them spend a weekend together and measure the mutual attraction. We could compare their attraction with other pairs who spent the same amount of time together but with a third person also present. Would the degree of attraction two people feel for each other be increased, decreased, or left unchanged by the presence of a third person? Indeed, would two people forced to spend a weekend together show an increase or decrease in attraction to each other? The pretest-posttest method answers these questions because we can compare the attraction two persons have toward each other prior to the weekend and after it.

2. *Size of the effect.* Along with the direction of the effect, the pretest-posttest design would reveal how much was gained by the treatment. It is often important to know whether the size of a change is large enough to warrant additional effort or expenditures. For example, if you were working in a business and were given the chance to start a new training program for your employees, you could do a pretest-posttest experiment. The training program would cost some money to implement, and if the gains from the training program were small, even if significant, it may not be cost effective to adopt the program.

3. *Increased sensitivity to the independent variable.* Situations exist where a manipulation may have a consistent effect, but the effect may be small but important. Suppose, for example, we give a group of students practice on techniques for speed reading. If we then compared their performance on a test for reading comprehension, we might not find a difference between these students and a control group not given any special training on speed reading. If we had a pretest on these subjects, then gave them the speed-reading techniques, and followed this with a posttest, we might well find improvement in reading comprehension. By learning how to read faster, these subjects might have more time to review what they have read and thus show improved comprehension scores. The effect may be relatively small because speed of reading is an indirect influence on comprehension. The within-subjects procedure allows us to see the effect, even though it may be a relatively small one. You might think in terms of seasoning food. A taste of the soup (pretest) followed by adding salt or pepper to it and a second taste (posttest) can produce a noticeable change that is easily detected by the "pretaste-posttaste" procedure.

4. *Insurance against mortality.* Recall that when subjects fail to complete the experiment, the mortality confound can threaten the internal validity of the study. Subjects may discontinue participation at different rates in different conditions, and thus comparison of once-equated groups becomes impossible. We recommended in chapter 6 that mortality could

be corrected if it was not serious by randomly dropping subjects from the larger group until the groups were again of equal numbers. If pretest scores were available, when a subject failed to complete the experiment, a subject from the other condition could be eliminated not at random but by finding one with the same pretest score as the dropout.

5. *Insurance for random assignment.* Although random assignment guards against rival hypotheses, it does so by chance. It is possible, therefore, that a disproportionate amount of a confounding variable could occur in one condition compared with another. With studies using only a few subjects, this possibility becomes more likely. In such cases, a pretest might be advisable simply to check on the (admittedly rare) cases when random assignment does not distribute the variables across conditions.

6. *Ceiling and floor effects.* In some experiments, knowing the initial position of the subjects would be useful. Ceiling effects and floor effects, which could reduce the probability of an effect of the independent variable, would be easily discerned in the pretest data. For example, with an after-only procedure comparing two training procedures, the experimenter might observe very high, statistically identical scores in the two conditions. This could indicate that both conditions were equally effective or that subjects were already at the ceiling on the task and could not get better. If one training procedure were better than another, we could not tell because the task was too easy to allow a difference to be detected.

7. *Generalizing to the population.* Another reason to know the initial position of the subjects is to help determine to which population the results should be generalized. For example, if designing a training procedure to help poor readers, the experimenter would expect to see pretest scores indicative of their low reading abilities. If, instead, the scores were average, or above average, the study would relate to a different population. The study could either be continued with this change, or the experimenter could resample to get a more appropriate sample.

Reasons Not to Pretest

Should we always use the pretest-posttest methodology? The answer is no for at least two reasons. If none of the above reasons is important for your experiment, then there is no reason to prefer the pre-post procedure to the simple between-groups designs that require less effort on your part. Second, a problem with the pre-post procedure that does not appear in the between-groups designs is the testing confound. It is a special type of sequencing confound (chapter 10). The **testing** confound occurs when the first test of a pretest-posttest experiment influences the performances on the second test.

Consider the following study. A developmental psychologist is interested in whether children who do not have "object permanence" can be trained to acquire it. Object permanence refers to the fact that young children will act as if an object no longer exists if it is taken from view. To use only children without object permanence, the psychologist gives children a pretest. Those without object permanence are randomly assigned to either the training group or the control group. Subjects are then given a posttest. The experimenter observes that in a posttest, the training group improved, whereas the control group did not.

A possible rival hypothesis is that the combination of a pretest and the treatment *together* is responsible for the change in the posttest. For example, the special class may be especially beneficial *only* if it is preceded by a pretest. If another educator tried to use only the special class, but did not give a pretest (the after-only design), he or she may not find any improvement.

With a pretest-posttest design, the pretest may have an influence on the posttest, either alone or in concert with the treatment. The experimenter can control for this in one of two ways. First, the experimenter can attempt to minimize the potential impact of the pretest. Second, the experimenter can attempt to assess the contribution of the pretest to the posttest performance.

Minimizing the Effects of the Pretest

In some cases, for example, with unobtrusive measurements of the dependent variable, the testing effect is likely to be absent, and therefore it could be assumed to have minimal effects on the posttest. The effect of the pretest can also be minimized by the experimenter. For example, a longer delay between pretest and posttest can, in some instances, reduce the effect of the pretest. In other cases, for example, when the subject must complete an achievement test at pretest and at posttest, the testing effect could be quite large, despite the length of the delay. In this instance, an experimenter may minimize testing effects by using **alternate forms** of the same test. Rather than give the same test at both points in time, the researcher finds two forms of the test that are comparable. Half of the subjects will receive Form A at pretest and half will receive Form B. Then at posttest, each subject will receive the other form.

To make certain that the alternate forms are comparable, the experimenter must ask other subjects to take *both* tests. Performance on Form A is then correlated with performance on Form B. Because performance on such tests are likely to be at least at the interval-scale level, the Pearson correlation coefficient can be computed to provide a quantification of the relationship. If the forms are highly correlated (usually positively), then they will serve well as alternate forms. This high correlation means that the tests have high **reliability** in that scores on one form are predictive of scores on the other form. As a reminder, the Pearson correlation coefficient appears at the end of the chapter.

Assessing the Effect of a Pretest:
Solomon's Four-Groups Design

How can we assess the effect of the pretest and the pretest/treatment combination? The **Solomon's four-groups design** is a partial solution to the problem. This design has four groups, as illustrated below, and subjects are randomly assigned to one of the four groups.

	Pretest	Treatment	Posttest
Group 1	Yes	Yes	Yes
Group 2	Yes	No	Yes
Group 3	No	Yes	Yes
Group 4	No	No	Yes

The groups above the line form the standard pretest-posttest design, and the groups below the line form the standard after-only design. We can now make a number of comparisons. For example, we can compare Group 1 with Group 2 to learn about the effect of the treatment when the pretest is present; we can compare Group 1 with Group 3 to learn about the effect of the pretest when the treatment is present; we can compare Group 1 with Group 4 to learn about the effect of the combination of pretest and treatment. Many other important comparisons can also be done in this design, but this is substantially more work for the experimenter than either of the other simpler designs. In addition, no statistic currently exists that will simultaneously take advantage of all the comparisons of the Solomon design. So, is the extra effort worth it? It will depend on the particular experiment; in general, however, if a pretest is not needed or its effects can be assumed irrelevant, then the experimenter should use a simpler design.

The pretest-posttest design is a true experimental design, because subjects are randomly assigned to the levels of the independent variable. However, several situations, such as the special class example, do not always lend themselves to random assignment. We discuss the situation where the control group may not be equivalent to the experimental group as an example of quasi-experimental methods.

The Experiment

We want to gain some insight into how subjects learn the spatial layout of a new area. We can capture many of the essentials of this process in a convenient way by looking at how people learn the path through a finger maze. A finger maze is a device (e.g., a piece of cardboard) with a maze or pathway cut into it. A *blindfolded* subject then tries to learn how to move his or her finger, or something held in the fingers such as a pencil, from point A to point B through the maze. With a finger maze we can ensure that subjects do not have any prior knowledge of the layout; we can vary the complexity of the layout if desired; and we can gain more control than would ever be possible in the field. We can ask people to practice solving a particular maze and measure how long it takes to complete the maze and the number of errors.

In chapter 8, we mentioned the concept of a cognitive map. A cognitive map is an intermediate mechanism. If the organism has or forms a cognitive map, then it has a mental representation of an area that has much in common with a physical map of the area. For example, the analogy would lead one to argue that, like a physical map, the cognitive map presents many relations of the area simultaneously. This can be contrasted to a situation where the organism has a list of directions stored in memory rather than a map. If there is some validity to the idea of a cognitive map, we should be able to see a difference between a group given a list of directions for navigating the maze and those given a physical map.

In the current experiment, we are interested in the formation of a cognitive map of the path through an unfamiliar area (i.e., a maze) and how a physical map of the maze may be useful in establishing a cognitive representation of the maze. We will contrast the cognitive representation acquired from studying a map with the representation acquired from studying a list of directions (e.g., right, left, left, continue). Studying will be simply looking at a representation of the maze for 1 minute.

The map representation will be a line-drawing map of the maze. As with all maps, it will be smaller than the maze it represents. The map can be defined further by reference to the mazes and maps at the end of the chapter. The other representation will be a verbal listing of directions to take through the maze from a local point of view. That is, a direction to "go left" would mean to go up the maze if coming from the left and would mean to go down the maze if coming from the right.

Blindfolded subjects will trace through a map at pretest while errors and time to complete the maze are recorded. Then the subjects will study a representation (i.e., map or list). Following this 1-minute study period, a posttest will be given with the subjects again being blindfolded and allowed to trace through the maze. The expectation is that if cognitive maps are a useful construct, then supplying a person with a physical map should facilitate the construction of the cognitive map and thus allow a greater gain than would be expected with another representation.

The easiest way of doing the experiment is to use the template at the end of this chapter and cut out the indicated route from a piece of cardboard. The cardboard may then be put over a blank piece of paper and a pencil or pen used by the subjects to trace the route. The blank piece of paper will therefore provide a tracing of the route the subject used to get through the maze. The experimenter should also record the time it takes the subject to go from point A to point B. The pretest is given first; the subject is then given one of the two descriptions provided at the end of the chapter to study, either the map or the list, depending on which condition the subject is in. The subject then traces through the maze a second time. The difference in posttest from pretest for subjects shown the map versus list of the maze are the results of interest.

The design, as it stands now, could be subject to a testing confound. Clearly tracing the maze once should result in learning even with no treatment. In addition, the treatment may prove especially helpful if it serves to help the subject integrate the prior experience of going through the maze. Let us consider some possible solutions.

1. A delay between pretest and treatment could minimize the effect. On the other hand, the subjects may review the trial mentally if the delay is short and thus form a cognitive map during the intertrial interval. Although a delay is a good idea, it is not sufficient in this case.

2. Using alternate forms of the maze, perhaps together with a delay, would help ensure that the testing effect would be minimized. Two mazes are supplied at the end of the chapter. These mazes have given us reasonable reliability scores. They are similar in the number of choice points, and so forth. However, it may turn out that one maze is a little easier than another. If that maze was always the pretest, it would work against us finding a gain from studying. If that maze was always the posttest, it would give a bias in favor of studying, which might not exist. A solution is to use Maze A as a pretest for half of the subjects and Maze B as a pretest for the other half of the subjects. This procedure is a simple form of counterbalancing, which is covered in more detail in the next chapter.

3. Finally, we could decide to use the Solomon's four-groups design and assess the effect of the pretest. However, as the current study is framed, we have no particular interest in the pretest, and by using a delay and alternate forms we can reduce the testing confound considerably.

Thus, we plan to increase the delay between pretest and treatment to 5 minutes and use alternate forms of the maze. Other procedural details of this experiment will be left to you. For example, should the subjects be given feedback when they make a wrong turn? Why or why not? Can you anticipate *any* possible problems that may arise and then develop a procedure for handling these problems before they arise?

Data Analysis

There are several comparisons in which we will have some interest. First is a comparison of the difference scores for the two groups. However, we will also be interested in whether the gains made by the groups were significant. In other words, are the posttest scores different from the pretest scores? Thus, we plan to conduct three tests on each dependent variable. We can use an independent *t*-test to compare the difference scores between the two groups, and two correlated *t*-tests to compare posttest scores with pretest scores for each group of subjects.

However, we stated in chapter 7 that simply performing these tests will inflate the probability of a Type I error from the conventional .05 to .15. Researchers differ in how to correct this problem. Some argue that if the test is a **planned comparison,** that is, one that you were going to make before you started to collect the data, you can simply continue with the use of *t*-tests. The fact that they are planned *before* the experiment gives additional information that should be taken into account when conducting the statistical test. If, instead, the test is a post-hoc comparison (see chapter 7), then some correction must be applied to keep your Type I error rate at the conventional level. The Tukey *HSD* discussed in chapter 7 is a post-hoc comparison test that controls for the probability of a Type I error.

Whether planned comparisons or post-hoc comparisons are conducted is a decision that hinges as much on the individual's philosophy of science as it does on statistical principles. We leave this aspect of the analysis to you.

Finally, the graphic representation should be similar to that in Figure 9−2. Pretest and posttest are marked on the abscissa and the dependent

Figure 9–2 Plot of results for a pretest-posttest study.

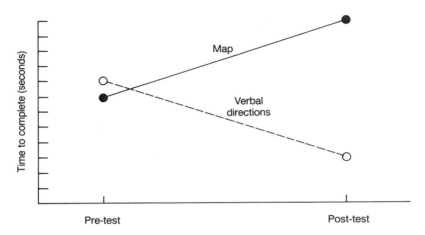

variable (time to complete the maze or number of errors made getting through the maze) is on the ordinate. Each group of subjects is represented by a line, often differentiated in some graphic way (e.g., dotted lines vs. solid lines), and the name of the group appears near the line. A line is used to connect the pretest score and the posttest score for each group because the pretest and posttest vary on the dimension of time, a continuous variable.

Key Words

after-only design   pretest-posttest design
alternate forms   reliability
difference score   Solomon's four-groups design
gain score   testing
planned comparison   within-subjects manipulation

Additional Reading

Higginson, G. D. (1937). Maze learning with knowledge of pattern similarity. *Journal of Experimental Psychology, 20,* 223–243.

Kozlowski, L. T., & Bryant, K. J. (1976). Sense of direction, spatial orientation, and cognitive maps. *Journal of Experimental Psychology: Human Perception and Performance, 3,* 590–598.

Langhorne, M. C. (1948). The effects of maze rotation on learning. *Journal of General Psychology, 38,* 191–205.

Reed, S. K. (1974). Structural descriptions and limitations of visual images. *Memory & Cognition, 2,* 329–336.

Thorndyke, P. W., & Goldin, S. E. (1983). Spatial learning and reasoning skill. In H. L. Pick, Jr. & L. P. Acredolo (Eds.), *Spatial orientation, theory, research, and application* (pp. 195–217). New York: Plenum Press.

Warden, C. J. (1924). The relative economy of various modes of attack in the mastery of a stylus maze. *Journal of Experimental Psychology, 7,* 243–275.

Pearson's Product-Moment Correlation Coefficient

Indices of correlation are useful descriptive statistics for describing the strength (and direction) of a relationship between two variables. We discussed the idea of correlation in chapter 4 and again here in chapter 9. We may want to compare performance on the first trial (pretest) of the finger maze with performance on the second trial (posttest). There are several indices of correlation depending on whether the dependent variable is continuous or dichotomous, interval or ordinal, and whether the relationship is assumed to be linear or nonlinear. Here we review the Pearson product-moment correlation coefficient, which is useful for continuous interval data in which a linear relationship is assumed to exist.

$$r = \frac{SS_{xy}}{\sqrt{SS_x \, SS_y}}$$

where SS_{xy} is the sum of the squared cross products:

$$SS_{xy} = \Sigma XY - \frac{(\Sigma X)(\Sigma Y)}{p}$$

where p = number of pairs

STEP 1.   *Table the data.*

Finger Maze Pretest (X)	Finger Maze Posttest (Y)
5	7
3	5
2	3
4	5
1	2

STEP 2.   *Square the Xs; Square the Ys; Multiply X with Y.*

X	X^2	Y	Y^2	XY
5	25	7	49	35
3	9	5	25	15
2	4	3	9	6
4	16	5	25	20
1	1	2	4	2

STEP 3.   *Sum each column from step 2.*

$X = 15$ $X^2 = 55$ $Y = 22$ $Y^2 = 112$ $XY = 78$

STEP 4.   *Compute r.*

$$r = \frac{78 - \dfrac{(15)(22)}{5}}{\sqrt{55 - \dfrac{15^2}{5} \quad 112 - \dfrac{22^2}{5}}} = +.9733$$

STEP 5.   *Interpret the results.*

If performance was good on the first trial, it was good on the second; and if it was poor on the first, it was poor on the second. The subjects maintained their relative position on the pretest to the posttest even though they all improved on the posttest.

Finger Maze

Experimenter: _____

Map Condition

Subject		Pretest	Posttest	Difference Score
1	Time to complete (Seconds)			
	Errors to completion			
2	Time to complete (Seconds)			
	Errors to completion			
3	Time to complete (Seconds)			
	Errors to completion			

Comments:

Finger Maze

Experimenter: _____

		Directions Condition		
Subject		Pretest	Posttest	Difference Score
1	Time to complete (Seconds)			
	Errors to completion			
2	Time to complete (Seconds)			
	Errors to completion			
3	Time to complete (Seconds)			
	Errors to completion			

Comments:

Finger Maze

Experimenter: _____ Date: _____

DV: TIME to complete maze or ERRORS (circle one)

Pretest maze: _____
Posttest maze: _____

Subject #	COND	Pretest	Posttest	Difference (Gain) Score

MAP PRE: $\bar{X} =$; Var =
MAP POST: $\bar{X} =$; Var =   ; $t_{observed} =$ $t_{crit} =$

NONMATCHING PRE: $\bar{X} =$; Var =
DIRECTIONS   POST: $\bar{X} =$; Var =   ; $t_{observed} =$ $t_{crit} =$

COMPARISON OF GAIN SCORES:

independent $t_{obs} =$ $t_{crit} =$

Finger Maze

Experimenter: _____ Date: _____

DV: TIME to complete maze or ERRORS (circle one)

Pretest maze: _____

Posttest maze: _____

Subject #	COND	Pretest	Posttest	Difference (Gain) Score

MAP PRE: $\bar{X} =$; Var =
MAP POST: $\bar{X} =$; Var =   ; $t_{observed} =$ $t_{crit} =$

NONMATCHING PRE: $\bar{X} =$; Var =
DIRECTIONS   POST: $\bar{X} =$; Var =   ; $t_{observed} =$ $t_{crit} =$

COMPARISON OF GAIN SCORES:

independent $t_{obs} =$ $t_{crit} =$

General Idea (Previous Research, Curiosity, Theory)

Tie the current idea into the idea from chapter 8. Can you also see connections to the study on the method of loci?

Explanatory Statement

Discuss how *cognitive map* fits into an explanatory statement.

Can you generate an alternative theory that could be tested with the current experiment?

Research Hypothesis/Descriptive Statement

Possible hypothesis: Presenting subjects with a physical map, because it facilitates the formation of a cognitive map, will lead to superior performance.

Alternative hypothesis: Formation of a cognitive map . . . (for you to complete)

Continued

196

Continued
Methods (Natural Observation, Survey, Field Experiment, Lab Experiment)

Lab experiment.

Dependent Variable(s)

Two dependent variables were discussed in the text. Why were both the number of wrong turns and time to get through the maze included as a measure of performance?

Operational Definition   Time is a relatively easy measure to define operationally.

In what sense is the maze itself a part of the operational definition? How is the maze operationally defined?

Predictor or Independent Variable

Type of studied representation.

Operational Definition   Operationally define
Map:

Directions:

In what sense is the maze itself a part of the operational definition? How is the maze operationally defined?

Continued

Design (Between, ► Pre-Post)

Pre-Post: Why did we choose the pre-post methodology? Below are the seven reasons scientists have given for using the pretest-posttest experimental design. Some, but not all, of the reasons below could be important in the current work. First, select those you believe to be important to the study at hand, then rank them from most to least important, and finally discuss how they would apply to the current work. Be specific.

Direction of the effect

Size of the effect

Increased sensitivity to the independent variable

Insurance against mortality

Insurance for random assignment

Continued

198

Continued
Ceiling and floor effects

Generalizing to the population

Subjects

(Complete the following for your institution according to its guidelines and procedures.)

Ethical considerations

Characteristics and Availability

Sampling Procedure and Number of Subjects

Continued

Control

Subject Assignment (Randomization, Matching)
Randomization:

Matching: The chapter does not specify matching. The pretest-posttest design does not require matching, but it is possible to match on the pretest score before introducing the treatment. Specify how this might be done. Does this change your answer about why the pre-post design was chosen?

Environment (Insured Equivalence, Yoking)
Insured equivalence:

Yoking: Not applicable.

Procedural Command Decisions (Ceiling Effect, Floor Effect)

How could you determine if a finger maze was likely to yield a ceiling effect or a floor effect? What would such effects do to the specific comparison of the current study?

Retrospective Confound Check (Assumed, Statistical, Rethink)

Selection, Mortality, History, Maturation, Reactivity,
► Testing, Instrumentation)
Assuming good experimental procedures, most of the typical rival hypotheses should be controlled. The short, nonthreatening nature of the experiment also aids in eliminating confounds as does the relative ease with which time can be measured.

Continued

Continued

Rethink: The only concern about measuring time would be to work out a method that would reduce the reaction time of the experimenter in stopping the timer.

Testing was considered a serious problem. It was controlled by extending the delay between pretest and the studying of the map or directions. Further, it was decided to use alternate forms of the maze. *Rethink:* Can we improve on this procedure still further?

Data Analysis

Descriptive Mean time to complete the pretest and posttest mazes. Mean errors to complete the pretest and posttest mazes.

Inferential Dependent *t*-tests can be used to see if the gains are significant. An independent *t*-test can be used to compare the gain scores of the two groups. (If subjects were matched on pretests, what statistic would you use instead of the independent *t*-test?)

Hypothetical Outcome Analysis

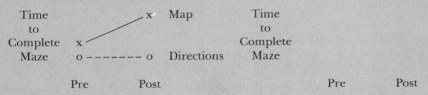

Transition Devices

For a paper to flow smoothly, the reader must be able to maintan a continuity of thought from one sentence to another and from one paragraph to another. Most of the time this continuity can be maintained by tieing some part of the new sentence back to some part of the previous sentence. When you cannot do this, you must warn the reader with an explicit transition device.

Sentences usually are associated by repeating propositions or ideas. There are two primary ways to repeat a proposition. You can repeat and then expand on a word or phrase used earlier. Alternatively, you can use a related word, including synonyms and pronouns, to repeat the proposition without repeating the exact wording.

Look at the above paragraph. Follow from sentence to sentence and see if you can identify the repetitions that held the paragraph together. In sentence three, the word *alternatively* is used to help make the transition. Sentence two helps hold the paragraph together by giving the reader an overview of what is to come; until the reader comes across "two primary ways," she or he will hold this sentence in mind.

Below are some particularly useful transition words and what they accomplish. These will serve you in a number of situations, but you will also often need a *transition paragraph*. It is usually a brief paragraph containing a summary of what has preceded it and an announcement of what is to come. Beginners *always* have too few transition paragraphs.

Device	Function
However, In contrast, On the other hand, But, Yet, Whereas, Alternatively, Nevertheless	Contrasts, contradicts, limits
In addition, Furthermore, Also, Moreover, Again, Likewise, Similarly	Adds to your previous point
In particular, Specifically	Provides support
First, Second, Finally	Lists
Thus, As a result, As a consequence, Therefore, Consequently	Leads to a conclusion
In summary, To summarize	Summarizes

Discussion Section

The discussion "funnels out" from the results section. It should begin with a summary (even if somewhat redundant) of the important findings of your work that were presented in the results section. Begin with the descriptive statements of the results to summarize the most important ones.

Following this summary, you now have an opportunity (for the first time) to tell how your descriptive statements relate to your theory, hypotheses, or explanatory statements. Tell the reader why something happened and what it means. A serious mistake made by some authors is to talk about the hypotheses as if the experiment was never even conducted. For example, one of our students was so convinced that our bookstore buy-back policy was so unfair that she conducted a phone survey. The data from the survey revealed little animosity on the part of the students in the poll toward the policy, yet she reached the same conclusion with which she began: they were really unhappy with the book buy-back policy.

The discussion should connect back to the introduction. Even if all did not go according to plan, it is important that this connection back to the introduction exist. The reader should be told whether the hypothesis was supported, disconfirmed, or a little of both. Other studies could be brought in from the literature at this time. This should be done judiciously but might include, for example, a paper that was not relevant given the introduction, but because of the results becomes important.

Finally, the discussion broadens in one of several ways. First, speculations on the importance of this study to the general issues of the introduction can be considered. Second, the author could consider future studies. Third, the discussion could consider the limitations of the current work. There is a danger in discussing the limitations of the research that should be considered. The experimenter may list problems without thinking about how the problem might affect the data. For example, minor changes in room temperature may be listed, but there may be no reason to suppose it would have had any noticeable affect on the results. Or the experimenter may try to explain the failure to get significant results by considering a confound that, if present, would have actually made it more likely to get a difference. For example, in our experiment in this chapter, we would be silly to explain failure to get a difference by saying that we discovered that all subjects in the map condition had photographic memories. The discussion section is a place to say what you think, but good sense must be exercised. You cannot say what you think without some support from your data.

General Information

Two maze configurations are given on succeeding pages. They may be taped to a piece of cardboard, such as the back of a tablet of paper, and cut out using sharp scissors or an X-ACTO knife. The subject will use a pencil or pen to trace his or her way through the maze. The pencil should be used in a vertical position. The maze could be elevated slightly off the table by placing small pieces of wood, the edge of magazines, match books, or other available things, under it. This will help ensure that the pencil does not slip out of the maze. A data sheet matching the maze should be placed on the table underneath the maze so the pencil directly marks the maze. Errors occur when entry into one of the dead ends is greater than 1 cm, marked by a dotted line on the data sheet.

The code for turns in the mazes are as follows:

Maze 1:   L R R S L L R L R S L R L L S S R R S L L S R L R R S L

Maze 2:   R S L R L R L L S R L R L S R R L L S R R L R S L L S R

Where L = left, R = right, S = straight, and the orientation of the movement is parallel to the direction of movement (i.e., the directions correspond to the movement of a Pac-man video game).

The maps for the mazes are reduced versions of the map templates.

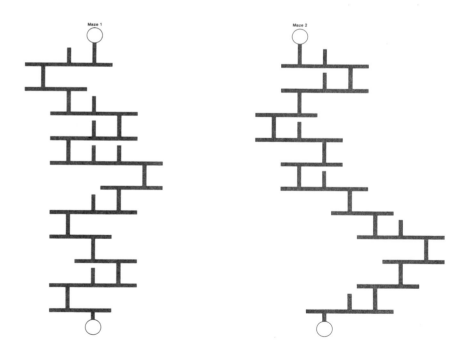

Maze 1

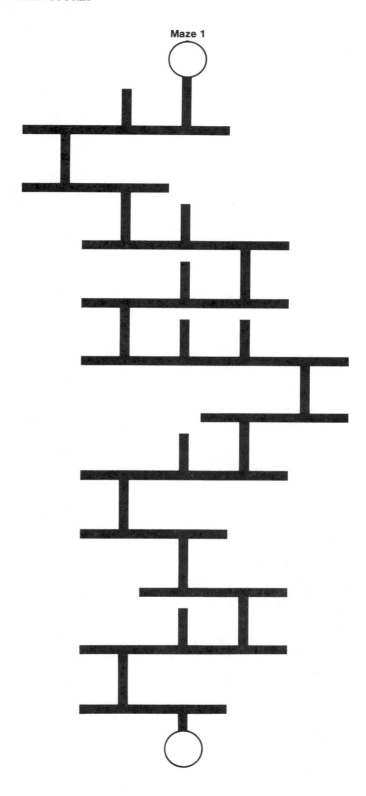

Maze 2

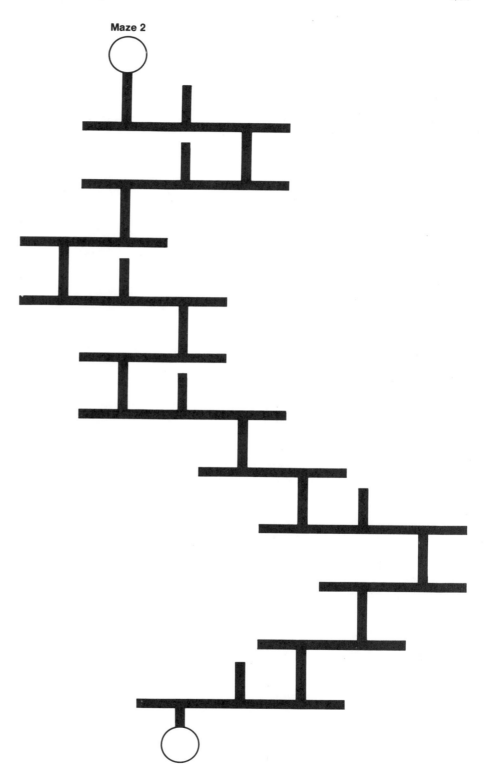

10 Sequencing & Counterbalancing

Overview

The idea of more precision introduced in chapter 8 and considered in chapter 9 is carried to its logical conclusion with the introduction of the repeated-measures design.

This chapter focuses on the sequencing confound and its two manifestations: order effects and carryover effects. Order effects add (or subtract) from behavior simply as a function of when, in a sequence of conditions, the observation is made. Carryover effects arise from the preceding experimental condition, adding (or subtracting) from behavior under current conditions. Counterbalancing techniques are related to these effects, and demonstrations of how the technique works are conducted in the context of a three-level within-subjects design. Complete counterbalancing requires $N!$ sequences, where N = the number of conditions in the experiment. Incomplete counterbalancing will also help to minimize the influence of a sequencing confound and requires fewer sequences than complete counterbalancing. The experiment is concerned with eye dominance in a sensory-motor task.

The repeated-measures ANOVA is introduced.

Tips on General Style focuses on the overall organization of the manuscript. Tips on Specific Style focuses on the shortest, most difficult to write, part of the psychology paper: the abstract.

Sequencing Confounds and Counterbalancing

"Who's the bigger fool, the fool or the fool who follows him?"

—*Obi-Wan Kenobi*

Most, about 90%, of those reading this chapter will be right-handed. The other 10%, with a few exceptions, show a preference for using their left hand. As with other minorities, left-handedness has been viewed negatively by society. For example, the words *sinister* and *gauche* make reference to the lefty, *dexterity* to the righty. These differences in handedness are not merely interesting individual differences but have been linked to other psychological functions. Most notably, differences in handedness appear to reflect differences in how and where language is represented in the hemispheres of the brain.

Although handedness is the most notable distinction between the left and right halves of our bodies, others exist as well. The study discussed in this chapter is concerned with eye dominance. Some people rely more on their right eye in focusing and locating visual objects in space, whereas others tend to rely on their left eye. This difference may also have deeper psychological implications. One possibility is that because English is read left to right, eye dominance may be a factor in reading time and comprehension. Another interesting example comes from the world of sports. In major league baseball, there are a greater number of players who are mixed dominant than would be expected by chance. A mixed-dominant person shows one handedness preference and a different eye preference. This may be a pattern of dominance that actually helps the player. For example, a left-handed batter who is right-eye dominant may have a fraction of a second more time between when he sees the ball and when he has to swing, or he may have a better view of the pitched ball because the left-handed batter has his right eye facing more directly toward the pitcher than a left-handed batter who is also left-eye dominant.

In this study we want to determine if eye dominance does, in fact, play a role in a general visual-motor task. This general information could then be combined with handedness information if we wanted also to answer some questions about mixed-dominance effects. However, we will not design the experiment to investigate mixed dominance because there will likely be very few available individuals falling into that category. Instead, we will focus on eye dominance alone but will record handedness information.

Several aspects of the experiment are relatively simple. First, we require only one independent variable: eye dominance. The simplest experiment would compare people using their dominant eye with people using their nondominant eye. However, we should also include a condition where subjects use both eyes, because if one eye really dominates when we use both eyes, then we should observe that performance with the dominant eye is similar to performance with both eyes. According to this working hypothesis, when people locate a visual object with two eyes, they are really only using one: their dominant eye. Thus, our independent variable will have three levels: dominant eye, nondominant eye, and both eyes.

A second simple decision is what the task subjects will perform and what dependent variable we will measure. This decision is easy because it is a command decision from among a number of alternatives. The task should be visual, require subjects to perform some action, and involve locating something in space. These criteria immediately suggest some task such as darts, ring toss, bean bag toss, or the like. More-sophisticated equipment exists, but any of these will meet our criteria. Thus, the decision will depend in large part on what apparatus is available. The dependent variable should simply be some measure of how far the tossed object is from the target.

A third decision is whether to use a between-subjects design or a within-subjects design. Some of the thinking behind this decision was discussed in chapter 9. In the pretest-posttest design, subjects were measured twice on the dependent variable. However, any particular subject received only one level of the independent variable. A pretest-posttest version of the current experiment would mean that subjects would be in either the Dominant-Eye, the Nondominant-Eye, or the Both-Eyes condition. On the other hand, if the subjects are used in all three conditions, we would have a **repeated-measures design.**

Repeated Measures

There are many advantages to testing a subject repeatedly under the different conditions of the experiment. Take the situation where we would like to measure some aspect of a person's ability to use his or her dominant eye, nondominant eye, or both eyes. We need three conditions for the experiment: one where the subject uses the dominant eye, another where the subject uses the nondominant eye, and a third where the subject uses both eyes. We could use the same subject in all conditions, having the subject sometimes use the dominant eye, sometimes the nondominant eye, and sometimes both eyes.

The above experiment can serve to exemplify the *economy gained* by the use of the repeated-measures procedure. The alternative experimental design would be the between-subjects procedure described in chapter 6. That design would require that we have three groups of subjects. One obvious advantage to the repeated-measures procedure is that three times as much data can be gathered from the same number of subjects as compared with the between-subjects procedure.

A second major advantage to the repeated-measures procedure is *perfect matching*. We discussed in chapter 8 the advantages of matching subjects in the different conditions of the experiment. If we use the same subject, we have matched on all possible variables. Thus, we have an incredibly sensitive experiment; one that is capable of picking up the smallest differences. Similarly, we can be certain that no selection confounds are present. That is, we can be certain that any differences that could have existed because of a bad randomization of subjects into conditions of the experiment are eliminated. The advantage here is that, although randomization works best with a large number of subjects, a within-subjects design ensures comparability with only a few subjects.

A third reason for the repeated-measures procedure is that sometimes it is *demanded by the nature of the experiment*. Suppose we want to scale a series of photographs for their beauty. It would not make much sense to have an individual rate only one of the photographs and then try to make sense of a scale based on each photograph being rated by a different person. Obviously a meaningful scale of beauty should be derived using the repeated-measures procedure. Experiments concerned with learning and practice effects also demand the use of repeated measures because the interest is in the change in behavior that comes with experience. Developmental changes are another example of a topic that often makes use of repeated measures (e.g., a longitudinal study).

Although there are many advantages of the repeated-measures procedure, there are also some potential problems with its use. Primary among the potential problems is the possibility of a sequencing confound. The sequencing confound or effect occurs when the conditions of one trial persist and thereby affect performance on the next trial. In a learning experiment we would expect such a sequencing effect and be interested in studying it, but in the kind of experiment considered here, it would clearly be undesirable. Using the dominant eye may affect how you later perform with the nondominant eye, or vice versa. **Sequencing** effects are those attributable to the sequence in which the subject experiences different levels of the independent variable.

Consider the following study. A doctor wants to compare two drugs reportedly capable of improving learning. The doctor gave the subjects Drug A and measured how long it took them to learn a list of historical dates. The doctor then gave the subjects Drug B and measured how long it took them to learn a different list of historical dates. The doctor found that Drug A led to faster learning than Drug B.

A rival hypothesis is that Drug A was still in the person's system when Drug B was administered, thus making the effect of B contaminated by A. The performance in B could have been poorer simply because it was the second list of dates that subjects learned and the first list confused the subject trying to learn the second set of dates.

How can such sequencing effects be controlled? One way is through the experimenter's knowledge of the topic and his or her ability to design the experiment in ways to prevent such unwanted effects. One way of reducing possible sequencing effects is to use a long spacing between trials (called the intertrial interval). This relatively simple technique can be an important way of ensuring a well-designed experiment.

Another way of dealing with sequencing effects is to make them part of the experiment. By presenting the conditions to the subjects in different orders, it is possible to eliminate *almost* all occurrences of sequencing effects. As we will see, the one confound that cannot be eliminated in a repeated-measures design is one where a condition has a unique and unusual effect on the conditions that follow it.

For the eye-dominance experiment using dart-throwing accuracy, several reasons point to a within-subjects, or repeated-measures, design. First, we can expect a great deal of random error if we had different subjects perform in different conditions. Second, we probably want to match on several factors, including handedness. Third, we can assume any sequencing effects present can be handled by the appropriate counterbalancing technique. Let us consider each of these points in turn.

The first reason for using a repeated-measures design is to increase the sensitivity of the experiment. In this study, we can expect that there will be vast differences between subjects in their performance on the task due to factors such as past experience and skill at darts. These individual differences would probably be so great that we would require a large number of subjects to reveal differences between the two monocular (one-eye) conditions (i.e., between the dominant and nondominant conditions). If we did choose a between-subjects design and we randomly assigned subjects to conditions, we would have an internally valid study. However, because there would be so much difference between subjects in dart-throwing ability within the same condition, our statistics would not be very powerful. The statistics might not be able to detect differences between conditions, and thus, our experiment would not be very sensitive.

Second, we want to be able to match on a number of factors. Recall that a variable we want to match should be one that is highly correlated with the dependent variable. Further, if we want to match on more than one variable that is highly correlated with the dependent variable, we must pick those that are not correlated with each other. This, as we discussed, becomes increasingly difficult. In this case, because only 10% of the population is left-handed, we may have difficulty obtaining enough lefties to represent them equally in the three conditions. In addition, other factors that could reduce the sensitivity of the experiment, such as previous experience with the task and visual acuity, may also be factors on which we wish to match. Again, these considerations lead to a repeated-measures design. By having the same subjects in all conditions, there is perfect matching.

The third consideration is the expected effects of sequencing confounds. If certain sequencing confounds may be present, this would be sufficient reason *not* to use a within-subjects design, despite the other advantages.

Sequencing Confounds

Begin by pretending that we will give all the subjects the three conditions in the following order: (1) both eyes, (2) nondominant eye, and (3) dominant eye. Further assume that there are no real differences among the three conditions. How might the order in which we presented the conditions produce differences in the dependent variable?

First, performance in the Nondominant-Eye condition might be worse than performance in the Dominant-Eye condition simply because it was first. This is one type of sequencing confound: an **order effect.** An order effect is a systematic bias in the data that is due to when a condition occurred. Order effects do not depend on the condition, but rather on the order.

For the three conditions in our experiment if there were an effect of order that contributed +1 to the second condition and +2 to the third condition, we would have:

Both	Nondominant	Dominant
0	1	2

If we reversed the order, the effect would be the same:

Dominant	Nondominant	Both
0	1	2

The effect is due to the order, not to what conditions preceded it. Thus, in the first case, Nondominant-Eye condition receives a systematic influence of +1 because it is second, not because it occurred after the Both-Eyes condition.

In some situations order effects are obvious, but in others they may be more subtle. Suppose you are a shoe manufacturer and you want to prove that your running shoe is superior to brand X running shoes. You could arrange for 20 persons to run a mile in your shoes and then have them switch to brand X and run a second mile. If you had your subjects run their hardest and gave them only a minute to change shoes between miles, clearly the order confound would work to your advantage. After just running a hard mile in your shoes, the subjects will run much slower in brand X shoes because they could still be tired from the first mile run. You have not proven anything by doing the experiment this way. Undoubtedly you can come up with additional cases where order effects would occur.

Second, performance in the Dominant-Eye condition might be affected because it followed the Nondominant-Eye condition. This is called a **carry-over effect.** A carryover effect refers to a confound that is due to which condition precedes which condition. The difference between an order effect and a carryover effect is that an order effect depends only on the position of the condition within a series, whereas a carryover effect depends on whether some aspect of one condition carries over to affect the subsequent condition(s).

If we assume that there is a carryover effect where both eyes help, nondominant hurts, and dominant has no effect and if we assume that the effects carry over for only a short time, we might have:

Both		Nondominant		Dominant
0	carryover	+ 1	carryover	− 1

If we reverse the order, we have:

Dominant		Nondominant		Both
0	carryover	0	carryover	− 1

Fortunately, both of these confounds are *usually* curable. Whether there is a cure depends on whether the effect of the confound can be assumed to be linear. Linear effects of either type are eliminated by counterbalancing; the first example is a linear effect because as order changed from first to second to third each condition benefited by 1 unit. If you plotted this on a graph, the effect of the confound would be a straight line. Nonlinear order effects can also be eliminated. If, however, the effect is nonlinear and is a carryover effect, there is *no* way to eliminate its impact on a within-subjects design. In this case the experimenter must switch to a between-subjects design or go to great lengths to ensure that the carryover effect has been eliminated by procedural means (e.g., wait a month). The second example above is nonlinear; try plotting the effect of the confound against the conditions.

We now turn to specific counterbalancing procedures designed to eliminate sequencing confounds when possible.

Complete Counterbalancing

Conceptually, the simplest thing to do to get rid of a sequencing confound is to present the conditions in all possible orders (B = Both, N = Nondominant, D = Dominant):

B	N	D
B	D	N
N	B	D
N	D	B
D	N	B
D	B	N

This counterbalancing is called **complete counterbalancing** because it uses all possible orders. The number of orders required for complete counterbalancing is $N!$ (N-factorial or $N \times N - 1 \times N - 2 \times \ldots \times 2 \times 1$) where N is the number of conditions. For our experiment, $N = 3$ so there are $3 \times 2 \times 1$ or 6 possible orders.

These six orders meet two very important criteria. If each subject received one of the orders, then by the end of the experiment we would be certain that (1) each condition occurred in each position equally often, and (2) each condition preceded and followed every other condition equally often. For example, N occurs twice in each position, and it precedes D twice and follows D twice. The first criterion guards against order effects while the second guards against carryover effects. See Table 10-1.

The problem with complete counterbalancing is that the number of orders and therefore the number of subjects we must use increases quite dramatically with increases in the number of conditions (e.g., $4! = 24$,

Table 10-1   Illustration of how the four sequencing effects accumulate in a counterbalanced design. The summation shows how counterbalancing equates the three conditions unless the effect is a nonlinear carryover effect.

LINEAR ORDER: Any condition in the second position is helped by +1, and any condition in the third position is helped by +2:

B	N	D		0	1	2
B	D	N		0	1	2
N	B	D		0	1	2
N	D	B		0	1	2
D	N	B		0	1	2
D	B	N		0	1	2

Total confound on:
B = 0+0+1+2+2+1 = 6
N = 1+2+0+0+1+2 = 6
D = 2+1+2+1+0+0 = 6

LINEAR CARRYOVER: Each condition helps *all* subsequent conditions by +1, and these effects accumulate. (For example, in the sequence BND, B helps N by +1 and helps D by +1; N also helps D by +1, making the total carryover to D a +2.)

B	N	D		0	1	2
B	D	N		0	1	2
N	B	D		0	1	2
N	D	B		0	1	2
D	N	B		0	1	2
D	B	N		0	1	2

Total confound on:
B = 0+0+1+2+2+1 = 6
N = 1+2+0+0+1+2 = 6
D = 2+1+2+1+0+0 = 6

NONLINEAR ORDER: Any condition in the second position is helped by +1, and any condition in the third position is helped by +5:

B	N	D		0	1	5
B	D	N		0	1	5
N	B	D		0	1	5
N	D	B		0	1	5
D	N	B		0	1	5
D	B	N		0	1	5

Total confound on:
B = 0+0+1+5+5+1 = 12
N = 1+5+0+0+1+5 = 12
D = 5+1+5+1+0+0 = 12

NONLINEAR CARRYOVER: B helps the subsequent condition by +1; N helps the subsequent condition by +5; and D has 0 carryover influence.

B	N	D		0	1	5
B	D	N		0	1	0
N	B	D		0	5	1
N	D	B		0	5	0
D	N	B		0	0	5
D	B	N		0	0	1

Total confound on:
B = 0+0+5+0+5+0 = 10
N = 1+0+0+0+0+1 = 2
D = 5+1+1+5+0+0 = 12

5! = 120, 6! = 720). Psychologists have devised a number of procedures that deal with order and carryover confounds but require many fewer subjects.

Incomplete Counterbalancing

To do **incomplete counterbalancing,** begin by writing down your conditions:

-----› B(oth) -------------› N(ondominant) -------------› D(ominant) ------
              !st   2nd   3rd & Last

This will not necessarily be one of your orders, but you will make reference to this starting point.

The trick to incomplete counterbalancing is to pick out the sequences that meet the two criteria above. There is a simple algorithm to help us, which is also illustrated in Figure 10–1.

For the first sequence use the following formula: 1st, 2nd, Last, 3rd, Next-to-Last, 4th, Next-to-Next-to-Last, 5th, and so forth.

Our first condition in our starting point is B, the second is N, and the last is D. Thus our first sequence would be:

B   N   D

The second order is created by following the arrows in our starting diagram for each condition in the first sequence. For example, the arrow from B leads to N; thus the first condition of our second sequence would be N. The arrow from N leads to D; thus D would be the second condition in the second sequence. Finally, the arrow leading from D takes us back to B, making B the third condition in our second sequence. The second sequence should be:

N   D   B

This idea of following the arrows can now create the third condition. Start with the second sequence and follow the arrows to generate the third sequence:

D   B   N

Because we have three conditions, we stop after we have generated three orders. This gives us the orders below:

B   N   D ←———————— (according to formula)
N   D   B ←———————— (following arrows in Fig. 10–1)
D   B   N ←———————— (following arrows in Fig. 10–1)

Each condition is in each position equally often, meeting our first criterion. However, N follows B twice (order 1 and order 3) and B follows N only once (order 2). Thus, these three orders do not satisfy our second criterion of counterbalancing. With an odd number of conditions, we will never be able to meet the second criterion with only this number of sequences. Alternatively, if we had an even number of sequences, we could stop now and would have met both criteria.

Figure 10–1   Illustration of algorithm to produce an incomplete counterbalancing scheme for N conditions. The results next to the algorithm are for $N = 7$, with labels for the conditions: A B C D E F G.

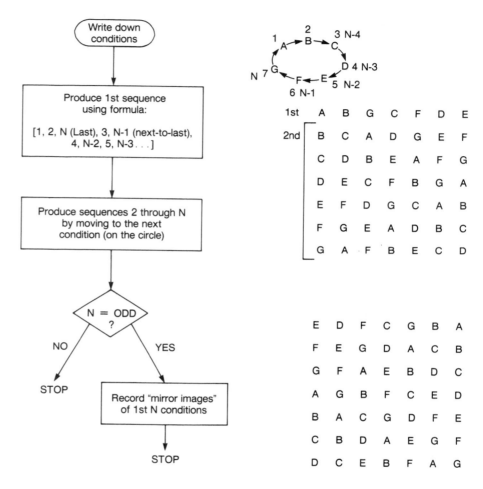

However, the third step in our algorithm is very simple: If there are an odd number of conditions, take each order from step 2 and create a mirror image of the orders.

Following this third step, we would have the three orders on the left and generate the three mirror image orders on the right. The line separating our first three orders from the last three is a representation of the mirror.

B	N	D		D	N	B
N	D	B		B	D	N
D	B	N		N	B	D

We now have all the conditions necessary to meet the two criteria. Every condition appears in every position twice. Every condition precedes and follows every other condition three times. For example, B precedes D in orders 1, 5, and 6, and follows D in orders 2, 3, and 4. In general, the number of conditions needed to do incomplete counterbalancing is not $N!$, but rather N if the number of conditions is even or $2N$ if the number of conditions is odd. However, when $N = 3$, $N! = 2N$. Thus, we actually have generated all possible conditions (complete counterbalancing) with incomplete counterbalancing when $N = 3$.

When the number of conditions is greater than three, the difference between the number of incomplete and complete counterbalancing sequences is quite dramatic. With four conditions, complete counterbalancing would require 24 orders, whereas incomplete counterbalancing would require only 4 orders. With five conditions, the comparison is between 120 and 10; with six conditions, the comparison is between 720 and 6.

The reader should try to work out the 10 orders required for incomplete counterbalancing of the conditions: A B C D E.

1st order from formula: A B E __ __
2nd–5th orders: B C A __ __
              C D B __ __
              D E C __ __
              E A D __ __
6th–10th orders (mirror reversals):
              __ __ A C B
              __ __ B D C
              __ __ C E D
              __ __ D A E

Random Counterbalancing

Another counterbalancing method that greatly reduces the number of orders required is **random counterbalancing.** In this method we begin with complete or incomplete counterbalancing and then randomly sample from those orders. This has one advantage over incomplete counterbalancing and one disadvantage. With incomplete counterbalancing, the number of subjects we use must be a multiple of the number of orders. So, for our particular study, we could use 6, 12, 18, or 24 subjects, but we could not use 25 subjects because it would destroy the counterbalancing. With random counterbalancing, no such restriction exists. However, with random counterbalancing we are ensuring that *in the long run* the sequencing effects would be controlled. Thus, the success of random counterbalancing depends on the number of subjects you use: the more subjects the more effective the random counterbalancing procedure.

The Experiment

People will perform a visual-motor task better using their dominant eye than using their nondominant eye. Further, dominant-eye use will lead to performance comparable to using both eyes.

This hypothesis must have some operationally defined terms before it is a good research hypothesis. First, we need a measure of eye dominance. Then we need to make command decisions about the visual-motor task and the measure of performance. We will assume for these last two decisions that you will have access to a dart board and that the dependent variable will be the distance the dart sticks from the center of the board. Further decisions concerning the task include the distance from the target, the number of trials under each condition, what to do with mechanical recording errors (i.e., the dart does not stick).

Our measure of eye dominance could simply be self-report. However, people may not have an opinion about eye dominance as they do with handedness. In fact, self-report of handedness is often misleading. For example, although it seems true that there are pure right-handers, left-handers differ in their degree of left-handedness. Tests such as having people use scissors to cut out a drawing are often used. In addition, familial sinistrality (history of left-handedness in the family) is also a factor. Thus, we will use a more objective measure than self-report.

Draw a small target on the blackboard. Have your subject overlap their hands in front of them so that there is a small hole through which to view the target. Then have your subject focus on the target through the slit in the hands. Make certain that they use both eyes to fixate on the target. With an index card, cover one of the eyes of the subject and ask if the object moved out of sight. Then have the subject fixate again with both eyes and repeat the procedure with the other eye. When the dominant eye is covered, the object will disappear. It is possible, although unlikely, that subjects will experience movement when each eye is covered. In these cases we could repeat the procedure and get a measure of how much movement the subject experienced, or we can dismiss the subject from the experiment as ambiocular. In most cases, however, when the dominant eye is covered, the target will completely disappear from the slit.

Assignment of Subjects to Order

The possible orders are:

B	N	D
B	D	N
N	B	D
N	D	B
D	B	N
D	N	B

We will randomly assign one of these orders to each subject in groups of six. In other words, the first subject will receive one randomly chosen order. This order will then be eliminated from consideration and the second subject will receive one order randomly chosen from the remaining five. We will continue in this way until we have assigned the six orders. Then we will repeat this procedure for the 7th subject through the 12th subject.

Procedural Details

Subjects will stand 6 ft away from a dart board that is covered with a sheet of paper that is blank except for a red bull's-eye that will serve as a target. For each condition in the experiment, subjects will throw five darts at the target. The dependent variable, distance of the dart from the target, will be measured after each throw. Subjects will then rest for 5 minutes and participate in the next condition.

Two factors in this design will handle the problem of darts that hit the board but do not stick. One is the use of sheets of paper over the dart board for each condition. Another is inherent in the collection of multiple data points for each subject for each condition. For example, if one dart misses the board, we will compute the mean miss-length on the basis of four trials. If we wanted to we could also keep track of the number of complete misses and analyze these data separately from the miss-length scores. These two methods should tend to be correlated. That is, if the miss-length is large in the Nondominant-Eye condition, we would be likely to observe that the most complete misses occurred in the Nondominant-Eye condition.

The remainder of the procedural details can be discussed in lab. The reader is left with the task of considering other factors important to this study.

Data Analysis

Data analysis will begin by finding the mean miss-distance for each subject in each condition. Each order should then be unscrambled so that the data can be recorded in a consistent manner:

	Mean Missed Distance		
	Both Eyes	Nondominant Eye	Dominant Eye
Subject			
1			
2			
etc.			

These means will then be submitted to a one-factor, three-level ANOVA. ANOVAs were first discussed in chapter 7. The main difference here is that because this was a within-subjects design, we can take advantage of this fact just as we were able to when we used a dependent t-test.

Once you have conducted the ANOVA and find a significant effect, you will want to isolate where the effect lies. For example, it may be that the Both-Eye and Dominant-Eye conditions are equivalent and that both conditions are superior to the Nondominant-Eye condition. The ANOVA does not tell you which conditions are different from which. You should follow a significant ANOVA with post-hoc comparisons (see chapter 7).

Key Words   carryover effect   random counterbalancing
                 complete counterbalancing   repeated-measures design
                 incomplete counterbalancing   sequencing
                 order effect

**Additional
Reading**
Ruggieri, V., Bergerone, C., Cei, A., & Ceridono, D. (1980). Relationship between ocular dominance and field dependence/independence. *Perceptual and Motor Skills, 51,* 1247–1251.

Ruggieri, V., Cei, A., Ceridono, D., & Bergerone, C. (1980). Dimensional approach to the study of sighting dominance. *Perceptual and Motor Skills, 51,* 247–251.

Woo, T. L. (1928). Dextrality and sinistrality of hand and eye, 2d memoir. *Biometrika, 20,* 79–148.

Repeated-Measures ANOVA

When the same subject participates in all conditions of an experiment or when the subjects from all conditions are matched on a variable, then the experimenter can eliminate random error from the statistical test. With two levels of the independent variable, this can be done with a correlated t-test. With three or more levels, the repeated-measures ANOVA removes random error by extracting the variance due to subjects, which would otherwise be in the error term.

SOURCE	DF	SS	MS	F
VISION	$v - 1$	$\dfrac{\overset{v\ s}{\Sigma(\Sigma X)^2}}{s} - \dfrac{\overset{v\ s}{(\Sigma\Sigma X)^2}}{vs}$	SS_v/df_v	MS_v/MS_e
SUBJECTS	$s - 1$	$\dfrac{\overset{s\ v}{\Sigma(\Sigma X)^2}}{v} - \dfrac{\overset{v\ s}{(\Sigma\Sigma X)^2}}{vs}$		
ERROR	$(v - 1)(s - 1)$	$\overset{v\ s}{\Sigma\Sigma X^2} - \dfrac{\overset{v\ s}{\Sigma(\Sigma X)^2}}{s} - \dfrac{\overset{s\ v}{\Sigma(\Sigma X)^2}}{v} + \dfrac{\overset{v\ s}{(\Sigma\Sigma X)^2}}{vs}$		

STEP 0. State the null and alternative hypotheses.

Null: Means from the v conditions are equal.
Alternative: The null is not true.

STEP 1. Table the data.

(Here we use the same data as statistics review of between-subjects ANOVA, chapter 7. The data *do not* convey any indication of matching or repeated trials by the same subject. Which analysis should be more powerful for these data, the between-subjects or repeated-measures ANOVAs?)

	Both Eyes	Vision Based On Dominant Eye	Nondominant Eye
S#1:	7	5	1
2:	6	4	0
3:	5	6	2
4:	4	5	3

STEP 2. Sum each column; square each sum; divide each squared sum by the number of subjects in that condition; total these values. (Note: Same as step 2 of between-subjects ANOVA.)

	$\overset{s}{\Sigma X}$	$\overset{s}{(\Sigma X)^2}$	$\dfrac{\overset{s}{(\Sigma X)^2}}{s}$
Both	22	484	121
Dominant	20	400	100
Nondom	6	36	$\dfrac{9}{230} = \dfrac{\overset{v\ s}{\Sigma(\Sigma X)^2}}{s}$

STEP 3.   *Sum all data in table; square that sum; divide it by total number of data points. (Note: Same as step 3 of between-subjects ANOVA.)*

$$\frac{(\Sigma\Sigma X)^2}{v \times s} = \frac{(48)^2}{3 \times 4} = \frac{2304}{12} = 192$$

STEP 4.   *Square each data point in the table; sum these squared values. (Note: Same as step 4 of between-subjects ANOVA.)*

$$\Sigma\Sigma X^2 = 7^2 + 6^2 + 5^2 + \ldots + 0^2 + 2^2 + 3^2 = 242$$

STEP 5.   *Sum each row (i.e., each subject); square each sum; divide each sum by the number of levels of the independent variable; total these results.*

	ΣX	$(\Sigma X)^2$	$(\Sigma X)^2/v$	
Subj #1:	13	169	56.33	
2:	10	100	33.33	
3:	13	169	56.33	
4:	12	144	48.00	
			$193.99 = \dfrac{\Sigma(\Sigma X)^2}{v}$	

STEP 6.   *Calculate the SSs.*

$SS_v = [\text{Step 2}] - [\text{Step 3}] = 230 - 192 = 38$

$SS_s = [\text{Step 5}] - [\text{Step 3}] = 193.99 - 192 = 1.99$

$SS_e = [\text{Step 4}] - [\text{Step 2}] - [\text{Step 5}] + [\text{Step 3}] = 242 - 230 - 193.99 + 192 = 10.01$

STEP 7.   *Calculate DFs.*

$$df_V = k - 1 = 3 - 1 = 2$$

$$df_s = s - 1 = 4 - 1 = 3$$

$$df_e = (v - 1)(s - 1) = (3 - 1)(4 - 1) = 6$$

STEP 8.   *Compute mean squares.*

$$MS_v = 38.3/2 = 19.15$$

$$MS_s = [\text{not necessary to compute } F]$$

$$MS_e = 10.0/6 = 1.668$$

STEP 9.   *Compute F.*

$$F = 19.15/1.668 = 11.48$$

Source	DF	SS	MS	F	Sig Level
V	2	38.3	19.15	11.48	.01
Subject	3	2.29			
Error	6	9.71	1.66		

STEP 10.   Compare the observed F *with the critical* F.

The observed $F(2, 6) = 11.48$. This should be compared with the critical F in Table C with 2 degrees of freedom in the numerator and 6 in the denominator. The observed F could have occurred if the three conditions were equal less than 1 chance in 100. Clearly, we would reject the null hypothesis and conclude that the conditions are not equal.

Comparison of repeated-measures and between-subjects ANOVA

The reader may have noticed some relationships between this repeated-measures ANOVA and the between-subjects ANOVA discussed in chapter 7. First, all computations for the independent variable effects were identical. Thus, the difference lies in the computation of the error term. The degrees of freedom for subjects (3) and error (6) in the repeated-measures designs sums to the degrees of freedom for the between-subjects ANOVA (9). The same is true of the sum-of-squares.

The repeated measures F is based on fewer degrees of freedom, but usually is accompanied by a smaller MS_{error}. In the current example, however, while power was lost with fewer degrees of freedom, it was not compensated by a corresponding decrease in the MS_{error}. Thus, we actually observed a smaller (though still significant) F in the current analysis. This highlights that bad matching is worse than no matching.

Ocular Dominance

Experimenter: _____
Distance from target: 6′   Rest Period: 5 min
Height from floor: _____

Orders:
1: _____   2: _____   3: _____   4: _____   5: _____   6: _____

Data are missed distances measured in _____.
Complete misses are indicated by an "x" in place of a score.

Scratch out one:
MEANS (M) DO NOT INCLUDE COMPLETE MISSES.

MEANS (M) INCLUDE ESTIMATES OF ALL COMPLETE MISSES.

Subject	Order	D-Eye	Dominant						Nondominant						Both					
			1	2	3	4	5	M	1	2	3	4	5	M	1	2	3	4	5	M

Ocular Dominance

Experimenter: _____ Date: _____

Complete Misses were handled by:

Distance from subject: 6′   From Floor: _____

Mean Missed Distance (in _____s)

Subject	Order	Dominant	Nondominant	Both

ANOVA Summary table:

Source	DF	SS	MS	F_{OBS}	Prob
Eye	2				
Subject					
Error					

Comments:

General Idea (Previous Research, Curiosity, Theory)

People's bodies are assymetric in function. The left hemisphere differs from the right hemisphere. The left hand differs in efficiency of function from the right hand.

Explanatory Statement

Assuming functional assymetry at other levels leads to the following explanatory statement based on the category principle:
The left and right half of the body differ in their efficiency at performing different functions. One half will always be superior to the other, often to the extent of being comparable to using both halves.

Research Hypothesis/Descriptive Statement

People will show a difference in a visual-motor task when allowed to use their dominant eye compared with the nondominant eye, and this dominance will be such as to equate the dominant eye with both eyes.

Methods (Natural Observation, Survey, Field Experiment, Lab Experiment)

Subjects are not randomly assigned to conditions. Is this still a true experiment? Can we make causal claims? What is the logic behind your answer?

Dependent Variable(s)

Missed distance.

Operational Definition   Operationally define Missed Distance: (Do not forget complete misses.)

Predictor or Independent Variable

Eye(s) used.

Operational Definition   Operationally define Dominant Eye:

Continued

230

Continued
Design (Between, Pre-Post, ► Within)

What is the difference between this within-subjects design and the pre-post design?

Subjects

Ethical Considerations

Characteristics and Availability

Are there any characteristics that would lead to the exclusion of subjects from your experiment? What does this do to external validity?

Sampling Procedure and Number of Subjects

Control

Subject Assignment (Randomization, Matching)
Randomization: Randomly assigned to counterbalancing order.
Matching: Perfect.

Environment (Insured Equivalance, Yoking, ► Counterbalancing)
Insured equivalence:

Continued

Yoking:

Counterbalancing: Complete counterbalancing; six orders.

Procedural Command Decisions (Ceiling Effect, Floor Effect)

Why was each subject given five darts to throw in each condition?

Deciding what type of dart board to use, how far away all subjects should stand from target, whether or not to count darts completely missing the target board, and so forth.

Retrospective Confound Check (Assumed, Statistical, Rethink)

(Selection, Mortality, History, Maturation, Reactivity, Testing/► Sequencing, Instrumentation)

Selection: Perfect matching eliminates any possible selection confound.

Testing/Sequencing: Complete counterbalancing should control for all but nonlinear carryover effects. Nothing in a dart-throwing experiment leads us to suspect such a carryover effect, so this rival hypothesis can be ruled out.

Continue for the remaining confounding variables.

Continued

232

Continued
Data Analysis

Descriptive   Mean missed distance will be computed for each subject for each condition. Complete misses can be excluded from the computation of the means, or an estimate can be made.

Inferential   A one-factor, three-level analysis of variance will be conducted on the means. Post-hoc tests will follow a significant F.

Hypothetical Outcome Analysis

Compare the following two patterns of outcomes and discuss them in terms of the explanatory statement and the research hypothesis. Is there a problem? With what?

PREDICTION 1	PREDICTION 2
Both > Dom > Nondom	Both = Dom > Nondom

Organization of the Manuscript

The sections and subsections of your manuscript supply a large step toward the overall organization of your report. This box, and future boxes, gives some advice on more subtle organizational questions. The reader must follow your thinking from the introduction of the concepts and problem, through your operationalization of the concepts (i.e., the methods) and the findings, to your conclusions. To do this, the paper must supply the right information *and supply it at the right time.* You must never use an idea, concept, or term until the reader is prepared for it.

A problem that often arises in method sections is that to explain one idea, you must make reference to another idea from later in the paper. For example, if the subject section requires that you classify subjects as right-eye dominant, the reader would like to know at that time what it means to be right-eye dominant, but the definition of right-eye dominant does not occur until the procedure section.

This problem can be eased by (1) remembering that the end of the introduction can supply valuable information about the experiment, (2) realizing that concepts and operational definitions can be used differently, and (3) moving the information. Using point 1, we could make an effort to explicate the idea of eye dominance in the introduction, so that by the time the reader reaches the subject section, he or she will have an idea of what the concept is. Using point 2, we could refer to the *concept* of eye dominance in the subject section even though the operationalization of the idea occurs later in the procedure section. Using point 3, we could actually move the eye-dominance procedure to the subject section. Even though it is really procedural information, if it makes it clearer to the reader, go ahead and move it. Later, in the procedure you can simply refer to the procedure because it has been previously defined.

The biggest problem writers have is that they leave out too much information. What seems to them to be a logical next step leaves the reader at a loss. Direct your paper to an intelligent but uninformed person. Give your paper to your roommate or classmate to read, one not afraid of offending you. Does he or she follow the logic of your paper?

The Abstract

The abstract is, in one sense, the most important part of your paper and is the most difficult section to write well. It is important because it is used by other scientists to decide whether or not to consider your work. It is difficult to write because it is seldom more than 100 (to 150) words and yet must include something about the problem, the methods, the results, and conclusions, with the results being most important. It must both interest and inform the reader. Stylistically it is placed on a separate page following the title page and is not indented.

(The above is, incidentally 100 words.)

The abstract should be accurate and exclude information not in the paper; it should be self-contained, nonevaluative, and specific.

Factorials
&
Interactions

Overview

This chapter discusses the most often used design in experimental psychology, the factorial design. The difference between a main effect and an interaction is discussed, and the limitations about conclusions of the main effect when an interaction is present are stressed. Higher order factorials are also considered. The experiment for the chapter is on personal space and the difference between subject characteristics as an independent variable (a blocking variable), and independent variables that are randomly assigned are mentioned. Three interpretive techniques for evaluating interactions are presented along with examples to be completed by the student. Crossover and synergistic interactions are illustrated. The use of the factorial experiment is justified to increase the efficiency of producing knowledge, explore the effects of a particular variable, discover new effects, and provide a closer approximation to the real world while maintaining the control inherent in an experiment. Caution about the factorial experiment becoming overly complex and difficult to interpret is also suggested.

The factorial ANOVA (2×2 between) is introduced. Tips on General Style discusses the concept of balance. Tips on Specific Style discusses the title page of a psychology paper.

Factorial Experiments and Interactions

"The happy combination of fortuitous circumstances."

—*Sir Walter Scott*

Which gender, male or female, is more conservative with personal space? We have all had our personal space violated. For example, in a crowded elevator (where we cannot escape the invasion) we have developed socially acceptable behaviors to minimize the intrusions (such as looking at the floor indicator or maybe just the floor). But do men and women behave differently? "It depends," you might say, "on the circumstances." Our tolerance for an invasion of our personal space may be greater in an elevator than a grocery store, and whether you are a male or a female may influence your tolerance for such circumstances.

While walking around campus, you may notice that there are a lot of factors affecting how people react to an intrusion on their personal space. Some people are more "touchy-feely" than others and allow others to be close to them without feeling uncomfortable. People do not seem to mind if

235

a person sits next to them, provided the intruder is occupied with some task such as reading a newspaper or book. They also do not seem to mind if there is no alternative place for the intruder to sit. In an elevator, everyone seems to adapt to crowded conditions.

When we suspect that the answer to an experimental question begins with the words *it depends*, we must learn a new design, perhaps the most useful design available to the psychologist, called a **factorial design.**

Factorial Designs

In the past experiments, we recognized the possibility that the effect we studied may only occur under some circumstances. We dealt with this by controlling or holding constant the circumstances that, if varied, might have made a difference in the experiment. However, psychologists are often interested in the effect of these other circumstances, or variables, as well as the primary independent variable. Most, if not all, interesting psychological questions require that psychologists look at two or more variables simultaneously.

In this experiment, we want to ask three questions. First, we want to know if men or women are more conservative with their personal space. Second, we want to know if personal space is different for an "occupied intruder" (e.g., one who is reading a paper) compared with an "unoccupied intruder" (e.g., one who just sits down). Third, we would like to know if the effect of the type of intruder depends on the gender of the subject. We could do one study to answer the first question and then another study to answer the second question. Unfortunately, even with the effort of conducting two separate studies, we could not supply any answer to the third question, because we did not know how to manipulate two independent variables at the same time.

Using a factorial design, we can answer all three of the above research questions in one experiment. The factorial design is illustrated in Table 11–1. In the factorial design shown in Table 11–1, two independent variables, type of intruder and subject gender, have been combined in all possible ways. Therefore, the upper left box is the condition where the male subject is intruded upon by an unoccupied experimenter. The upper right box is the condition where the male subject is intruded upon by an occupied experimenter. The bottom two boxes represent the female subjects given the same intruder conditions.

Many types of independent variables can serve as a factor in a factorial design. In some cases, treatment variables, such as the type of intruder, are

Table 11–1

Subject Gender	Type of Intruder		Main Effect
	Unoccupied	Occupied	
Male	Male-Unoccupied	Male-Occupied	Male
Female	Female-Unoccupied	Female-Occupied	Female
Main Effect	Unoccupied	Occupied	

Table 11–2

Subject Gender	Type of Intruder		Row Mean
	Unoccupied	Occupied	
Male	10	20	15
Female	50	26	38
Column Mean	30	23	

combined with other treatment variables, such as the distance to the subject. In other cases, treatment variables are combined with a factor based on a characteristic of the subjects, such as gender. When used as an independent variable, subject characteristics (e.g., gender, race, high vs. low IQ, and age) are called **blocking variables,** and the factorial design is referred to as a **Treatment × Block design.** Because subjects cannot be randomly assigned to levels of the blocking variable, statements about the blocking variable *causing* a change in the dependent variable are not appropriate. Rather, discussion is usually concerned with how the treatment affected members of each block. To make this point more clear, imagine a factorial design with two blocking variables and no treatment variable, for example, Race × Gender design. In such a design we could make no causal statements, and the study would not be a true experiment. It is the presence of the treatment variable or variables that allows us to make claims about causality.

The virtue of any factorial design is that it allows us to see main effects of each of the independent variables and how the combinations of each variable affect the results, that is, the possible **interaction** of the independent variables.

Table 11–2 illustrates the idea of main effects and interactions by presenting some hypothetical data. In the actual experiment, we will measure the time it takes for the subject to move away from the intruder. The numbers in Table 11–2 are fictional "times-to-move" in seconds averaged over 10 observations for each of the four cells in the factorial design.

If we had simply compared occupied and unoccupied intruders without attending to the gender of the subject, the column means (23 seconds to move versus 30 seconds) would imply that an occupied intruder is slightly less intrusive than an unoccupied one. In a factorial design, an effect that ignores the effects of all other variables is called a **main effect.** If 30 seconds were significantly longer than 23 seconds, we could speak of a significant main effect of type of intruder. Similarly, if we did an experiment comparing males and females without paying any attention to the occupied and unoccupied nature of the intruder, we would conclude that males (15 seconds) move away faster than females (38 seconds), as indicated in a comparison of the row means. In our factorial experiment, we call this a main effect of subject gender.

Interactions

If we conducted either of these simple experiments with other than a factorial design, we would be tempted to generalize our findings about intruders to both males and females or about gender to different types of intruders. In a factorial design, we can actually test statistically whether this type of generalization is warranted. This is the important contribution of factorial designs: It lets us look at interactions between two or more independent variables.

There are a number of different ways to think about interactions. Some students easily grasp one way of looking at the interaction whereas other students grasp another. It is important that you grasp at least one; which one is less important. However, an understanding of all of them would certainly aid you when you observe a significant interaction in your own data. In the following discussion, we assume that the experiment is very powerful and any difference between means is a significant one. In real life, statistics will tell you whether an interaction is there. However, it is then up to you, the scientist, to interpret the interaction.

The data in Table 11−2 will be used to illustrate the different interpretive techniques for thinking about interactions. Each of these techniques leads to the same conclusion: The effect of one variable depends on the value, or level, of the other, because this is the basic nature of an interaction.

Interpretive Technique 1

Does the effect of one variable depend on the level of other variable(s)? In Table 11−2, for male subjects the Occupied Intruder condition results in the subject being 10 seconds slower to leave than subjects in the Unoccupied condition. Does the type of intruder have the same effect on female subjects? No. In fact, female subjects in the Occupied Intruder condition are 24 seconds *faster* to depart than in the Unoccupied condition. Because the simple main effect of type of intruder is different for males and females, there is an interaction in the data.

Interpretive Technique 2

Do the two variables combine in a way that produces a unique effect? When we speak of unoccupied intruders *and* females, we notice a large jump in the time to depart. This jump is larger than we would have expected looking at the number in the margins (i.e., we expect to go up by 7 seconds when we go from occupied to unoccupied but, in fact, we go up 24).

Interpretive Technique 3

Plot the two variables on graph paper. Do the lines intersect or diverge? (If the lines diverge, then if you extended the lines they would intersect.) If the answer is yes, then you have an interaction. Or, you could ask if the lines are parallel. If they are, then there is no interaction.

All of these interpretive techniques lead to the conclusion that there is an interaction between subject gender and type of intruder in the data. This is usually reported in results sections as a Subject Gender × Type of Intruder interaction.

The interaction and the main effects are not dependent on each other in any way. In other words, it is possible to observe none of the effects, any one, any two, or even all three. In the above example, all three effects are

Figure 11–1   Illustration of a crossover interaction from a 2 × 2 factorial design.

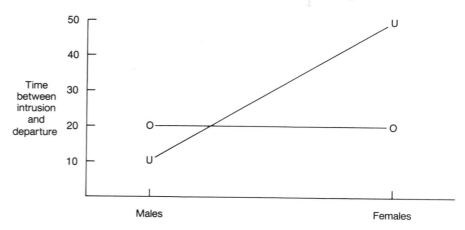

present. As a test of your understanding of main effects and interactions, see if you can complete the following factorial designs for the kinds of effects specified by making up appropriate numbers to complete the tables.

1. ONLY a main effect of type of intruder.

Subject Gender	Type of Intruder		Mean
	Unoccupied	Occupied	
Male	10		16
Female		22	
Mean	10	22	

2. ONLY a main effect of subject gender.

Subject Gender	Type of Intruder		Mean
	Unoccupied	Occupied	
Male	15	15	15
Female		25	
Mean		20	

3. ONLY a two-way interaction between subject gender and type of intruder (i.e., no main effects).

Subject Gender	Type of Intruder		Mean
	Unoccupied	Occupied	
Male	30		20
Female		30	
Mean		20	

4. A main effect of type of intruder, an interaction, but no effect of subject gender.

Subject Gender	Type of Intruder		Mean
	Unoccupied	Occupied	
Male	10		20
Female			
Mean	15		

5. BOTH main effects, but no two-way interaction.

Subject Gender	Type of Intruder		Mean
	Unoccupied	Occupied	
Male			
Female			
Mean			

For each of the above, now try writing a one- or two-statement description of each pattern of results. If an interaction is present, always explain that pattern before trying to interpret the main effects. This is especially important if the interaction is a **crossover interaction.** In a crossover interaction, the effect of a variable present for one level of the other variable is reversed at the other level. The term *crossover* comes from the fact that on a graph the lines cross, as in Figure 11–1. In other interactions, the main effect may correctly characterize the direction of the effect in all cases; the interaction is due only to relative size of the effect under different conditions. The interaction thus represents a magnification of the main effect when moving from one level to the next of the other variable. This is sometimes called a **synergistic interaction.**

A written description of the example in Table 11–2 might read as follows:

> Both the preoccupation of the intruder and the gender of the subject affected the time to depart. Males departed more quickly if the intruder was unoccupied, whereas females departed more quickly if the intruder was occupied. In general, for both types of intruders, males departed more quickly than females, and this was especially true if the intruder was unoccupied.

Provide similar descriptions for the other examples.

1. Main effect of type of intruder: (Remember that you should also mention what did not obtain.)

2. Main effect of subject gender:

3. Interaction, no main effects:

4. Main effect of type of intruder and an interaction: (Remember to discuss the interaction first.)

5. Both main effects, no interaction:

More Complex Two-Factor Designs

Factorial designs can be more complicated than the one above. The one above is called a two-factor design because it involves two independent variables. It can also be referred to as a 2 × 2 (read as "2 by 2") factorial design. There are two numerals, one for each independent variable; further, we know that each independent variable had two levels, as indicated by the actual numerals. Suppose just sitting next to someone is not sufficient to violate the person's space. We might want the intruder to speak to the subject so that the invasion of space is maximal. Now we have a 2 × 3 factorial experiment with the "3" referring to the three levels of intruders: occupied, unoccupied, and talking. This design is illustrated in Table 11–3. The main effect of type of intruder now has three levels to consider and is directly analogous to the experiment with three independent conditions described in chapter 7.

The 3 × 2 factorial experiment represented by Table 11–3 is slightly more complicated to interpret than the 2 × 2 design represented by Table 11–1. Suppose we have conducted the experiment with the intruder sitting next to an unsuspecting student studying in the library. We have the intruder simply sit down and stare into space (unoccupied), sit down and begin reading a book (occupied), or sit down and ask the subject what they are studying, where they are from, what their major is, and so forth (talking). The male or female subject leaves after the interval indicated in Table 11–4 (these are again hypothetical data, not to be taken too seriously as representative of the actual results you might obtain if you did this study).

You should know that there are main effects of type of intruder and subject gender by looking at the column and row means. The question for these hypothetical data is whether there is an interaction between the two independent variables. The answer is no.

Table 11–3

Subject Gender	Type of Intruder		
	Unoccupied	Occupied	Talking
Male	Male-Unoccupied	Male-Occupied	Male-Talking
Female	Female-Unoccupied	Female-Occupied	Female-Talking

Table 11–4

Subject Gender	Type of Intruder			Row Mean (Main Effect)
	Unoccupied	Occupied	Talking	
Male	18	53	33	34.67
Female	10	45	25	26.67
Column Mean (Main Effect)	14	49	29	

**Figure
11–2**   Illustration of a pattern of results suggesting two main effects but no interaction. The design was a 2 × 3 factorial.

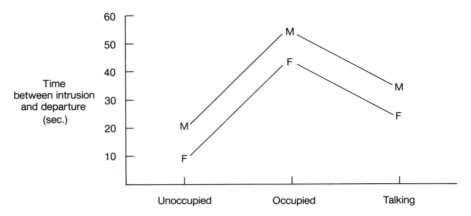

Interpretive Technique 1

Does the effect of one variable depend on the level of the other variable? Consider the male-female subject differences. Females leave sooner than males when the intruder is unoccupied (10 seconds vs. 18 seconds). The same is true when the intruder is occupied (45 seconds vs. 53 seconds) and when the intruder talks to the subject (25 seconds vs. 33 seconds). In each of these three comparisons, the female leaves 8 seconds sooner than the male. Therefore, we can conclude that there is *not* an interaction in these data.

Interpretive Technique 2

Do the two variables combine in a way that produces a unique effect? Again, the answer is no. The different types of intruders result in both males and females leaving after different times, but there is no unique effect due to the combination of the two variables.

Interpretive Technique 3

Plotting the two variables on a graph, do the lines intersect or diverge? The data are plotted for males and females in Figure 11–2. The lines are parallel, not intersecting or diverging, meaning that there is no interaction present in these results.

Higher Order Factorials

The factorial design can be made more complex in another way. We can add an additional independent variable to make it a three-factor experiment. In our experiment, the gender of the intruder may be an important variable. For example, we might hypothesize that males, being more aggressive by usual social stereotypes, would not cause as great of a reaction by the subject as that caused by a female violating personal space. To test

Table 11—5

Subject Gender	Intruder Gender Male — Type of Intruder				Female — Type of Intruder		
	Unoccupied	Occupied	Talking		Unoccupied	Occupied	Talking
Male				Male			
Female				Female			

the importance of gender of intruder, we will include it as a factor (an independent variable), and the design now appears as in Table 11—5. There are 12 squares in the table, the result of the combination of the 2 × 2 × 3 factorial design (multiplying the numerals together tells you how many separate conditions there are in the experiment.

Three-factor and higher order designs are basically the same as our simple 2 × 2. The more complex design allows us to test more hypotheses. For example, in our three-factor design we could test hypotheses about each of the following:

Main effect of Subject Gender

Main effect of Type of Intruder

Interaction of Subject Gender × Type of Intruder

These are the same main effects and interactions contained in our previous examples in Tables 11—1 and 11—3. Using the three-factor design, the additional effects will be:

Main effect of Intruder Gender

Interaction of Intruder Gender × Subject Gender

Interaction of Intruder Gender × Type of Intruder

Finally, a three-way interaction:

Intruder Gender × Type of Intruder × Subject Gender

Factorial designs, such as *t*-tests and simple one-way designs, can vary in whether the independent variable is between subjects, matched, or within subjects. If all the independent variables are between subjects, it is called a *completely between factorial design*. If all the independent variables are within, then it is called a *completely within factorial*. If both types of variables are present, then we call it a *mixed factorial design*.

Why Do a Higher Order Factorial Experiment?

A higher order factorial experiment is a way to test several hypotheses. If you do not have hypotheses that require higher order interactions to test them, then you should prefer a simpler design. A common mistake among new researchers is to "throw in" every variable that may make a difference. Then when the researcher discovers a significant interaction between three or four independent variables, he or she is at a loss to understand it.

Why should we want to do experiments that are so complicated? Factorial experiments are often used because experimenters want to *explore the effects of a particular variable* under a wide range of conditions. For example, in the experiment we have been discussing, we are mostly interested in how people react to the violation of personal space. Our intuitions tell us that violation of personal space may be linked to the gender of the subject and the intruder. The most efficient way to find out if our intuitions are correct is to do the factorial experiment. By combining many independent variables, *new effects may be discovered* that may be pursued using somewhat simpler procedures in follow-up experiments.

Another reason for doing a factorial experiment is that it comes *closer to the way the real world works*, yet maintains the control and precision of an experiment. In most real-world situations many factors will influence our behavior, and the factorial experiment is useful because it allows many factors to be present in the experiment.

Finally, we can justify factorial experiments because they are *efficient*. In one experiment the effect of several variables can be measured instead of doing a whole series of smaller experiments on each independent variable. In addition to the information about the main effect of each independent variable, the factorial experiment provides information about how the independent variables interact, and doing single experiments with each independent variable manipulated separately will never yield information about interactions. Remember, however, that the virtues of the higher order factorial design must be tempered by the fact that these designs may be difficult for the experimenter to interpret. We now turn to the interpretation of a three-factor design.

Interpretation of a Three-Factor Design

Interpretation of the three-way interaction requires a simple generalization of the interpretations of two-way interactions. The easiest way to think of this type of interaction is to follow interpretive technique 1, but rather than speak of simple main effects we speak now of simple interactions. If there is a three-way interaction, it means that one of the two-way interactions depends on the level of the third variable. For example, it may be that the interaction plotted above only holds for male intruders. If we observe some other interaction for female intruders, then we would have a three-way interaction.

Try solving the interpretations of Table 11–6 given below. Some of the problems have been solved for you; the key to answering these questions is

Table 11–6		Intruder Gender			
Subject Gender		Male		Female	
		Unoccupied	Occupied	Unoccupied	Occupied
Male		10	20	20	30
Female		50	26	60	36

to *average across all variables that are not part of the effect.* The answers appear at the end of the chapter. Which of the following effects are present in the data?

Subject Gender:

Yes, the male-subject average time [$\bar{m} = (10 + 20 + 20 + 30)/4 = 20$] is different than the female-subject average time [$\bar{f} = (50 + 26 + 60 + 36)/4 = 43$].

Type of Intruder:

Subject Gender × Type of Intruder:

(Hint: Reduce the above matrix to one containing only the two factors of interest by averaging across the Intruder Gender factor.)

	Intruder	
	Occupied	Unoccupied
Subj: Male	25	15
Female	31	55

Yes, males were 10 seconds faster if the intruder was unoccupied (15) than if occupied (25), whereas females were 24 seconds slower if the intruder was unoccupied (55) than if occupied (31).

Intruder Gender:

Intruder Gender × Subject Gender:

Intruder Gender × Type of Intruder:

Intruder Gender × Intruder Preoccupation × Subject Gender:

The Experiment

Research Hypotheses

Time to depart will be less for females than males. Time to depart will be longer if the intruder is occupied compared with unoccupied. The difference between males and females will be greater when the intruder is unoccupied. (You may wish to alter the experiment to fit your own ideas and situation.)

Independent Variables

The gender variable is defined by its nature. The intruder preoccupation variable requires some operationalization. For the Occupied condition, the intruder will read the student newspaper or a book. For the Unoccupied Intruder condition, the intruder will stare straight ahead.

Control

You should provide answers to the following questions or discuss them in class. Should the intruders be male or female or some of each? If using both gender intruders, whom should they approach? What should the intruder wear? How should the intruder handle attempts at communication? How close should the intruder be to the subject?

Dependent Variables

The primary dependent variable will be the time it takes for the subject to move away from the intruder. Who will measure the time? What if a subject moves closer to the intruder? How long should the intruder intrude before deciding to move on to another subject?

The remainder of the design issues will be left for you and your lab to solve. Do not forget consideration of control methods and practical considerations.

Answer to exercise: All main effects, the SG × TI interaction were present in the data. The SG × IG, IG × TI, and the three-way interaction are not suggested by the data.

Key Words

blocking variables	main effect
crossover interaction	synergistic interaction
factorial design	Treatment × Block design
interaction	

Additional Reading

Ahmed, S. (1980). Reactions to crowding in different settings. *Psychological Reports, 46,* 1279–1284.

Ford, J., & Hoeboke, S. (1980). Distance: Interpersonal spacing and psychological distance. *Psychological Reports, 46,* 1299–1303.

Little, K. (1965). Personal space. *Journal of Experimental Social Psychology, 1,* 237–247.

Slane, S., Petruska, R., & Cheyfitz, S. (1981). Personal space: A validational comparison. *Psychological Record, 31,* 145–151.

2×2 Between-Subjects Factorial

A factorial design can be analyzed using an ANOVA. The ANOVA will supply an F statistic for each main effect and each interaction. With two factors there will be 3 tests; with three factors, 7 tests; with four factors, 14 tests (4 main effects, 6 two-way interactions, 4 three-way interaction, 1 four-way interaction); and so on.

Source	DF	SS	MS	F
Intruder	$(i - 1)$	$\dfrac{\overset{i}{\Sigma}(\overset{g}{\Sigma}\overset{s}{\Sigma}X)^2}{gs} - \dfrac{(\overset{i}{\Sigma}\overset{g}{\Sigma}\overset{s}{\Sigma}X)^2}{igs}$	$SS_I/(i-1)$	MS_I/MS_{ERR}
Gender	$(g - 1)$	$\dfrac{\overset{g}{\Sigma}(\overset{i}{\Sigma}\overset{s}{\Sigma}X)^2}{is} - \dfrac{(\overset{i}{\Sigma}\overset{g}{\Sigma}\overset{s}{\Sigma}X)^2}{igs}$	$SS_G/(g-1)$	MS_G/MS_{ERR}
$I \times G$	$(i - 1)(g - 1)$	$\dfrac{\overset{i}{\Sigma}\overset{g}{\Sigma}(\overset{s}{\Sigma}X)^2}{s} - \dfrac{\overset{i}{\Sigma}(\overset{g}{\Sigma}\overset{s}{\Sigma}X)^2}{gs} - \dfrac{\overset{g}{\Sigma}(\overset{i}{\Sigma}\overset{s}{\Sigma}X)^2}{is} + \dfrac{(\overset{i}{\Sigma}\overset{g}{\Sigma}\overset{s}{\Sigma}X)^2}{igs}$	$\dfrac{SS_{IG}}{(i-1)(g-1)}$	MS_{IG}/MS_{ERR}
Error	$ig(s - 1)$	$\overset{i}{\Sigma}\overset{g}{\Sigma}\overset{s}{\Sigma}X^2 - \dfrac{\overset{i}{\Sigma}\overset{g}{\Sigma}(\overset{s}{\Sigma}X)^2}{s}$	$\dfrac{SS_{ERROR}}{ig(s-1)}$	

STEP 0. State the nulls.

Main effect of Intruder: Occupied intruders have the same effect as unoccupied intruders.

Main effect of Gender: Males will be the same as females.

Interaction: The effect of intruder will be the same for both genders.

STEP 1. Table the data.

	Column 1 (Occupied)	Column 2 (Unoccupied)
	Cell 1	Cell 2
ROW 1	0	8
(Males)	2	7
	0	7
	0	6
	1	5
	Cell 3	Cell 4
ROW 2	0	0
(Females)	0	1
	2	1
	2	2
	1	0

STEP 2.   Sum each column; square the sums; divide the sums by the number of scores in each column (s × g); total these values.

	$\overset{s\,g}{\Sigma\Sigma X}$	$\overset{s\,g}{(\Sigma\Sigma X)^2}$	$\overset{s\,g}{(\Sigma\Sigma X)^2/(s \times g)}$
Occupied	8	64	6.4
Unoccupied	37	1369	$\dfrac{136.9}{143.3} = \dfrac{\overset{i}{\Sigma} \overset{s\,g}{(\Sigma\Sigma X)^2}}{s \times g}$

STEP 3.   Sum each row; square these sums; divide each sum by the number of scores in each sum (s × i); total these values.

	$\overset{s\,i}{\Sigma\Sigma X}$	$\overset{s\,i}{(\Sigma\Sigma X)^2}$	$\overset{s\,i}{(\Sigma\Sigma X)^2/(s \times i)}$
Males	36	1296	129.6
Females	9	81	$\dfrac{8.1}{137.7} = \dfrac{\overset{g\,s\,i}{\Sigma(\Sigma\Sigma X)^2}}{s \times i}$

STEP 4.   Sum all scores; square this sum; divide by total number of scores (s × i × g).

$\overset{s\,i\,g}{\Sigma\Sigma\Sigma X}$	$\overset{s\,i\,g}{(\Sigma\Sigma\Sigma X)^2}$	$\overset{s\,i\,g}{(\Sigma\Sigma\Sigma X)^2/(s \times g)}$
45	2025	101.25

STEP 5.   Sum each cell; square these sums; divide by the number of scores in each cell (i.e., number of subjects, s); total these values.

	$\overset{s}{\Sigma X}$	$\overset{s}{(\Sigma X)^2}$	$\overset{s}{(\Sigma X)^2/s}$
Cell 1 (M-Occ)	3	9	1.8
Cell 2 (M-Un)	33	1089	217.8
Cell 3 (F-Occ)	5	25	5.0
Cell 4 (F-Un)	4	16	$\dfrac{3.2}{227.8} = \dfrac{\overset{i\,g\,s}{\Sigma\Sigma(\Sigma X)^2}}{s}$

STEP 6.   Square each score; sum these values.

$$0^2 + 2^2 + 0^2 + \ldots + 1^2 + 2^2 + 0^2 = \overset{s\,i\,g}{\Sigma\Sigma\Sigma X^2} = 243$$

STEP 7.   *Compute SSs.*

$$SS_I = [\text{Step 2}] - [\text{Step 4}] = 143.3 - 101.25 = 42.05$$

$$SS_G = [\text{Step 3}] - [\text{Step 4}] = 137.7 - 101.25 = 36.45$$

$$SS_{I \times G} = [\text{Step 5}] - [\text{Step 2}] - [\text{Step 3}] + [\text{Step 4}] = $$
$$227.8 - 143.3 - 137.7 + 101.25 = 48.05$$

$$SS_{\text{error}} = [\text{Step 6}] - [\text{Step 5}] = 243 - 227.8 = 15.2$$

STEP 8.   *Calculate DFs.*

$$df_I = (i - 1) = 1$$

$$df_G = (g - 1) = 1$$

$$df_{I \times G} = (i - 1)(g - 1) = 1$$

$$df_{\text{error}} = ig(s - 1) = 2 \times 2 \times 4 = 16$$

STEP 9.   *Calculate MSs.*

$$MS_I = 42.05/1 = 42.05$$

$$MS_G = 36.45/1 = 36.45$$

$$MS_{I \times G} = 48.05/1 = 48.05$$

$$MS_{\text{error}} = 15.2/16 = .95$$

STEP 10.   *Calculate Fs.*

$$F_I = 42.05/.95 = 44.26$$

$$F_G = 36.45/.95 = 38.37$$

$$F_{I \times G} = 48.05/.95 = 50.58$$

Source	df	SS	MS	F	Sig Level
I	1	42.05	42.05	44.26	.01
G	1	36.45	36.45	38.37	.01
I × G	1	48.05	48.05	50.58	.01
Error	16	15.2	.95		

STEP 11.   *Compare Observed Fs to critical F.*

All tests are Fs with 1 and 16 degrees of freedom. At 0.05 the critical F is 4.49, and at 0.01 it is 8.53. All effects are clearly significant.

Personal Space

Experimenter: _____

Subject #	Gender (M/F)	Intruder (O/U)	Depart Time	Comments (including intruder gender?)

Locations:

Times:

General situations:

Personal Space

Experimenter: _____   Date: _____

Departure times:

Subject #	Male-Occ	Male-Un	Female-Occ	Female-Un

Means:

ANOVA Summary Table

SOURCE	df	SS	MS	F	SIG?
Intruder					
Gender					
I × G					
Error					

General Idea (Previous Research, Curiosity, Theory)

General observations and research have given rise to the construct of personal space. This study explores some of the factors that might affect reactions to the violation of that space.

Explanatory Statement

Personal space is, in fact, viewed as an intermediate mechanism. That is, personal space is placed between observables such as "someone moving closer" and "departure time." This study is designed to explore this mechanism further.

Research Hypothesis/Descriptive Statement

There are three hypotheses of interest:
  1. Given an intrusion, females will depart sooner than males.
  2. Intrusion by an unoccupied intruder will lead to faster departure than intrusion by an occupied intruder.
  3. The difference between males and females will be primarily when the intruder is unoccupied.
Restate hypothesis 3 by completing the following:
The difference between occupied and unoccupied intruders will be primarily for MALES/FEMALES/EITHER (pick one).

Methods (Natural Observation, Survey, Field Experiment, Lab Experiment)

Field experiment.

Dependent Variable(s)

Operational Definition

Predictor or Independent Variable(s)

Treatment variable: Type of intruder.
Blocking variable: gender.

Operational Definition   Operationally define Type of Intruder:

Design (Between, Pre-Post, Within, ➤ Factorial)

Factorial (Treatment × Block)

Subjects

Ethical Considerations   In any field experiment, ethical guidelines must be carefully considered. List the considerations and discuss whether your procedures allow you to continue. How would you modify the procedures to minimize problems and still conduct the study?

Continued

Continued

Characteristics and Availability   Are there any characteristics of the subjects or their situation that would lead you to exclude them from your sample?

Sampling Procedure and Number of Subjects   How can you avoid selecting your subjects in a biased way?

Control

Subject Assignment (Randomization, Matching)
Randomization:

Environment (Insured Equivalence, Yoking, Counterbalancing)
Insured equivalence:

Gender of the intruder?

Other characteristics of intruder?

Distance from subject?

Procedural Command Decisions (Ceiling Effects, Floor Effects)

Continued

Retrospective Confound Check (Assumed, Statistical, Rethink)

Selection: Remember subject gender cannot be randomly assigned.

Mortality: Interestingly, time to depart is related to mortality. Because this is the dependent variable, we are measuring mortality in a sense.

History:

Maturation:

Reactivity: Pesonal space works both ways. It is important that the experimenter samples unbiasedly and implements the procedure in the same way, regardless of whether his or her personal space is violated.

Testing/Sequencing: N/A

Instrumentation:

Data Analysis
Descriptive

Inferential   The analysis will be a 2 × 2, Type of Intruder × Subject Gender, between-subjects ANOVA.

Hypothetical Outcome Analysis

Below is a plot of the outcome if all hypotheses are confirmed. Write statements describing the effects present. On the right-hand side below, generate the plot you would obtain if only the main effect hypotheses are confirmed. How would you discuss this pattern in your results section?

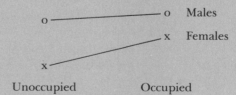

```
o ———————————— o  Males
                    x  Females

x ———————————/

Unoccupied       Occupied
```

Continued

Balance of Information

Two concepts, if mastered, will improve the organization of your manuscript. One is the idea of **emphasis** and the other is its cousin, **balance.** Here we consider how they apply to the manuscript as a whole (rather than how they apply to a sentence). Appropriate emphasis means that your paper devotes more space to important issues and less space to less important issues. Similarly, balance means that issues of comparable importance receive equal time. These very simple concepts are not always implemented in the paper.

Balance and emphasis are measured by a number of factors. The more text devoted to an issue, the more important it appears. A figure of data, as compared to a table or presentation of data in the text, makes the data in the figure more important. The author usually violates these principles either by not discriminating between important and less important issues and findings or by actually overemphasizing unimportant information.

How can this happen? This imbalance and misemphasis occurs because of one or both of the following related reasons: (1) the minor effects are often unexpected and difficult to interpret; the author therefore feels compelled to spend a good deal of manuscript space on these difficult-to-understand, but actually minor, issues. (2) the major effects have been predicted and seem to be obvious. The author will often devote very little space to the most important part of the paper because it seems so obvious. In the discussion, the author might go as far as simply mentioning the major effect and then spend the rest of the discussion on unexpected, small effects. This distracts the reader from the main point of the experiment.

There are two solutions. One is to resist the temptation of spending a great deal of time on secondary issues. Rewrite these paragraphs until they are more tightly constructed. Leave out some of the nuances of the effect. Second is to write more about the major work. Rather than shortchange the important effects, write more, even if it means introducing some redundancy. You may think you "already said that" but saying it at the right time and in the right way will give the reader a new perspective (and jog his or her memory about the main point of the experiment).

Formatting the Title Page

The first page of every article is the title page. You should follow this example. The title should be informative, without extraneous words, such as
"A study on . . .", and be about 8–12 words in length. Remember from
chapter 2 that a literature search depends on the informativeness of the
title. You should follow . . .

How to Set

1

How to Set Up a Title Page: An Example

I. M. Scientist and U. M. Knott

University of Oklahoma

Running Head: THE PSYCHOLOGY PAPER

12 Reactivity & Blinds

Overview

This chapter focuses on the reactivity confound and the number of techniques designed to eliminate this pervasive threat to internal validity. Within the context of an attraction study, we consider several techniques for dealing with the reactivity confound, including blind, double-blind, and partial-blind procedures. Also discussed is the disguised experiment and the unrelated experiment, as well as the use of deception and cover stories. The success of these methods in preventing the subject from learning of the true nature of the experiment is assessed by a postexperimental interview. Ethical concerns are discussed and the importance of debriefing the subject at the end of the experiment is emphasized.

Two nonparametric statistical techniques are introduced: the Wilcoxon signed-rank test and the Mann-Whitney U-test.

Tips on General Style extols the benefits of rewriting the manuscript.

Tips on Specific Style focuses on the format of figures and tables of a manuscript in psychology.

Reactivity and Blind Techniques

"I never seen anybody but lied, one time or another, without it was Aunt Polly, or the widow, or maybe Mary."

—*Huckleberry Finn*

What factors influence our attraction toward another human being? This question has been seriously considered by all of us from the time we entered puberty, through the turbulent teenage years, to adulthood. The importance of attraction has not escaped the notice of social psychologists. In this chapter we explore one very interesting factor that, according to some theories, should influence the degree of liking or disliking we feel toward another.

Some psychologists have proposed that our feelings toward another person often depend on physiological cues from our bodies and how we interpret those cues. For example, John is on his first date with Mary. While driving her to the movie theater another driver runs a red light and nearly hits John's car. The arousal from this near accident may persist for some time and may not be completely dissipated until well after the date is over. Later, John feels very positively toward Mary and asks her out again. It has been argued that at least part of this attraction is due to John misattributing the arousal from the near accident to being with Mary.

In one study, experimenters gave people shots of epinephrine (i.e., adrenalin) or shots of a saline solution (i.e., a placebo). Some people in each group were informed about the effects they should expect because of the injection. Others were told it was a vitamin. Subjects were then asked to wait in a room until they were called to take some tests. While the real subjects were waiting, a **confederate,** a person pretending to be a subject but who was working with the experimenters, entered the waiting room. For half of the subjects he acted euphoric and for the other half of the subjects he acted angry. Observers watched the subject and recorded his or her behaviors. Interestingly, the subjects who were not informed that they had been given the epinephrine modeled the behavior of the confederate, whereas subjects from the other groups (placebo injected and the informed subjects given either drug) did not behave like the confederate.

The researchers interpreted their results as support for the idea that physiological arousal may result in the person interpreting the arousal to fit the context in which it occurs. So, an aroused person around a euphoric person becomes happy and joyful, but a similarly aroused person around an angry person becomes hostile and angry.

How often, you may ask, are we aroused but do not know why? Rarely does someone stop by to give us an injection of epinephrine. Another study, however, suggests that our attraction toward a person can be influenced without a drug.

In a field experiment, experimenters had a male or female interviewer approach males who were crossing a high and unsteady bridge or who were crossing a low and sturdy bridge. Later the subjects were called by the experimenters and asked follow-up questions including questions about their opinion of the interviewer. Subjects rated female interviewers more positively if they were interviewed on the high bridge rather than the low bridge. Opinions about male interviewers were not affected. The subjects on the high bridge were aroused and apparently misattributed some of this arousal to the female interviewer. Male interviewers were presumably not viewed differently in the two bridge conditions because another male would not be a potential romantic target, and therefore the subjects would be less likely to misattribute their arousal to the interviewer.

After reading the first 11 chapters of this book, you should be able to find a number of aspects of the procedure described above that limit our ability to make causal statements. As one example, you could argue that males who tend to walk on high, unsturdy bridges are more likely to be womanizers than those who walk on low bridges. How could we bring this study under better experimental control?

We can begin by bringing the question into the laboratory, but we will immediately be faced with the problem of *reactivity.* As you recall, reactivity refers to confounds due to the subjects' biases about the experiment and the experimenter as well as experimenter expectancies and biases. Fortunately, a number of techniques exist that will reduce reactivity, thus increasing the internal validity of the experiment.

In the laboratory we must find a way to increase the arousal of some subjects and not others. We must do this without their realization that arousal is our independent variable. Further we must get a measure of attraction that is not subject to demand characteristics.

Our task is made difficult if we must use subjects from an advanced psychology methodology class. One interesting (and ethical) way to manipulate arousal for such a group is to tell subjects that they will be asked to prepare a short speech about some aspect of experimental methodology (e.g., a particular confound). We can then tell half of them that they have been randomly selected to be videotaped while making the speech. To increase arousal further, we could tell them that this videotape will be presented to another group who will evaluate their speech, their style, and their general personal appearance. Further, as in the bridge study, we must provide the subject with a romantic target. This can be accomplished by creating mixed-sex pairs to work together on the speech.

Reactivity Control Techniques

Experimenter Biases

How can we implement such a procedure and avoid **experimenter biases** and **subject biases?** The first procedure that comes to mind is the **double-blind technique.** In this procedure neither the subject nor the experimenter knows which condition the subject was assigned. Unfortunately, any effective way of increasing arousal will likely be evident to the subjects receiving that manipulation. The subjects who are told their presentation will be recorded will certainly know they are being treated differently from others in the class who were not told their speech will be recorded.

We can, however, try to keep the experimenter unaware of the subject's condition. At this point you may be asking yourself: How can the experimenter *not* know what condition a subject is in? The answer is two experimenters. One who codes the relevant information in a way that is unknown to the second experimenter, and a second experimenter who actually interacts with the subjects. In several cases even this **experimenter-blind technique** may be impossible. For example, subjects will be likely to react in different ways when they are actually assigned to a condition. Some may show relief whereas others may not, thus alerting the experimenter to their condition.

We can, however, keep the experimenter blind as long as possible by using a **partial-blind technique.** We can, for example, have sealed envelopes with information about the relevant condition inside. In this way, everything before the actual administration of the independent variable is identical for the two groups. The experimenter before this point cannot treat one group differently from the other because he or she does not know to what condition they will ultimately be assigned.

In general, to minimize the effect of the experimenter, we must try to make it impossible for the experimenter to treat the groups differently. In other words, we want to "take the experimenter out of the experiment" as much as possible. In this experiment we will do this with the partial-blind technique. In addition, we will supplement this by having as much as possible of the experiment standardized. For example, instructions will be read from a typed sheet of paper, the experimenter will not interact with the subjects except in prescribed ways, and so on.

Subject Biases

The partial-blind technique has minimized to an extent the biases and expectancies of the experimenter. Clearly, however, the subject will bring biases and expectancies to the experiment as well. In this case we may want to employ a **deception technique.** To a psychologist, deception can be accomplished in many ways. The simplest and most often used method is to tell the subject that they are in the experiment for some reason that has nothing to do with the real research hypothesis. The logic behind this **cover-story technique** is that if all subjects think they are in the experiment for the same reason, any differences between groups because of the subjects' expectations should be minimized. This is the same logic applied to the use of a placebo in drug studies.

A more extreme version of deception involves trying to collect data from subjects without them even realizing that they are in an experiment. The bridge study above was just such an experiment. However, the bridge study, like most uses of the **disguised-experiment technique,** was a field experiment. In our experiment, if we are clever, we can convince our subjects that they are performing their speeches as a class exercise and that the tapes will be used elsewhere including, perhaps, an attempt to start a video library for use in the course.

As you have probably guessed, in many situations we would be unable to use the disguised experiment. Instead we can use the **unrelated-experiment technique.** With this procedure the subject actually participates in two experiments which he or she believes are unrelated to each other. In the first experiment, the subject is administered the independent variable but the dependent variable is not measured. The subject is then contacted and asked to be in another experiment. No mention of the first experiment is made. During the second experiment, the dependent variable associated with the first experiment is measured. The logic behind this technique is that if subjects formed any biases or expectancies based on the independent variable, it will not be attached to the new experiment. The follow-up interview of the bridge study has much of this flavor. In our case, as with several other situations, it is often impossible or impractical to measure the dependent variable removed from the independent variable.

We have considered a number of ways to eliminate biases of the subjects. We chose the disguised-experiment technique with a cover story as our best bet. It is important to realize, however, that subjects may see through even the most clever deceptions. When reactivity confounds are suspected, subjects can be presented with a **postexperimental interview** during which the experimenter tries to ascertain what the subject thought the experiment was about.

The Dependent Variable

Thus far we have discussed the major issues involved in administering the independent variable. We still need to decide how to measure the dependent variable that will reflect the attachment one person feels toward another. Clearly, as evident from our preceding discussion, simply asking a subject to tell us how he or she feels about her partner would lend itself to many demand characteristics. It would be nice if we could find a less obtrusive measure. Perhaps in keeping with our disguised experiment, a measurement can be taken without the subjects realizing that they are evaluating their partner.

One possibility comes to mind based on our lab experiment concerning personal space. Generally, your attraction toward a person is correlated with how closely you choose to stand to that person. We can take advantage of this finding by measuring the distance between members of a pair. How and when should we take these measurements? We can ask each pair of subjects to come to the instructor's desk under the pretense of informing the instructor about their topic. When they arrive at the desk, the experimenter/instructor can then count the number of floor tiles between the subjects. If floor tiles were not available, other unobtrusive markings could have been made to minimize the difficulty of measuring distance.

Finally, these measurements can be taken twice: once before the pairs work on the problem and once 5 minutes after they have started working. This pretest-posttest design will allow us to determine the extent and direction of the change. Our hypothesis is not merely that the aroused pairs will stand closer together than control pairs but that liking will increase. Without a pretest-posttest design, it might be the case that the control group participants began to dislike their partners and that arousal served only to mitigate this dislike. Clearly such a pattern of results would go against our hypothesis.

Ethical Considerations

Whenever the experiment necessitates deception of one kind or another, the researcher is faced with serious ethical questions. In our previous work, some ethical concerns were present. In some cases the concerns were small (e.g., door holding), and in other cases they were moderate (e.g., asking to cut in line). In no case, however, were the experimental participants asked to face risks and discomfort beyond those normally expected in life.

However, in most of the techniques described in the current chapter, the risks are potentially greater. In our experiment, manipulating anxiety is, by definition, a manipulation that will cause subjects some discomfort. In the general population, we cannot assume that the anxiety produced by being videotaped is within the discomfort normally experienced by the majority of the population. People may choose to avoid situations, such as college, where such participation is a normal part of the activities. Fortunately, by using only college students, our experiment falls within ethical guidelines. Presentations to a class are an appropriate activity for college students, even if it is not a favorite activity. Even in such a situation, however, the experimenter should be sensitive enough to realize when a subject is likely to undergo undue stress. Being excused from the experiment is *always* the subject's right. Further, this should in no way result in a penalty to the subject. From an objective viewpoint of scientific methods, this would lead to the possibility of a mortality confound. From the subjective viewpoint of an ethical scientist, this would lead to the possibility of compassion.

If the experimenter decides that the deception is necessary to the experiment, *and* that the potential contribution of the work warrants it being conducted, *and* if the Internal Review Board approves, then he or she must still consider the effects of the experiment on the subjects. Ideally, the subject should leave the experiment in the same condition, or better, than he or she was before entering the experiment. He or she should learn something from the experiment, either about himself or herself or about science or about the world. Further, the subject should leave with good feelings about the experience. Even selfishly motivated researchers recognize the value of presenting a positive experience if only to obtain subjects for future experiments.

Many of these goals can be accomplished by **debriefing** the subject at the end of the experiment. In a debriefing, a subject should be made to feel as he or she did before entering the experiment. This can sometimes mean revealing the deception. For example, if the subject has been given a number of very difficult problems, many of which were not solved, he or she should be told that this was meant to be a difficult or impossible task. In other cases, reassuring the subject may require the experimenter to present a less-than-accurate depiction of the subject's performance. For example, if the problems were not particularly difficult, yet the subject performed poorly, we see no reason to tell the subject about his or her relative performance. Simply saying "you did okay" is sufficient. Finally, as part of the debriefing, if the subjects wish to ask any questions, the experimenter should make certain that they are answered to the best of his or her ability.

The Experiment

This study was motivated by the descriptive statement produced by an earlier study: Males interviewed on a high bridge rated a female interviewer more positively than those interviewed on a low bridge. Male interviewers were evaluated similarly under either condition. One possible explanation for this finding is that "People in an aroused state will misattribute their arousal to the presence of romantic targets."

If that is true, then students who expect to be videotaped and criticized while reading a speech should stand closer to their partner than students who do not expect to be videotaped or criticized. Subjects will be a convenience sample from a laboratory-methods-in-psychology class. The external validity of such a study is thus poor because psychology majors cannot, in this experiment, be assumed to be representative of most larger populations. However, because other studies with more external validity (but less internal validity) already exist in the literature, the lack of external validity will only be problematic if the present study does not agree with the literature. In that case the effect may be due to a different causal factor (i.e., our lab study is correct), or the effect may only manifest itself in certain situations (i.e., our lab study is too contrived).

The design will be a two-group pretest-posttest with pairs of subjects being randomly assigned to one of the two groups. Pairs of mixed-sex subjects will receive videotape instructions or control instructions. The videotape instructions will inform subjects that they are to present a 5-minute speech on one of the confounds and that the speech will be videotaped. The videotape will then be shown to the methodology lecture class of 60 people. The students will criticize the content of the speech, the presentation style of the pair, and the personal appearance of the speakers. This group will be informed that the tape will ultimately become part of a new videotape library for future use in the course. The control instructions will inform subjects that they are to prepare a short description of one of the studied confounds. Both groups will be informed that we do not have time to make videotapes of all of the pairs and thus only some of them will be selected.

Random assignment of pairs to groups should eliminate most confounds. However, effects of history and the like can be introduced after the experiment has begun if we are not careful. Reactivity confounds may exist despite the random assignment. Mortality may also be a confound, but using members of the class should reduce this.

Reactivity was controlled explicitly by using a partial-blind technique within a disguised experiment. In addition, the measurement of the DV was unobtrusive. Finally, subjects will be given a postexperimental interview as a final check for reactivity.

The dependent variable will be the distance between the members of the pair when they come to the front of the class to speak with the instructor about the exercise. Floor tiles will be counted and converted to centimeters. This pretest is very unobtrusive and makes it very unlikely that there will be an effect from the pretest on the posttest. The posttest measurements will be subtracted from the pretest measurements to create gain scores.

Previously, we analyzed the pretest-posttest design with a combination of correlated and independent t-tests. The t-test makes several assumptions about the data to which it is applied. Two assumptions that concern us here are (1) the t-test assumes the data are on at least an interval scale and (2) the scores will approximate **normal distribution** (i.e., bell-shaped). The distance between two people would usually be considered as ratio data; however, in the current situation the experimenter was forced to estimate the distance in order to be unobtrusive. Estimates of distance are not perfect (see chapter 15), and some researchers might be willing to assume that the estimates are only sensitive to an ordinal level. Second, the distribution of distance will likely tend to be skewed. That is, most people will tend to stand at an acceptable, relatively close distance. No one will stand intimately close in this public situation. However, we can expect a small proportion of people to stand quite far apart. In other words, it will be a **skewed distribution.** Some researchers would again suggest that the t-test is inappropriate.

We can solve both of these concerns about the *t*-test by using statistical tests that do not make as many assumptions. These tests are called **nonparametric** or **distribution-free statistics.** The Wilcoxon signed-rank test is the distribution-free counterpart to the correlated *t*-test. The Mann-Whitney U-test is the distribution-free counterpart to the independent *t*-test.

Key Words

confederate	nonparametric/distribution-free statistics
cover-story technique	normal distribution
debriefing	partial-blind technique
deception technique	postexperimental interview
disguised-experiment technique	skewed distribution
double-blind technique	subject biases
experimenter biases	unrelated-experiment technique
experimenter-blind technique	

Additional Reading

Dutton, D. G., & Aron, A. P. (1974). Some evidence for heightened sexual attraction under conditions of high anxiety. *Journal of Personality and Social Psychology, 30,* 510–517.

Green, S. K., Buchanan, D. R., & Heuer, S. K. (1984). Winners, losers, and choosers: A field investigation of dating initiation. *Personality and Social Psychology Bulletin, 10,* 502–511.

Schachter, S., & Singer, J. E. (1962). Cognitive, social, and physiological determinants of emotional state. *Psychological Review, 69,* 379–399.

Valins, S. (1966). Cognitive effects of false heart-rate feedback. *Journal of Personality and Social Psychology, 4,* 400–408.

Wilcoxon Signed-rank Test

The Wilcoxon signed-rank test is useful when the same subjects or matched subjects participate in both levels of the independent variable. As a distribution-free test, it is especially useful when the median is a better average than the mean (e.g., badly skewed distributions, ordinal data). However, if several ties occur in the data, the assumption of a continuous variable may have been violated.

STEP 1. Table the data into pairs as with the correlated t-test and compute the difference score for each subject.

Subject	Pre	Post	Difference
1	5	7	2
2	4	1	−3
3	10	9	−1
4	5	11	6
5	9	11	2
6	10	27	17

STEP 2. Rank the differences from smallest to largest, ignoring the sign. If there is a tie, sum the ranks of the tied scores and divide by the number of ties.

Difference	Rank	
2	2.5	(tie)
−3	4	(sign ignored)
−1	1	(sign ignored)
6	5	
2	2.5	(tie)
17	6	

STEP 3. Find the signed-rank values by summing the ranks for the negative *differences and for the* positive *differences separately. Differences of 0 should have their ranks evenly distributed to the negative and the positive.*

Negative: $4 + 1 = 5$ Positive: $2.5 + 5 + 2.5 + 6 = 16$

STEP 4. Compare the smaller signed-rank value to the critical values in the Wilcoxon signed-rank probability table (Appendix, Table E).

Assume a two-tailed test at .05. Because 5 (the smaller signed-rank value) is *larger* than the critical value for a six-pair test, we conclude the observed difference is *not* significant.

Mann-Whitney U-Test

The Mann-Whitney U-test is useful when different subjects have participated in the two levels of the independent variable. As a distribution-free statistic, it is particularly useful when medians are a more appropriate average than the mean (e.g., ordinal data, skewed distribution). However, if there are many tied ranks, the Mann-Whitney U-test should not be chosen for the analysis.

U is based on the number of subjects in each condition (n_1, n_2) and the sum of the ranks for each condition (R_1, R_2) according to the following formula. U_e, for our example, refers to the experimental group, and U_c to the control group.

$$U_e = n_e n_c + \frac{n_e(n_e + 1)}{2} - \Sigma R_e$$

$$U_c = n_e n_c + \frac{n_c(n_c + 1)}{2} - \Sigma R_c$$

Begin with the following data:

Experimental		Control	
S1	10	S9	3
S2	5	S10	4
S3	8	S11	1
S4	7	S12	5
S5	11	S13	4
S6	18	S14	5
S7	10	S15	0
S8	22	S16	9

STEP 1. Combine the two groups and rank the subjects from 1 to N, in this case 1 to 16.

Cond:	C	C	C	C		C	E	C	C	E	E	C	E	E	E	E	E
Score:	0	1	3	4		4	5	5	5	7	8	9	10	10	11	18	22
Rank:	1	2	3	4.5		4.5	7	7	7	9	10	11	12.5	12.5	14	15	16

The U-test answers the question: Are the Cs and Es randomly intermixed, or do they tend to fall at one end versus the other?

STEP 2. Sum the ranks for each group separately.

For C group: $1 + 2 + 3 + 4.5 + 4.5 + 7 + 7 + 11 = 40 = R_c$
For E group: $7 + 9 + 10 + 12.5 + 12.5 + 14 + 15 + 16 = 96 = R_e$

STEP 3. Solve for U_e and U_c using the formulas above:

$$U_e = (8)(8) + \frac{8(8 + 1)}{2} - 96 = 4$$

$$U_c = (8)(8) + \frac{8(8 + 1)}{2} - 40 = 60$$

STEP 4. The smaller of the two is the Mann-Whitney U and is compared to the critical value in Table F in the Appendix. Because the obtained U is smaller than the critical U(8,8 at .05), we can reject the null hypothesis.

Note: With the sample sizes over 20, the U approximates a normal distribution and can thus be transformed to a z-statistic and compared in t table with infinite degrees of freedom, because $t(\infty) = z$.

$$z = \frac{X - mu}{sigma} = \frac{U - \dfrac{n_c n_e}{2}}{\sqrt{\dfrac{n_c n_e (n_c + n_e + 1)}{12}}}$$

Attraction

Experimenter: _____

Pair #	Videotape (Y/N)	Pretest Estimate	Posttest Estimate	Interview Suspicion?	Comments

Attraction

Experimenter: _____ Date: _____

Note: Only those subjects who passed the postexperimental interview are included. Exclusion for aroused was _____; for control was _____.

Subject #	Pre	Aroused Post	Gain	Pre	Control Post	Gain

Sign tests:

Aroused   Control

Mann-Whitney on gain scores:

General Idea (Previous Research, Curiosity, Theory)

The idea was based on previous research and theory. A descriptive statement from one study was: Males interviewed on a high bridge liked their female interviewer more than those interviewed on a low bridge.

Explanatory Statement

The following statement supplies an explanation of the above descriptive statement:

People in an aroused state will misattribute their arousal to the presence of romantic targets.

Research Hypothesis/Descriptive Statement

Students expecting to be videotaped and criticized while reading a speech will stand closer to their partner than students who do not expect to be videotaped and criticized.

Methods (Natural Observation, Survey, Field Experiment, Lab Experiment)

Field experiment: Why is this a field experiment when it is conducted in the lab?

Dependent Variable(s)

Distance between partners.

Operational Definition Normally a very easy variable to define, distance becomes more difficult in this context because of the need for the experimenter to estimate distance unobtrusively. How is this handled in the text?

Predictor or Independent Variable(s)

Arousal level: High or low.

Operational Definition Operationally define arousal level:

Continued

Continued
Design (Between, Pre-Post, Within, Factorial)

Pre-Post: What reasons for choosing the pre-post design over the between design are relevant here?

Subjects

Ethical Considerations   The chapter discusses many of the ethical considerations associated with this study. List these considerations in order of importance, state what the negative impact might be, and note the ethical resolution.

Characteristics and Availability   Subjects will be all of the members of an intact class.

Continued

Sampling Procedure and Number of Subjects   If all members of an intact class are used, what is the sample and what is the population?

Control

Subject Assignment (Randomization, Matching)   Random assignment: Control or videotape condition.

Environment (Insured Equivalence, Yoking, Counterbalancing)   Insured equivalence:

Yoking: Although not discussed, how might you yoke pairs of subjects and what would you gain?

▶ *Reactivity (Blinds, Deception, Disguised, etc.)*   Partial blind: The experimenter removes a slip of paper designating the condition for a pair of subjects. (Why did the chapter settle for this procedure rather than the preferred double-blind technique?)

Disguised experiment: The subjects are led to believe that they are participating in a class exercise, not an experiment. This obviously involves deception, in particular a cover story. In addition, the measurement of the dependent variable was unobtrusive. (What would you do to faciliate deceiving a group of "lab-wise" psychology students?)

Continued

Continued

Postexperimental interview: With a well-phrased interview, it may be possible to discover if any subjects thought they were in an experiment. The form of the questions must be such that they do not invite the suspicion. For example, one question might be: "Do you think this exercise should be done again later, on a different topic, in order to build up the videotape library? Why or why not?" or perhaps, "What do you believe was the main purpose of this exercise?"

Procedural Command Decisions (Ceiling Effect, Floor Effect)

Retrospective Confound Check (Assumed, Statistical, Rethink)

Selection: Okay, random assignment of pairs.

Mortality: Subjects in aroused state could drop out, but being in a class could reduce this. Another version of this confound could appear if the postexperimental interview is used to eliminate subjects from the final analysis. Perhaps the aroused pairs will catch on more often and thus more of these subjects will be omitted.

History: Should be okay assuming good procedures.

Maturation:

Reactivity: Anything more that can be done?

Testing/Sequencing: Unobtrusive measure minimizes this.

Instrumentation: Because the dependent variable is estimated, this confound could be problematic if ignored. However, it can be easily accomplished. How?

Continued

Data Analysis

Descriptive   Estimates of intrapair distance.

Inferential   Distribution-free statistics: Mann-Whitney and Wilcoxon. Why were these tests chosen over the *t*-test?

Hypothetical Outcome Analysis

Consider the following plots. Which one is consistent with your research hypothesis? What would the other one tell you?

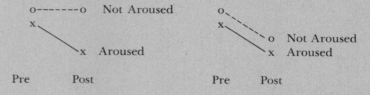

Rewriting, Rewriting, Rewriting

It is a truth that every good paper has gone through more than one draft. Rewrites are important for a number of reasons. Interestingly, some beginning writers choose to agonize during their first draft; make certain that each sentence is "perfect" before they move on to the next. We suggest, instead, that you write as a painter paints. *Do not* agonize over a sentence or a paragraph. Instead, like the painter, cover the whole canvas with vague forms and figures. Make sure you have said what you want to say. Then go over your "canvas" with more detail, adding transitions, precise wording, and better organization. Rewrite your work.

We have already advised you in an appropriate order for writing the sections. But during the rewrite, things may change. One common observation that students have when they read the literature is that the scientist never seems to be incorrect in the introduction, at least about the major issues. In other words, was the scientist really in touch with the experiment and its results to the extent implied by the introduction? Probably not!

Is this unethical? Again, probably not. The object of the research article is to convey to the reader *your current state of understanding*. You are supposed to inform and enlighten the readers, not give them a tour through chaos, dead ends, and stupid mistakes. Why should you subject the readers to the confusion and misunderstandings that you had when you first planned the study? Thus, the data will often lead to a rethinking, which in turn leads to a rewriting. There is a not-so-old saying that says if the introduction you wrote before the experiment is identical to the introduction after the experiment, you have not learned anything.

Figures and Tables

Figures, tables, and in-text presentations are the three ways that data are communicated in the journal article. Figures and tables are costly to publish, so their use should serve a clear purpose. In this box we discuss the formatting of these two costly, but often effective, ways to present data.

Tables

Tables supplement (rather than duplicate) the text. Each table should be understandable without reference to the text.

Give every table an arabic number (e.g., Table 13) followed on the next line by an underlined title that is clear and *explanatory*. For example:

Too cryptic: *Relation between Instructions and Performance*

Too detailed: *Mean Performance Scores on Test A, Test B, and Test C of*
(Duplicates *Students with Psychology, Physics, English, and Engineering*
Table Headers) *Majors*

Good: *Mean Recall Scores of Students with Different College Majors*

Following the table are headings for the columns. These headers should be as short as possible while still being informative.

Following the table can be notes to clarify the entire table or abbreviations used (e.g., *Note.* All responses were based on 100 questionnaires. TH = Try hard instructions). Superscripts are used to clarify a particular entry, row, or column (e.g., $*p < .05$).

Figures

Figure numbers and figure titles (captions) are placed on a separate page called *figure captions,* which is placed immediately prior to the figures. Other than this, the requirements above hold. Thus, to identify a figure do not write Figure 1 on the front of the figure. (If your instructor agrees, for a class paper, you may type Figure 1 on the figure at the bottom, but include a caption page as well.)

Figures convey only essential facts, should be easy to read (make the components a little bigger than you think), and should not be cluttered or contain distracting elements (e.g., use simple circles and squares to represent your data points). Figures are reproduced in actual articles exactly as provided by the author. Therefore, care should be taken to make figures as presentable as possible.

13 Baselines & Low N

Overview

In this chapter, the baseline design is presented, and its usefulness when one or a small number of subjects are available is emphasized. An experiment involving reinforcement (feedback) of gestures during conversation is designed, and the problem of the recovery of the baseline following treatment is discussed. Because a single subject is used, there is no need for statistics in presenting the results. The multiple baseline design, multiple time-series design, and combination baseline design are complications of the regular baseline procedure and are used to deal with problems of a nonrecoverable baseline or to assess more than one treatment at a time. Baseline designs are particularly useful when measuring performance effects, when variability between subjects is great, and when the availability of subjects is limited. The dependent variable measured in most baseline designs is the rate of a behavior across time.

No statistics are introduced in this chapter.

Tips on General Style discusses the use of word processing packages to prepare manuscripts. Tips on Specific Style covers the fine point of whether to use the word or a figure for a number.

Baselines and Small Numbers of Subjects Procedures

And the earth was without form and void (1:2)
God created man (1:27)
And every living substance was destroyed (7:23)
　　　　　　　　—Genesis

I have a friend I like to talk to whenever I have a problem. He seems to really hear what I say, and after I have talked to him I feel better, as though the weight of my problems are not so great as they were before. Why does this friend play the role of a psychotherapist for me? Why are other friends not equally able counselors? It always seems that among a group of friends, one or two individuals become the ones who hear the problems, doubts, goals, and innermost feelings of the other members of the group. What makes one person an amateur psychotherapist and another not? We hope to explore at least one reason why in this chapter.

Obviously an individual who plays the role of psychotherapist in a group must be what we would usually call a good listener. What makes one

person a good listener and another person not? This question is too broad
and general to answer by doing one experiment, just as determining who
will make a good psychotherapist cannot be answered by a single word or
sentence. We can, however, try to get an idea of what characteristics might
make a person a good listener (and, by implication, a potentially good psychotherapist) by analyzing the things that the good listener does when
interacting with another person. Back in the 1950s, psychologists Joel
Greenspoon, Leonard Krasner, and others reasoned that a listener can
have an influence on what another person says by agreeing with the talker
in various subtle ways. Such agreements as saying "yes" or "umm-humm"
or giving nonverbal cues such as smiles or nodding the head in agreement
serve as reinforcers.

They argued that a good listener uses these reinforcers to encourage
the talker to utter certain categories of statements. If you nod or voice
agreement every time your friend says something about himself or herself,
you may find your friend telling you more and more about personal feelings and problems. The hypothesis is that how we act, what we say and do
in a conversation, can be conditioned by the feedback provided by a listener. The feedback is the agreement or interest shown by the listener. In
the technical literature, this kind of strengthening of behavior through
feedback is called reinforcement.

To investigate the effect that reinforcement has on a *friend* places severe restrictions on our experiment. We may only have a few friends, or
perhaps one friend, who would ever feel comfortable disclosing personal
problems. With only one subject available for an experiment, the designs
discussed thus far would be inappropriate for methodological and statistical reasons. This situation occurs more often than the example of at-
tempting to have a friend make self-disclosing statements. For example, an
experimenter would be lucky to find one person who suffered from the
multiple personalities discussed in chapter 2. Even if more subjects could
be found, scientists are sometimes interested in how treatments affect individuals, rather than "groups on the average."

With one subject, we could take a pretest, apply the treatment, and
then take a posttest. However, because we have no control group, we would
not be able to rule out rival hypotheses that could have resulted from the
presence of confounding variables. The **baseline** design is a procedure that
is useful in many situations but requires only one subject.

The area of psychology most commonly associated with the use of baseline procedures is the experimental analysis of behavior that derives from
the influential work of B. F. Skinner. These procedures were originally
used in animal studies, but have now been widely applied to human studies.
This applied area is known as behavior modification. Behavior modification has been useful in dealing with such diverse problems as the behavior
of patients in mental hospitals to controlling bed-wetting problems in young
children. The use of baselines and the deviation of behavior from baseline
in response to independent variable manipulations are the keys to understanding this area of psychology. Because the problems of individuals in
mental hospitals are often unique, the baseline approach is particularly
appropriate.

Defining a Target Behavior

We have suggested that a person's behavior can be manipulated by another person's interactions or feedback. In a clinical situation a therapist might use this procedure to get the patient to talk about his or her problem. A target behavior of "talking about yourself" is a little too general to illustrate the baseline design. Indeed, most verbal categories are both difficult to define and to record as they happen. For example, if I say "I think the New York Yankees are the best team in baseball this year," am I making a self-revealing statement? Is it important from a clinical standpoint what I think about a baseball team? The answers to these questions are probably no. What we want to do is an experiment that addresses the issue "Is it at least possible that feedback can influence the behavior of a person in an interaction?" To get an answer to this question we need to find a clear and unambiguous behavior to treat as the target of the feedback. Self-referent statements are too vague for our purposes.

Rather than concentrating on the verbalizations of the subject as a target behavior, we suggest that gestures might be more easily defined and recorded. Specifically, we suggest that any part of the hand coming into contact with another part of the body (including the opposite hand) is a behavior that will suit our needs. When a person talks to another person, the hands are often used as nonverbal punctuation. Emphasis through hand gestures and thoughtfulness gestures, such as scratching the head or rubbing the chin with a hand, are all part of our everyday conversations. We suggest that such gestures can be modified in their frequency of occurrence through a process of reinforcement. Therefore, the target behavior in the experiment will be a discrete touch of the hand to a part of the body. During the feedback, or reinforcement, part of the experiment, each discrete touch will result in the feedback stimulus. Suppose the subject has his hands folded together and unfolds them and then puts them back together. This would count as one response. The point when the subject put his hands back together is the target behavior and should result in you, the experimenter, saying "good" or "right." Suppose the subject was sitting with her chin in her hand. Now she removes her hand and scraches her head. Once again the scatching would constitute an instance of the target behavior and result in an "umm-humm" or other feedback for its occurrence.

To create a situation where the subject will talk and do so under reasonably standard conditions, the experiment will use a form of deception in which a cover story will be told to the subject (chapter 12 discusses the use of a disguised experiment to control for the reactivity confound).

The Baseline Procedure

The baseline procedure is particularly effective in dealing with individual subject variability because the subject serves as its own control. In the most simple application of the baseline design, we begin by observing the subject under a baseline, or control, condition. The frequency of hand-to-body touches will be recorded over a 10-minute period without any reactions to

Figure 13–1   Two baseline studies that differ in the stability of the baseline before the treatment is introduced. Study B effects suggest the subject was improving before treatment (e.g., maturation), making it difficult to argue for a causal role of the treatment.

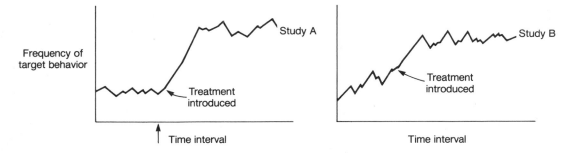

the subject by the experimenter. The data of interest are the total number of touches over the 10 minutes. Unlike a pretest, during a baseline, *several* measurements of the dependent variable are made. This change from a pretest to a baseline is a partial solution to the problem of confounds. For example, with a single-group pre-post design, maturation could explain any change in the dependent variable. In a baseline design, however, this confound is much less likely because if the subject was maturing, maturation should also be evident across the baseline measurements. Figure 13–1 illustrates the results from two baseline studies. In Study A, the frequency of behavior across the baseline changes very little, yielding a **stable baseline.** When the treatment is introduced, the frequency of behavior increases dramatically. In Study B, the frequency of behavior across the baseline is unstable. When the treatment is introduced, the frequency of behavior is now at the same high level as in Study A. However, the results of Study A are much more compelling than those of Study B. In Study B, the subjects were improving anyway, perhaps because of maturation. In our conversation study, this might mean that the subjects were simply becoming more and more comfortable as the experiment progressed.

Even for Study A, however, someone could argue that another confounding variable, for example, history, occurred at the time that the treatment was implemented. In our study, after recording the frequency of hand-to-body touches in the baseline condition, a 20-minute period of reinforcement will occur. The treatment condition will involve reinforcing each hand touch, immediately as it occurs, with a head nod, smile, and verbal reinforcer of "good," "right," or "umm-humm." How might a rival hypothesis be introduced in this study? One possibility is that when the experimenter begins to reinforce the subject's behavior, the additional concentration required by the experimenter distorts his or her role in the conversation, making the subject feel less at ease, more jittery.

Consider another common use of the baseline design. An overweight man is given a membership to a health spa by his girlfriend. Any subsequent weight loss may not be due to the health spa, but rather to the realization that his obesity was noticeable and something his girlfriend wanted to change.

Figure 13–2   If the baseline is not recovered in a BTB design, the possibility of a rival hypothesis, perhaps due to a history confound, exists. The recovery of the baseline makes it less likely that the effect was due to a confound because the rival hypothesis would have to claim that the confound was removed when the treatment was removed.

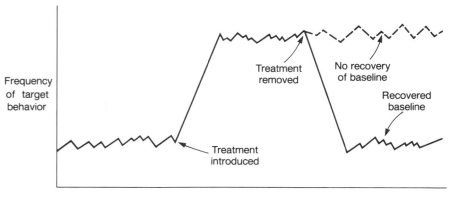

The logic of a baseline design is that the change in behavior that occurs with the change from baseline to the experimental treatment conditions is caused by the change in the independent variable. Obviously the change in condition is confounded with the passage of time in the experiment. To assess the possibility that something other than the change to the experimental treatment condition caused a change in behavior, a return to the baseline condition is the minimal baseline experimental design. If we let B stand for the baseline condition and T stand for the experimental treatment condition, then the minimal baseline design may be characterized as a BTB design. To conclude that the experimental treatment caused the change in behavior, we must be able to **recover the baseline.** The behavior under the second administration of the baseline condition must reasonably match the behavior observed under the first baseline condition. Figure 13–2 illustrates a recovered baseline in a BTB design.

The logic that the baseline must be recovered to show a cause-and-effect relationship between the experimental treatment and behavioral change rules out using the BTB design with an experimental treatment that produces permanent or long-lasting effects on behavior. For example, we might want to measure the social distance two persons maintain as a function of their familiarity with each other. The baseline would be an unfamiliar relationship, and the experimental condition would be that the subjects become familiar with each other; once familiar with each other, there is no way they can return to the baseline condition of being strangers. Thus the minimal conditions of a baseline design could not be met in this case.

In our experiment, the baseline condition is to withhold reinforcement for hand-to-body touches. Thus we will return to the baseline condition for a 10-minute period after the 20-minute reinforcement condition. The re-

Figure 13–3 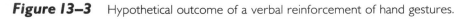 Hypothetical outcome of a verbal reinforcement of hand gestures.

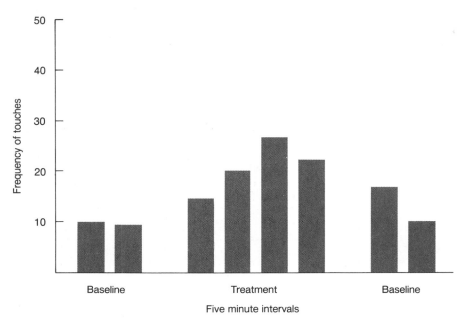

sults, when plotted on a bar graph, might look like those shown in Figure 13–3.

There are two main complications to consider when interpreting the result of the BTB design. First, can we be sure that the increase in hand-to-body touches was really caused by the experimental treatment? The alternative is to assume that the increase seen in Figure 13–3 during the treatment condition was due to random fluctuations in the data. In other designs, the researcher would be able to conduct statistical tests to show that the changes apparent in the graph were not due to chance. However, with one subject those techniques would not apply. One solution is to hope that our experimental treatment has a *large effect*. If the number of hand touches quadrupled between baseline and treatment, the magnitude of the effect might be great enough to convince us that the experimental treatment had the effect. Without such a large effect, what can we do to convince ourselves that the effects such as those illustrated in Figure 13–3 are real?

The second complication is that the subject is now in the same situation as before the experiment began. This is not a problem for the current study because the procedure was designed to determine if reinforcement could influence hand gestures. However, when self-destructive behavior in an autistic child is reduced by treatment, the return to baseline means that the child is again committing the self-destructive acts and at the same frequency. This presents a dilemma. On the one hand, if the experiment does not recover the baseline, scientific conclusions about the causal effect of the treatment are weak; on the other hand, if the baseline is recovered, the patient is no better than before the treatment.

The solution to both the statistical problem, where the effects of the treatment are not large, and the scientific/ethical problem, where the researcher wants to leave a person in a better state and prove the causal impact of the treatment, is the same: *repeat the experimental treatment* after the second baseline. The design would now be BTBT. If the experimental treatment caused the first increase, it should cause an increase on the second occurrence. If doubt still exists, the baseline could be reinstituted and again followed by another period of the experimental treatment. In principle, the repetition of baseline and treatment conditions are limited only by the patience of the experimenter and subject. The more times the baseline and treatment have been administered and produced predictable changes, the greater our confidence in the causal effect of the treatment.

In all of these derivatives of the BTB design, it has been assumed that the baseline is recoverable. What happens if the baseline is not recovered on its second occurrence? Suppose the number of hand touches in our experiment remains high when the subject is returned to the baseline condition. If this happens, we cannot be sure if the experimental treatment increases hand touches or if some other factor (passage of time, feeling comfortable in the situation, etc.) might have caused the change. Thus the failure to recover the baseline represents a serious problem for the interpretation of the effect of the experimental treatment. Alternative baseline designs that get around the problem of the lack of recovery of the baseline will be considered next.

Multiple Baseline Design

Suppose we cannot recover the baseline. A **multiple baseline design** is an experimental design that solves the nonrecovery-of-the-baseline problem, but still can be used with one subject. Suppose we identify five topic areas on which to focus under the guise of our cover story: social life, academics, sports, employment, and family. We can devote 30 minutes to each of these topics, perhaps over several days. (The cost associated with an unrecoverable baseline in a single-subject design is often extra time and effort on the part of the experimenter.) With the multiple baseline design, the subjects will experience the following baseline and treatment conditions.

Topic	30-Minute Intervals					
	1	2	3	4	5	6
Social Life (Day 1)	B	T	T	T	T	T
Academics (Day 2)	B	B	T	T	T	T
Sports (Day 3)	B	B	B	T	T	T
Employment (Day 4)	B	B	B	B	T	T
Family (Day 5)	B	B	B	B	B	T

If we are to make a causal statement about the treatment and changes in hand-touching behavior, then hand touching should increase *only* when the experimental treatment is introduced. So, during the social life conversation, hand touching should show an increase during the second 30-minute interval, but the other topics should not show an increase that early in the conversation because they are still under the baseline condition. Similarly, the sports conversation should show an increase in hand touching during the fourth interval, but not before. The employment and family conversations should remain at baseline levels of response during the fourth interval, whereas the social life and academics conversations should remain at treatment levels of response.

In effect, a multiple baseline design uses an introduction of the experimental treatment at different intervals for different situations, locations, topics, or, if available, subjects. With five topics and five introductions of the experimental treatment, it is unlikely that a consistent change in behavior can be accounted for by anything but the treatment.

A limitation of the multiple baseline design is that the treatment implemented for one topic may generalize to the other topics. For example, if, after the first 30-minute conversation, the subject returns for the second conversation but is emitting gestures at a high rate, then multiple baselines could not be measured. As another example, a behavior modification program designed to reduce smoking may require the subject to quit smoking at home during the first week, then at work during the second week, then at school, and so on. If the subject generalizes the treatment to all locations, that is, if the person quits smoking in all locations during the first week, it will not demonstrate the causal influence of the treatment even though it would be fantastic for the subject.

Other Baseline Designs

Multiple Time-Series Design

The **multiple time-series design** is similar to the multiple baseline design in that it is an attempt to overcome the limitations of the BTB design. Unlike the multiple baseline design, the multiple time-series design overcomes the inability or unwillingness to return to baseline by using a second subject strictly as a control. Essentially, *the control subject remains in the baseline phase for the duration of the experiment.* In our example, one subject would be in a B-T condition while the other subject is placed in a B-B condition. This helps to eliminate such confounds as history because the B-B subject should be affected by history in the same way and at the same time as the B-T subject.

Combination Baseline Design

Thus far, the baseline design is unable to reveal anything about interactions. As discussed in chapter 11, the interaction revealed by factorial designs is often more interesting to psychologists than the effect of a single variable. The **combination baseline design** allows for the study of interactions in a baseline procedure.

In our hand-touching experiment we could look at the effects of punishment in the form of disagreement such as shaking our head no, showing disinterest by yawning, averting our eyes, and so forth. Suppose we deliver a punishment when the subject fails to show one hand touch over a 60-second period. Whenever the subject fails to have a hand touch for 60 seconds, we will show displeasure (our punishment). The questions we can ask include whether punishment of the undesired behavior (non-touches) will result in an increase in the desired behavior and whether such a punishment procedure will increase the effectiveness of our reinforcement procedure when the two are used together.

The design of a combination baseline experiment is shown in the diagram below.

Subject	\multicolumn{7}{c}{10-Minute Interval}

Subject	1	2	3	4	5	6	7
1	Baseline	Reinforce	Baseline	Reinforce	Reinforce + Punish	Reinforce	Reinforce + Punish
2	Baseline	Punish	Baseline	Punish	Reinforce + Punish	Punish	Reinforce + Punish

Phases 1-2-3-4 is really a BTBT design for each subject. For Subject 1, the T is reinforcement (as in our earlier example), and for Subject 2, it is punishment. Pretend for a moment that our standard condition for Subject 1 is reinforcement, and for Subject 2, it is punishment. In other words, pretend that the baseline for Subject 1 is reinforcement and for Subject 2 is punishment. Then Phases 4-5-6-7 can be viewed as a BTBT design as well. In these phases, however, we can tell what effect reinforcement + punishment has over just receiving reinforcement; we can also tell what this effect would be when compared with just receiving punishment. In this way, the baseline design can tell us about interactions. However, because it is essentially a BTB design, the issue of recovery of baseline is important to the combination design.

When to Use a Baseline Design

As we mentioned earlier in this chapter, an influential group of researchers following the lead of B. F. Skinner and others (see *Tactics of Scientific Research* by Sidman for a methodological and philosophical review of this approach) advocates the exclusive use of single-subject baseline designs for experiments. Some of the issues addressed by those interested in the experimental analysis of behavior have already been discussed (e.g., recovery of the baseline). Additional issues are presented below.

Lack of Statistics

The baseline design has no required statistics. The data in the raw form must be sufficient to convince the researcher of the effect of the treatment.

The use of statistics from this standpoint is an admission of ignorance. Taking a mean of a group of subjects and comparing it with the mean of another group obscures the true nature of the effect of a variable: the change it causes in the behavior of the individual. The view is not just that statistics are not needed, but that they are inappropriate because the true effect is at the level of the individual subject, not group means.

Antitheoretical

The position taken by Skinner and his followers is that experiments done to test a theory are only as good as the theory they are designed to test. If the theory proves wrong (which it probably will be, according to this view), then the experiments done only to test the theory are uninteresting and of no permanent value. In this antitheoretical view, experiments should be done to satisfy the experimenter's curiosity about how nature might work, not to test formal theories. The approach may be characterized as being radically inductive in nature (chapter 1 discusses the difference between inductive and deductive approaches) or empirically based.

Rate of Behavior as the Dependent Variable

The baseline design is clearly most easily done when behavior is continuously occurring, such as occurs in a conversation or other interactions. The rate of behavior is thus seen as the fundamental unit of analysis.

In summary, the main belief of researchers in this tradition is that the individual subject is the appropriate unit of analysis for psychology. The baseline design is the obvious choice of experimental techniques when a single subject is the unit of analysis. An extreme position that some have argued is that a baseline design is always appropriate and is the only legitimate design except for unusual cases. We adopt a less extreme position than this. We see six main reasons that a baseline design may be preferable to a separate-group design.

1. *Performance effects.* The baseline design is a sensitive method for measuring the effects of a variable that does not have permanent effects on the subject. A variable that does not have permanent effects on the subject's behavior is called a **performance variable.** As we discussed above, an independent variable that has a permanent (or at least long-lasting) effect is not easily studied with a baseline design because the baseline cannot be recovered (BTB design) or it may be difficult to stop the treatment from generalizing to other situations (multiple baseline design).

2. *Variability between subjects.* When the variability of behavior between different subjects is great, the baseline design can be useful because the effect of the independent variable is measured within the same subject. Thus, it has many of the advantages of the more powerful repeated-measures designs.

3. *Availability of subjects.* If we were interested in using a chimpanzee as the subject of our research, an independent-groups design would be very expensive and perhaps impossible. Availability can also be restricted because of the problem studied. As we learned in chapter 2, multiple-personality disorder is extremely rare in the population. If we wished to

study this phenomenon, we would be lucky to have one subject. The trade-off between the baseline design and the between-groups design is that the baseline design requires the subject to be studied over a relatively long period of time, but not many subjects are needed, whereas the between-groups design requires a larger number of subjects, but the time needed to study each one is much less than the baseline design. A limitation to keep in mind is that the ability to generalize from a single subject may be limited. In other words, the external validity of these studies are often questioned.

4. *Substantial effects*. These designs typically ensure that any effects observed are substantial ones. Thus, no statistics are usually employed. In fact, the existing statistics are inaccurate measures of the effects in baseline designs. The disadvantage of this is that small but important effects will often go undetected.

5. *Experimenter-oriented experiments*. In the baseline design, the experimenter does not need to plan every action prior to collecting the data. In other words, the experimenter can introduce a manipulation when certain conditions have been met by the subject. In this way, he or she interacts more dynamically with the experiment and can take advantage of factors that could not be considered in other designs.

6. *Pilot studies*. An experimenter sometimes comes up with a novel idea or hypothesis to test. If the idea is an interesting one, but the experimenter is not sure about its correctness, a pilot study may be the answer. A pilot study is a partial experiment, or one done in a drastically reduced manner. A baseline procedure, because it typically uses just one or a few subjects, may serve as a pilot study to provide the experimenter with a clue about the correctness of his or her hypothesis. The pilot study allows the researcher to get an indication of whether an idea is worth pursuing and minimizes the costs of the indicator experiment.

Baselines and Many Subjects

Even though the baseline design was motivated as a methodology for single subjects, it can be used with several subjects. With additional subjects, the baseline design overcomes the low external validity associated with using a single subject. Several of the advantages we mentioned above apply even when more than one subject is available. For example, the fact that the experimenter can adjust the procedure as the study progresses can be useful in several situations. However, baseline designs often require more effort than do other designs. The researcher must assess the strengths and weaknesses (including cost) of the various designs against the purpose of the experiment when making the final decision.

The Experiment

In this experiment we will use a BTB design with 10 minutes of baseline, followed by 20 minutes of reinforcement, followed by a 10-minute return to baseline. Below is some of the thinking about the details of the study.

Cover Story and Deception

In the previous chapter we discussed the idea that some experiments must be done so that the subject is fooled by the experimenter. If the subject is aware of what the experimenter is trying to study, this awareness may alter the results of the experiment (the possible reactivity confound). If we tell our subject we are trying to condition him or her to use hand gestures while talking to us, the results of the experiment would be questionable. The subject who cooperated would be reacting to the demand characteristics of the experiment, not the effects of the reinforcers being given by the experimenter. For this reason we must engage in a mild bit of deception to do the experiment.

We will tell the subject that we are interested in doing an open-ended opinion survey, and we would like to solicit his or her opinion on a number of topics. This cover story will allow us to use a clipboard and write things down without arousing suspicion about the true nature of the experiment. Also, this story will encourage the subject to talk. After all, we are supposed to be getting his or her opinion about a series of topics, and this story should be sufficient to allow you, the experimenter, to conduct the real experiment.

As part of the planning for the experiment, you should create a list of topics of current concern. These topics might include political events, current movies or TV shows, campus issues, and so forth. You should make your questions vague so that the subject has plenty of room to answer. Remember, you are not really doing an opinion survey, you are only using it to get your subject to talk so you can condition him or her to touch hands.

It is a good idea to practice as the experimenter on a fellow classmate before actually doing this experiment. Research has shown that the effectiveness of the procedures we are studying depend on the skill of the experimenter in recognizing the appropriate behavior to reinforce and then delivering the reinforcer ("umm-humm") immediately and naturally. There are no bad subjects, only bad experimenters. Failure to do the experiment correctly will occur only if the experimenter has not been appropriately prepared. The data sheet/survey form at the end of the chapter may be used to help create the cover story and keep the subject from becoming aware of the true nature of the experiment. Once the experiment is over, you should inform the subject of the true nature of the experiment and explain what you hoped to find.

Key Words

baseline	performance variable
combination baseline design	recover the baseline
multiple baseline design	stable baseline
multiple time-series design	

Additional Reading

Greenspoon, J. (1955). The reinforcing effect of two spoken sounds on the frequency of two responses. *American Journal of Psychology, 68,* 409–416.

Greenspoon, J. (1962). Verbal conditioning and clinical psychology. In A. J. Bachrach (Ed.), *Experimental foundations of clinical psychology* (pp. 510–553). New York: Basic Books.

Krasner, L. (1965). Verbal conditioning and psychotherapy. In L. Krasner & L. P. Ullmann (Eds.), *Research in behavior modification* (pp. 211–228). New York: Holt, Rinehart, & Winston.

Verbal Reinforcement

Opinion Survey

Experimenter: _____ Date: _____

Subject: _____ Time started: _____

Opinion about (topics to be covered—fill in before beginning the experiment)

1. _____

2. _____

3. _____

4. _____

5. _____

6. _____

7. _____

8. _____

9. _____

10. _____

Real Data: Frequency of
hand touches in 5-minute
intervals

		Touches	Total
baseline	Start(S) to S + 5	____ : _____	_____
	S + 5 ____ to S + 10	____ : _____	_____
treatment	S + 10 ____ to S + 15	____ : _____	_____
	S + 15 ____ to S + 20	____ : _____	_____
	S + 20 ____ to S + 25	____ : _____	_____
	S + 25 ____ to S + 30	____ : _____	_____
baseline	S + 30 ____ to S + 35	____ : _____	_____
	S + 35 ____ to S + 40	____ : _____	_____

Use this space to make general comments and to occasionally write things down so as to make it appear that you are really interested in your subject's opinions about the issues listed above.

General Idea (Previous Research, Curiosity, Theory)

Put the general idea in your own words.

Explanatory Statement

This experiment follows a radically inductive approach. What does this mean?

Research Hypothesis/Descriptive Statement

State the research hypothesis:

Methods (Natural Observation, Survey, Field Experiment, Lab Experiment)

Is this a field experiment or a lab experiment?

Dependent Variable(s)

Frequency of target behavior

Operational Definition   Operationally define target behavior:

Also try your hand at the variable avoided in the text, Self-referring Statements:

Predictor or Independent Variable(s)

Reinforcement.

Operational Definition   Operationally define Reinforcement

Design (Between, Pre-Post, Within, Factorial, ▶ Baseline)

Baseline: A BTB design was developed in the chapter.

Continued

Continued
Subjects

Ethical Considerations

Characteristics and Availability

Sampling Procedure and Number of Subjects

Control

Subject Assignment (Randomization, Matching)   N/A

Environment (Insured Equivalence, Yoking, Counterbalancing)   N/A

Reactivity (Blinds, Deception, Disguised, etc.)
   Cover story (expand):

Continued

Procedural Command Decisions (Ceiling Effect, Floor Effect)

Retrospective Confound Check (Assumed, Statistical, Rethink)

Several of the following would present no problem. Which are they? Note how the baseline controls, where appropriate, and note where the return to baseline controls, where appropriate.

Selection:

Mortality: What does this mean in a single-subject experiment?

History:

Maturation:

Reactivity: Is the cover story in a disguised experiment enough?

Testing/Sequencing:

Instrumentation: Rethink: The experimenter may get better at doing the experiment.

Data Analysis

Descriptive

Inferential

Continued

Continued
Hypothetical Outcome Analysis

Word Processing

Like any other skill, the best way to improve your writing is to practice. By increasing the amount you write and the amount you rewrite, you not only polish your mastery of the rules of grammar, but also develop a style of your own.

A great drawback to this advice is the tedium associated with the mechanical aspects of writing: also known as the typewriter. Fortunately, the rapid advances in computer technology have made word processing software available to almost everyone. Using a typewriter to draft a manuscript is like using a slide rule to do an analysis of variance.

Word processors facilitate editing by providing powerful cut-and-paste functions, word wrapping to eliminate the need to hit the carriage return, and formatting. In fact, it is possible to set up the formatting according to the APA guidelines once and then use it for all of your papers. Word processors can also be used with spelling checkers, grammar checkers, and outline programs.

We recognize that computers and word processing packages can sometimes be expensive. There are some inexpensive machines and inexpensive word processors that will allow you a great amount of power compared with the typewriter, although some of the more esoteric features of the better word processors will be absent. In addition, the price of such a system is trivial when compared with the effort and expenses associated with four years of college.

Numbers

When should you spell out a number and when should you use the numeral?

Use numerals to express all numbers 10 and above unless it begins a sentence, as in "Ten subjects . . ."

Numbers below 10 should also appear as figures when:

1. they are in a series with a number over 10, as in "3 of the 12 subjects."
2. they precede a unit of measurement, as in "4 cm," "$4.00," "3 hr," "7%," "2-year-olds," "1:00 a.m."
3. they act as a mathematical function, as in "divided by 8."
4. they represent sample size or points on a scale, as in "3 subjects" or "scored 2 on a 7-point scale."

Thus you should use words to express numbers below 10 that do not represent precise measurements and that are not grouped for comparison with numbers 10 and above, as in "three or four times before," "nine conditions," "two-way interaction," or "one-fifth."

Combine words and figures to avoid awkwardness, as in rounded large numbers ("almost 3 billion subjects") or back-to-back modifiers ("2 two-way interactions," "twenty 2-year-olds").

Quasi-Experiments & Nonequivalent Controls

Overview

In this chapter we discuss the quasi-experiment, which is used when subjects cannot be assigned to conditions using randomization. In particular we focus on the nonequivalent control group design. A major confound, statistical regression, is given an in-depth treatment. In an attempt to evaluate the effectiveness of a "help session" for an experimental methodology course, we illustrate how the pattern of results obtained in a quasi-experiment can be useful in ruling out potential rival hypotheses. Local history and maturation confounds are discussed in this context, and comparisons are made to pretest-posttest methods.

Pairwise comparisons are used to analyze the data, although advanced techniques applicable to quasi-experiments are mentioned.

Tips on General Style discusses the value of obtaining reviews of the manuscript and some strategies for obtaining useful criticism. Tips on Specific Style discusses the psychology paper that reports more than one experiment.

Quasi-Experiments: When Randomization Is Impossible

"There is very little difference between one man and another; but what little there is, is very important."

—*William James*

In the last chapter, we talked about how to get around some of the requirements of true experiments and still be able to make some conclusions about causality. With baseline designs we get around the fact that we have only one subject by using a baseline and making it increasingly unlikely that some other variable could have produced the same pattern of results. What do we do when the problem is not the lack of subjects, but the fact that we cannot place our subjects into the experimental conditions using random assignment?

This problem occurs in several situations. For example, how do we evaluate a program for quitting smoking? What is the control group? We could use smokers who chose not to participate in the program, but there could be many differences between the people who took the program and those who did not. In our experiment, we will try to determine the effectiveness of a help session for improving an understanding of experimental methodology.

303

Let us consider the situation. The instructor has just given a quiz on research methods. After the quiz, he offers a special help session for those who wish to attend. Some of the students in class choose to attend and some choose not to attend. Some time after the help session the instructor gives another quiz, and the students who attended the help session score higher than those who did not. Can we conclude that the help session was effective? What can we do to improve the experiment?

We could do the following (unethical) *true* experiment. It is a true experiment because subjects will be randomly assigned. We give the first quiz as before. We then randomly assign half of the class to the help session (invite them to the review session) and half of the class to the control condition (we forbid them from attending). We then give the second quiz as before. Because subjects have been randomly assigned to either the Review or No-Review conditions we have a standard pre-post design and could procede as discussed in chapter 9. However, we should not use such a pre-post design in this situation. Imagine being one of the people not allowed to attend the help session. Or one of the people forced to go!

Thus, we are forced into using a procedure that does not assume that subjects have been randomly assigned to conditions. These designs are called **quasi-experimental designs** and are used when true experiments are impossible or impractical. There are several types of quasi-experimental designs; however, we will focus on only the **nonequivalent control group design.**

Nonequivalent Control Group Design

The nonequivalent control group design is identical to the pre-post design with the exception that subjects are not randomly assigned to conditions. This difference makes the conclusions about causality difficult to make with quasi-experiments. You should not reach the conclusion that this design is as good as the true experimental designs we have already discussed.

In addition to the confounding variables we have discussed thus far, one additional confound, statistical regression, can threaten the internal validity of the nonequivalent control group design. **Statistical regression** occurs when extreme scores tend to become less extreme on repeated testing.

Assume that students who did poorly on the first quiz (the pretest) decide to attend the help session. Students who did well choose not to attend. On the second quiz, statistical regression leads us to expect that the poor group will do better and the good group will do more poorly, *even if the help session had no effect.* Figure 14-1 illustrates this effect. The distribution on the ordinate represents the underlying (unknown) distribution of both Frank's and Roger's quiz scores. That is, the population of "ability" is exactly the same for both students. From this distribution, Roger happens to score an extremely low score on the first quiz (e.g., 0), whereas Frank scores a sample that is unusually high. If we now randomly sampled from this distribution a second time, we would expect the scores to be closer to the mean than was the case on the first quiz (e.g., at least greater than 0). Statistical regression is reflected in the commonly held student belief that they "are

Figure 14-1   Illustration of statistical regression.   Both students are equally competent, but one appears to perform more poorly, while the other appears to improve.

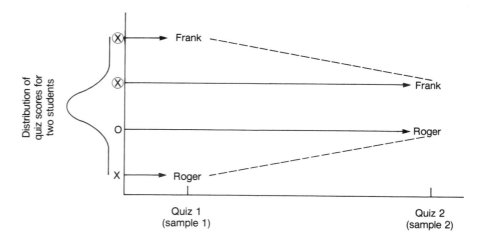

bound to do better" on the next test because they did so poorly on the first. Such a statement assumes that the initial poor showing was a deviant score for the student and not characteristic of his or her underlying distribution.

Consider the following study. A teacher wants to gain better classroom control over her third-grade class. She decides to reward students who behave and punish students who do not. The teacher gives students positive reward and special assignments if they meet the criteria of good deportment, and she places them in the naughty corner if they misbehave. She discovers that students who were punished were better behaved the next day, but that those who were rewarded actually had poorer deportment the next day. She decides to eliminate the reward component of the discipline program and only punish those who misbehave.

What is a possible rival hypothesis? Those who were rewarded had high scores that would, by chance, become lower over repeated testing. Those who were punished had low scores that would, by chance, become higher over repeated testing. Thus, even if the program were completely ineffective, statistical regression could have led to the pattern of results that the teacher observed.

Matching in the nonequivalent control group design does not eliminate these problems. First, matching does not control for unknown influences. Second, even if we match on pretest performance to equate the groups initially, statistical regression could still be a rival hypothesis. To understand this second point, consider the data in Figure 14-2 from a hypothetical help-session experiment. The data are pretest scores on the first quiz, and we want to match subjects on the pretest. The matched subjects will be included in our experiment, and any unmatched subjects will not be included. (We will still let them come to the help session of course.)

Clearly, the poorer students chose to come to the help session. If we attempt to match individual by individual, we would match the five highest scores of those choosing to come with the five lowest scores of those choos-

Figure 14-2 Matching without random assignment may force the experimenter into the tails of two different underlying distributions in order to equate the subjects at pretest (a). At posttest, subjects will regress to the mean of their underlying distribution, yielding an interaction even when no variable was manipulated (b).

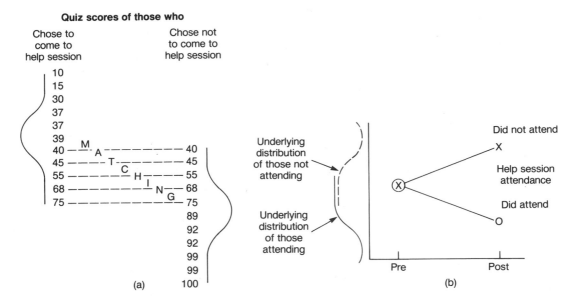

ing not to come. What would we expect to happen on the posttest, *even if the help session had no effect?* Extremely high scores tend to become lower and extremely low scores tend to become higher. Because the groups are different (no random assignment), we would expect each subject to regress to the mean of his or her particular group: the high scores of the people coming to the review session to get lower (they come from a population with a lower mean) and the low scores of the people who did not come to get higher (they come from a population with a higher mean). This is exactly the opposite of what a review session should do to the scores.

Because matching does not guarantee internal validity, we must be content with the fact that our groups may differ in their pretest scores. How they differ, and how they change at posttest, fortunately gives us clues as to what potential confounds to suspect. In other words, once we see the data, we no longer need to fear *every* possible confound. If one or two confounds still exist as rival hypotheses, we must then evaluate the extent to which these hypotheses are reasonable competitors with our treatment for the role of causal agent. Consider the pattern illustrated in Figure 14-3, which might be called *the rich-get-richer pattern.*

Here we would be tempted to conclude that going to our help session improved people's scores. However, our help-session attendees did better on the pretest. This suggests the possibility that this group was improving at a faster rate than those who did not attend the help session. This is a local maturation effect; local because it affects only one group, and maturation

Figure 14-3   The rich-get-richer pattern occurs when subjects who perform better initially are given the independent variable and improve still further.

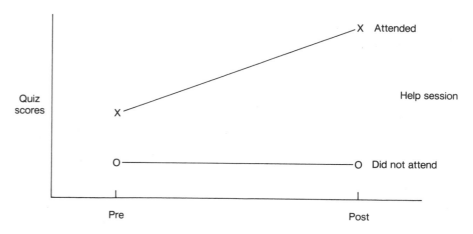

because it refers to an internal change within the subject (i.e., increasing understanding of the material). Similarly, another possible confound with this pattern of results is a local history effect. The people going to the review session have spent more time with the instructor; in fact, the instructor may have rewarded these people with a definite hint or two. Or knowing they were going to the review session may have led to more studying; in that case it may be the extra studying, not the review session, that caused the improvement.

What can be done about these problems? If possible, we could get evidence about the local maturation effect by looking at an even earlier quiz. If the difference between this earlier quiz and the pretest was the same, it would suggest that one group was not maturing at a faster rate; if they were maturing faster, they should show the improvement earlier. Obtaining several pretest measures is similar to the baseline design we discussed in the last chapter. However, this comparison may not be possible because there may not have been any earlier quizzes.

Another approach is to try to gather evidence in the data you have that would help you decide if a local maturation effect is present. Assume first that there is no local maturation confound operating. If we compute the variance of the pretest scores and the variance of the posttest scores, we would expect them to be comparable because both should be estimates of random error. If, instead, a maturation confound was operating, we would expect the posttest scores to reflect this growth factor, and thus the variability should be higher for the posttest. Thus, if we find greater variability at posttest compared with pretest, we should suspect a local maturation effect.

Some local history effects can be controlled by a cooperative instructor of the review session. Others may be considered as part of the help-session complex. In other words, you may say, "so what if the help-session people studied more because they went to the help session; if I consider the help session plus any side effects it may have as being one manipulation, then I have evidence for the effect of the help session—even if the cause is indirect." There is nothing wrong with this, but keep in mind that you have changed your hypothesis. Someone could say, "I'll bet the help session itself is useless!"

Finally, these effects may remain as alternatives. On the one hand, you might believe that the confounds should lead to disregarding the experiment as providing any evidence for your hypothesis. On the other hand, you may feel that their influence is minimal and be willing to accept the treatment as the causal agent. You will get support for your hypothesis only if the reviewers of your work agree with you.

Consider the second general pattern that may result as shown in Figure 14-4. This pattern, which could be called the *them-that-needs-it-gets-it pattern*, differs from the earlier pattern in that the help-session attendees started out lower than those who chose not to attend. This pattern is the one desired by most instructors of help sessions. That is, they hope that the people who need the help come to get the help.

If this pattern results, we should be concerned about local history effects and statistical regression effects. (Do you understand why local maturation is no longer a serious possibility?) The local history effect has already been discussed. The more likely confound in this pattern is statistical regression. We expect, by chance, that poor performers will improve. (Notice that the improvement does not place the help-session participants above the nonattendees.) Again, we could obtain further evidence for a regression effect by looking at even earlier quizzes. If performance of the poor performers had stayed at a low point over a number of previous quizzes, it would suggest that the true mean of the group was, in fact, low. Thus, any regression toward the mean could not account for the increase to the higher point observed in the study. Again, such previous quizzes may be nonexistent, leaving the statistical regression confound as a serious contender for our attention.

Figure 14-4　　The them-that-needs-it-gets-it pattern occurs when subjects who perform poorer initially are given the independent variable and show a large improvement.

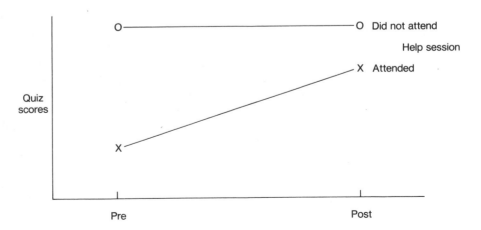

Figure 14-5   The crossover pattern occurs when subjects who were initially performing poorly receive the treatment and subsequently surpass the other subjects.

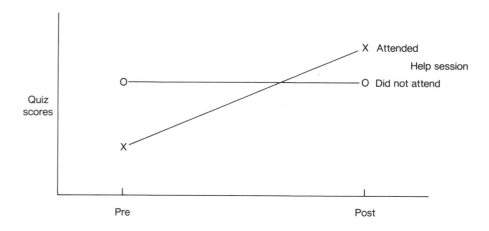

The third possible pattern of results, as illustrated in Figure 14-5, is the one that makes interpretation easier than either of the previous two patterns. Recall from chapter 11 that such a pattern is a crossover interaction.

In this pattern the poor performers attend the review session and improve to a point beyond those who did not attend. Local history may still be a confound, but both statistical regression and local maturation can be ruled out. The former is unlikely because regression should not move the experimental group to a point significantly better than the control group. Local maturation can be ruled out because it is typically the students scoring higher on the pretest who are learning or growing at a faster rate.

Other Quasi-Experimental Designs

Although there exist a number of other quasi-experimental designs, discussion of each of them is beyond the scope of this book. They do tend to share a number of characteristics, however. Besides a lack of random assignment, each of the designs involves some type of measurement of the dependent variable *before* the manipulation is introduced. In some designs this measurement resembles a pretest (as in the nonequivalent control group design) and in others it resembles a baseline.

Quasi-experimental designs, as a group, also share characteristics with true experimental designs. Two such characteristics may prove particularly confusing. First, consider the completely within-subjects design and its relative, the baseline design. Are subjects randomly assigned in the within-subjects design? No, and yet we treated this design as a true experimental design. The difference between the quasi-experimental and wtihin-subjects designs is that in the latter we are certain that all sources of error variance are equivalent in all conditions; with the quasi-experimental designs, we have no such assurance because with different people we could never match on *all* variables. Second, consider the factorial designs in which one of the factors is a blocking variable, such as gender. We did not randomly assign subjects to levels of gender, yet we treated that design as a true experimental design. The difference between these Treatment × Block designs and the quasi-experimental designs is that the former designs have at least one manipulated variable. It is in this manipulated variable that the power of causal explanation rests. We did not make claims in chapter 11 about gender causing any effects. Rather, we used the blocking factor to modify the causal statements based on the manipulated variable. This modification is correlational, just as the conclusions from the quasi-experimental designs are correlational.

The Experiment

We would like to test the possibility that help sessions improve student performance. We expect that students who attend a help session will improve more than an equivalent group of students who do not attend the help session.

Because attendance at a help session cannot be forced or prohibited, we will use a nonequivalent control group design. The pretest will consist of a short quiz on research methodology, and the posttest will be a similar test on the same material.

In our experiment, we will give a class of psychology majors taking experimental methodology a short, 15-minute quiz covering problems in experimental design. We will then announce to the class that we will be holding a help session for anyone who wishes to attend. The help session will last 1 hour. On the next class day following the help session, we will give another 15-minute quiz on the same topics as the pretest.

Data Analysis

The appropriate analysis for a nonequivalent control group design depends on why randomization was impossible. In our case, the groups differed because the students self-selected the condition they would be in (as opposed to being divided on the basis of a pretest or on demographic characteristics). In our case, a form of the analysis of covariance (ANCOVA) is the suggested analysis. Recall from chapter 6 that statistical control could be accomplished after the data had been collected. The ANCOVA is one such statistical control procedure. The differences observed at pretest between the two groups can be accounted for by ANCOVA in its analysis of the data.

The ANCOVA is a reasonably complex procedure, the details of which should be considered in an upper-level undergraduate or graduate-level statistics course. Because statistics have been used as a simple tool in this text, we will analyze this design with correlated t-tests comparing pre and post for each group and an independent t-test comparing the gain scores. (Distribution-free tests, such as Mann-Whitney and Wilcoxon, may also be used.) You should be aware, however, that the more sophisticated ANCOVA would be more appropriate.

Key Words   nonequivalent control group design
quasi-experimental designs
statistical regression

Additional   Curby, V. M. (1984; October). Analysis of an academic assistance program's success
Reading   in retaining students. Paper presented at the Annual Conference of the Southern Association for Institutional Research, Little Rock.

Goodson, M. L., & Okey, J. R. (1976; April). The effects of diagnostic tests and help
sessions on science achievement. Paper presented at the Annual Meeting of the
National Association for Research in Science Teaching, San Francisco.

Bell, P. E. (1970; March). An exploration of alternative methods for teaching large
sections of general education biology. Paper presented at the Annual Meeting
of the National Association for Research in Science Teaching, Minneapolis.

Help Session

Experimenter: _____

Class: _____ Instructor: _____

Help-session moderator: _____

Date of pretest: _____

Date of help session: _____

Date of posttest: _____

Subject #	Help?	Pretest Score	Posttest Score	Gain

Note: It would be difficult to conduct this experiment with the class using this text. However, you may be able to interview students from another class. If so, you will not have control over many factors. Be sure to note these possible rival hypotheses.

General Idea (Previous Research, Curiosity, Theory)

Help sessions for courses are usually assumed to be beneficial for students in those courses, yet the evaluation of the success of such experiences is often difficult. The following study is designed to determine if a help session is a useful pedagogical device.

Explanatory Statement

There are many explanatory statements that could be constructed to explain why a help session would be beneficial. The current work, however, is designed merely to demonstrate that a help session does, in fact, help.

Research Hypothesis/Descriptive Statement

State the research hypothesis:

Methods (Natural Observation, Survey, Field Experiment, Lab Experiment, ► Quasi-Experiment)

Quasi-experiment.

Dependent Variables

Quiz performance.

Operational Definition   The operational definition of performance will be the quizzes constructed and the score subjects receive on those quizzes. With a different type of quiz, you would have a different operational definition.

Predictor or Independent Variables

Attendance at a help session.

Operational Definition   Operationally define
    Help Session:

Continued

Continued

No Help Session:

Design (Between, Pre-Post, Within, Factorial, Baseline, ➤ Nonequivalent Control Group)

Nonequivalent Control Group: Subjects cannot be randomly assigned to the two conditions.

Subjects

Ethical Considerations   In addition to the usual considerations, state how ethical considerations led to the adoption of the quasi-experimental design used here.

Characteristics and Availability

Sampling Procedure and Number of Subjects   If the whole class is used, are you dealing with the population or a sample? If a sample, a sample of what?

Control

Subject Assignment (Randomization, Matching)   Subjects will self-select whether they will attend the help session. Thus, subject assignment is in no way controlled.

Continued

Environment (Insured Equivalence, Yoking, Counterbalancing)

Reactivity (Blinds, Deception, Disguised, etc.)   The subjects participate in a disguised experiment. Explain.

Procedural Command Decisions (Ceiling Effect, Floor Effect)

Retrospective Confound Check (Assumed, Statistical, Rethink)

(Selection, Mortality, History, Maturation, Reactivity, ► Statistical Regression, Testing/Sequencing, Instrumentation)   The potential threats to internal validity in this design depend, to an extent, on the pattern of results observed. For example, maturation, history, and statistical regression are more or less problematic with different outcomes. For each of the three patterns discussed in the text, state the possible confounds and what, if anything, you could do. Statistical control could be used to help acknowledge selection effect.

Continued

318

Continued

In addition, the experimenter can still take steps to reduce many rival hypotheses.

Instrumentation: The person running the help session should not be allowed to grade the quizzes. In most classes, this would be difficult to achieve. *Rethink:* Is there a procedure that would minimize this confound?

Testing: The early quiz (pretest) could have an effect on the later quiz (posttest). Clearly, the measurement of the quizzes is not unobtrusive. How could you minimize any testing effect? Why would the Solomon's four-groups design make little sense in this situation?

Continue by reconsidering other rival hypotheses.

Data Analysis

Descriptive Quiz scores for at least the pretest and posttest. Quizzes prior to the pretest may also prove of use.

Inferential Independent and dependent t-tests will be used in lieu of the statistical control provided by the analysis of covariance.

Continued

Hypothetical Outcome Analysis

Sketch the three patterns discussed in the chapter. Which of these patterns do you believe will most likely occur? What would you conclude in the results section if that pattern occurs? In the discussion section?

Proofreading and Feedback

In the prior two TOGS we have attempted to give you advice about rewriting your manuscript. There will come a point, however, when your manuscript must leave your hands and enter those of someone else. Many students make the mistake of picking the hands of the person about to grade the paper as the first reader. Much can be gained by allowing someone else to read the paper before it is given to the instructor or the editor of a journal. Picking the person to do you this favor is relatively easy: Ask a naive but intelligent person who is not a close friend. If this person does his or her job, many ambiguities, nonfluencies, grammatical problems, and just plain confusing or awkward sections will be noted. With this information, you should *make every change* suggested unless it alters the meaning of what you want to say or unless you *know* it is wrong. Many novice writers of technical prose make the mistake of assuming that their way was "just as good" or that the change is simply a matter of style. Most of time this is not the case, and if it is the case, why not make the change?

To facilitate the proofreading and feedback process, a standardized system of marks are used. A standardized system is of value not only in the publishing process but also in the exchange of papers for class. Below are some of the more common ones.

ℯ	Delete letter or ~~the~~ words	Delete letter or word
ℯ	Delete and close up	Delete and close-up
/	Make it lower case	Make it lower case
.....	Ignore the correction	Ignore the correction
≡	make it capital	Make it capital
#	Insert a space	Insert a space
⁋	Start a new paragraph	
⋀	Insert a comma	
⊙	Insert a period	

Reporting a Series of Experiments

Many, if not most, articles published today in psychology report programmatic results of a number of experiments. This requires some modification of the general organizational procedures we have discussed thus far.

The general organization would now be something like:

I.   Introduction

II. Experiment 1
    A. Methods
       1. Subjects
       2. Apparatus
       3. Procedure
    B. Results and discussion

III. Experiment 2
    A. Methods
    B. Results and discussion

IV. General discussion

The results and discussion sections are now placed together. The general discussion serves to integrate the two or more experiments and ties the entire paper together. Also, because Experiment 2 is likely to share much of the same methodology as Experiment 1, the second methods section is usually much shorter than the first. Often the new methods section is so short that no subheadings are used. Anything in the second methods section that is identical to the first is simply noted. For example, "The procedure was identical to the first experiment," or "subjects were sampled from the same pool as Experiment 1," or "except for the above changes, the methodology was the same as that of Experiment 1."

15 Quantitative IVs & Regression

Overview

This chapter discusses quantitative independent variables and how they can be analyzed. Some time is spent on data transformation and the relationship between physical (phi) and psychological (psi) measures. In particular, the logarithmic transformation and Steven's power law are discussed. In addition, the value of regression analysis is discussed and compared with the ANOVA. An experiment is developed that requires subjects to estimate the length of lines in the Mueller-Lyer illusion

Statistics introduced include data transformations and simple linear regression.

Tips on General Style discusses the oral presentation. Tips on Specific Style discusses the value of keeping a diary of your research and how it aids in writing the psychology paper.

Quantitative Independent Variables

". . . the aim of exact science is to reduce the problems of nature to the determination of quantities by operations with numbers."

—*James Clerk Maxwell*

If a 30-watt bulb is turned on in a dark room, how much brighter will the room seem? Obviously, the bulb will make a difference in the perception of brightness. But what if the room is already lit by two 100-watt bulbs? Will the addition of the 30-watt bulb make a difference in the perception of brightness? If so, how much of a difference?

We mentioned early in the text that physical scales and psychological scales are not necessarily the same. For example, if the amount of shock a person receives is doubled, that person is likely to estimate the amount of shock at more than double. However, if the sound pressure level of a tone doubles, the subject is likely to perceive it as less than twice as loud. In this chapter, we will try to determine the function relating the physical magnitude of a stimulus to the psychological magnitude.

The difference between the psychological and the physical is never more obvious than in visual illusions. Which line in Figure 15–1 is longer? People usually estimate the line on the left to have greater extent than the line on the right. Can we characterize this illusion more specifically? What is the function that relates our perception to the physical stimulus?

Thus far in this text we have discussed only qualitative independent variables. That is, we introduced variability in our independent variables by

Figure 15-1   The Mueller-Lyer illusion.   Both lines are the same length, but the one on the left appears longer.

comparing one level of the IV against a different example of the IV (see chapter 5). For example, we compared a reason with a no reason, observers with hiders, dominant eye with nondominant eye. Often psychologists prefer to vary the IV quantitatively. They may do this after they have a basic understanding of the effect of the variable. They may also use quantitative manipulations if they are interested in *how* the IV is related to the DV rather than just *if* the IV causes the DV. Finally, some interesting independent variables are naturally quantitative, and ignoring that quantitative aspect of the variable would be foolish. For example, the intensity of a light is a variable that could be manipulated in an experiment. It would be silly to do an experiment comparing no light with light. Rather we could easily look at precisely specified levels of light intensity.

Background: The Psychophysical Law

The purpose of the current experiment is to determine the function relating the length of a line, its physical extent, to our perception of extent as it occurs in the Mueller-Lyer illusion. We are interested in whether the same function characterizes length perception for both forms of the Mueller-Lyer illusion. For simplicity, however, the following discussion focuses on only one of the functions. We will return to the comparison of the two functions later in the chapter.

Regression Analysis

Analysis of Quantitative Independent Variables

The analysis of quantitative independent variables differs from what we have done in other analyses. Previously, we would have conducted an ANOVA to see if there was an effect of physical extent and if this effect interacted with the two forms of the Mueller-Lyer figures. This is not the best approach for at least three reasons: (1) the ANOVA does not "realize" that length is a quantitative IV and will not take advantage of this additional information; (2) we want to know what form the function takes that relates psychological estimates of length to physical length, not just if a relationship exists (obviously, and uninterestingly, a relationship does exist); and (3) besides establishing the general form of a relationship (e.g., power function or log function), we want to characterize the situation more specifically by estimating the parameters of the model. In our case, we may find that people can be "good" length estimators either because they are able to estimate absolute length or because they are sensitive to relative changes in length even if they are unable to give accurate estimates in an absolute sense. (For example, a person may not know the length is 100 cm but may know that it is twice the length of the 50 cm line.) Let us consider each point in turn.

ANOVAS and Quantitative IVs

There are several analyses that can take advantage of the quantitative nature of the independent variable, including some ANOVA-based analyses such as trend analysis. However, the standard ANOVA that we have used thus far does not care whether the IVs are qualitative or quantitative. Even though physical length in our study is clearly a ratio scale, the ANOVA will treat the IV as a nominal variable. What does this matter? Consider the two graphs shown in Figure 15–2. They represent the same data. The graph on the right is the hypothetical length estimates collected from one of our subjects. There is a slight increase in estimates of length with increasing objective length. To the ANOVA, this pattern is no different than the pattern on the left. Because the ANOVA does not use the quantitative information in the IV, it is likely to fail to detect a relationship between the estimates and the physical length.

The Form of the Function

When we have a quantitative IV, we often are interested in simply what the function looks like: is it linear or not? What is its general form? How well does the function fit the data, or how much of the variance in the data can be accounted for by the function? Regression and correlational techniques are better suited to answer these questions than is the ANOVA.

Estimation of Parameters

Once the form of a function is established, we will also want to estimate the parameters of the function. What is the slope of the function? What is the intercept? Often, it is the parameter that is of primary interest. An ANOVA obviously cannot give us any idea what these estimates should be. In our case we will want to know the *relative differences* in how people judge length. For example, if a person estimates a 50 cm line to be 10 cm and a 100 cm line to be 20 cm, then the person is doing a good job because his or her

Figure 15–2   Both plots display the same data. However, the linear increase apparent in *b* is not evident in *a*. The standard ANOVA would, similarly, treat the independent variable as a qualitative one and thus may fail to detect the systematic effect of the IV.

estimate of the second line is twice as large as the first estimate, even though the person is not being very accurate in an absolute sense. Psychologists realize that people are not very good at making absolute judgments (such as how many people were at the football game), but they are good at making relative judgments (such as were more people at this week's game than last week's game).

Because of these three reasons, we will use **regression analyses** rather than the ANOVA to analyze the data. If you need assistance in the statistical principles of regression analysis, you should refer to the statistics review.

In this experiment, we present subjects with stimuli that vary in their length and have subjects estimate the length. There are many ways of having subjects estimate the length, but the easiest of these has also proven to be one of the best. The procedure is called *magnitude estimation* and simply requires the subject to assign a number to each stimulus in such a way that the number represents the perceived magnitude of the attribute of interest. The only constraint placed on the subject is that if one stimulus is, for example, twice as large as another, then the subject should give a number twice as large, and so forth. (Another constraint is that the subject must give only positive numbers; he or she cannot give zero or negative numbers. Such an estimate would, of course, make no sense, but you may find that a subject will do this occasionally.)

The stimuli will consist of eight lines (for each form of the Mueller-Lyer) varying in length over a 30 : 1 range. That is, the largest line will have a length at least 30 times as large as the smallest line. This 30 : 1 ratio will give us a range large enough to gain a good understanding of the nature of the function relating physical length and psychological length. Each subject will be exposed to the lines in a different order. All subjects will be told how to make magnitude estimations and will be told that we are interested in their general impression of the length and that they should not try to figure out the length.

For each stimulus line, we will find an average response for each subject. Then we will average across all subjects for each of the 16 lines and thus end with 16 averages,[1] 8 for Form A and 8 for Form B.

A Linear Relationship

Let us assume that we observe the following data across 20 subjects for our line experiment.

---

[1] Because subjects are free to use any numbers that they choose (e.g., centimeters, inches), the arithmetic average is not a good estimate when averaging across subjects. One subject could greatly influence the arithmetic mean. Psychophysicists use the **geometric mean** because it is less sensitive to extreme scores than is the arithmetic mean, and yet, unlike the median, still uses all of the scores in the distribution. The geometric mean is, formally:

$$GM = \sqrt[N]{Y1 \times Y2 \ldots \times Y_N}$$

However, it is computationally simpler to find the arithmetic mean of the natural logarithms of the estimates.

$$\ln GM = \frac{\ln Y_i}{N}; \quad GM = e^{(\ln GM)}$$

Phi (physical length in cm)	Psi (psychological length in unitless estimates)
5	8
10	23
16	35
25	54
40	79
60	123
100	202
182	368

We can then plot out results on standard (i.e., linear-linear) graph paper, as shown in Figure 15–3. The data come very close to a straight line. We can characterize a straight line as:

$$Psi = b \, (Phi) + a$$

where Psi is psychological magnitude, Phi is physical magnitude, and b and a are **parameters** of the equation. More specifically, b is the slope of the line and a is the intercept. The size of b tells us the relative differences in psychological magnitude as a function of Phi. In magnitude estimation procedures, the parameter a is relatively uninteresting because our subjects could use any numbers they want to describe the line. Some may have given numbers reflecting estimates in inches, some in centimeters, or even in miles. The point is that whatever differences there were all go into the parameter a.

By using regression analysis, we can find the best-fit straight line for our data, and we can tell how well such a function (i.e., straight line) fits the data. That is, we can tell how much of the variance in the data can be accounted for by a straight line. In addition, we will obtain an estimate of b. For our data, $b = 2.014$, $a = 1.222$, and the line accounts for $r^2 = 0.9997$ or 99.97% of the variance. If you need a reminder of how to obtain these values from regression analysis, refer to the statistics review in this chapter and the one in chapter 9 on correlation.

A Nonlinear Relationship

Imagine, instead of the above data, we observed the following from the subjects.

Phi	Psi
5	3
10	8
16	22
25	40
40	110
60	180
100	360
182	950

Figure 15–3   Graph of a linear relationship with the best-fit line superimposed. The equation for the line is given on the figure.

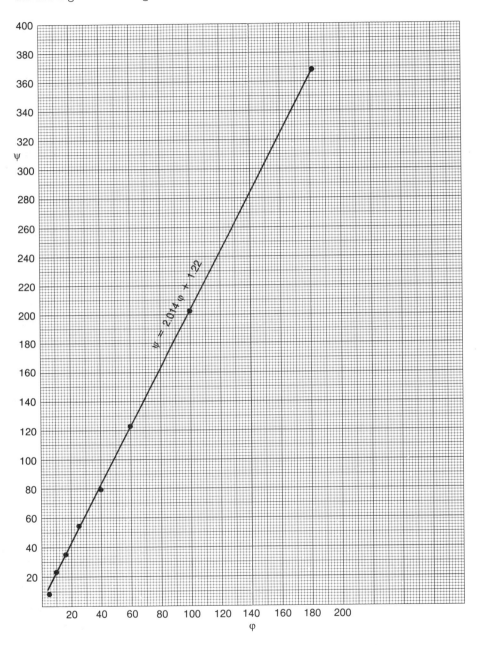

A graph of these data, as shown in Figure 15–4, confirms that Psi is not linearly related to Phi. If the data are not linear, is it still possible to characterize the function, and is it still possible to·estimate parameters? The answer is yes, but it is somewhat more difficult. One approach, the one taken here, is to perform a **transformation** on the data. For any set of data, there

Figure 15–4 Graph of a curvilinear relationship on standard graph paper.

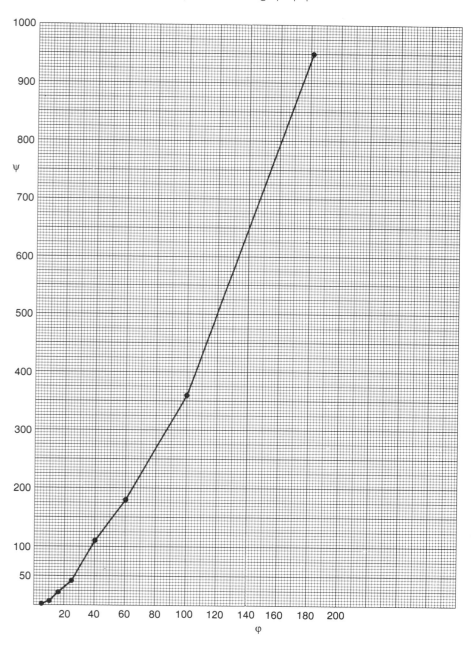

does exist some transformation that will produce a linear relationship between the transformed Phi and transformed Psi. Transformations are only
useful if they are done in the context of a theory or model.

S. Stevens (the author of the four types of measurement scales discussed early in the book) contends that the relationship between the physi-

cal and the psychological is a power function. Power functions are also familiar to most of us. When we plotted $Y = X^2$ in high school, we were plotting a power function; that is, we were saying that Y is equal to X raised to the power of 2. The more general formula of Steven's power law is:

$$\text{Psi} = K \text{ Phi}^{\text{Beta}}$$

We can turn this equation into a linear one by taking the *logarithm* of both sides. (It is irrelevant whether we use the natural logarithm, 1n, or base 10 logarithms. In our work, we will use the natural logarithm.)

$$\text{1n Psi} = \text{Beta (1n Phi)} + \text{1n } K$$

Comparing this equation to the equation for a straight line, Psi = b (Phi) + a, we see that Beta is the slope of the linearized power function and 1n K corresponds to a.

Below are the original data from above and the natural logarithm transformations.

Phi	Psi	In Phi	In Psi
5	3	1.609	1.099
10	8	2.303	2.079
16	22	2.773	3.091
25	40	3.219	3.689
40	110	3.689	4.700
60	180	4.094	5.193
100	360	4.605	5.886
182	950	5.204	6.856

If we plot the transformed data on standard graph paper, as shown in Figure 15–5, we will obtain a straight line. Submitting the transformed data to standard linear regression analysis also allows us to estimate Beta and to determine the percentage of variance accounted for by the power function. However, rather than plotting the transformed scores on standard graph paper, we can plot the original values on log-log graph paper as shown in Figure 15–6. Log-log paper has performed a logarithmic transformation on both its ordinate and its abscissa. The paper should also give you a better idea of exactly what a log transformation does to the data: It compresses the higher ends of the scale. For our data, the estimate of Beta is 1.62, 1n a = -1.50, a = .224 (exponentiate 1n a, $e^{\ln a}$). The correlation, r, is .998, leading to an r^2 of .996, which indicates that the function accounts for 99.6% of the variance in the empirical estimates.

The percentage of variance accounted suggests that for these data, the power function provides a good characterization of the relationship of physical and psychological magnitude. Further, the estimate of Beta tells us a great deal about the function. Because Beta is less than 1, we know that an increase in physical magnitude for small lengths has a larger psychological effect than does a similar physical increase for large stimuli. In other words, the difference between a very small line and a small line is larger, psychologically, than is the difference between a large line and a very large line. As another example, the difference between $10 and $12 is psycho-

Figure 15–5   Graph of same relationship as Figure 15–4.   Natural logs of both variables were calculated and these transformed scores were plotted on standard graph paper. The curvilinearity in Figure 15–4 is not evident in this figure.

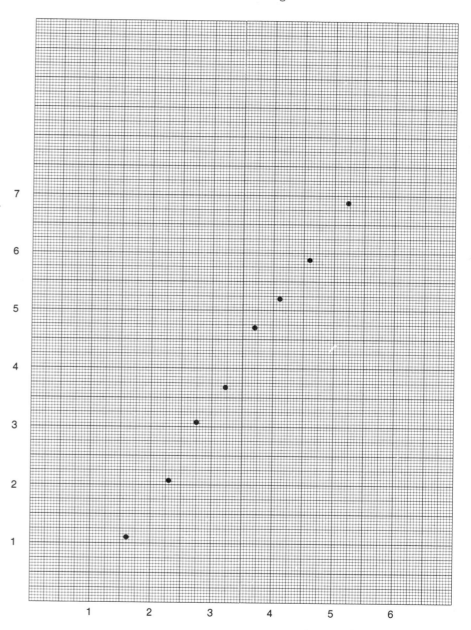

logically larger than the difference between $50,000 and $50,002. If Beta were larger than 1, it would mean that changes at the high end of the physical scale have larger psychological effects than changes at the small end. Finally, if Beta were exactly 1, the function would be linear. Try taking the data illustrating a linear relationship and determining the value of Beta: it

Figure 15–6   Power function in log-log coordinates.   Both the linearized equation and the best-fit power equation are shown.

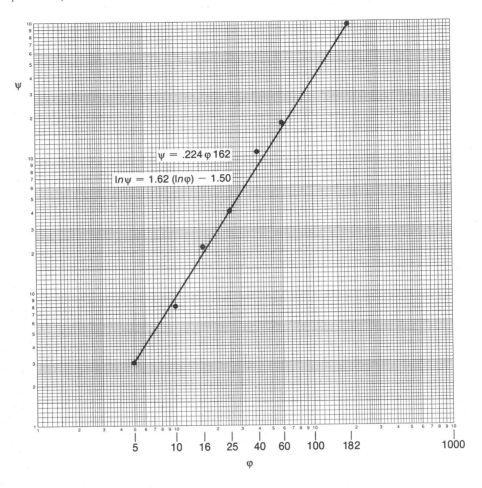

$$\psi = .224\, \varphi\, 162$$

$$\ln\psi = 1.62\,(\ln\varphi) - 1.50$$

should be 1.0. Plot those data on log-log paper. It should also be straight, but should have a different slope than the function based on nonlinear data.

The Experiment

In the experiment, we will present subjects with a mix of 16 Mueller-Lyer figures. Eight will be of one form and eight of the other. For each subject, we will scramble the stimuli (i.e., randomize the stimuli) to obtain a different order for each subject.

Subjects will be told to estimate the length of the lines. More specifically, they will be told that if one stimulus seems twice as long as another, they should give it a number twice as large. They can use any numbers they would like (except negative numbers). They should be told that we are interested in how well people can *estimate* length, and thus they do not need to make protracted deliberations.

After all subjects have made estimates, geometric means can be computed, or for easier computation, the median can be used. This will produce 16 averages. Then the IV (physical length) and the DV (estimated length) will be transformed into natural logarithms and a regression analysis will be performed twice: once on the eight Form A stimuli, and once on the eight Form B stimuli.

For our study we want to answer several questions. We want to know what type of function characterizes the relationship between physical and psychological estimates of size. If a power function is a good characterization of the relation, then we want to know if Beta is larger than 1, less than 1, or equal to 1.

Finally, we will fit one function for Form A of the Mueller-Lyer illusion and one function for Form B of the Mueller-Lyer illusion. We could reach several conclusions after comparison of the two functions. First, it would be important to determine if both forms are fit by a power function. If so, we would like to determine if the functions are the same. If not, do they differ in their exponents (i.e., nonparallel lines) or their intercepts (i.e., parallel lines)? Differences in exponents would mean that the Mueller-Lyer forms lead to different assessments of relative length. Differences in intercepts would mean that the Mueller-Lyer forms lead to different assessments of absolute length.

At the end of this chapter you will find lines that vary in size so you may perform the experiment outlined in the chapter. In addition, other stimuli are available that could be scaled instead: frequency of causes of death in our society, or frequency of English words, to mention two. You can determine the psychological scale using magnitude estimation and the procedures outlined here for any physical dimension for which you have measures.

Key Words   geometric mean   regression analysis
                 parameters   transformation

Additional Reading   Engen, T. (1971). Psychophysics II: Scaling methods. In J. W. Kling & L. A. Riggs (Eds.), *Woodworth & Schlosberg's Experimental Psychology* (3rd ed., pp. 47–86). New York: Holt, Rineheart, and Winston.

Gregory, R. L. (1966). *Eye and brain* (1st ed.). New York: McGraw-Hill.

Judd, C. H. (1899). A study of geometrical illusions. *Psychological Review, 6,* 241–261.

Robinson, J. O. (1972). *The psychology of visual illusion.* London: Hutchinson & Co.

Linear Regression

Note: Students should refamiliarize themselves with the statistics review on the Pearson product-moment correlation coefficient before proceeding with this review.

Linear regression is a procedure for fitting a linear function to correlated variables so as to allow prediction from one variable (IV) to the other (DV). The line fit is the "best-fit line" in the sense that it minimizes the deviations of the values predicted by the line from the actual observations. Usually the researcher wants to know the formula for the line and how well the line fits the data (that is, the percentage of variance accounted for). A straight line has the form: $Y = bX + a$, where b is the slope of the line and a is the intercept.

The formula for slope is $b = SS_p/SS_x$.

The formula for the intercept is $a = \bar{Y} - b\bar{X}$.

The formula for proportion of variance accounted for is r^2.

STEP 1.   Table the data.

X	Y
1	3
2	12
4	48
8	192
16	768

STEP 2.   Perform transformations, if any, on the data.

ln X	ln Y
0.0000	1.0986
0.6931	2.4849
1.3863	3.8712
2.0794	5.2575
2.7726	6.6438

STEP 3.   Compute SS_p. (See review of Pearson, chapter 9.)

$$SS_p = \Sigma xy - \frac{(\Sigma x)\,(\Sigma y)}{p} = 36.442 - \frac{(6.93)\,(19.36)}{5} = 9.609$$

STEP 4.   Compute SS_x. (See review of independent t-test.)

$$SS_x = \Sigma x^2 - \frac{(\Sigma x)\,(\Sigma x)}{p} = 14.413 - \frac{(6.93)\,(6.93)}{5} = 4.805$$

STEP 5.   Compute slope.

$$b = SS_p/SS_x = 2.00$$

STEP 6.   Compute intercept.

$$a = \bar{Y} - b\bar{X} = 3.8712 - (2.00 \times 1.3863) = 1.0986$$

STEP 7.   State the formula for the transformed data.

$$\ln \hat{Y} = 2.00\,(\ln X) + 1.0986$$

STEP 8. Retransform the formula to account for the original data, if appropriate.

$$\hat{Y} = 3X^{2.0}$$

STEP 9. Compute Pearson's r, *and square it. (See correlation review.)*

$$r = 1.00; \quad r^2 = 1.00;$$

thus the straight line accounts for 100% of the variance in Y.

STEP 10. Plot the line.

Given the equation from step 8, we can now substitute a value of X and observe a predicted value of Y (i.e., $\hat{Y}$). Two points are needed to define a line. We recommend using the arithmetic mean of X as one input to your equation (which should produce $\overline{Y}$ in order to check your calculations.

Mueller-Lyer

Experimenter: _____ Date: _____

Subject #   Stimulus

	Form A ($\succ$——$\prec$)								Form B ($\longleftrightarrow$)							
1	2	3	4	5	6	7	8	9	10	11	12	13	14	15	16

Medians:

ln GMs:

GMs:

General Idea (Previous Research, Curiosity, Theory)

Psychophysicists have argued that a power function relates physical stimuli to psychological perceptions. A severe test of this model would be to determine how well such a function fits the data in a situation where perceptual processes break down, as in a visual illusion.

Explanatory Statement

In one sense, the idea that a power function describes the transformation of the physical world into the psychological world may be viewed as an "explanation." Discuss in what sense you believe that this is an explanation and in what sense you believe that it is not.

Research Hypothesis/Descriptive Statement

1. Both functions should be power functions.
2. Both should have Betas less than unity.
3. Subject should be more sensitive to relative changes with (Form A/Form B/Neither). Pick one that reflects your research hypothesis.

Methods (Natural Observation, Survey, Field Experiment, Lab Experiment, Quasi-Experiment)

Lab experiment.

Dependent Variables

Estimates of length.

Operational Definition   Describe the magnitude estimation procedure:

Predictor or Independent Variables

Physical line length under two forms of the Mueller-Lyer illusion.

Operational Definition   A ruler and the figures drawn at the end of the chapter.

Design (Between, Pre-Post, Within, Factorial, Baseline, Nonequivalent Control Group)

Within.

Continued

340

Continued
Subjects

Ethical Considerations

Characteristics and Availability

Sampling Procedure and Number of Subjects   Can this experiment be conducted with only one subject? Discuss.

Control

Subject Assignment (Randomization, Matching)   Completely within.

Environment (Insured Equivalence, Yoking, Counterbalancing)   Materials should be randomly ordered for each subject, or a form of randomized counterbalancing can be conducted. With this counterbalancing, all orders are constructed (in this case only two: AB and BA). Then the experimenter randomly picks orders until the ordering of the 16 stimuli is determined: ABBAABABBBABABAAB.

Reactivity (Blinds, Deception, Disguised, etc.)

Procedural Command Decisions (Ceiling Effect, Floor Effect)

Retrospective Confound Check (Assumed, Statistical, Rethink)

(Selection, Mortality, History, Maturation, Reactivity, Statistical Regression, Testing/Sequencing, Instrumentation)

Data Analysis

▶ ***Transformation*** 1n-1n: natural log transforms on both the IV and the DV prior to analysis.

Descriptive Geometric means (or medians). Parameter of the equation will be Beta (1n a is also a parameter, but not of interest). Proportion variance: r^2.

Inferential No inferential tests are planned in this chapter. However, the motivated student could explore how to test the difference between two slopes by consulting the appropriate statistics text.

Continued

Continued

Hypothetical Outcome Analysis

State the hypothesized outcome according to your research hypothesis. What would the plots look like on standard graph paper? On log-log paper?

The Oral Presentation

We have discussed in depth the processes required to communicate your work in written form. That is, we have assumed that the work will be read by someone who has your manuscript or article in front of them. This form of communication allows the reader to reread sections, flip pages, underline sections, and take notes. Thus, the printed journal article need not contain much redundancy because you can expect the reader to review that which he or she does not grasp immediately.

The other means of communicating your efforts is at a convention where you will orally tell an audience in about 15 minutes what you did and what you found. Although 15 minutes may seem like a long time, you will discover that it is surprisingly short.

Writing something to be spoken differs greatly from writing something that will be read. In the speech you can expect to communicate very few details. The speech must be constructed so that it sounds as though you are speaking; it must include a lot of redundancy to aid the listeners' processing capacity; and it must be constructed to be of interest to all levels of your potential audience.

In general, if you speak at a normal rate, a 7-page, double-spaced manuscript will occupy 12 to 15 minutes. You should expect to be able to present one complex figure or table (via slide projector or overhead projector) for every 5 minutes of speech. The listener will be able to grasp *one* or *two* major points. So before you start preparing your talk, decide what those one or two points will be and keep them in mind throughout the entire talk.

Professionals differ on whether or not students should be allowed to read their papers. (They do not disagree about how professionals should present their papers—definitely no reading!) We take the view that it is better for a student to read the paper, assuming good eye contact, than to not present a paper at all. However, you should try to present your paper without reading. Some tips on how to do this are (1) carry a triple-spaced version of your paper to the podium as a security blanket, (2) memorize the first paragraph *at most,* (3) use a lot of simple slides and overheads to serve as prompts to you, and (4) practice!

Keep a Diary

When you begin a research project in earnest, it is a good idea to keep a diary or a journal of your thoughts and activities as you progress. This is important for writing because it will allow you to recover your thinking of many months ago. Often, the scientist's thinking will change dramatically as he or she continues reading and as new data from the laboratory become available. The way the scientist views the problem now will be different than the way he or she viewed the problem at the beginning of the project. Experimental outcomes that at one time were interesting or even surprising, may now seem trite and expected.

Yet, for those of us who have not been involved in the project, our expectations and understanding are like the scientist's at the beginning of the experiment. The journal article must take us from our state of understanding through to the author's current understanding. To do this, the author must capture the thoughts he or she had at the beginning of the experiment. If the author were to begin with his or her current thinking, the reader would be denied several months of a logical progression.

A diary or a journal that includes the reasons certain decisions were made can be a valuable tool. Although it is true, as we discussed earlier, that the author should not take the reader down blind alleys and dead ends, the author should take the reader from the original starting point along the smoothest path to the current understanding.

Mueller-Lyer

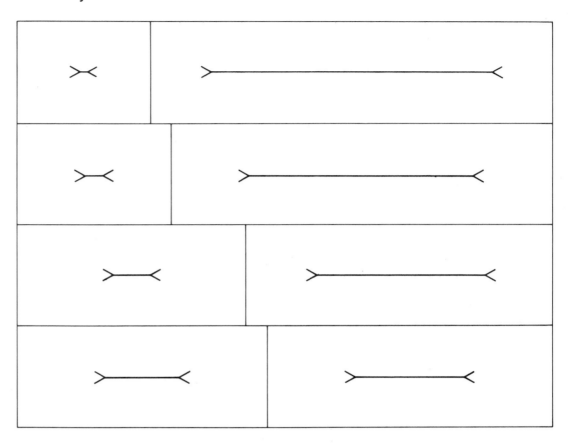

Mueller-Lyer

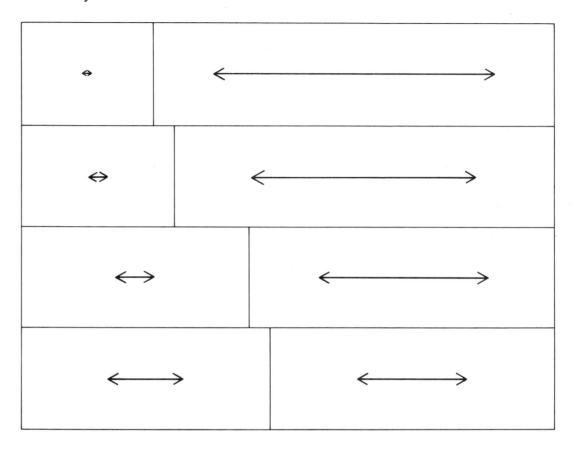

Mueller-Lyer

Mueller-Lyer

16 Publishing & Publishing

◼ Overview

In the closing chapter, we recount the steps involved in the publication of a psychology journal article, from inception of the idea, through the review process, to publication of the article.

No new statistics are introduced, but the value of computer packages is discussed.

Tips on General Style provides a number of words of wisdom. Tips on Specific Style traces through the publication process.

Final Thoughts: Diary of a Journal Article

"You know my methods, Watson."
—Sherlock Holmes

We have taken you through a number of empirical investigations and have introduced you to the methods used by research psychologists to gain a better understanding of cognition and behavior. We have tried to give you an idea of the thought processes that go into any scientific study. If we have been successful, you should have a better understanding of what experimental psychologists do and how they do it. What you do with this information will depend on your professional goals. Some of you will use this information to help refine your thinking and planning in an area other than psychology. Some of you will become practitioners, rather than researchers, and will use this information in evaluating the literature and your own work. Finally, a few of you will become research psychologists. To those of you who hope to contribute to the puzzle of humankind, who hope to publish creative, original work, we dedicate this chapter.

Below we sketch the processes involved in publishing a journal article. Much of the detail about methodology and day-to-day problems has been omitted, but the reader should be able to take what he or she has learned from the first 15 chapters and determine where each issue was addressed. The article was published in the *Journal of Personality and Social Psychology*, and the reader is directed to that journal for the final version of this work.

The Idea

In spring of 1982, I was listening to a lecture given by Richard Reardon on individual differences. Dr. Reardon is an experimental psychologist studying social cognition and individual differences. The lecture was about an individual difference variable called Field-Independence/Field-Dependence (FI-FD). FI-FD, he was explaining, influenced a number of different tasks, and people were beginning to understand how these two types of people differed in the way they approached their world. FD individuals, apparently, depended a great deal on the surrounding context of their world (i.e., the field) to help them orient themselves. FI persons did not seem to require or make use of the field. In an early experiment, subjects were given a rod-and-frame task (see Figure 16–1) and asked to move the rod until it was vertical to the room, ignoring the frame. With the lights out in the room, the subjects could see only the rod and the frame and nothing else in the room. Interestingly, some subjects (FD) were unable to ignore the frame, whereas other subjects (FI) were much better able to adjust the rod appropriately regardless of the position of the frame.

Since that early study, psychologists have apparently found an impact of this difference on a number of other tasks, including such things as reading comprehension and memory. There was now a paper-and-pencil test of FI-FD that made it easier to test people without having to shut off the lights in the room. This test, called the Embedded Figures Test, required subjects to try to find a hidden object in a more complex picture. FI people can do this task easily, whereas FD people cannot.

So much information had accumulated on this individual difference that some psychologists (i.e., Witkin & Goodenough) had developed a theory to account for the existing data. As Dr. Reardon was discussing the theory, he noted that FD people are theoretically less able to separate the self from the nonself. I asked what this meant. The class joined the discussion, considering statements such as "Field dependent people are one with the universe" and "The guy on *Kung Fu* must have been field dependent." We discovered that FD people are more socially adroit, and FI people are more analytical. As the discussion continued we thought of a concrete example: People sometimes get confused about whether they said something or whether someone else said it. In fact, in the discussion some of us were uncertain as to who made the statement about *Kung Fu*, while others were quite certain they knew who it was.

Figure 16–1 The rod-and-frame test. The illuminated rod and frame were in an otherwise dark room. The subject's task was to adjust the rod to be vertical to the room, not the frame.

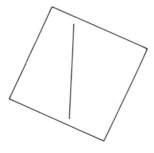

I had been reading some work by Johnson and Raye on a process they called reality monitoring. Reality monitoring refers to people's ability to remember whether some event was created by them or created in the environment and simply perceived by them. In other words, Johnson and Raye were interested in how people distinguish between thoughts and perceptions. We discussed this work and realized that distinguishing between something you thought and something you heard was the same thing as distinguishing between the self and the nonself. Thus the Johnson and Raye reality monitoring model might let us test the theory from the FI-FD literature.

This example is a good illustration of how an original idea often seems like a simple combination of two ideas or logical next step to the person who had the idea. Your original ideas will also be simple next steps. No one in the country is likely to be taking the same courses as you, reading the same articles as you, having the same interests as you, and experiencing the same events as you. From the interplay of these unique forces affecting you, there will emerge the original.

Finding Out More

By this time, a graduate student named Eric Jolly had become interested in the problem as well. Thus, Dr. Reardon, Jolly, and I decided to work on the project. Jolly went to the library to see what had been done recently in these two areas, with an eye toward whether anyone had integrated the areas before. Dr. Reardon contacted friends in the FI-FD area to see what they knew. I wrote to Marcia Johnson, my major professor in graduate school, asking for information about her recent work in reality monitoring. Jolly uncovered a number of useful sources, but none integrating the two areas. Dr. Reardon reported that none of his colleagues knew of an integration of the two areas. Dr. Johnson wrote back with a great deal of useful information about her recent work on reality monitoring. It looked as if we had (maybe) a good idea!

The Hypothesis

Our hypothesis was a simple one. We thought that FD people would be more likely to confuse the origin of a memory. More specifically, they would have a relatively difficult time deciding whether a memory was one that they generated or one that they heard.

Designing the Experiment

We decided to use a standard reality-monitoring procedure. In such a procedure people hear sentences such as "Frozen water is called _____" or "Frozen water is called ice." Sometimes the subject must fill in the missing word, and other times the person simply hears the word. Later the subject is given the word *ice* and asked whether he or she thought it or heard it.

To determine whether the subjects were FI or FD, we asked them to complete the Embedded Figures Test (EFT). The EFT required subjects to find hidden, camouflaged objects within a specific period of time. Thus we had the basics of our design. It would be something like a 2×2 factorial with FI/FD as one between-subjects blocking factor and Origin (heard/ thought) as one within-subjects factor. As our hypothesis suggests, we planned to find the average number of confusions for FI and FD people regardless of whether the original source was heard or thought; thus, when we did our statistics, we averaged across the Origin factor of the design. Therefore, the experimental design, a 2×2 factorial, was not the same as our statistical design, a one-factor ANOVA.

Materials

We next had to develop sentences which, when the last word was omitted, subjects would be able to complete with the word we had in mind. The three of us went to Mr. Bill's, a local speakeasy, and stayed until we created 100 sentences we thought would be easy to complete.

We then conducted a norming study by asking 150 students to complete our incomplete sentences for us. We were, of course, surprised that our little gems of sentences were not as good as we believed. However, we did manage to find 40 sentences that were completed by all 150 of our subjects.

The next step was to decide how to present the materials to the subject. We decided to use an audiotape deck as the simplest approach. We also decided to create different tapes so that the sentences could be presented in different orders. Finally, because Origin was a within-subjects factor, we had to present half of the sentences completed and half of the sentences incomplete to each subject. Then we flipped the sentences, creating tapes similar to the first but which had changed the completed sentences to incomplete and vice versa. This assignment of materials to condition and the randomization of the order of the sentences was sufficient to counterbalance the materials.

The Pilot Study

Much of the above had taken place during the summer of 1982. The fall semester was underway and subjects were back in Introductory Psychology. We decided to start with a small version of the experiment for several reasons: (1) we wanted to work out any kinks in our procedure, (2) we wanted to see if the hypothesis would be worth pursuing with more time and subjects, and (3) we wanted to take a look at the data and then play the role of devil's advocate to see what a reviewer might say about our findings.

When the pilot data were analyzed later that semester, we noticed a kink in our procedure. The data showed an extraordinary number of some types of confusions, suggesting that people were thinking about an answer to the completed sentences. We went back and listened carefully to our tapes. Several of the sentences sounded like this "Frozen water is called . . . ice." In other words, the maker of our tape had waited too long before completing the sentence. We had not noticed this originally, but the floor effect in our data caused us to look back at our materials.

Even with this problem, it looked to us as though the FD people were performing more poorly than the FI people, as our hypothesis predicted. So, in this sense, we were encouraged.

Next, we speculated on what the article would be like after we had corrected the problem. Dr. Reardon and I spent an evening trying to criticize our study as much as possible. One of us, I don't remember who (reality-monitoring failure?), said that if FD people do worse in this memory-monitoring task, it may be because they are bad in all memory-monitoring tasks, not only self-nonself. Clearly, this would not be consistent with what we really wanted to say. Thus, we planned other experiments to see if FD people were bad memory monitors in general or if they were only bad at self-nonself, thought-heard, types of tasks. We decided we would conduct three experiments: Experiment 1 would be the same as our pilot study with the appropriate corrections made. Experiment 2 would compare what one person said with what another person said, or nonself-nonself. Experiment 3 would compare what the subject thought with what the subject wrote, a self-self task.

Finally, we worried that we may not have been fair to the FD subjects. Becuse they are more socially oriented, they may do better if they actually saw the people who were speaking to them. This was easily accomplished and allowed Reardon to use his new video recorder.

New Hypotheses

Experiment 1: FD people would make more memory confusions than FI people.

Experiment 2: FD people would do just as well as FI people.

Experiment 3: FD people would do just as well as FI people.

The Experiments

Collecting and analyzing the data for the three experiments took most of the spring of 1983.

Communicating the Results

Starting late that spring, we began presenting the preliminary results of our work at conventions and talks. In particular, we presented our work at the Psychology Department Colloquium Series and at the Annual Meeting of the Southwestern Psychological Association.

During the summer of 1983, we began writing the first draft of our work. Reardon and I rewrote the work five separate times, each time improving (we hoped) on our last version. We decided to begin by quickly putting all the ideas in a coherent order. We then went back and polished each transition. Finally, we met several times to talk about the conclusions, modifying those many more times. After our rewriting, we gave the manuscript to a number of colleagues and asked them to do us the favor of making comments and suggestions. Not having any enemies, we could not follow the old advice to give your manuscript to an enemy rather than a friend. We gave the work to faculty members and graduate students who had no idea what we were doing before they read the manuscript. These in-house reviewers gave us a number of important comments about sections of the manuscript that were unclear or ambiguous. We incorporated most of their suggestions into the next draft.

Our next decision was where to send the work. We identified several journals for which the work might be appropriate. If the editor does not think the work is appropriate for the journal, he or she may return it unreviewed. The journals we identified as appropriate differed in their calibre. Obviously, some journals enjoy a wider readership, are more selective in the manuscripts they accept, and are more likely to have their work cited by other researchers. These top-level journals, in short, publish the best work. To decide whether one's work will be well received by a top-level journal is an important decision. If the author evaluates the importance of his or her work too highly, the publication of the manuscript will be delayed. If the author undervalues the importance of his or her work, the publication may not reach the widest possible audience.

Why publish something that does not qualify for the top level? There are several reasons: The paper may be good, but not great. It may supply interesting empirical data, but not a good theory; it may be meant for a select audience and thus the editor and reviewers may not think that the readership will benefit from your (good) article compared with another; finally, the reviewers of top-level journals sometimes make mistakes and your work really is better than they think. In this case, what do you do? Publish it somewhere or let it sit in your desk.

We thought our work met all the criteria of a top-level journal: The data were interesting; the experiments were theory driven; and our conclusions were provocative. Thus, we decided to send it to the APA journal that publishes work on individual differences: *Journal of Personality and Social Psychology.* We knew that it had a large readership, a high rejection rate (87%), and was often cited by others. So, we read the instructions to authors printed in an issue of the journal, held our breath, and mailed four copies of the work to the journal's editor.

The Publication Process

Within 2 weeks we received word from *JPSP* that the work had been received and was given a manuscript number. We were also informed that Dr. Jones would serve as **action editor** and that we should communicate with him in the future, if need be.

The next step in the process was to wait until the reviews of our work were returned. *JPSP* usually picks two experts in the field to review each manuscript. Thus, the opinions of the editors and two anonymous experts would be returned to us. These reviews are very useful in improving your manuscript. This feedback can sometimes be useful not only for the current work but also for getting ideas for future studies. Had we made a logical error? Had we let a confound slip through?

It was now October, 1983. About 3 months had passed since we sent in the manuscript. The reviews had arrived. The action editor had accepted the manuscript with revisions. The editor usually classifies each manuscript in one of the following categories: **accepted** as is (very rare); **accepted with revisions; rejected without prejudice** (rejected but invited to resubmit); **rejected.**

Needless to say, we were quite happy that our work had been well received. We studied the reviews thoroughly and over the next months, rewrote the manuscript a few more times to address the issues raised by the reviewers. We returned the work to Dr. Jones who soon wrote back that the manuscript was ready for publication. At that time, we signed over our copyright to the APA.

During 1984, we received the technical editor's manuscript. This was a copy of our manuscript prepared by a **technical editor** for the printer. The technical editor's job is to correct any minor grammatical errors, any deviation from APA style, and any sexist language. At this point these errors were slight because the work would have never been accepted if violations were great. This is also the last stage of the publication process where you, the author, can make any small changes in wording (e.g., add a reference, correct a phrase). We returned this to Washington, D.C., within 48 hours as instructed.

During 1985, we received the **galleys** of the manuscript. This is a copy of what the article will look like when it appears in the journal. At this phase, we read the galleys word for word against the original manuscript to check for typos, omitted phrases, and other mistakes. We returned the work in 48 hours. We finished! The work we started in the beginning of 1982 appeared in the literature near the end of 1985.

Now it is your turn. Following is the complete frame for research that has been evolving over the semester. Use it as a guide to conduct your own research. Happy Breakthrough!

Key Words

accepted
accepted with revisions
action editor
galleys

rejected
rejected without prejudice
technical editor

Additional Reading

Durso, F. T., Reardon, R., & Jolly, E. J. (1985). Self-nonself segregation and reality monitoring. *Journal of Personality and Social Psychology, 48,* 447–455.
Johnson, M. K., & Raye, C. L. (1981). Reality monitoring. *Psychological Review, 88,* 67–85.
Goodenough, D. R. (1976). The role of individual differences in field dependence as a factor in learning and memory. *Psychological Bulletin, 83,* 675–694.

General Idea (Previous Research, Curiosity, Theory)

Explanatory Statement

Research Hypothesis/Descriptive Statement

Methods (Natural Observation, Survey, Field Experiment, Lab Experiment, Quasi-Experiment)

Dependent Variables

Operational Definition

Predictor or Independent Variables

Operational Definition

Design (Between, Pre-Post, Within, Factorial, Baseline, Nonequivalent Control Group)

Subjects

Ethical Considerations

Characteristics and Availability

Sampling Procedure and Number of Subjects

Control

Subject Assignment (Randomization, Matching)

Environment (Insured Equivalence, Yoking, Counterbalancing)

Reactivity (Blinds, Deception, Disguised, etc.)

Procedural Command Decisions (Ceiling Effect, Floor Effect)

Retrospective Confound Check (Assumed, Statistical, Rethink)

Selection, Mortality, History, Maturation, Reactivity, Statistical Regression, Testing/Sequencing, Instrumentation)

Data Analysis

Transformation

Descriptive

Inferential

Continued

Continued
Hypothetical Outcome Analysis

Targeted Oral Presentation

Length of Talk

Location, Cost of Next Meeting

Targeted Publication Outlet

Requirements of Journal (Format, Topic)

Typical Articles (Number of Experiments, Length)

Computer Packages

In this text we have reviewed the computational steps required to calculate the appropriate statistic. Today much of these calculations can be done using a computer and various statistical packages. We believe, however, that any person who uses a statistical package on a computer should, at least in principle, be able to calculate the statistic by hand. There is nothing more disturbing than to see psychologists offer up their data at the electronic altar, wait while it is transmogrified by some mystical process, and then take the fatted data to a quantitative cleric as penance.

With this disclaimer aside, if you are able to perform the calculation by hand, it does not mean that you should. Depending on your institution, you may have access to one of several statistical packages: SAS, SPSS, BMDP, and so forth. As an upper-level undergraduate who has successfully completed a course on research methodology and statistics, you may be allowed to have access to these systems. This is likely to be especially true if you decide to continue your involvement in research by working with a faculty member. We cannot overemphasize the value of mastering these systems for your research and for your transition to graduate school.

In addition to the large systems, such as SAS, SPSS and BMDP, there are an ever-increasing number of systems designed for the personal computer. We suggest that you first explore the possibility of using the more sophisticated, large packages before committing your financial resources to systems for the personal computer.

Epilogue

You write with ease to show your breeding,
But easy writing's curst hard reading.
>—Richard Sheridan

It you would not be forgotten, as soon as you are dead and rotten, either write things worth reading, or do things worth writing.
>—Benjamin Franklin

Of all those arts in which the wise excell,
Nature's chief masterpiece is writing well.
>—John Sheffield

Don't forget to write!
>—Frank Durso & Roger Mellgren

The Publication Process

Once the paper has been rewritten to your satisfaction, you will want to submit the work for publication. To do this you must follow steps similar to the following:

1. Identify an appropriate journal.

2. Make enough copies to meet the submission requirements (usually 3 to 5).

3. Write a cover letter to the editor requesting your work be considered for publication.

4. Wait 2 to 4 weeks to receive an acknowledgment of receipt.

5. Wait 3 to 9 months to receive reviews by experts in the field (probably people you cited). At this time you will also recieve a decision about whether your work is to be published in the journal. It may be accepted as is (a rare event), or accepted with revisions.

6. Make any revisions suggested or collect new data as indicated in the review.

7. Return the manuscript to the editor or return to step 1.

8. Wait for the second reviews.

9. Receive final acceptance or go to step 6.

10. Wait for manuscript edited by a technical editor.

11. Wait for galley proofs. Order reprints.

12. See your work published!

13. Send reprint to Mom.

14. Write another paper so you can cite yourself.

Statistical Tables

Table A   Distribution of χ^2

Alpha Level

n	.10	.05	.02	.01	.001
1	2.706	3.841	5.412	6.635	10.827
2	4.605	5.991	7.824	9.210	13.815
3	6.251	7.815	9.837	11.345	16.266
4	7.779	9.488	11.668	13.277	18.467
5	9.236	11.070	13.388	15.086	20.515
6	10.645	12.592	15.033	16.812	22.457
7	12.017	14.067	16.622	18.475	24.322
8	13.362	15.507	18.168	20.090	26.125
9	14.684	16.919	19.679	21.666	27.877
10	15.987	18.307	21.161	23.209	29.588
11	17.275	19.675	22.618	24.725	31.264
12	18.549	21.026	24.054	26.217	32.909
13	19.812	22.362	25.472	27.688	34.528
14	21.064	23.685	26.873	29.141	36.123
15	22.307	24.996	28.529	30.578	37.697
16	23.542	26.296	29.633	32.000	39.252
17	24.769	27.587	30.995	33.409	40.790
18	25.989	28.869	32.346	34.805	42.312
19	27.204	30.144	33.687	36.191	43.820
20	28.412	31.410	35.020	37.566	45.315
21	29.615	32.671	36.343	38.932	46.797
22	30.813	33.924	37.659	40.289	48.268
23	32.007	35.172	38.968	41.638	49.728
24	33.196	36.415	40.270	42.980	51.179
25	34.382	37.652	41.566	44.314	52.620
26	35.563	38.885	42.856	45.642	54.052
27	36.741	40.113	44.140	46.963	55.476
28	37.916	41.337	45.419	48.278	56.893
29	39.087	42.557	46.693	49.588	58.302
30	40.256	43.773	47.962	50.892	59.703

continued

Table A   (Continued)

Alpha Level

n	.10	.05	.02	.01	.001
32	42.585	46.194	50.487	53.486	62.487
34	44.903	48.602	52.995	56.061	65.247
36	47.212	50.999	55.489	58.619	67.985
38	49.513	53.384	57.969	61.162	70.703
40	51.805	55.759	60.436	63.691	73.402
42	54.090	58.124	62.892	66.206	76.084
44	56.369	60.481	65.337	68.710	78.750
46	58.641	62.830	67.771	71.201	81.400
48	60.907	65.171	70.197	73.683	84.037
50	63.167	67.505	72.613	76.154	86.661
52	65.422	69.832	75.021	78.616	89.272
54	67.673	72.153	77.422	81.069	91.872
56	69.919	74.468	79.815	83.513	94.461
58	72.160	76.778	82.201	85.950	97.039
60	74.397	79.082	84.580	88.379	99.607
62	76.630	81.381	86.953	90.802	102.166
64	78.860	83.675	89.320	93.217	104.716
66	81.085	85.965	91.681	95.626	107.258
68	83.308	88.250	94.037	98.028	109.791
70	85.527	90.531	96.388	100.425	112.317

Tables A and B are taken from Tables IV and III of Fisher & Yates': *Statistical Tables for Biological, Agricultural and Medical Research* published by Longman Group UK Ltd. London (previously published by Oliver and Boyd Ltd, Edinburgh) and by permission of the authors and publishers.

Table B Distribution of *t*

Alpha Level (Two-Tailed)

n	.1	.05	.02	.01	.001
1	6.314	12.706	31.821	63.657	636.619
2	2.920	4.303	6.965	9.925	31.598
3	2.353	3.182	4.541	5.841	12.924
4	2.132	2.776	3.747	4.604	8.610
5	2.015	2.571	3.365	4.032	6.869
6	1.943	2.447	3.143	3.707	5.959
7	1.895	2.365	2.998	3.499	5.408
8	1.860	2.306	2.896	3.355	5.041
9	1.833	2.262	2.821	3.250	4.781
10	1.812	2.228	2.764	3.169	4.587
11	1.796	2.201	2.718	3.106	4.437
12	1.782	2.179	2.681	3.055	4.318
13	1.771	2.160	2.650	3.012	4.221
14	1.761	2.145	2.624	2.977	4.140
15	1.753	2.131	2.602	2.947	4.073
16	1.746	2.120	2.583	2.921	4.015
17	1.740	2.110	2.567	2.898	3.965
18	1.734	2.101	2.552	2.878	3.922
19	1.729	2.093	2.539	2.861	3.883
20	1.725	2.086	2.528	2.845	3.850
21	1.721	2.080	2.518	2.831	3.819
22	1.717	2.074	2.508	2.819	3.792
23	1.714	2.069	2.500	2.807	3.767
24	1.711	2.064	2.492	2.797	3.745
25	1.708	2.060	2.485	2.787	3.725
26	1.706	2.056	2.479	2.779	3.707
27	1.703	2.052	2.473	2.771	3.690
28	1.701	2.048	2.467	2.763	3.674
29	1.699	2.045	2.462	2.756	3.659
30	1.697	2.042	2.457	2.750	3.646
40	1.684	2.021	2.423	2.704	3.551
60	1.671	2.000	2.390	2.660	3.460
120	1.658	1.980	2.358	2.617	3.373
∞	1.645	1.960	2.326	2.576	3.291

Tables A and B are taken from Tables IV and III of Fisher & Yates': *Statistical Tables for Biological, Agricultural and Medical Research* published by Longman Group UK Ltd. London (previously published by Oliver and Boyd Ltd, Edinburgh) and by permission of the authors and publishers.

Table C 5% (Roman Type) and 1% (Bold Face Type) Points for the Distribution of F

f_1 Degrees of Freedom (for greater mean square)

f_2	1	2	3	4	5	6	7	8	9	10	11	12	14	16	20	24	30	40	50	75	100	200	500	∞	f_2
1	161	200	216	225	230	234	237	239	241	242	243	244	245	246	248	249	250	251	252	253	253	254	254	254	1
	4,052	**4,999**	**5,403**	**5,625**	**5,764**	**5,859**	**5,928**	**5,981**	**6,022**	**6,056**	**6,082**	**6,106**	**6,142**	**6,169**	**6,208**	**6,234**	**6,261**	**6,286**	**6,302**	**6,323**	**6,334**	**6,352**	**6,361**	**6,366**	
2	18.51	19.00	19.16	19.25	19.30	19.33	19.36	19.37	19.38	19.39	19.40	19.41	19.42	19.43	19.44	19.45	19.46	19.47	19.47	19.48	19.49	19.49	19.50	19.50	2
	98.49	**99.00**	**99.17**	**99.25**	**99.30**	**99.33**	**99.36**	**99.37**	**99.39**	**99.40**	**99.41**	**99.42**	**99.43**	**99.44**	**99.45**	**99.46**	**99.47**	**99.48**	**99.48**	**99.49**	**99.49**	**99.49**	**99.50**	**99.50**	
3	10.13	9.55	9.28	9.12	9.01	8.94	8.88	8.84	8.81	8.78	8.76	8.74	8.71	8.69	8.66	8.64	8.62	8.60	8.58	8.57	8.56	8.54	8.54	8.53	3
	34.12	**30.82**	**29.46**	**28.71**	**28.24**	**27.91**	**27.67**	**27.49**	**27.34**	**27.23**	**27.13**	**27.05**	**26.92**	**26.83**	**26.69**	**26.60**	**26.50**	**26.41**	**26.35**	**26.27**	**26.23**	**26.18**	**26.14**	**26.12**	
4	7.71	6.94	6.59	6.39	6.26	6.16	6.09	6.04	6.00	5.96	5.93	5.91	5.87	5.84	5.80	5.77	5.74	5.71	5.70	5.68	5.66	5.65	5.64	5.63	4
	21.20	**18.00**	**16.69**	**15.98**	**15.52**	**15.21**	**14.98**	**14.80**	**14.66**	**14.54**	**14.45**	**14.37**	**14.24**	**14.15**	**14.02**	**13.93**	**13.83**	**13.74**	**13.69**	**13.61**	**13.57**	**13.52**	**13.48**	**13.46**	
5	6.61	5.79	5.41	5.19	5.05	4.95	4.88	4.82	4.78	4.74	4.70	4.68	4.64	4.60	4.56	4.53	4.50	4.46	4.44	4.42	4.40	4.38	4.37	4.36	5
	16.26	**13.27**	**12.06**	**11.39**	**10.97**	**10.67**	**10.45**	**10.29**	**10.15**	**10.05**	**9.96**	**9.89**	**9.77**	**9.68**	**9.55**	**9.47**	**9.38**	**9.29**	**9.24**	**9.17**	**9.13**	**9.07**	**9.04**	**9.02**	
6	5.99	5.14	4.76	4.53	4.39	4.28	4.21	4.15	4.10	4.06	4.03	4.00	3.96	3.92	3.87	3.84	3.81	3.77	3.75	3.72	3.71	3.69	3.68	3.67	6
	13.74	**10.92**	**9.78**	**9.15**	**8.75**	**8.47**	**8.26**	**8.10**	**7.98**	**7.87**	**7.79**	**7.72**	**7.60**	**7.52**	**7.39**	**7.31**	**7.23**	**7.14**	**7.09**	**7.02**	**6.99**	**6.94**	**6.90**	**6.88**	
7	5.59	4.74	4.35	4.12	3.97	3.87	3.79	3.73	3.68	3.63	3.60	3.57	3.52	3.49	3.44	3.41	3.38	3.34	3.32	3.29	3.28	3.25	3.24	3.23	7
	12.25	**9.55**	**8.45**	**7.85**	**7.46**	**7.19**	**7.00**	**6.84**	**6.71**	**6.62**	**6.54**	**6.47**	**6.35**	**6.27**	**6.15**	**6.07**	**5.98**	**5.90**	**5.85**	**5.78**	**5.75**	**5.70**	**5.67**	**5.65**	
8	5.32	4.46	4.07	3.84	3.69	3.58	3.50	3.44	3.39	3.34	3.31	3.28	3.23	3.20	3.15	3.12	3.08	3.05	3.03	3.00	2.98	2.96	2.94	2.93	8
	11.26	**8.65**	**7.59**	**7.01**	**6.63**	**6.37**	**6.19**	**6.03**	**5.91**	**5.82**	**5.74**	**5.67**	**5.56**	**5.48**	**5.36**	**5.28**	**5.20**	**5.11**	**5.06**	**5.00**	**4.96**	**4.91**	**4.88**	**4.86**	
9	5.12	4.26	3.86	3.63	3.48	3.37	3.29	3.23	3.18	3.13	3.10	3.07	3.02	2.98	2.93	2.90	2.86	2.82	2.80	2.77	2.76	2.73	2.72	2.71	9
	10.56	**8.02**	**6.99**	**6.42**	**6.06**	**5.80**	**5.62**	**5.47**	**5.35**	**5.26**	**5.18**	**5.11**	**5.00**	**4.92**	**4.80**	**4.73**	**4.64**	**4.56**	**4.51**	**4.45**	**4.41**	**4.36**	**4.33**	**4.31**	
10	4.96	4.10	3.71	3.48	3.33	3.22	3.14	3.07	3.02	2.97	2.94	2.91	2.86	2.82	2.77	2.74	2.70	2.67	2.64	2.61	2.59	2.56	2.55	2.54	10
	10.04	**7.56**	**6.55**	**5.99**	**5.64**	**5.39**	**5.21**	**5.06**	**4.95**	**4.85**	**4.78**	**4.71**	**4.60**	**4.52**	**4.41**	**4.33**	**4.25**	**4.17**	**4.12**	**4.05**	**4.01**	**3.96**	**3.93**	**3.91**	
11	4.84	3.98	3.59	3.36	3.20	3.09	3.01	2.95	2.90	2.86	2.82	2.79	2.74	2.70	2.65	2.61	2.57	2.53	2.50	2.47	2.45	2.42	2.41	2.40	11
	9.65	**7.20**	**6.22**	**5.67**	**5.32**	**5.07**	**4.88**	**4.74**	**4.63**	**4.54**	**4.46**	**4.40**	**4.29**	**4.21**	**4.10**	**4.02**	**3.94**	**3.86**	**3.80**	**3.74**	**3.70**	**3.66**	**3.62**	**3.60**	
12	4.75	3.88	3.49	3.26	3.11	3.00	2.92	2.85	2.80	2.76	2.72	2.69	2.64	2.60	2.54	2.50	2.46	2.42	2.40	2.36	2.35	2.32	2.31	2.30	12
	9.33	**6.93**	**5.95**	**5.41**	**5.06**	**4.82**	**4.65**	**4.50**	**4.39**	**4.30**	**4.22**	**4.16**	**4.05**	**3.98**	**3.86**	**3.78**	**3.70**	**3.61**	**3.56**	**3.49**	**3.46**	**3.41**	**3.38**	**3.36**	
13	4.67	3.80	3.41	3.18	3.02	2.92	2.84	2.77	2.72	2.67	2.63	2.60	2.55	2.51	2.46	2.42	2.38	2.34	2.32	2.28	2.26	2.24	2.22	2.21	13
	9.07	**6.70**	**5.74**	**5.20**	**4.86**	**4.62**	**4.44**	**4.30**	**4.19**	**4.10**	**4.02**	**3.96**	**3.85**	**3.78**	**3.67**	**3.59**	**3.51**	**3.42**	**3.37**	**3.30**	**3.27**	**3.21**	**3.18**	**3.16**	
14	4.60	3.74	3.34	3.11	2.96	2.85	2.77	2.70	2.65	2.60	2.56	2.53	2.48	2.44	2.39	2.35	2.31	2.27	2.24	2.21	2.19	2.16	2.14	2.13	14
	8.86	**6.51**	**5.56**	**5.03**	**4.69**	**4.46**	**4.28**	**4.14**	**4.03**	**3.94**	**3.86**	**3.80**	**3.70**	**3.62**	**3.51**	**3.43**	**3.34**	**3.26**	**3.21**	**3.14**	**3.11**	**3.06**	**3.02**	**3.00**	
15	4.54	3.68	3.29	3.06	2.90	2.79	2.70	2.64	2.59	2.55	2.51	2.48	2.43	2.39	2.33	2.29	2.25	2.21	2.18	2.15	2.12	2.10	2.08	2.07	15
	8.68	**6.36**	**5.42**	**4.89**	**4.56**	**4.32**	**4.14**	**4.00**	**3.89**	**3.80**	**3.73**	**3.67**	**3.56**	**3.48**	**3.36**	**3.29**	**3.20**	**3.12**	**3.07**	**3.00**	**2.97**	**2.92**	**2.89**	**2.87**	
16	4.49	3.63	3.24	3.01	2.85	2.74	2.66	2.59	2.54	2.49	2.45	2.42	2.37	2.33	2.28	2.24	2.20	2.16	2.13	2.09	2.07	2.04	2.02	2.01	16
	8.53	**6.23**	**5.29**	**4.77**	**4.44**	**4.20**	**4.03**	**3.89**	**3.78**	**3.69**	**3.61**	**3.55**	**3.45**	**3.37**	**3.25**	**3.18**	**3.10**	**3.01**	**2.96**	**2.89**	**2.86**	**2.80**	**2.77**	**2.75**	
17	4.45	3.59	3.20	2.96	2.81	2.70	2.62	2.55	2.50	2.45	2.41	2.38	2.33	2.29	2.23	2.19	2.15	2.11	2.08	2.04	2.02	1.99	1.97	1.96	17
	8.40	**6.11**	**5.18**	**4.67**	**4.34**	**4.10**	**3.93**	**3.79**	**3.68**	**3.59**	**3.52**	**3.45**	**3.35**	**3.27**	**3.16**	**3.08**	**3.00**	**2.92**	**2.86**	**2.79**	**2.76**	**2.70**	**2.67**	**2.65**	
18	4.41	3.55	3.16	2.93	2.77	2.66	2.58	2.51	2.46	2.41	2.37	2.34	2.29	2.25	2.19	2.15	2.11	2.07	2.04	2.00	1.98	1.95	1.93	1.92	18
	8.28	**6.01**	**5.09**	**4.58**	**4.25**	**4.01**	**3.85**	**3.71**	**3.60**	**3.51**	**3.44**	**3.37**	**3.27**	**3.19**	**3.07**	**3.00**	**2.91**	**2.83**	**2.78**	**2.71**	**2.68**	**2.62**	**2.59**	**2.57**	

f_1 Degrees of Freedom (for greater mean square)

Each cell: upper value (roman) = 0.05 point; lower value (**bold**) = 0.01 point.

f_2	∞	500	200	100	75	50	40	30	24	20	16	14	12	11	10	9	8	7	6	5	4	3	2	1
19	1.88 **2.49**	1.90 **2.51**	1.91 **2.54**	1.94 **2.60**	1.96 **2.63**	2.00 **2.70**	2.02 **2.76**	2.07 **2.84**	2.11 **2.92**	2.15 **3.00**	2.21 **3.12**	2.26 **3.19**	2.31 **3.30**	2.34 **3.36**	2.38 **3.43**	2.43 **3.52**	2.48 **3.63**	2.55 **3.77**	2.63 **3.94**	2.74 **4.17**	2.90 **4.50**	3.13 **5.01**	3.52 **5.93**	4.38 **8.18**
20	1.84 **2.42**	1.85 **2.44**	1.87 **2.47**	1.90 **2.53**	1.92 **2.56**	1.96 **2.63**	1.99 **2.69**	2.04 **2.77**	2.08 **2.86**	2.12 **2.94**	2.18 **3.05**	2.23 **3.13**	2.28 **3.23**	2.31 **3.30**	2.35 **3.37**	2.40 **3.45**	2.45 **3.56**	2.52 **3.71**	2.60 **3.87**	2.71 **4.10**	2.87 **4.43**	3.10 **4.94**	3.49 **5.85**	4.35 **8.10**
21	1.81 **2.36**	1.82 **2.38**	1.84 **2.42**	1.87 **2.47**	1.89 **2.51**	1.93 **2.58**	1.96 **2.63**	2.00 **2.72**	2.05 **2.80**	2.09 **2.88**	2.15 **2.99**	2.20 **3.07**	2.25 **3.17**	2.28 **3.24**	2.32 **3.31**	2.37 **3.40**	2.42 **3.51**	2.49 **3.65**	2.57 **3.81**	2.68 **4.04**	2.84 **4.37**	3.07 **4.87**	3.47 **5.78**	4.32 **8.02**
22	1.78 **2.31**	1.80 **2.33**	1.81 **2.37**	1.84 **2.42**	1.87 **2.46**	1.91 **2.53**	1.93 **2.58**	1.98 **2.67**	2.03 **2.75**	2.07 **2.83**	2.13 **2.94**	2.18 **3.02**	2.23 **3.12**	2.26 **3.18**	2.30 **3.26**	2.35 **3.35**	2.40 **3.45**	2.47 **3.59**	2.55 **3.76**	2.66 **3.99**	2.82 **4.31**	3.05 **4.82**	3.44 **5.72**	4.30 **7.94**
23	1.76 **2.26**	1.77 **2.28**	1.79 **2.32**	1.82 **2.37**	1.84 **2.41**	1.88 **2.48**	1.91 **2.53**	1.96 **2.62**	2.00 **2.70**	2.04 **2.78**	2.10 **2.89**	2.14 **2.97**	2.20 **3.07**	2.24 **3.14**	2.28 **3.21**	2.32 **3.30**	2.38 **3.41**	2.45 **3.54**	2.53 **3.71**	2.64 **3.94**	2.80 **4.26**	3.03 **4.76**	3.42 **5.66**	4.28 **7.88**
24	1.73 **2.21**	1.74 **2.23**	1.76 **2.27**	1.80 **2.33**	1.82 **2.36**	1.86 **2.44**	1.89 **2.49**	1.94 **2.58**	1.98 **2.66**	2.02 **2.74**	2.09 **2.85**	2.13 **2.93**	2.18 **3.03**	2.22 **3.09**	2.26 **3.17**	2.30 **3.25**	2.36 **3.36**	2.43 **3.50**	2.51 **3.67**	2.62 **3.90**	2.78 **4.22**	3.01 **4.72**	3.40 **5.61**	4.26 **7.82**
25	1.71 **2.17**	1.72 **2.19**	1.74 **2.23**	1.77 **2.29**	1.80 **2.32**	1.84 **2.40**	1.87 **2.45**	1.92 **2.54**	1.96 **2.62**	2.00 **2.70**	2.06 **2.81**	2.11 **2.89**	2.16 **2.99**	2.20 **3.05**	2.24 **3.13**	2.28 **3.21**	2.34 **3.32**	2.41 **3.46**	2.49 **3.63**	2.60 **3.86**	2.76 **4.18**	2.99 **4.68**	3.38 **5.57**	4.24 **7.77**
26	1.69 **2.13**	1.70 **2.15**	1.72 **2.19**	1.76 **2.25**	1.78 **2.28**	1.82 **2.36**	1.85 **2.41**	1.90 **2.50**	1.95 **2.58**	1.99 **2.66**	2.05 **2.77**	2.10 **2.86**	2.15 **2.96**	2.18 **3.02**	2.22 **3.09**	2.27 **3.17**	2.32 **3.29**	2.39 **3.42**	2.47 **3.59**	2.57 **3.82**	2.74 **4.14**	2.98 **4.64**	3.37 **5.53**	4.22 **7.72**
27	1.67 **2.10**	1.68 **2.12**	1.71 **2.16**	1.74 **2.21**	1.76 **2.25**	1.80 **2.33**	1.84 **2.38**	1.88 **2.47**	1.93 **2.55**	1.97 **2.63**	2.03 **2.74**	2.08 **2.83**	2.13 **2.93**	2.16 **2.98**	2.20 **3.06**	2.25 **3.14**	2.30 **3.26**	2.37 **3.39**	2.46 **3.56**	2.57 **3.79**	2.73 **4.11**	2.96 **4.60**	3.35 **5.49**	4.21 **7.68**
28	1.65 **2.06**	1.67 **2.09**	1.69 **2.13**	1.72 **2.18**	1.75 **2.22**	1.78 **2.30**	1.81 **2.35**	1.87 **2.44**	1.91 **2.52**	1.96 **2.60**	2.02 **2.71**	2.06 **2.80**	2.12 **2.90**	2.15 **2.95**	2.19 **3.03**	2.24 **3.11**	2.29 **3.23**	2.36 **3.36**	2.44 **3.53**	2.56 **3.76**	2.71 **4.07**	2.95 **4.57**	3.34 **5.45**	4.20 **7.64**
29	1.64 **2.03**	1.65 **2.06**	1.68 **2.10**	1.71 **2.15**	1.73 **2.19**	1.77 **2.27**	1.80 **2.32**	1.85 **2.41**	1.90 **2.49**	1.94 **2.57**	2.00 **2.68**	2.05 **2.77**	2.10 **2.87**	2.14 **2.92**	2.18 **3.00**	2.22 **3.08**	2.28 **3.20**	2.35 **3.33**	2.43 **3.50**	2.54 **3.73**	2.70 **4.04**	2.93 **4.54**	3.33 **5.42**	4.18 **7.60**
30	1.62 **2.01**	1.64 **2.03**	1.66 **2.07**	1.69 **2.13**	1.72 **2.16**	1.76 **2.24**	1.79 **2.29**	1.84 **2.38**	1.89 **2.47**	1.93 **2.55**	1.99 **2.66**	2.04 **2.74**	2.09 **2.84**	2.12 **2.90**	2.16 **2.98**	2.21 **3.06**	2.27 **3.17**	2.34 **3.30**	2.42 **3.47**	2.53 **3.70**	2.69 **4.02**	2.92 **4.51**	3.32 **5.39**	4.17 **7.56**
32	1.59 **1.96**	1.61 **1.98**	1.64 **2.02**	1.67 **2.08**	1.69 **2.12**	1.74 **2.20**	1.76 **2.25**	1.82 **2.34**	1.86 **2.42**	1.91 **2.51**	1.97 **2.62**	2.02 **2.70**	2.07 **2.80**	2.10 **2.86**	2.14 **2.94**	2.19 **3.01**	2.25 **3.12**	2.32 **3.25**	2.40 **3.42**	2.51 **3.66**	2.67 **3.97**	2.90 **4.46**	3.30 **5.34**	4.15 **7.50**
34	1.57 **1.91**	1.59 **1.94**	1.61 **1.98**	1.64 **2.04**	1.67 **2.08**	1.71 **2.15**	1.74 **2.21**	1.80 **2.30**	1.84 **2.38**	1.89 **2.47**	1.95 **2.58**	2.00 **2.66**	2.05 **2.76**	2.08 **2.82**	2.12 **2.89**	2.17 **2.97**	2.23 **3.08**	2.30 **3.21**	2.38 **3.38**	2.49 **3.61**	2.65 **3.93**	2.88 **4.42**	3.28 **5.29**	4.13 **7.44**
36	1.55 **1.87**	1.56 **1.90**	1.59 **1.94**	1.62 **2.00**	1.65 **2.04**	1.69 **2.12**	1.72 **2.17**	1.78 **2.26**	1.82 **2.35**	1.87 **2.43**	1.93 **2.54**	1.98 **2.62**	2.03 **2.72**	2.06 **2.78**	2.10 **2.86**	2.15 **2.94**	2.21 **3.04**	2.28 **3.18**	2.36 **3.35**	2.48 **3.58**	2.63 **3.89**	2.86 **4.38**	3.26 **5.25**	4.11 **7.39**
38	1.53 **1.84**	1.54 **1.86**	1.57 **1.90**	1.60 **1.97**	1.63 **2.00**	1.67 **2.08**	1.71 **2.14**	1.76 **2.22**	1.80 **2.32**	1.85 **2.40**	1.92 **2.51**	1.96 **2.59**	2.02 **2.69**	2.05 **2.75**	2.09 **2.82**	2.14 **2.91**	2.19 **3.02**	2.26 **3.15**	2.35 **3.32**	2.46 **3.54**	2.62 **3.86**	2.85 **4.34**	3.25 **5.21**	4.10 **7.35**
40	1.51 **1.81**	1.53 **1.84**	1.55 **1.88**	1.59 **1.94**	1.61 **1.97**	1.66 **2.05**	1.69 **2.11**	1.74 **2.20**	1.79 **2.29**	1.84 **2.37**	1.90 **2.49**	1.95 **2.56**	2.00 **2.66**	2.04 **2.73**	2.07 **2.80**	2.12 **2.88**	2.18 **2.99**	2.25 **3.12**	2.34 **3.29**	2.45 **3.51**	2.61 **3.83**	2.84 **4.31**	3.23 **5.18**	4.08 **7.31**
42	1.49 **1.78**	1.51 **1.80**	1.54 **1.85**	1.57 **1.91**	1.60 **1.94**	1.64 **2.02**	1.68 **2.08**	1.73 **2.17**	1.78 **2.26**	1.82 **2.35**	1.89 **2.46**	1.94 **2.54**	1.99 **2.64**	2.02 **2.70**	2.06 **2.77**	2.11 **2.86**	2.17 **2.96**	2.24 **3.10**	2.32 **3.26**	2.44 **3.49**	2.59 **3.80**	2.83 **4.29**	3.22 **5.15**	4.07 **7.27**

continued

Table C (Continued)

f_1, Degrees of Freedom (for greater mean square)

f_2	1	2	3	4	5	6	7	8	9	10	11	12	14	16	20	24	30	40	50	75	100	200	500	∞	f_2
44	4.06 **7.24**	3.21 **5.12**	2.82 **4.26**	2.58 **3.78**	2.43 **3.46**	2.31 **3.24**	2.23 **3.07**	2.16 **2.94**	2.10 **2.84**	2.05 **2.75**	2.01 **2.68**	1.98 **2.62**	1.92 **2.52**	1.88 **2.44**	1.81 **2.32**	1.76 **2.24**	1.72 **2.15**	1.66 **2.06**	1.63 **2.00**	1.58 **1.92**	1.56 **1.88**	1.52 **1.82**	1.50 **1.78**	1.48 **1.75**	44
46	4.05 **7.21**	3.20 **5.10**	2.81 **4.24**	2.57 **3.76**	2.42 **3.44**	2.30 **3.22**	2.22 **3.05**	2.14 **2.92**	2.09 **2.82**	2.04 **2.73**	2.00 **2.66**	1.97 **2.60**	1.91 **2.50**	1.87 **2.42**	1.80 **2.30**	1.75 **2.22**	1.71 **2.13**	1.65 **2.04**	1.62 **1.98**	1.57 **1.90**	1.54 **1.86**	1.51 **1.80**	1.48 **1.76**	1.46 **1.72**	46
48	4.04 **7.19**	3.19 **5.08**	2.80 **4.22**	2.56 **3.74**	2.41 **3.42**	2.30 **3.20**	2.21 **3.04**	2.14 **2.90**	2.08 **2.80**	2.03 **2.71**	1.99 **2.64**	1.96 **2.58**	1.90 **2.48**	1.86 **2.40**	1.79 **2.28**	1.74 **2.20**	1.70 **2.11**	1.64 **2.02**	1.61 **1.96**	1.56 **1.88**	1.53 **1.84**	1.50 **1.78**	1.47 **1.73**	1.45 **1.70**	48
50	4.03 **7.17**	3.18 **5.06**	2.79 **4.20**	2.56 **3.72**	2.40 **3.41**	2.29 **3.18**	2.20 **3.02**	2.13 **2.88**	2.07 **2.78**	2.02 **2.70**	1.98 **2.62**	1.95 **2.56**	1.90 **2.46**	1.85 **2.39**	1.78 **2.26**	1.74 **2.18**	1.69 **2.10**	1.63 **2.00**	1.60 **1.94**	1.55 **1.86**	1.52 **1.82**	1.48 **1.76**	1.46 **1.71**	1.44 **1.68**	50
55	4.02 **7.12**	3.17 **5.01**	2.78 **4.16**	2.54 **3.68**	2.38 **3.37**	2.27 **3.15**	2.18 **2.98**	2.11 **2.85**	2.05 **2.75**	2.00 **2.66**	1.97 **2.59**	1.93 **2.53**	1.88 **2.43**	1.83 **2.35**	1.76 **2.23**	1.72 **2.15**	1.67 **2.06**	1.61 **1.96**	1.58 **1.90**	1.52 **1.82**	1.50 **1.78**	1.46 **1.71**	1.43 **1.66**	1.41 **1.64**	55
60	4.00 **7.08**	3.15 **4.98**	2.76 **4.13**	2.52 **3.65**	2.37 **3.34**	2.25 **3.12**	2.17 **2.95**	2.10 **2.82**	2.04 **2.72**	1.99 **2.63**	1.95 **2.56**	1.92 **2.50**	1.86 **2.40**	1.81 **2.32**	1.75 **2.20**	1.70 **2.12**	1.65 **2.03**	1.59 **1.93**	1.56 **1.87**	1.50 **1.79**	1.48 **1.74**	1.44 **1.68**	1.41 **1.63**	1.39 **1.60**	60
65	3.99 **7.04**	3.14 **4.95**	2.75 **4.10**	2.51 **3.62**	2.36 **3.31**	2.24 **3.09**	2.15 **2.93**	2.08 **2.79**	2.02 **2.70**	1.98 **2.61**	1.94 **2.54**	1.90 **2.47**	1.85 **2.37**	1.80 **2.30**	1.73 **2.18**	1.68 **2.09**	1.63 **2.00**	1.57 **1.90**	1.54 **1.84**	1.49 **1.76**	1.46 **1.71**	1.42 **1.64**	1.39 **1.60**	1.37 **1.56**	65
70	3.98 **7.01**	3.13 **4.92**	2.74 **4.08**	2.50 **3.60**	2.35 **3.29**	2.23 **3.07**	2.14 **2.91**	2.07 **2.77**	2.01 **2.67**	1.97 **2.59**	1.93 **2.51**	1.89 **2.45**	1.84 **2.35**	1.79 **2.28**	1.72 **2.15**	1.67 **2.07**	1.62 **1.98**	1.56 **1.88**	1.53 **1.82**	1.47 **1.74**	1.45 **1.69**	1.40 **1.62**	1.37 **1.56**	1.35 **1.53**	70
80	3.96 **6.96**	3.11 **4.88**	2.72 **4.04**	2.48 **3.56**	2.33 **3.25**	2.21 **3.04**	2.12 **2.87**	2.05 **2.74**	1.99 **2.64**	1.95 **2.55**	1.91 **2.48**	1.88 **2.41**	1.82 **2.32**	1.77 **2.24**	1.70 **2.11**	1.65 **2.03**	1.60 **1.94**	1.54 **1.84**	1.51 **1.78**	1.45 **1.70**	1.42 **1.65**	1.38 **1.57**	1.35 **1.52**	1.32 **1.49**	80
100	3.94 **6.90**	3.09 **4.82**	2.70 **3.98**	2.46 **3.51**	2.30 **3.20**	2.19 **2.99**	2.10 **2.82**	2.03 **2.69**	1.97 **2.59**	1.92 **2.51**	1.88 **2.43**	1.85 **2.36**	1.79 **2.26**	1.75 **2.19**	1.68 **2.06**	1.63 **1.98**	1.57 **1.89**	1.51 **1.79**	1.48 **1.73**	1.42 **1.64**	1.39 **1.59**	1.34 **1.51**	1.30 **1.46**	1.28 **1.43**	100
125	3.92 **6.84**	3.07 **4.78**	2.68 **3.94**	2.44 **3.47**	2.29 **3.17**	2.17 **2.95**	2.08 **2.79**	2.01 **2.65**	1.95 **2.56**	1.90 **2.47**	1.86 **2.40**	1.83 **2.33**	1.77 **2.23**	1.72 **2.15**	1.65 **2.03**	1.60 **1.94**	1.55 **1.85**	1.49 **1.75**	1.45 **1.68**	1.39 **1.59**	1.36 **1.54**	1.31 **1.46**	1.27 **1.40**	1.25 **1.37**	125
150	3.91 **6.81**	3.06 **4.75**	2.67 **3.91**	2.43 **3.44**	2.27 **3.14**	2.16 **2.92**	2.07 **2.76**	2.00 **2.62**	1.94 **2.53**	1.89 **2.44**	1.85 **2.37**	1.82 **2.30**	1.76 **2.20**	1.71 **2.12**	1.64 **2.00**	1.59 **1.91**	1.54 **1.83**	1.47 **1.72**	1.44 **1.66**	1.37 **1.56**	1.34 **1.51**	1.29 **1.43**	1.25 **1.37**	1.22 **1.33**	150
200	3.89 **6.76**	3.04 **4.71**	2.65 **3.88**	2.41 **3.41**	2.26 **3.11**	2.14 **2.90**	2.05 **2.73**	1.98 **2.60**	1.92 **2.50**	1.87 **2.41**	1.83 **2.34**	1.80 **2.28**	1.74 **2.17**	1.69 **2.09**	1.62 **1.97**	1.57 **1.88**	1.52 **1.79**	1.45 **1.69**	1.42 **1.62**	1.35 **1.53**	1.32 **1.48**	1.26 **1.39**	1.22 **1.33**	1.19 **1.28**	200
400	3.86 **6.70**	3.02 **4.66**	2.62 **3.83**	2.39 **3.36**	2.23 **3.06**	2.12 **2.85**	2.03 **2.69**	1.96 **2.55**	1.90 **2.46**	1.85 **2.37**	1.81 **2.29**	1.78 **2.23**	1.72 **2.12**	1.67 **2.04**	1.60 **1.92**	1.54 **1.84**	1.49 **1.74**	1.42 **1.64**	1.38 **1.57**	1.32 **1.47**	1.28 **1.42**	1.22 **1.32**	1.16 **1.24**	1.13 **1.19**	400
1000	3.85 **6.66**	3.00 **4.62**	2.61 **3.80**	2.38 **3.34**	2.22 **3.04**	2.10 **2.82**	2.02 **2.66**	1.95 **2.53**	1.89 **2.43**	1.84 **2.34**	1.80 **2.26**	1.76 **2.20**	1.70 **2.09**	1.65 **2.01**	1.58 **1.89**	1.53 **1.81**	1.47 **1.71**	1.41 **1.61**	1.36 **1.54**	1.30 **1.44**	1.26 **1.38**	1.19 **1.28**	1.13 **1.19**	1.08 **1.11**	1000
∞	3.84 **6.64**	2.99 **4.60**	2.60 **3.78**	2.37 **3.32**	2.21 **3.02**	2.09 **2.80**	2.01 **2.64**	1.94 **2.51**	1.88 **2.41**	1.83 **2.32**	1.79 **2.24**	1.75 **2.18**	1.69 **2.07**	1.64 **1.99**	1.57 **1.87**	1.52 **1.79**	1.46 **1.69**	1.40 **1.59**	1.35 **1.52**	1.28 **1.41**	1.24 **1.36**	1.17 **1.25**	1.11 **1.15**	1.00 **1.00**	∞

Reprinted by permission from *Statistical Methods, Seventh Edition* by G. W. Snedecor and W. G. Cochran © 1980 by Iowa State University Press, Ames, IA.

Table D Percentage points of the studentized range, q

Upper 5% points

v \ n	2	3	4	5	6	7	8	9	10	11	12	13	14	15	16	17	18	19	20
1	18.0	27.0	32.8	37.1	40.4	43.1	45.4	47.4	49.1	50.6	52.0	53.2	54.3	55.4	56.3	57.2	58.0	58.8	59.6
2	6.09	8.3	9.8	10.9	11.7	12.4	13.0	13.5	14.0	14.4	14.7	15.1	15.4	15.7	15.9	16.1	16.4	16.6	16.8
3	4.50	5.91	6.82	7.50	8.04	8.48	8.85	9.18	9.46	9.72	9.95	10.15	10.35	10.52	10.69	10.84	10.98	11.11	11.24
4	3.93	5.04	5.76	6.29	6.71	7.05	7.35	7.60	7.83	8.03	8.21	8.37	8.52	8.66	8.79	8.91	9.03	9.13	9.23
5	3.64	4.60	5.22	5.67	6.03	6.33	6.58	6.80	6.99	7.17	7.32	7.47	7.60	7.72	7.83	7.93	8.03	8.12	8.21
6	3.46	4.34	4.90	5.31	5.63	5.89	6.12	6.32	6.49	6.65	6.79	6.92	7.03	7.14	7.24	7.34	7.43	7.51	7.59
7	3.34	4.16	4.68	5.06	5.36	5.61	5.82	6.00	6.16	6.30	6.43	6.55	6.66	6.76	6.85	6.94	7.02	7.09	7.17
8	3.26	4.04	4.53	4.89	5.17	5.40	5.60	5.77	5.92	6.05	6.18	6.29	6.39	6.48	6.57	6.65	6.73	6.80	6.87
9	3.20	3.95	4.42	4.76	5.02	5.24	5.43	5.60	5.74	5.87	5.98	6.09	6.19	6.28	6.36	6.44	6.51	6.58	6.64
10	3.15	3.88	4.33	4.65	4.91	5.12	5.30	5.46	5.60	5.72	5.83	5.93	6.03	6.11	6.20	6.27	6.34	6.40	6.47
11	3.11	3.82	4.26	4.57	4.82	5.03	5.20	5.35	5.49	5.61	5.71	5.81	5.90	5.99	6.06	6.14	6.20	6.26	6.33
12	3.08	3.77	4.20	4.51	4.75	4.95	5.12	5.27	5.40	5.51	5.62	5.71	5.80	5.88	5.95	6.03	6.09	6.15	6.21
13	3.06	3.73	4.15	4.45	4.69	4.88	5.05	5.19	5.32	5.43	5.53	5.63	5.71	5.79	5.86	5.93	6.00	6.05	6.11
14	3.03	3.70	4.11	4.41	4.64	4.83	4.99	5.13	5.25	5.36	5.46	5.55	5.64	5.72	5.79	5.85	5.92	5.97	6.03
15	3.01	3.67	4.08	4.37	4.60	4.78	4.94	5.08	5.20	5.31	5.40	5.49	5.58	5.65	5.72	5.79	5.85	5.90	5.96
16	3.00	3.65	4.05	4.33	4.56	4.74	4.90	5.03	5.15	5.26	5.35	5.44	5.52	5.59	5.66	5.72	5.79	5.84	5.90
17	2.98	3.63	4.02	4.30	4.52	4.71	4.86	4.99	5.11	5.21	5.31	5.39	5.47	5.55	5.61	5.68	5.74	5.79	5.84
18	2.97	3.61	4.00	4.28	4.49	4.67	4.82	4.96	5.07	5.17	5.27	5.35	5.43	5.50	5.57	5.63	5.69	5.74	5.79
19	2.96	3.59	3.98	4.25	4.47	4.65	4.79	4.92	5.04	5.14	5.23	5.32	5.39	5.46	5.53	5.59	5.65	5.70	5.75
20	2.95	3.58	3.96	4.23	4.45	4.62	4.77	4.90	5.01	5.11	5.20	5.28	5.36	5.43	5.49	5.55	5.61	5.66	5.71
24	2.92	3.53	3.90	4.17	4.37	4.54	4.68	4.81	4.92	5.01	5.10	5.18	5.25	5.32	5.38	5.44	5.50	5.54	5.59
30	2.89	3.49	3.84	4.10	4.30	4.46	4.60	4.72	4.83	4.92	5.08	5.09	5.15	5.21	5.27	5.33	5.38	5.43	5.48
40	2.86	3.44	3.79	4.04	4.23	4.39	4.52	4.63	4.74	4.82	4.91	4.98	5.05	5.11	5.16	5.22	5.27	5.31	5.36
60	2.83	3.40	3.74	3.98	4.16	4.31	4.44	4.55	4.65	4.73	4.81	4.88	4.94	5.00	5.06	5.11	5.16	5.20	5.24
120	2.80	3.36	3.69	3.92	4.10	4.24	4.36	4.48	4.56	4.64	4.72	4.78	4.84	4.90	4.95	5.00	5.05	5.09	5.13
∞	2.77	3.31	3.63	3.86	4.03	4.17	4.29	4.39	4.47	4.55	4.62	4.68	4.74	4.80	4.85	4.89	4.93	4.97	5.01

continued

Table D (Continued)

Upper 1% points

v \ n	2	3	4	5	6	7	8	9	10	11	12	13	14	15	16	17	18	19	20
1	90.0	135	164	186	202	216	227	237	246	253	260	266	272	277	282	286	290	294	298
2	14.0	19.0	22.3	24.7	26.6	28.2	29.5	30.7	31.7	32.6	33.4	34.1	34.8	35.4	36.0	36.5	37.0	37.5	37.9
3	8.26	10.6	12.2	13.3	14.2	15.0	15.6	16.2	16.7	17.1	17.5	17.9	18.2	18.5	18.8	19.1	19.3	19.5	19.8
4	6.51	8.12	9.17	9.96	10.6	11.1	11.5	11.9	12.3	12.6	12.8	13.1	13.3	13.5	13.7	13.9	14.1	14.2	14.4
5	5.70	6.97	7.80	8.42	8.91	9.32	9.67	9.97	10.24	10.48	10.70	10.89	11.08	11.24	11.40	11.55	11.68	11.81	11.93
6	5.24	6.33	7.03	7.56	7.97	8.32	8.61	8.87	9.10	9.30	9.49	9.65	9.81	9.95	10.08	10.21	10.32	10.43	10.54
7	4.95	5.92	6.54	7.01	7.37	7.68	7.94	8.17	8.37	8.55	8.71	8.86	9.00	9.12	9.24	9.35	9.46	9.55	9.65
8	4.74	5.63	6.20	6.63	6.96	7.24	7.47	7.68	7.87	8.03	8.18	8.31	8.44	8.55	8.66	8.76	8.85	8.94	9.03
9	4.60	5.43	5.96	6.35	6.66	6.91	7.13	7.32	7.49	7.65	7.78	7.91	8.03	8.13	8.23	8.32	8.41	8.49	8.57
10	4.48	5.27	5.77	6.14	6.43	6.67	6.87	7.05	7.21	7.36	7.48	7.60	7.71	7.81	7.91	7.99	8.07	8.15	8.22
11	4.39	5.14	5.62	5.97	6.25	6.48	6.67	6.84	6.99	7.13	7.25	7.36	7.46	7.56	7.65	7.73	7.81	7.88	7.95
12	4.32	5.04	5.50	5.84	6.10	6.32	6.51	6.67	6.81	6.94	7.06	7.17	7.26	7.36	7.44	7.52	7.59	7.66	7.73
13	4.26	4.96	5.40	5.73	5.98	6.19	6.37	6.53	6.67	6.79	6.90	7.01	7.10	7.19	7.27	7.34	7.42	7.48	7.55
14	4.21	4.89	5.32	5.63	5.88	6.08	6.26	6.41	6.54	6.66	6.77	6.87	6.96	7.05	7.12	7.20	7.27	7.33	7.39
15	4.17	4.83	5.25	5.56	5.80	5.99	6.16	6.31	6.44	6.55	6.66	6.76	6.84	6.93	7.00	7.07	7.14	7.20	7.26
16	4.13	4.78	5.19	5.49	5.72	5.92	6.08	6.22	6.35	6.46	6.56	6.66	6.74	6.82	6.90	6.97	7.03	7.09	7.15
17	4.10	4.74	5.14	5.43	5.66	5.85	6.01	6.15	6.27	6.38	6.48	6.57	6.66	6.73	6.80	6.87	6.94	7.00	7.05
18	4.07	4.70	5.09	5.38	5.60	5.79	5.94	6.08	6.20	6.31	6.41	6.50	6.58	6.65	6.72	6.79	6.85	6.91	6.96
19	4.05	4.67	5.05	5.33	5.55	5.73	5.89	6.02	6.14	6.25	6.34	6.43	6.51	6.58	6.65	6.72	6.78	6.84	6.89
20	4.02	4.64	5.02	5.29	5.51	5.69	5.84	5.97	6.09	6.19	6.29	6.37	6.45	6.52	6.59	6.65	6.71	6.76	6.82
24	3.96	4.54	4.91	5.17	5.37	5.54	5.69	5.81	5.92	6.02	6.11	6.19	6.26	6.33	6.39	6.45	6.51	6.56	6.61
30	3.89	4.45	4.80	5.05	5.24	5.40	5.54	5.65	5.76	5.85	5.93	6.01	6.08	6.14	6.20	6.26	6.31	6.36	6.41
40	3.82	4.37	4.70	4.93	5.11	5.27	5.39	5.50	5.60	5.69	5.77	5.84	5.90	5.96	6.02	6.07	6.12	6.17	6.21
60	3.76	4.28	4.60	4.82	4.99	5.13	5.25	5.36	5.45	5.53	5.60	5.67	5.73	5.79	5.84	5.89	5.93	5.98	6.02
120	3.70	4.20	4.50	4.71	4.87	5.01	5.12	5.21	5.30	5.38	5.44	5.51	5.56	5.61	5.66	5.71	5.75	5.79	5.83
∞	3.64	4.12	4.40	4.60	4.76	4.88	4.99	5.08	5.16	5.23	5.29	5.35	5.40	5.45	5.49	5.54	5.57	5.61	5.65

n is the size of the sample from which the range is obtained and v is the number of degrees of freedom of s_v.

Reprinted from Biometrika Tables for Statisticians (Vol. 1) 3rd Edition (1966) with permission of the Biometrika trustees.

Table E Critical Values for the Wilcoxon *T*

n	Level of Significance for a Two-Tailed Test				n	Level of Significance for a Two-Tailed Test			
	.10	.05	.02	.01		.10	.05	.02	.01
5	0	—	—	—	28	130	116	101	91
6	2	0	—	—	29	140	126	110	100
7	3	2	0	—	30	151	137	120	109
8	5	3	1	0	31	163	147	130	118
9	8	5	3	1	32	175	159	140	128
10	10	8	5	3	33	187	170	151	138
11	13	10	7	5	34	200	182	162	148
12	17	13	9	7	35	213	195	173	159
13	21	17	12	9	36	227	208	185	171
14	25	21	15	12	37	241	221	198	182
15	30	25	19	15	38	256	235	211	194
16	35	29	23	19	39	271	249	224	207
17	41	34	27	23	40	286	264	238	220
18	47	40	32	27	41	302	279	252	233
19	53	46	37	32	42	319	294	266	247
20	60	52	43	37	43	336	310	281	261
21	67	58	49	42	44	353	327	296	276
22	75	65	55	48	45	371	343	312	291
23	83	73	62	54	46	389	361	328	307
24	91	81	69	61	47	407	378	345	322
25	100	89	76	68	48	426	396	362	339
26	110	98	84	75	49	446	415	379	355
27	119	107	92	83	50	466	434	397	373

Table F   Critical Values for the Mann-Whitney U[a]

n_2 \\ n_1	1	2	3	4	5	6	7	8	9	10	11	12	13	14	15	16	17	18	19	20
1	—[b]	—	—	—	—	—	—	—	—	—	—	—	—	—	—	—	—	—	0	0
2	—	—	—	—	0	0	0	1	1	1	1	2	2	2	3	3	3	4	4	4
	—	—	—	—	—	—	—	**0**	**0**	**0**	**0**	**1**	**1**	**1**	**1**	**1**	**2**	**2**	**2**	**2**
3	—	—	0	0	1	2	2	3	3	4	5	5	6	7	7	8	9	9	10	11
	—	—	—	—	**0**	**1**	**1**	**2**	**2**	**3**	**3**	**4**	**4**	**5**	**5**	**6**	**6**	**7**	**7**	**8**
4	—	—	0	1	2	3	4	5	6	7	8	9	10	11	12	14	15	16	17	18
	—	—	—	**0**	**1**	**2**	**3**	**4**	**4**	**5**	**6**	**7**	**8**	**9**	**10**	**11**	**11**	**12**	**13**	**13**
5	—	0	1	2	4	5	6	8	9	11	12	13	15	16	18	19	20	22	23	25
	—	—	**0**	**1**	**2**	**3**	**5**	**6**	**7**	**8**	**9**	**11**	**12**	**13**	**14**	**15**	**17**	**18**	**19**	**20**
6	—	0	2	3	5	7	8	10	12	14	16	17	19	21	23	25	26	28	30	32
	—	—	**1**	**2**	**3**	**5**	**6**	**8**	**10**	**11**	**13**	**14**	**16**	**17**	**19**	**21**	**22**	**24**	**25**	**27**
7	—	0	2	4	6	8	11	13	15	17	19	21	24	26	28	30	33	35	37	39
	—	—	**1**	**3**	**5**	**6**	**8**	**10**	**12**	**14**	**16**	**18**	**20**	**22**	**24**	**26**	**28**	**30**	**32**	**34**
8	—	1	3	5	8	10	13	15	18	20	23	26	28	31	33	36	39	41	44	47
	—	**0**	**2**	**4**	**6**	**8**	**10**	**13**	**15**	**17**	**19**	**22**	**24**	**26**	**29**	**31**	**34**	**36**	**38**	**41**
9	—	1	3	6	9	12	15	18	21	24	27	30	33	36	39	42	45	48	51	54
	—	**0**	**2**	**4**	**7**	**10**	**12**	**15**	**17**	**20**	**23**	**26**	**28**	**31**	**34**	**37**	**39**	**42**	**45**	**48**
10	—	1	4	7	11	14	17	20	24	27	31	34	37	41	44	48	51	55	58	62
	—	**0**	**3**	**5**	**8**	**11**	**14**	**17**	**20**	**23**	**26**	**29**	**33**	**36**	**39**	**42**	**45**	**48**	**52**	**55**
11	—	1	5	8	12	16	19	23	27	31	34	38	42	46	50	54	57	61	65	69
	—	**0**	**3**	**6**	**9**	**13**	**16**	**19**	**23**	**26**	**30**	**33**	**37**	**40**	**44**	**47**	**51**	**55**	**58**	**62**
12	—	2	5	9	13	17	21	26	30	34	38	42	47	51	55	60	64	68	72	77
	—	**1**	**4**	**7**	**11**	**14**	**18**	**22**	**26**	**29**	**33**	**37**	**41**	**45**	**49**	**53**	**57**	**61**	**65**	**69**
13	—	2	6	10	15	19	24	28	33	37	42	47	51	56	61	65	70	75	80	84
	—	**1**	**4**	**8**	**12**	**16**	**20**	**24**	**28**	**33**	**37**	**41**	**45**	**50**	**54**	**59**	**63**	**67**	**72**	**76**
14	—	2	7	11	16	21	26	31	36	41	46	51	56	61	66	71	77	82	87	92
	—	**1**	**5**	**9**	**13**	**17**	**22**	**26**	**31**	**36**	**40**	**45**	**50**	**55**	**59**	**64**	**67**	**74**	**78**	**83**
15	—	3	7	12	18	23	28	33	39	44	50	55	61	66	72	77	83	88	94	100
	—	**1**	**5**	**10**	**14**	**19**	**24**	**29**	**34**	**39**	**44**	**49**	**54**	**59**	**64**	**70**	**75**	**80**	**85**	**90**
16	—	3	8	14	19	25	30	36	42	48	54	60	65	71	77	83	89	95	101	107
	—	**1**	**6**	**11**	**15**	**21**	**26**	**31**	**37**	**42**	**47**	**53**	**59**	**64**	**70**	**75**	**81**	**86**	**92**	**98**
17	—	3	9	15	20	26	33	39	45	51	57	64	70	77	83	89	96	102	109	115
	—	**2**	**6**	**11**	**17**	**22**	**28**	**34**	**39**	**45**	**51**	**57**	**63**	**67**	**75**	**81**	**87**	**93**	**99**	**105**
18	—	4	9	16	22	28	35	41	48	55	61	68	75	82	88	95	102	109	116	123
	—	**2**	**7**	**12**	**18**	**24**	**30**	**36**	**42**	**48**	**55**	**61**	**67**	**74**	**80**	**86**	**93**	**99**	**106**	**112**
19	0	4	10	17	23	30	37	44	51	58	65	72	80	87	94	101	109	116	123	130
	—	**2**	**7**	**13**	**19**	**25**	**32**	**38**	**45**	**52**	**58**	**65**	**72**	**78**	**85**	**92**	**99**	**106**	**113**	**119**
20	0	4	11	18	25	32	39	47	54	62	69	77	84	92	100	107	115	123	130	138
	—	**2**	**8**	**13**	**20**	**27**	**34**	**41**	**48**	**55**	**62**	**69**	**76**	**83**	**90**	**98**	**105**	**112**	**119**	**127**

[a] For a two-tailed test at $\alpha = .10$ (roman type) and $\alpha = .05$ (boldface type).
[b] Dashes in the body of the table indicate that no decision is possible at the given α.

Table F (Continued)[a]

n_2	1	2	3	4	5	6	7	8	9	10	11	12	13	14	15	16	17	18	19	20
1	—[b]	—	—	—	—	—	—	—	—	—	—	—	—	—	—	—	—	—	—	—
2	—	—	—	—	—	—	—	—	—	—	—	—	0	0	0	0	0	0	1	1
	—	—	—	—	—	—	—	—	—	—	—	—	—	—	—	—	—	—	0	0
3	—	—	—	—	—	—	0	0	1	1	1	2	2	2	3	3	4	4	4	5
	—	—	—	—	—	—	—	—	0	0	0	1	1	1	2	2	2	2	3	3
4	—	—	—	—	0	1	1	2	3	3	4	5	5	6	7	7	8	9	9	10
	—	—	—	—	—	0	0	1	1	2	2	3	3	4	5	5	6	6	7	8
5	—	—	—	0	1	2	3	4	5	6	7	8	9	10	11	12	13	14	15	16
	—	—	—	—	0	1	1	2	3	4	5	6	7	7	8	9	10	11	12	13
6	—	—	—	1	2	3	4	6	7	8	9	11	12	13	15	16	18	19	20	22
	—	—	—	0	1	2	3	4	5	6	7	9	10	11	12	13	15	16	17	18
7	—	—	0	1	3	4	6	7	9	11	12	14	16	17	19	21	23	24	26	28
	—	—	—	0	1	3	4	6	7	9	10	12	13	15	16	18	19	21	22	24
8	—	—	0	2	4	6	7	9	11	13	15	17	20	22	24	26	28	30	32	34
	—	—	—	1	2	4	6	7	9	11	13	15	17	18	20	22	24	26	28	30
9	—	—	1	3	5	7	9	11	14	16	18	21	23	26	28	31	33	36	38	40
	—	—	0	1	3	5	7	9	11	13	16	18	20	22	24	27	29	31	33	36
10	—	—	1	3	6	8	11	13	16	19	22	24	27	30	33	36	38	41	44	47
	—	—	0	2	4	6	9	11	13	16	18	21	24	26	29	31	34	37	39	42
11	—	—	1	4	7	9	12	15	18	22	25	28	31	34	37	41	44	47	50	53
	—	—	0	2	5	7	10	13	16	18	21	24	27	30	33	36	39	42	45	48
12	—	—	2	5	8	11	14	17	21	24	28	31	35	38	42	46	49	53	56	60
	—	—	1	3	6	9	12	15	18	21	24	27	31	34	37	41	44	47	51	54
13	—	0	2	5	9	12	16	20	23	27	31	35	39	43	47	51	55	59	63	67
	—	—	1	3	7	10	13	17	20	24	27	31	34	38	42	45	49	53	56	60
14	—	0	2	6	10	13	17	22	26	30	34	38	43	47	51	56	60	65	69	73
	—	—	1	4	7	11	15	18	22	26	30	34	38	42	46	50	54	58	63	67
15	—	0	3	7	11	15	19	24	28	33	37	42	47	51	56	61	66	70	75	80
	—	—	2	5	8	12	16	20	24	29	33	37	42	46	51	55	60	64	69	73
16	—	0	3	7	12	16	21	26	31	36	41	46	51	56	61	66	71	76	82	87
	—	—	2	5	9	13	18	22	27	31	36	41	45	50	55	60	65	70	74	79
17	—	0	4	8	13	18	23	28	33	38	44	49	55	60	66	71	77	82	88	93
	—	—	2	6	10	15	19	24	29	34	39	44	49	54	60	65	70	75	81	86
18	—	0	4	9	14	19	24	30	36	41	47	53	59	65	70	76	82	88	94	100
	—	—	2	6	11	16	21	26	31	37	42	47	53	58	64	70	75	81	87	92
19	—	1	4	9	15	20	26	32	38	44	50	56	63	69	75	82	88	94	101	107
	—	0	3	7	12	17	22	28	33	39	45	51	56	63	69	74	81	87	93	99
20	—	1	5	10	16	22	28	34	40	47	53	60	67	73	80	87	93	100	107	114
	—	0	3	8	13	18	24	30	36	42	48	54	60	67	73	79	86	92	99	105

[a] For a two-tailed test at $\alpha = .02$ (roman type) and $\alpha = .01$ (boldface type).
[b] Dashes in the body of the table indicate that no decision is possible at the given α.

From *Elementary Statistics*, 2nd Edition by R. E. Kirk. Copyright © 1984, 1978 by Wadsworth, Inc. Reprinted by permission of Brooks/Cole Publishing Company, Pacific Grove, California 93950.

Methodology: Selected Bibliography

American Psychological Association. (1981). Ethical principles of psychologists (revised). *American Psychologist, 36,* 633–638.

American Psychological Association. (1984). *Publication manual of the American Psychological Association* (3rd ed.). Washington, DC: Author.

American Psychological Association. (1985). *Thesaurus of psychological index terms.* Washington, DC: Author.

Anastasi, A. (1976). *Psychological testing.* New York: Macmillan.

Anderson, D.C., & Borkowski, J. G. (1978). *Experimental psychology: Research tactics and their applications.* Glenview, IL: Scott, Foresman.

Babbie, E. (1973). *Survey research methods.* Belmont, CA: Wadsworth.

Barber, T. X., & Silver, M. J. (1968). Fact, fiction, and the experimenter bias effect. *Psychological Bulletin Monograph, 70,* 1–29.

Calder, R. (1955). *Science makes sense.* London: George Allen and Unwin Ltd.

Campbell, S. K. (1974). *Flaws and fallacies in statistical thinking.* Englewood Cliffs, NJ: Prentice-Hall.

Campbell, D. T., & Stanley, J. C. (1963). *Experimental and quasi-experimental designs for research.* Chicago: Rand McNally.

Christensen, L. B. (1988). *Experimental methodology* (4th ed.). Boston: Allyn and Bacon.

Cochran, W. G., & Cox, G. M. (1957). *Experimental designs.* New York: Wiley.

Cook, T. D., Bean, J. R., Calder, B. J., Frey, R., Krovetz, M. L., & Reisman, S. R. (1970). Demand characteristics and three conceptions of the frequently deceived subject. *Journal of Personality and Social Psychology, 14,* 185–194.

Cook, T. D., & Campbell, D. T. (1979). *Quasi-experimentation: Design and analysis issues for field settings.* Skokie, IL: Rand McNally.

Cross, D. V. (1973). Sequential dependencies and regression in psychophysical judgments. *Perception and Psychophysics, 14,* 547–552.

D'Amato, M. R. (1970). *Experimental psychology methodology: Psychophysics and learning.* New York: McGraw-Hill.

Dukes, W. F. (1965). N = 1. *Psychological Bulletin, 64,* 74–79.

Elmes, D. G., Kantowitz, B. H., & Roediger, H. L. III. (1985). *Research methods in psychology* (2nd ed). St. Paul, MN: West.

Epstein, T. M., Suedfeld, P., & Silverstein, S. J. (1973). The experimental contact: Subject's expectations of and reactions to some behavior of experimenters. *American Psychologist, 28,* 212–221.

Fisher, R. A. (1935). *The design of experiments* (1st ed.). London: Oliver and Boyd.

Gaito, J. (1961). Repeated measurements designs and counterbalancing. *Psychological Bulletin, 58,* 46–54.

Gottman, J. M., McFall, R. M., & Barnett, J. T. (1969). Design and analysis of research using time series. *Psychological Bulletin, 72,* 299–306.

Goyder, J. (1985). Face-to-face interviews and mailed questionnaires: The net difference in response rate. *Public Opinion Quarterly, 49,* 234–252.

Granik, L. (Ed.). *Psychological abstracts.* Arlington, VA: American Psychological Association.

Hays, W. L. (1981). *Statistics* (3rd ed.). New York: McGraw-Hill.

Helmstadter, G. C. (1970). *Research concepts in human behavior.* New York: Appleton-Century-Crofts.

Howell, D. C. (1987). *Statistical methods for psychology.* Boston: Duxbury Press.

Institute for Scientific Information. *Social science citation index.* Philadelphia, PA: Author.

Irwin, D. M., & Bushner, M. M. (1980). *Observational strategies for child study.* New York: Holt, Reinhart, and Winston.

Johnson, R. W., & Ryan, B. J. (1976). Observer/recorder error as affected by different tasks and different expectancy inducements. *Journal of Experimental Research in Personality, 10,* 201–214.

Keppel, G., & Saufley, W. H. (1980). *Introduction to design and analysis: A student's handbook.* San Francisco: W. H. Freeman.

Kerlinger, F. N. (1964). *Foundations of behavioral research.* New York: Holt.

Kimmel, H. D., & Terrant, F. R. (1968). Bias due to individual differences in yoked control design. *Behavior Research Methods and Instrumentation, 1,* 11–14.

Kirk, R. E. (1968). *Experimental design: Procedures for the behavioral sciences.* Monterey, CA: Brooks/Cole.

Kratochwill, T. R. (1978). Foundations of time-series research. In T. R. Kratochwill (Ed.), *Single subject research: Strategies for evaluating change.* New York: Academic Press.

Kratochwill, T. R., & Brody, G. H. (1978). Single subject designs: A perspective on the controversy over employing statistical inference and implications for research and training in behavior modification. *Behavior Modification, 2,* 291–308.

Krejcie, R. V., & Morgan, D. W. (1970). Determining sample size for research activities. *Educational and Psychological Measurement, 30,* 607–610.

Lana, R. (1959). Pretest-treatment interaction effects in longitudinal studies. *Psychological Bulletin, 56,* 293–300.

Lana, R. E. (1969). Pretest sensitization. In R. Rosenthal & R. L. Rosnow (Eds.), *Artifact in behavioral research.* New York: Academic Press.

Martin, D. W. (1977). *Doing psychology experiments.* Monterey, Ca: Brooks/ Cole.

McGuigan, F. J. (1983). *Experimental psychology methods of research.* Englewood Cliffs, NJ: Prentice-Hall.

McInnis, R. (1982). *Research guide for psychology.* Westport, CT: Greenwood Press.

Mook, D. G. (1983). In defense of external invalidity. *American Psychologist, 38,* 379–387.

Neale, J. M., & Liebert, R. M. (1973). *Science and behavior: An Introduction to methods of research.* Englewood Cliffs, NJ: Prentice-Hall.

Rosenthal, R. (1976). *Experimenter effects in behavioral research* (2nd ed.). New York: Irvington.

Saudargras, R. A., & Lintz, F. E. (1986). Estimating percent of time and rate via direct observation: A suggested observational procedure and format. *School Psychology Review, 15,* 36–48.

Selltiz, C., Jahoda, M., Deutsch, M., and Cook, S. W. (1959). *Research methods in social relations.* New York: Holt.

Sidman, M. (1960). *Tactics of Scientific Research: Evaluating Experimental Data in Psychology.* New York: Basic Books.

Stevens, S. S. (1975). *Psychophysics: Introduction to its perceptual, neural and social prospects.* New York: Wiley.

Toothaker, L. E. (1986). *Introductory statistics for the behavioral sciences.* New York: McGraw-Hill.

Underwood, B. J. (1966). *Experimental psychology* (2nd ed.). New York: Appleton-Century-Crofts.

Waksberg, J. (1978). Sampling methods for random digit dialing. *Journal of American Statistical Association, 73,* 40–46.

Wason, P., and Johnson-Laird, P.N. (1972). *Psychology of reasoning: Structure and content.* Cambridge: Harvard University Press.

Webb, E. J., Campbell, D. T., Schwartz, R. D., & Sechrest, L. (1966). *Unobtrusive measures: Nonreactive research in the social sciences.* New York: Rand McNally.

Weber, S. J., & Cook, T. D. (1972). Subject effects in laboratory research: An examination of subject roles, demand characteristics, and valid inference. *Psychological Bulletin, 77,* 273–295.

Winer, B. J. (1971). *Statistical principles in experimental design* (2nd ed.). New York: McGraw-Hill.

Writing Appendix

In psychological journals it is customary to follow certain conventions when presenting an experiment. Typically an article that reports empirical work is divided into four major sections: introduction, method, results, and discussion. Each part of an experimental write-up has certain important information and ideas contained in it, and this overall format is followed to facilitate communication. Presenting ideas and information in a fairly standard pattern makes an experimental report more understandable and easier to read.

In addition to following a certain progression of ideas and information, psychologists also adhere to conventions of style. Basically, these conventions involve writing in the most concise, nonverbose manner possible. Individual turn-of-phrase, use of personal reference, subjective phrases, and overly literate style are discouraged.

A characteristic of good scientific reporting is the careful use of language. Everyone seems to think he or she knows what psychology is all about; if the vocabulary used in a research report is not carefully defined, there is considerable risk of misunderstanding. Much of the scientific vocabulary consists of words from everyday English such as fear, frustration, and affection. To insure effective communication, these terms always receive operational definitions. Throughout the chapters of this book we have stressed the importance of clear thinking and exposition. In this appendix the various components of the TOSS and TOGS features will be used and cross-referenced in an example research report.

On the following pages we will present, in manuscript form, an example of what a research report should look like. To illustrate some of the common errors made by students, there are two versions of the report: one correct version and one with errors. The version with errors has been marked with reference to the specific (TOSS) and general (TOGS) style boxes that were presented in each chapter. The actual report is entirely fictitious. Each section is shorter than ones you would actually write for class assignments.

As a final prefatory note, the correct and the incorrect manuscripts have been formatted to ensure that they can be compared on a page-by-page basis. This sometimes led to larger bottom margins. Normally the manuscript will have 1.5" margins.

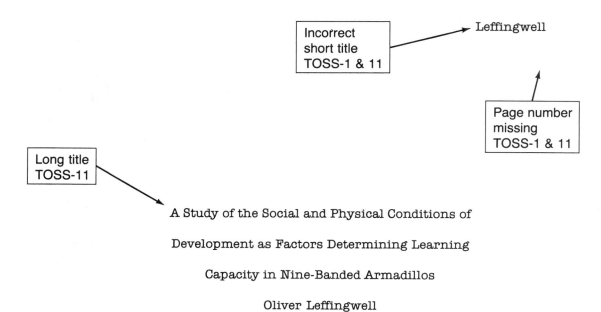

Incorrect
short title
TOSS-1 & 11

Leffingwell

Page number
missing
TOSS-1 & 11

Long title
TOSS-11

A Study of the Social and Physical Conditions of

Development as Factors Determining Learning

Capacity in Nine-Banded Armadillos

Oliver Leffingwell

Southern Brazil University

Running head: DEVELOPMENT AND LEARNING

Abstract

Genetically identical armadillos were raised together or apart (social conditions) in a plain environment or an environment full of objects (physical conditions). **The enriched environment contained a tire, a piece of pipe, 10 concrete blocks, and two wood balls; the plain environment had none of these objects present.** The effect of the factorial combination of social and physical rearing conditions was assessed in a discrimination learning task where the armadillo had to poke its nose at a target displaying the correct stimulus in order to receive a piece of food. The armadillos raised with their conspecifics made significantly **fewer errors.** The presence or absence of physical objects did not have a significant **affect** on the rate of learning the discrimination. These results suggest that social interactions at a young age may be an important determiner of later intellectual ability, consistent with social learning theories of development.

Too much detail
TOSS-10

Faulty comparison
TOGS-3

Wrong word
TOGS-6

Leffingwell

3

See TOSS-7

Spacing
TOSS-1

A Study of the Social and Physical Conditions of Development as
Factors Determining Learning Capacity in Nine-Banded Armadillos

Attempts to assess experiential factors during development

Wrong
word
TOSS-6

which may influence adult cognitive functioning have had a mixed

history of success (Popoff, 1988). Social learning theory, **Binbra,**

Incorrect
format &
order
TOSS-8

1983, 1968, predicts that the interaction of the developing organism

with other conspecifics is a critical factor in causing successful

intellectual development. Other theories, notably Rolex's (1979)

physical interaction theory, stress the importance of interactions

with the physical (nonsocial) environment during development

and later cognitive functioning. In her review of previous research,

Popoff (1988) found support for each theory but very few attempts

Split
infinitive
TOGS-3

to simultaneously test the relative influence of social and **phy-**

sical factors within a single experiment.

Inappropriate
transition
device
TOGS-9

    However, two problems exist for tests of theories of cognitive

development. One problem is that control cannot be maintained over

the developmental experiences of human infants. Therefore nonhuman

species are often used so that control of relevant physical and social

Hyphenation
TOSS-1

experiences is possible. A second problem is that genetic variability in

individual subjects can be a major influence in their learning capacity

in addition to developmental experiences. To control for genetic effects,

> Citation
> needed
> TOSS-7 & 8

identical twins have often been studied.

In the present experiment the armadillo was the subject of choice.

As Lorenzo (1982) reports, the armadillo gives birth to litters of eight

identical offspring, thus solving the problem of different genetic

> Irrelevant
> TOGS-8

makeup influencing the results. **Lorenzo also notes that otters often**

> Unwanted
> detail
> TOSS-7

have triplets. Furthermore, armadillos may be raised by artificial

feedings **using evaporated milk or whole milk from cows,** so the

social conditions of development may be controlled.

To evaluate the relative influence of social and physical stimuli

on subsequent learning ability, the armadillos were either **raised**

> Unclear
> punctuation
> TOGS-4

together, social, or individually, nonsocial, in an enclosure

that was empty, except for food and water, or stocked with

numerous objects, enriched. The design of the experiment was a

factorial combination of these two factors, making a total of four

conditions in the experiment. The influence of these rearing

Leffingwell

5

> **Awkward sentence structure TOGS-1**

conditions on cognitive functioning **when the subjects were**

40 years old was assessed by administering a discrimination

learning task.

Method

> **See TOSS-4**

> **Insufficient information TOSS-4**

Subjects. Armadillos from 4 litters were used. They were

obtained from the Willie Nelson Armadillo Ranch, Lone Star, Texas.

> **Wrong Selection headings format TOSS-3**

Apparatus. The rearing enclosures were 2.8 × 2.8 m with dirt

floors and concrete walls. The stimuli present in the enclosure for the

physically enriched conditions were a tire; a .5 m long, .2 m diameter

piece of pipe; 10 concrete blocks, .2 × .2 × .1 m; and two solid wood

balls, .25 m in diameter. When the armadillo touched the correct **disk**

> **Sexist language TOGS-7**

with **his** nose, a pellet of food was automatically delivered to a

food cup mounted midway between the two disks. **It** was manually

> **Ambiguous referent TOGS-2**

lowered into the enclosure for each trial. The discrimination

apparatus consisted of two plastic disks, 10 cm in diameter that were

20 cm apart. One disk was red and the other was green. **They were**

> **Too much detail TOSS-4**

.16 cm thick, weighed 10.6 g each, and were polished around

the edges to prevent the armadillos from cutting themselves.

Procedure. Twenty-four hours after birth, a litter of 8

> **See TOSS-5**

> **Net yet defined TOGS-10**

Verb-subject
agreement
TOGS-2

Redundant
TOGS-3

armadillos **were** divided in 4 pairs **of 2 each.** The animals were then

randomly assigned to a rearing condition. Two of the pairs were

raised together (social) and two pairs were isolated in individual

enclosures (nonsocial). One of the social pair was placed in an empty

enclosure (impoverished environment), and the other pair was

placed in the enclosure containing the various objects described

Not a
sentence
TOGS-2

above (enriched environment). Two of the isolated subjects were

placed in impoverished environments. **Two in enriched**

environments. Food and water were continuously available for the

next 39 days. On the 40th day all food was removed from the

enclosure and testing using the discrimination learning apparatus

was done 24 hours after the food had been removed.

Discrimination learning was done in a spare enclosure, so each

Spell out
a number
TOSS-13

subject was transported to the testing situation for a series of 50

trials. The trials consisted of the **2** disks and food cup being lowered

into the enclosure, a response (nosing the disk), a food reward for a

correct response (.4 g of chopped liver), or withdrawal of the disks

for an incorrect response. A 2-minute pause occurred between trials.

For half of the subjects, **the green disk was designated as correct**

| Unparallel TOGS-3 | → **and red was correct** for the other half of the subjects. The left-right

position of the red and green disks was counterbalanced, ensuring

that the target disk appeared on the left or right equally often.

Correct and incorrect responses and the time between presentations

of the disks and the response were recorded.

Results | See TOSS-6 |

| Weak paragraph TOGS-5 | → **Physical development of the armadillos was normal as**

evidenced by equal weight gain in subjects in the different

| Analysis missing TOSS-6 | → **experimental conditions (see Table 1).**

_____

Insert Table 1 about here

| Data not described TOSS-6 | → _____

A 2 × 2 Physical Condition × Social Condition analysis of

variance was conducted for the percentage of correct data and for the

| Describe effect TOSS-6 | → time-to-respond data. **The effect of rearing conditions was**

significant, $\underline{F}(1,28) = 7.93$, $\underline{p} < .01$. The physical environment did

not have an effect on the percentage correct, $\underline{F}(1,28) = $ **1.05, the**

| Comma splice TOGS-4 |

Leffingwell

8

two variables did not show an interaction, $\underline{F}(1,28) = 1.39$. The superiority of the subjects in the social rearing conditions over those in the nonsocial conditions **is interesting.**

Refer to figure TOSS-6

_____

Insert Figure 1 about here

_____

Whereas the rearing conditions influenced how well the armadillos learned the discrimination, they did not affect the time-to-respond measure: All $\underline{p}$ values were greater than .10.

Discussion   See TOSS-9

Long paragraph TOGS-5

The social learning theory of cognitive development predicts that superior intellectual functioning will result from being reared in a

Date needed TOSS-8

social context (presence of other conspecifics). The results of this experiment support this theory and suggestions by **Binbra** that maximizing social interactions during development may be a way of increasing the intellectual capacities of children. It is somewhat surprising that a physically enriched environment did not improve the learning capacity of the subjects as compared **to** those raised in

Wrong word TOGS-6

an impoverished environment. Perhaps the discrimination learning task is relatively insensitive for measuring the effects of the physical environment during development. The fact that the time-to-respond

Wrong
word
TOGS-6

data does not differ as a function of the different rearing conditions reduces the possibility that the observed learning differences might have been due to motivational differences. If motivation for food were to explain the differences in the percentage of correct choices, then similar differences should have been evident in the time-to-respond data.

Needs to
summarize
TOSS-9

References

Binbra, A. (1968). The social learning approach to cognitive develop-

ment. **Psycho. Iss.,** <u>17</u>, 471−489.

Binbra, A. (1983). Social learning theory: A developmental perspec-

tive on cognition. <u>Journal</u> <u>of</u> <u>Great</u> <u>Ideas</u>, <u>31</u>, 1−17.

Lorenzo, K. (1982). Armadillos on my mind. In N. Tinderberger (Ed.),

<u>Animals</u> <u>of</u> <u>the</u> <u>World</u> (Vol. 3, pp. 87−106). Hamburg: Ethology

Press.

Popoff, I. R. (1988). Developmental aspects of cognitive functioning.

<u>Journal</u> <u>of</u> <u>Psychological</u> <u>Reviews</u>, <u>76</u>, 246−281.

Rolex, **Jean.** (1979). <u>The</u> <u>physical</u> <u>environment</u> <u>and</u> <u>cognition</u>. Paris:

Mais Oui Press.

Incorrect reference Citation TOSS-8

Table 1

Cryptic
title
TOSS-12

Weight at Day 39 of Life

	Social Conditions	
Environment	Together	Isolated
Enriched	6.41	6.39
Impoverished	6.51	6.29

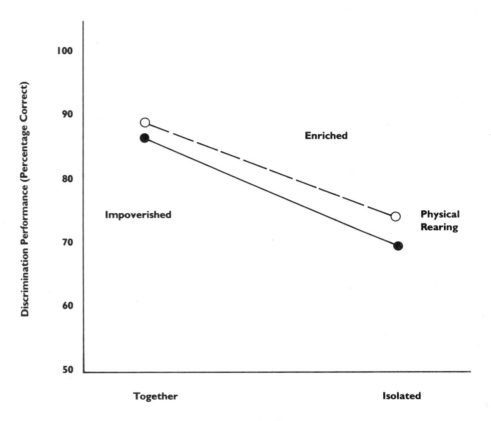

Figure caption out of place TOSS-12

Figure 1.

Discrimination learning (percentage correct) as a function of rearing conditions.

Social and Physical Conditions of Development:

Learning Capacity in Nine-Banded Armadillos

Oliver Leffingwell

Southern Brazil University

Running head: DEVELOPMENT AND LEARNING

Social and Physical

2

Abstract

Genetically identical armadillos were raised together or apart (social conditions) in a plain environment or an environment full of objects (physical conditions). The effect of the factorial combination of social and physical rearing conditions was assessed in a discrimination learning task where the armadillo had to poke its nose at a target displaying the correct stimulus in order to receive a piece of food. The armadillos raised with their conspecifics made significantly fewer errors than those raised alone. The presence or absence of physical objects did not have a significant effect on the rate of learning the discrimination. These results suggest that social interactions at a young age may be an important determiner of later intellectual ability, consistent with social learning theories of development.

Social and Physical Conditions of Development:

Learning Capacity in Nine-Banded Armadillos

Attempts to assess experiential factors during development that

may influence adult cognitive functioning have had a mixed history

of success (Popoff, 1988). Social learning theory (Binbra, 1968,

1983) predicts that the interaction of the developing organism with

other conspecifics is a critical factor in causing successful

intellectual development. Other theories, notably Rolex's (1979)

physical interaction theory, stress the importance of interactions

with the physical (nonsocial) environment during development and

later cognitive functioning. In her review of previous research, Popoff

(1988) found support for each theory but very few attempts to test

simultaneously the relative influence of social and physical factors

within a single experiment.

Two problems exist for tests of theories of cognitive development.

One problem is that control cannot be maintained over the

developmental experiences of human infants. Therefore nonhuman

species are often used so that control of relevant physical and social experiences is possible. A second problem is that genetic variability in individual subjects can be a major influence in their learning capacity in addition to developmental experiences. To control for genetic effects, identical twins have often been studied (Yin & Yang, 1953).

In the present experiment the armadillo was the subject of choice. As Lorenzo (1982) reports, the armadillo gives birth to litters of eight identical offspring, thus solving the problem of different genetic makeup influencing the results. Furthermore, armadillos may be raised by artificial feedings, so the social conditions of development may be controlled.

To evaluate the relative influence of social and physical stimuli on subsequent learning ability, the armadillos were either raised together (social) or individually (nonsocial) in an enclosure that was empty (except for food and water) or stocked with numerous objects (enriched). The design of the experiment was a factorial combination of these two factors, making a total of four conditions in the experiment. The influence of these rearing conditions on cognitive functioning was assessed by administering a discrimination learning

task when the subjects were 40 days old.

Method

Subjects

A total of 32 armadillos, 4 litters of 8 each, were used. They were

obtained from the Willie Nelson Armadillo Ranch, Lone Star, Texas.

Apparatus

The rearing enclosures were 2.8 × 2.8 m with dirt floors and

concrete walls. The stimuli present in the enclosure for the physically

enriched conditions were a tire; a .5 m long, .2 m diameter piece of

pipe; 10 concrete blocks, .2 × .2 × .1 m; and two solid wood balls,

.25 m in diameter. The discrimination apparatus consisted of two

plastic disks, 10 cm in diameter that were 20 cm apart. One disk was

red and the other was green. When the armadillo touched the correct

disk with its nose, a pellet of food was automatically delivered to a

food cup mounted midway between the two disks. The discrimination

apparatus was manually lowered into the enclosure for each trial.

Procedure

Twenty-four hours after birth, a litter of 8 armadillos was divided in 4 pairs. The animals were then randomly assigned to a rearing condition. Two of the pairs were raised together (social) and two pairs were isolated in individual enclosures (nonsocial). One of the social pair was placed in an empty enclosure (impoverished environment), and the other pair was placed in the enclosure containing the various objects described above (enriched environment). Two of the isolated subjects were placed in impoverished environments and two were placed in enriched environments. Food and water were continuously available for the next 39 days. On the 40th day all food was removed from the enclosure and testing using the discrimination learning apparatus was done 24 hours after the food had been removed.

Discrimination learning was done in a spare enclosure, so each subject was transported to the testing situation for a series of 50 trials. The trials consisted of the two disks and food cup being lowered into the enclosure, a response (nosing the disk), a food reward for a correct response (.4 g of chopped liver), or withdrawal of the disks for an incorrect response. A 2-minute pause occurred between trials. For half of the subjects, the green disk was designated as correct; for the other half of the subjects, red was correct. The left-right position of the red and green disks was counterbalanced, ensuring that the target disk appeared on the left or right equally often. Correct and incorrect responses and the time between presentations of the disks and the response were recorded.

Results

Physical development of the armadillos was normal as evidenced by equal weight gain in subjects in the different experimental conditions (see Table 1). An analysis of variance (ANOVA) confirmed the similar weight gains, $F(1,28) < 1.0, \underline{p} > .10$.

Insert Table 1 about here

Mean percentage correct and mean time to respond were computed for each subject. A 2 × 2 Physical Condition × Social Condition ANOVA was conducted for the percentage of correct data and for the time-to-respond measures. For the percentage of correct data the analysis indicated that the subjects in the social conditions made fewer errors than those in the nonsocial condition, $F(1,28) = 7.93$, $p < .01$. The physical environment did not have an effect on the percent correct, $F(1,28) = 1.05$, and the two variables did not show an interaction, $F(1,28) = 1.39$. The superiority of the subjects in the social rearing conditions over those in the nonsocial conditions is shown in Figure 1. Whereas the rearing conditions influenced how well the armadillos learned the discrimination, they did not affect the time-to-respond measure: All p values were greater than .10.

Insert Figure 1 about here

Discussion

The social learning theory of cognitive development predicts that superior intellectual functioning will result from being reared in a social context (presence of other conspecifics). The results of this experiment support this theory and suggestions by Binbra (1983) that maximizing social interactions during development may be a way of increasing the intellectual capacities of children.

It is somewhat surprising that a physically enriched environment did not improve the learning capacity of the subjects as compared with those raised in an impoverished environment. Perhaps the discrimination learning task is relatively insensitive for measuring the effects of the physical environment during development.

The fact that the time-to-respond data do not differ as a function of the different rearing conditions reduces the possibility that the observed learning differences might have been due to motivational differences. If motivation for food were to explain the differences in the percentage of correct choices, then similar differences should have been evident in the time-to-respond data. Thus the effects of social rearing conditions seem due to differences in learning capacity and are consistent with one theory (Binbra, 1983) of cognitive development.

References

Binbra, A. (1968). The social learning approach to cognitive

development. Psychological Issues, 17, 471–489.

Binbra, A. (1983). Social learning theory: A developmental

perspective on cognition. Journal of Great Ideas, 31, 1–17.

Lorenzo, K. (1982). Armadillos on my mind. In N. Tinderberger (Ed.),

Animals of the World (Vol. 3, pp. 878–106). Hamburg: Ethology

Press.

Popoff, I. R. (1988). Developmental aspects of cognitive functioning.

Journal of Psychological Reviews, 76, 246–281.

Rolex, J. (1979). The physical environment and condition. Paris: Mais

Oui Press.

Yin, A., & Yang, B. (1953). Twins in psychological research. Applied

Genetics, 1, 11–22.

Table 1

Weight in Kg. at Day 39 of Life as a Function of Rearing Conditions

	Social Conditions	
Environment	Together	Isolated
Enriched	6.41	6.39
Impoverished	6.51	6.29

Figure Caption

Figure 1.

Discrimination learning (percentage correct) as a function of rearing

conditions.

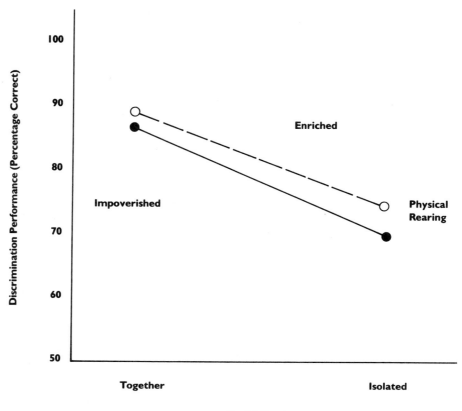

Index